3D Studio MAX 3
Fundamentals

Michael Todd Peterson

Cover art by Steve Burke

New Riders

201 West 103rd Street, Indianapolis Indiana 46290

3D Studio MAX 3 Fundamentals

International Standard Book Number: 0-7357-0049-4

Library of Congress Catalog Card Number: 99-63012

Printed in the United States of America

First Printing: July, 1999

03   02   01   00   99   5   4   3   2   1

Interpretation of the printing code: The rightmost double-digit number is the year of the book's printing; the rightmost single-digit number is the number of the book's printing. For example, the printing code 99-1 shows that the first printing of the book occurred in 1999.

Executive Editor
Steve Weiss

Acquisitions Editor
Laura Frey

Development Editor
Jennifer Eberhardt

Managing Editor
Sarah Kearns

Project Editor
Clint McCarty

Copy Editor
Malinda McCain

Indexer
Craig Small

Technical Editor
Jeff Solenberg

Software Development Specialist
Jason Haines

Proofreaders
Sheri Replin
Elise Walter

Layout Technicians
Darin Crone
Steve Gifford
Cheryl Lynch
Heather Moseman
Louis Porter, Jr.

Trademarks

Warning and Disclaimer

Dedication

In memory of Eric Baker

Contents at a Glance

Table of Contents

About the Author

Michael Todd Peterson is the owner of MTP Graphics (www.mtpgrafx.com), a full-service 3D animation shop that specializes in Architectural Rendering, Multimedia Development, Render Farm, and Special FX. In the past, Todd has taught at universities and community colleges. In addition to this book, Todd has also authored or coauthored a variety of other books for New Riders Publishing, including *Inside AutoCAD 14* and *Inside 3D Studio MAX 2, Volumes II* and *III*.

Acknowledgments

I would like to thank all the folks at New Riders for allowing me to write and update this book for the third time and for putting up with me. I would especially like to thank Laura, Jennifer, Jeff, and Clint for the excellent work they did on this book. I would also like to thank and congratulate Discreet on the creation of MAX 3 and what I think is a wonderful 3D graphics package. Also, thanks to the folks at Digimation for giving me advice and answering my questions when I needed them to be answered. Thanks, Beau!!!

Tell Us What You Think!

As the reader of this book, *you* are our most important critic and commentator. We value your opinion and want to know what we're doing right, what we could do better, what areas you'd like to see us publish in, and any other words of wisdom you're willing to pass our way.

As the Executive Editor for the Graphics team at New Riders Publishing, I welcome your comments. You can fax, email, or write me directly to let me know what you did or didn't like about this book—as well as what we can do to make our books stronger.

Please note that I cannot help you with technical problems related to the topic of this book, and that due to the high volume of mail I receive, I might not be able to reply to every message.

When you write, please be sure to include this book's title and author, as well as your name and phone or fax number. I will carefully review your comments and share them with the author and editors who worked on the book.

Fax: 317-581-4663

Email: editors@newriders.com

Mail: Steve Weiss
       Executive Editor
       Professional Graphics Design Team
       New Riders Publishing
       201 West 103rd Street
       Indianapolis, IN 46290 USA

PART I

Overview of 3D Graphics and 3D Studio MAX 3

CHAPTER 1

3D Graphics and Animation Fundamentals

In today's world, we are getting more and more used to seeing computer-generated imagery (CGI) on the television or movie screen and even in magazines and newspapers. The field of computer graphics (CG) has grown from a haven for computer scientists to a mainstream career that many people would like to have. The leading computer graphics software package for use on a PC is 3D Studio MAX.

This book covers three-dimensional computer graphics and explains how to create images and animations with 3D Studio MAX. Before you begin to learn this wonderful software package and all its intricacies, however, you need to learn the basic terminology and concepts behind the beautiful CGI scenes and imagery that surround us. This chapter explores the terminology and concepts behind computer graphics. In particular, this chapter covers

- Defining 3D graphics
- Moving from 2D to 3D graphics
- Principles of 3D computer graphics in 3D Studio MAX

Defining 3D Graphics

Saying "3D" means you are working with three dimensions—in other words, width, depth, and height. If you look around your room, everything you see is three-dimensional: the chair, desk, building, plants, and even you. But, when you look at three-dimensional computer graphics, calling them 3D is a distortion of the truth. In reality, 3D computer graphics are a *two-dimensional* representation of a *virtual* three-dimensional world.

To help illustrate this, imagine that you have a video camera and are filming the room around you. As you move around the room, you encounter various 3D objects, but when you play back the video on your VCR, you are looking at a flat, two-dimensional image that is *representative* of the 3D world you filmed a minute ago. The scene appears realistic, thanks to the lights, colors, and shadows that appear to give the scene life and three-dimensional depth, even though it is, in fact, 2D.

In computer graphics, objects exist only in the memory of the computer. They have no physical form—they are just mathematical formulas and little electrons running around. Because the objects don't exist outside the computer, the only way to record them is to add more formulas to represent lights and cameras. Fortunately for you, 3D Studio MAX (often referred to as just MAX) takes care of the mathematical side of things, enabling you to explore the artistic side. Figure 1.1 shows you 3D Studio MAX with a 3D scene loaded.

Figure 1.1   *3D Studio MAX with a scene loaded.*

In many ways, using a program such as 3D Studio MAX is much like videotaping a room full of objects that you construct. MAX enables you to design the room and its contents, using a variety of basic 3D objects such as cubes, spheres, cylinders, and cones that you can select and add to the scene. MAX also gives you the necessary tools—such as patch modeling or NURBS—to create more complex objects.

After you have created and positioned all of the objects in the scene, you can choose from a library of predefined materials and textures such as plastic, wood, or stone and apply them to the objects. You can also create your own materials through 3D Studio MAX's Material Editor, in which you can control color, shininess, and transparency or even use painted or scanned images to make surfaces appear any way you like.

After you have added materials to the scene, you can create a "camera" to record and view the scene. By adjusting the settings of the virtual camera, you can create wide-angle effects or zoom in on a small detail. Correct positioning of cameras always adds to the drama or realism of the scene. MAX provides camera objects with real-world controls you can use to create the views you are looking for in your scene.

To further the realism of the scene, you can add lighting. With MAX, you can add several different kinds of lights and define their properties, such as their color or brightness. By positioning the lights in the scene, you can control how the objects are illuminated and how they cast shadows into the scene and onto other objects.

Then, you can bring the scene to life by moving the objects themselves, as well as the lights and cameras. You can make objects move mechanically or appear to take on human characteristics. You can use filmmaking techniques to tell a story with your animation, or simply create something that looks cool.

Finally, you can render the animation to videotape or a digital video file so you can view the finished results and share them with others. Using 3D Studio MAX, you can create just about anything you can imagine and then use it as a portfolio piece, a portion of a computer game, a scene from a science fiction epic, or any number of other possibilities. The possibilities are limitless with MAX at your side.

Moving from 2D to 3D Graphics

Working with MAX can be frustrating if you don't have a solid handle on the principles and theories you're using. Although the theory is not as interesting as working with MAX itself, understanding the theory now will save you time and trouble later.

The easiest way to start is with a look at how 2D and 3D skills overlap. If you have any past experience with 2D programs such as AutoCAD or Illustrator, you can make good use of what you already know about making objects such as rectangles or circles (called *shapes* in MAX). The main difference between 2D and 3D is depth. 2D drawings have only height and width, with no depth whatsoever. A 2D object can be drawn to look like it's in 3D, but if you want to change the perspective or viewpoint in any way, you have to redraw the object from scratch. Figure 1.2 illustrates this.

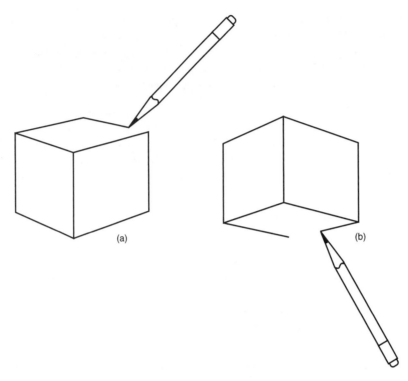

FIGURE 1.2   *2D drawing programs can be used to create images that look 3D, but if you want to view the object from a different perspective, you have to draw it again.*

Because objects have depth (at least in the virtual world), you only have to "draw" them once. Then, you can view them from any angle or perspective without starting from scratch. When you have a view of the objects in the scene, you can apply materials and lighting. At this point, MAX automatically calculates highlight and shadow information for the scene, based on how you arrange the objects and lighting (see Figure 1.3).

When using MAX, not only can you redraw your subject from any angle you choose, but MAX can also create a painting (called a *rendering* in CG terms) of the scene, based on the colors, textures, and lighting you decided on when you built the model. With all of these benefits, it's no wonder many artists rarely go back to traditional ·drawing and painting after they get into 3D.

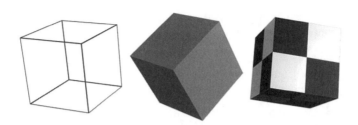

Figure 1.3 *After you construct an object in 3D Studio MAX, you can give it color and texture, light it, and then render it from any angle.*

Although major differences exist between 2D and 3D, many of the 2D drawing tools you might be familiar with are implemented in MAX as well. Tools such as line, arc, circle, and polygon are available and used in much the same ways as in an illustration program. The difference is that instead of using them to create a finished shape in a 2D environment, you use these tools as a starting point for creating a 3D object. Some of the most common 3D forms that start with a 2D shape are lofts, sweeps, lathes, and extrudes. Objects such as wineglasses, bananas, phone handsets, and many others are constructed with these methods. Actually constructing these types of objects is covered later in this book. What's important at this time is to remember that they rely on 2D techniques.

Although 2D programs make use of "layers" to separate objects and organize their drawings, MAX makes use of a powerful object-naming scheme whereby each object in the scene has a distinct name. Object-naming in MAX applies to 2D objects as well as 3D and is combined with advanced display controls as well as groups to accomplish the same things. With grouping, you can choose a related collection of objects and then temporarily combine them into a single unit. This makes it much easier to move, scale, or perform other operations on the group as a whole, because you don't have to choose elements individually every time you want to do something to them. Also, you can add objects to a group, remove them, or reassign them as you wish.

Principles of 3D Computer Graphics in 3D Studio MAX

When working with 3D Studio MAX, you must remember that you are dealing with a virtual computer world. As such, you must understand how objects are represented and stored in this world.

tip

If you are familiar with 2D programs such as AutoCAD or Adobe Illustrator, you can import 2D drawings from these programs into MAX and then convert them to 3D objects. See Chapter 2, "Touring the 3D Studio MAX 3 Interface," for more on importing files.

Within this virtual world, you'll encounter such things as coordinate systems, polylines, cameras, and more. The following sections provide tips to help you better navigate 3D space.

Understanding 3D Space

3D space is a mathematically defined cube of cyberspace inside your computer and controlled by MAX. Cyberspace differs from physical space in that it exists only inside of a piece of software.

Like real space, however, 3D space is infinitely large. Even with MAX, it's easy to get disoriented or to "lose" an object in cyberspace. Fortunately, avoiding this is made easier through the use of coordinates.

Coordinates

In 3D space, the smallest area it is possible to "occupy" is a *point*. Each point is defined by a unique set of three numbers, called *coordinates*. For example, the coordinates 0,0,0 define the center point of 3D space, also called the *origin point*. Other examples of coordinates include 12,96,200 or 200,–349,–303.

Each point in cyberspace has three coordinates, representing the height, width, and depth position of the point. As such, each coordinate represents a single axis in cyberspace.

Axes

An *axis* is an imaginary line in cyberspace that defines a direction. The three standard axes in MAX, referred to as the X, Y, and Z axes, are shown in Figure 1.4. In MAX, you can consider the X axis to be the width, the Y axis to be the depth, and the Z axis to be the height.

The intersection point of the three axes in MAX is the origin point 0,0,0. If you plot a point 1 unit away from the origin along the "right" side of the X axis, that point will be 1,0,0. (A *unit* can be defined as anything you want—such as a foot, an inch, a millimeter, or a centimeter.) If you move another unit in the same direction, the point becomes 2,0,0, and so on. If you move to the left of the origin point, the first point will be –1,0,0, followed by –2,0,0, and so on.

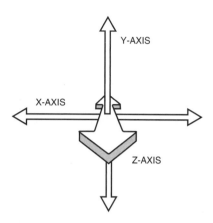

Figure 1.4   *An axis is an imaginary line in 3D space that defines a direction. The standard axes used in MAX are called X, Y, and Z.*

The same holds true for the other axes. When you are traveling up the Y axis, numbers are positive; when you are traveling down, they are negative. For example, 0,–1,0 represents a point 1 unit below the origin, along the Y axis. The same rules apply for the Z axis. Therefore, if you are trying to determine where the coordinate 128,–16,25 is, you will find it 128 points to the right, 16 points below the X axis, and 25 points up in the Z direction.

Lines, Polylines, and Polygons

If you connect two points in cyberspace, you create what is called a *line*. For example, by connecting point 0,0,0 to 5,5,0, you create a line (see Figure 1.5). If you continue the line to 9,3,0, you create a *polyline*, which is a line with more than one segment (a segment is a line that exists between two vertices). In MAX, lines and polylines are called *splines*. If you connect the last point back to the origin, you create a closed shape, with an "inside" and an "outside." This closed shape is a simple three-sided polygon (also called a triangle or a face) and is the basis of objects created in the 3D environment. The concept of a closed shape versus an open shape is very important in 3D Studio MAX. Many 2D objects cannot be converted to 3D shapes without being closed first. You will see this in later chapters.

When you take a look at a polygon, you need to understand its basic components. These basic components, which you can manipulate in MAX, are vertices, edges, and faces. Figure 1.6 shows a diagram of these components.

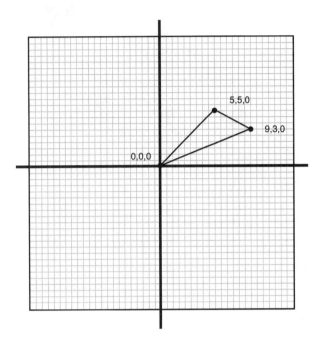

FIGURE 1.5   *When a connection is made between two points, a line is formed. If that line is extended to additional points, it is a polyline. If the line is further extended to the starting point, it forms a polygon or closed shape.*

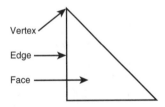

FIGURE 1.6   *Polygons are composed of vertices, edges, and faces.*

A *vertex* (the plural is "vertices") is a point where any number of lines come together and connect to each other—in other words, an intersection point in 3D space. In the previous example, each point that was drawn became one of the vertices in the polygon. Similarly, each line formed a boundary, or *edge*, of the polygon. Finally, when you closed the shape, you created an "inside" and an "outside." The area enclosed by the edges of the polygon—the "inside"—is called a *face*.

Although three-sided polygons (also called *triangles*) are used often in 3D Studio MAX, they are by no means the only type. Polygons (called *quads* or *quadrilaterals*) are also common. Four-sided polygons are the most heavily used in MAX, but a polygon can have any number of sides, as shown in Figure 1.7. Although these dull-looking polygons are not much by themselves, they form complex objects when combined.

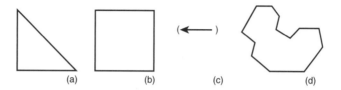

(a)   (b)   (c)   (d)

FIGURE 1.7   *Many polygons in 3D Studio MAX are either triangles, or quads. However, there is no limit to the number of sides a polygon can have.*

3D Objects

In 3D Studio MAX, objects are made up of polygons, patches, or nonuniform rational B-spline modeling surfaces (NURBS). Most objects are created as polygons. Even advanced object types such as patches and NURBS must be converted by MAX to polygons before rendering. In some cases, only a few polygons are necessary to construct a convincing object. Most of the time, however, hundreds or thousands are needed, creating a massive amount of data. Thankfully, because computers are so good at handling reams of complex numbers, they are able to keep track of all the polygons, vertices, edges, and faces in the scene.

For example, in the case of a simple cube, MAX has to keep track of eight vertices, six faces, and 12 visible edges (see Figure 1.8). For more complex objects, the number of polygon elements can soar into the tens of thousands.

tip

Even though polygons can have many sides, they are almost always made up of triangles with one or more edges hidden. For example, in MAX, a quad is two triangles that share a hidden edge, and this is true of more complex polygons as well. In other words, a polygon might look simple, but, in reality, probably has more detail than you see on the screen.

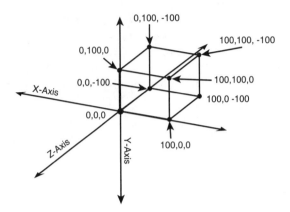

FIGURE 1.8   *A simple cube has eight vertices. Complex objects can have hundreds or thousands of vertices.*

Because these objects are made up of polygons, which are in turn defined by coordinates in cyberspace, the objects themselves take up space in our mathematical universe. For example, a cube might have one corner resting at the origin point and be 101 points wide in each direction, like the one in Figure 1.8. That would mean that the corner of the cube immediately "above" the origin point resides at coordinates 0,100,0, which should be considered the "upper left front" of the cube. Because the cube is on the positive ("right") side of the X axis (the horizontal one), the next set of corners is at 100,0,0 (lower right front) and 100,100,0 (upper right front). Finally, because the cube is positioned "behind" the origin point along the Z axis (depth), the remaining corners are at 0,0,–100 (lower left rear), 0,100,–100 (upper left rear), 100,0,–100 (lower right rear), and 100,100,–100 (upper right rear).

Understanding Viewpoints and Viewports

Just as it would be rather challenging to drive your car if it didn't have windows, manipulating the objects in 3D space is much easier when you can define a viewpoint (see Figure 1.9). A *viewpoint* is a position in or around cyberspace that represents the user's location. Viewpoints are analogous to the *viewports* in 3D Studio MAX, which provide you with the view into 3D space from the viewpoint.

MAX has a default set of four viewports, the Top, Left, Right, and Perspective views. By default, the Top viewport has the X axis running horizontally, the Y axis vertically, and the Z axis coming out of the screen at you, indicating depth. The viewpoint in the Top view is centered on the origin. The other viewports are similarly configured but view the 3D space from different angles. Figure 1.9 shows you an example of how the Top viewport is configured.

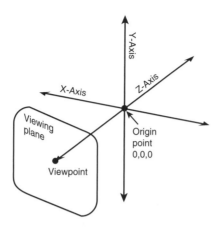

FIGURE 1.9   *The viewpoint represents the current vantage point of the user. The viewing plane indicates the limits of the user's view, because only objects in front of that plane are visible.*

Surrounding the viewpoint at a perpendicular angle is the *viewing plane*—an imaginary flat panel that defines the limits of the user's "sight." In other words, the user can see only things that are in front of the viewing plane, and everything else is "clipped off." In fact, another name for the viewing plane is the *clipping plane*.

To see anything "behind" the viewing plane, the user's viewpoint must change. In a sense, the viewing plane is like the limits of your peripheral vision. If you want to see something that's in back of you, you have to either turn your head (in other words, *rotate* the viewing plane) or step backward until the object is in front of you (*move* the viewing plane).

The monitor screen itself is akin to the viewing plane, because the user can only see what is "beyond" the monitor in cyberspace. This perspective is bound on the sides by the size of the viewport. In MAX, three of the four default views are orthographic, where objects are shown as orthographic projections, which might sound familiar if you have ever taken any mechanical drawing courses. *Orthographic* means that the viewer's location is infinitely distant from the object so that all lines along the same axis are parallel. The fourth default viewport in MAX, the Perspective viewport, is not orthographic and represents a truer view of 3D space, where lines converge to vanishing points as they do in real life.

tip

MAX 3 now supports viewport clipping in addition to camera clipping. Through viewport clipping, you can clip off the front or back of the geometry in the viewport so you can see what is happening inside of it. See Chapter 2, "Touring the 3D Studio MAX 3 Interface" for more info on this feature.

Understanding Display Modes

Just what do you see when peering into cyberspace from your chosen perspective? Because it takes time to convert all of the polygons and data into a form you can see, MAX provides several ways of viewing 3D objects to keep things moving along at a reasonable pace, as shown in Figure 1.10.

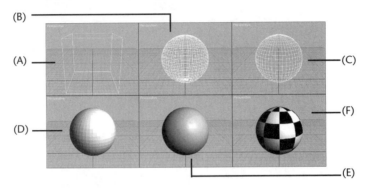

FIGURE 1.10   *MAX is capable of displaying geometry in the viewports in many ways, a few of which are shown here: (A) Bounding Box, (B) Wireframe, (C) Hidden Line, (D) Flat Shaded, (E) Smooth Shaded, (F) Smooth Textured.*

The fastest and simplest display format in MAX is the *bounding box*—a box with the same overall dimensions as the object. The bounding box is a very fast way to indicate an object's position and rough shape and is frequently used in MAX when you're playing back animations or moving an object around in the scene.

Wireframe mode draws the object by using lines to represent the visible edges of the polygon, making it resemble a sculpture made of wire mesh. This enables the user to see the true form of the object and have access to individual vertices for editing and modification.

For a higher level of realism, opt for a shaded display mode. In MAX, a *shaded* view is capable of displaying textures if the material definition is set to display the textures in the viewport. *Flat shaded* mode shows off the surface and color of the object in a coarse manner. The objects appear faceted, but the effects of lighting can be seen for the first time. *Smooth shaded* mode shows the surface of the object with color and smoothing and provides the highest level of realism in MAX. You can also opt for a combination mode called *shaded + edges*, with both shaded and wireframe displays.

MAX 3 also supports a special display mode called *X-Ray*. When this mode is active, all objects are drawn in a light gray color that is semitransparent. The X-Ray mode enables you to easily see inside of an object. It's especially helpful when you have objects, such as bones, inside of other objects.

Coordinate Systems

Until now, the focus has been on the fundamental coordinate system of 3D space, called the *world coordinate system*, as shown in Figure 1.11. Although world coordinates are used by MAX to keep track of everything in 3D space, you might want to switch to different coordinate systems for convenience and more precise control over objects. Two of the most common alternatives for the world coordinate system are view coordinates and local coordinates.

The more accurate or detailed the display mode, the longer it takes to redraw the viewport when something is changed. This can amount to quite a bit of time over the course of a project, especially with complex models or a scene with many objects. If you find things bogging down, hide unneeded objects or switch to a simpler display mode. These topics are covered in full detail in Chapter 2.

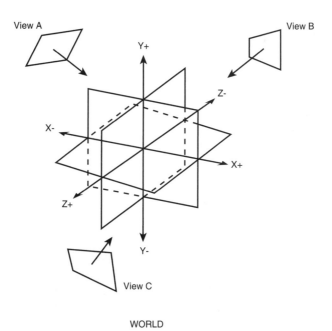

FIGURE 1.11   *The fundamental coordinate system of 3D space is world coordinates. They remain the same, regardless of the viewpoint.*

View coordinates use the viewport as the basis for the X, Y, and Z axes and remain the same, no matter how your viewpoint on the 3D scene changes (see Figure 1.12).

This can be convenient for repositioning objects. For example, to move an object to the right in your scene, you always have to move it positively along the X axis when you're using view coordinates. Almost all of MAX's default transformations (such as Move, Rotate, and Scale) make use of view coordinates as their default coordinate system.

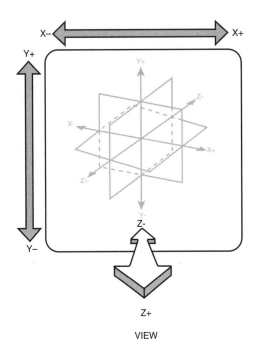

FIGURE 1.12   *View coordinates are tied to the viewport and are always oriented in the same manner.*

Even though you have world coordinate systems, each object in MAX also maintains its own local coordinate system. When you rotate the object in world coordinates, the *local coordinates* rotate with the object, as shown in Figure 1.13. This is very desirable when you are rotating the object because using coordinate systems other than view or local can produce unexpected results. For example, say you rotated a box 45 degrees in the Front viewport and then 45 degrees in the Left viewport. When you look at this box in the Top viewport, you'll need local coordinates to rotate the box correctly along its long axis.

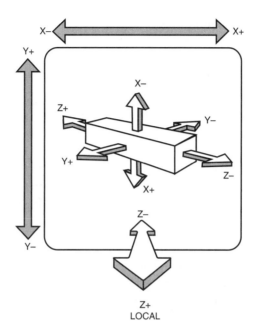

FIGURE 1.13   *Local coordinates are assigned on an object-by-object basis, making it easier to rotate individual objects predictably.*

Coordinate Systems and Rotation

When you rotate an object, three factors influence the way it turns:

- Which coordinate system (world, view, local, or user) is currently active
- The location of the rotational center point (the pivot point in MAX)
- Which axis you choose to rotate the object around

As you know, the current coordinate system can have a big impact on how the axes are oriented, so which one to use is the first thing you should decide. In general, you will want to use the local coordinate system when rotating an object around one of its own axes.

When local coordinates are selected, the center point is usually in the center of the object (unless it has been repositioned) and is located at the origin of the local coordinate system.

The final factor, the selected axis, determines which of the three axes to spin the object around, subject to the position of the center (pivot) point.

To illustrate why you must often switch to using the local coordinate system for rotation, imagine that you have created an elongated box like the one in Figure 1.14.

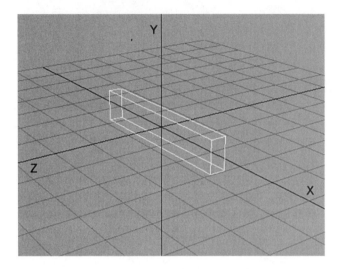

FIGURE 1.14   *When an object is in alignment with the world coordinates, the world coordinates can be used to manipulate it predictably.*

By default, the box is created in alignment with the world coordinate system. At this point, then, you could rotate the object by using world coordinates without any problems. After you rotate the box at something other than a 90-, 180-, or 270-degree angle, however, the object's local axes are no longer aligned to the world coordinates (see Figure 1.15). Therefore, you'll be out of luck if try to use anything except the local coordinates to rotate the object along its X axis because the object's local X axis and the world X axis are not the same anymore. Indeed, the object would rotate at some oddball angle and it would take some effort to get it rotated in the proper manner.

There are some ways to accomplish a controlled rotation without relying on the local axis. One way is to carefully position the viewpoint to make the view and local axes align and then rotate the object by using the viewpoint coordinate system axes.

A better method is to define a user coordinate system, as shown in Figure 1.16. A *user axis* is just what it sounds like—an axis you define. A user axis can be at any angle, or it can be aligned to an existing axis. In this case, you could define your axis along the same line as the object's local X axis. Then, you could rotate the object around the user axis to accomplish the same result.

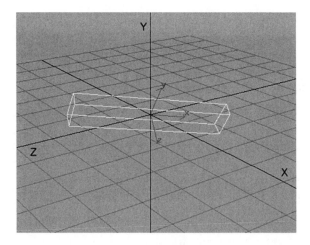

FIGURE 1.15   *When an object is no longer aligned with the world coordinate system, you must switch to local or view coordinates to properly rotate the object around one of its axes.*

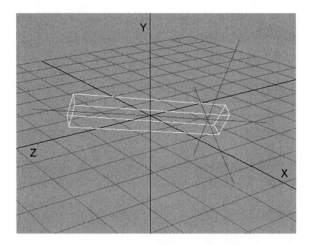

FIGURE 1.16   *An alternative to using the local or view coordinates is to define a user axis, which can be at any angle. User axes are often used for defining joint rotation points in character animation.*

Lights

So far, you've been wandering around in MAX's 3D universe practically in the dark. You need some lights to illuminate the objects so you can see them in the finished rendering. (MAX actually creates two default lights to illuminate the scene until you create your own, which makes life a little easier).

3D lights work much like real photography studio lights except that you can position them anywhere (including inside an object) and they don't fall down if objects bump into them. Each light type has its own set of configuration parameters with which you can control features such as light color and intensity. Also, most lights can cast shadows (different sorts), which add a great deal of realism to a scene. Following are the four main lights used in MAX:

- **Omni lights:** These are like bare bulbs and cast light in all directions.
- **Spot lights:** These are directional sources and are often used to highlight portions of an object or provide the main source of illumination for a scene.
- **Distant lights:** Also directional, but used to simulate very distant light sources, such as the sun, that cast parallel shadows.
- **Ambient light:** Present everywhere in the 3D space, illuminating all surfaces equally. Ambient lights generally are used to define a consistent brightness throughout the scene.

MAX allows you to use as many lights in a scene as you like, but adding more lights to a scene increases the rendering time. Lights are covered in full detail in Chapter 11, "Working with Lights and Cameras."

Cameras

Cameras are non-rendering objects that you can position in the 3D scene. They work like real world cameras in that they provide a viewpoint on the scene that can be adjusted and animated. This camera viewpoint is different from most of the ones users employ for modeling, because it enables the scene to be viewed in more realistic and natural perspective modes. Just like real cameras, MAX cameras have different settings for lens lengths and focal lengths, for example, which you can use to precisely control the view of the scene.

MAX gives you two types of cameras: a target camera and a free camera. A *target camera* makes use of a target—a point in 3D space where the camera is aimed—making it easy to see where a camera is aimed in non-camera viewports. A *free camera* doesn't have a target; its view is changed by rotating or moving the camera itself instead of by repositioning a target. Cameras are explored in further detail in Chapter 11.

Rendering

Rendering is the process by which MAX interprets all of the objects in the scene, in the context of lighting, materials, and viewpoint, to produce a finished image. The resulting image may be either a still or a frame in an animation sequence.

To understand how 3D Studio MAX takes a bunch of polygons and turns them into a finished rendering, you have to examine how the computer interprets polygon surfaces. First of all, to be "seen" by MAX as a surface, a polygon face must have a normal. A *normal*, represented by an arrow sticking out of the center of the face, indicates which side of the face is visible and which direction it's facing, as shown in Figure 1.17. If the normal faces away from the camera, the face is invisible. The opposite is true if the normal faces the camera. When MAX begins rendering, it calculates how much lighting is striking a particular polygon face (and from which direction), based on the orientation of the normal.

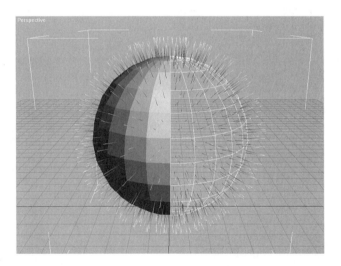

FIGURE 1.17   *Normals are imaginary lines extending from polygon faces. They are used by the software to calculate the intensity and direction of light striking the face. They also determine the visibility of a face. If a normal is facing away from the camera, the face is invisible.*

Most of the time, only one side of a polygon face has a normal, making it a *single-sided polygon*. Single-sided polygons can only be "seen" from the side with the normal, which can cause problems in some rendering situations (such as when a camera is moved to the inside of an object), as shown in Figures 1.18a and 1.18b. Therefore, the MAX rendering engine can be instructed to make a polygon double-sided, so it can be viewed from either side, as shown in Figures 1.18c and 1.18d.

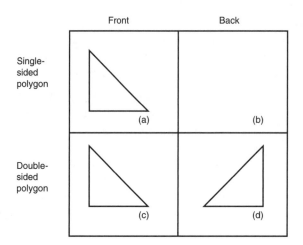

FIGURE 1.18   *Single-sided polygons have only one visible face, but double-sided polys are visible from either side.*

Rendering troubles such as "invisible" polygons also can arise if a polygon is nonplanar. Using a four-sided polygon, or quad, as an example, imagine that it's resting on a flat plane (see Figure 1.19a). If you take the right front vertex and pull it up away from the rest, the polygon becomes "bent," or nonplanar (see Figure 1.19b). Although it is still an acceptable polygon (remember, polygons can have any number of sides), part of it might not render properly because the normal won't be in the right position. One solution to this problem is to convert all objects to triangular polygons. Because they have only three sides, it is impossible for them to be become nonplanar.

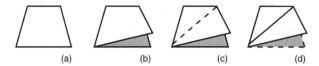

FIGURE 1.19   *Polygons with more than three vertices can become nonplanar if one of the vertices is out of alignment with the others. This can result in rendering errors.*

In addition to taking into account the position of normals, when the MAX rendering engine renders a scene, it considers any color or texture (material) that has been applied to a polygon, the positions of lights, their intensity and color, and many other factors. Then MAX renders the results of these calculations on the screen as an image.

MAX supports several rendering modes (either natively or through plug-ins) in a material-by-material method. In other words, you define the rendering modes on an object-by-object basis by assigning different materials with different types of properties. MAX 3 provides basic support for nine different shading modes.

MAX 3 supports the following rendering modes:

upgrader's note

MAX 2 supported only five shading modes. To get the most out of MAX 3, you will probably want to convert some of your materials over to the newer MAX 3 materials and shading modes. See Chapter 12, "Fundamentals of Materials," and Chapter 13, "More on Materials," for more on these features.

- **Wireframe.** This is the fastest and most basic rendering mode. It is very similar to a wireframe display in a viewport.

- **Phong.** In this mode, MAX calculates the color at each vertex of the face and then interpolates the result across the polygon face. The effect is smoothly blended object surfaces that are much more realistic than a flat rendering's surface. In addition, *specular highlights* (the bright reflections of light seen on glossy objects) are added for more realism.

- **Blinn.** Similar to Phong, but produces a more subtle highlight that tends to look a little more realistic.

- **Metal.** Provides enhanced highlights and deep rich colors within the material itself. This gives the material a deep metallic appearance.

- **Oren-Nayer Blinn.** Very similar to the Blinn mode; the difference is in the highlights. Oren-Nayer has a very subtle highlight, making this type of shading excellent for fabrics and other nonreflective surfaces.

- **Anisotropic.** A modified version of Ward anisotropic, which stretches the anisotropic shading in one direction only. Ward provides you with two directions of controls.

- **Strauss.** This shader is used to create enhanced metal effects and generally is better than the older metal shader. Strauss does a better job of handling the highlights and deep color effects that appear in metal objects when the shininess is high.

- **Multi-Layer.** This shader is the last anisotropic shader. It is called a multi-layer shader because it enables you to layer specular highlights on top of each other. If the highlights are different, you can create an anisotropic effect.

- **Raytracing.** The color and value of each pixel on the screen is calculated by casting an imaginary ray backward from the viewer's perspective into the model, to determine what light and surface factors are influencing it. The difference between raytracing and the other methods mentioned (collectively called *scanline rendering* techniques) is that the ray can be bounced off of surfaces and bent just-like real light, producing excellent shadows, reflections, and refractive effects.

MAX actually implements raytracing as a material instead of as a completely different rendering mode. This gives you the advantage of selectively raytracing objects in the scene, as well as increasing the speed.

Beyond these basic shading modes, you can make use of other modes in MAX through the use of plug-in rendering engines. Through plug-ins, you can add raytracing engines with advanced features or even make use of advanced radiosity rendering techniques. *Radiosity* is a global illumination system by which light is distributed throughout the entire model, enabling a single light to correctly illuminate the scene. Lightscape and RadioRay are examples of radiosity programs that work with MAX. With radiosity, you can produce extremely accurate lighting for a scene, but at the cost of very long rendering times. The materials mentioned here are explored in Chapters 12 and 13, and rendering is discussed in Chapter 14, "Rendering."

Animation

The last topic of 3D graphics to discuss here is *animation*, which can be defined as the movement of objects over time. Time in the digital world is interpreted as frames. By displaying still frames at a quick enough rate, you create the illusion of animation. This is the principle behind traditional animation and is also the principle that enables us to watch films. Three standards of time are used the most: NTSC, PAL, and FILM. NTSC is defined as 30 frames per second, PAL as 25 frames per second, and FILM as 24 frames per second.

Animation is created in MAX by creating keyframes. A *keyframe* is a frame in which a particular animation event must occur. Keyframes are placed in different frames along a timeline, and then animation is interpreted between the keyframes. This enables you to quickly and easily create animation without having to position the objects in every frame, as in stop animation or traditional cell animation.

MAX enables you to animate just about everything, from the position of an object to the actual object creation parameters (such as length and width in the case of a box). You can move and change objects, pieces of objects, lights, cameras, and even materials. You can view the animation as a timeline or function curve in MAX's TrackView utility. Chapter 15, "Understanding Animation Concepts," Chapter 16, "Exploring Basic Animation Methods," and Chapter 17, "Exploring Other Animation Methods," explore the methods by which MAX enables you to create animation.

Conclusion

In this chapter, you explored the following topics:

- 3D graphics defined
- Moving from 2D to 3D graphics
- Principles of 3D computer graphics

That's it for the basic 3D theory behind MAX. In other sections of the book, you will find more on 3D theory, with in-depth explanations of specific aspects of 3D theory, where applicable. This chapter provided an overview to help familiarize you with the terminology and basic process.

Now it is time to start becoming familiar with MAX. The next chapter gets you started by introducing you to the MAX 3 user interface and how to work with it.

CHAPTER 2

Touring the 3D Studio MAX 3 Interface

Before exploring how to make the most out of 3D Studio MAX 3, you need to learn how to navigate around in the program. In other words, you need to get a little practical experience working with the MAX 3 interface and some of the features it presents to you.

At the end of this chapter, you'll create an animation of a basic corporate logo. This exercise helps demonstrate the overall workflow process of MAX and gives you some practical experience in using the MAX interface. This same exercise is also used in other chapters in this book to explore relevant topics. In particular, this chapter covers the following topics:

- The MAX 3 Interface
- Working with Files
- Working with XRefs
- Working with Viewports
- Selecting Commands
- Customizing the MAX Interface
- Controlling the Display of Objects
- Object Naming
- Working with Groups
- Working with Object Selection
- Bringing It All Together
- Using the Asset Manager
- Using Plug-ins with MAX

The MAX 3 Interface

The 3D Studio MAX 3 interface is quite powerful and provides a highly streamlined workflow process. Thanks to this advanced interface, you will find working with MAX to be extremely intuitive, enabling you to learn the software quickly and grow with it well into the future. The interface in MAX 3 has been totally reworked from the MAX 1 and MAX 2 interfaces, and you can now customize the interface fully. Figure 2.1 shows you the new MAX 3 interface.

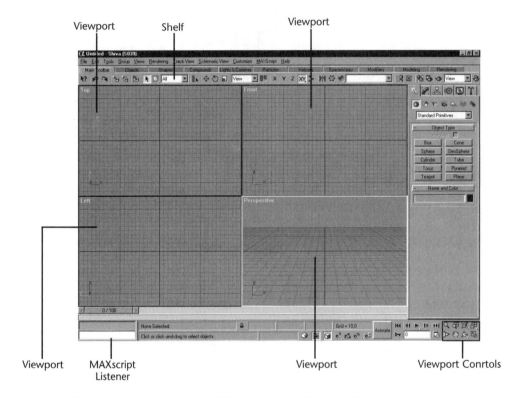

FIGURE 2.1   *Important areas of the MAX 3 interface include the viewports, the command panel, the Main toolbar, the Tab Panel, the viewport controls, and the MAXScript listener window. This screen shot uses the smaller toolbar icons.*

Working with Files

Before further exploring the interface, this is a good time to look at how MAX works with files. All 3D Studio MAX files are loaded and saved with a .**MAX** extension. By choosing File, Open or File, Save, you can use standard Windows Open and Save dialog boxes, but MAX provides you with more file functionality than that.

In MAX, you are also able to merge files, replace files, and import files.

File Properties

Another new feature to MAX 3 is the capability to save file properties with the MAX file. File properties are simply text-based information strings that are saved with the file, enabling you to fully describe the file. Some examples of properties include Title, Subject, Author, Category, and Keywords. You can access the File Properties dialog box, shown in Figure 2.2, by selecting File, Properties from the pull-down menus.

In addition to the basic file properties, the Contents tab of the File Properties dialog box displays important information about the file, such as objects, materials, number of faces, and even what plug-ins are used in the file. Last, the Custom tab enables you to add your own custom text fields, such as Checked By or Date Completed so you can perform basic project tracking through the file properties.

upgrader's note

MAX 3 does support the opening of MAX 1.x or 2.x files by simply opening the file with File, Open. In most cases, the file imports but you will need to make changes to the lights, materials, and antialiasing settings to take advantage of the new features in MAX 3. If, for some reason, the file will not load with File, Open, try using File, Merge and then saving the file, which converts it to MAX 3 format.

Unfortunately, MAX 3 files cannot be opened in MAX 1.X or 2.x. In this case, you need to use File, Export and export the file as a .3ds file.

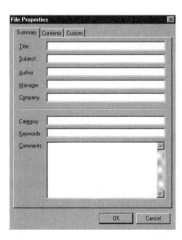

Figure 2.2   *In the File Properties dialog box, you can add full text descriptions to your file.*

The nice thing about file properties is that they are exposed directly in the MAX file itself. If you are browsing your system with the NT or Windows 98 Explorer and you run across a MAX file, you can right-click the file, choose Properties, and access this information. Figure 2.3 shows you an example of this in Windows NT 4.0.

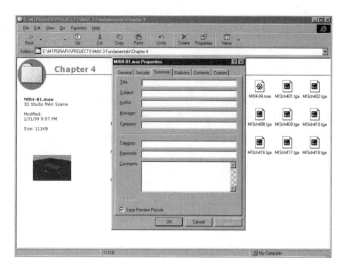

FIGURE 2.3   *The MAX file properties exposed through the NT Explorer. You can access these properties without loading the file.*

The last benefit of the MAX file properties involves the MAX File Finder. The MAX File Finder utility enables you to search your hard drive or network for files. In fact, it can use the file properties as a filter when searching for files. In other words, by using a custom file property field, you could search for all MAX files created by a particular animator in your company or for all files related to a specific client.

To access the MAX File Finder, go to the Utility command panel. Click the More button, select MAX File Finder from the list of utilities, and click OK. When a Start button appears in the command panel, click this button to launch the File Finder, shown in Figure 2.4.

FIGURE 2.4   *The MAX File Finder, where you can search your systems for MAX files, based on filename or file property information.*

Using the file properties and the MAX File Finder provides complete control over your MAX files, from information to organization. A good idea is to start using the file properties to document your MAX files as you create them. You'll find the files easier to work with in the future.

Merging Files

One of the nicer file features of MAX 3 is the capability to load a file and merge it with the current scene. This is handy anytime you want to bring an object in from another scene and use it in the current scene. Even more useful is that you don't have to merge the entire file. When you select the file, MAX prompts you with a Select by Name dialog box where you can select the objects, lights, camera, and such that you want to merge from that file. It's extremely easy to reuse components from scenes you have created in the past. Worth noting is that you can merge only other 3D Studio MAX files. To bring non-MAX files into your scene, you must use File, Import instead. The following exercise merges several objects from one MAX scene to another.

Merging a File into a Scene

1. Choose File, Merge. You are presented with a File Open dialog box.

2. Select the file **MF02-01.MAX** from the accompanying CD. The Object Selection dialog box appears, where you can select the objects from the file that you want to merge into your scene. Select all objects in the list and choose OK.

3. If you selected any objects that have the same name as objects in your current scene, you are prompted to rename them. At this point, you're merging a table with a teapot on it into the scene.

   A similar merge command available in MAX is File, Insert Tracks, which enables you to pull animation tracks from one file and insert them in another. This feature is covered in Chapter 16, "Exploring Basic Animation Methods."

Replacing Files

As an alternative to merging files, you can replace objects in your scene with objects from another MAX file. Select this option by choosing File, Replace. When you select a file with which to replace objects, MAX searches the selected file for object names that match those in your current scene. Because object-naming in MAX (discussed later in this chapter) is case sensitive, only exact matches are processed. If MAX finds any exact matches, the objects are replaced. This command relies on the naming of objects to perform the replacement. Make sure you do not give two objects in your scene the same name.

For example, if you are working on a complex animation, you can replace complex objects with simple stand-in objects to make editing the animation quicker. Then, when it comes time to render the file image, replace the proxy objects with the real objects.

Importing Files

The last file operation to look at is MAX's capability to import files from other formats. You can import other file formats by selecting File, Import. You can also export files by choosing File, Export. Natively, MAX supports 3D Studio 4 (3DS, PRJ, and SHP), Adobe Illustrator, IGES, StereoLithography (STL), and AutoCAD DWG and DXF for imports and supports 3D Studio 4, ASE, DXF, STL, DXF, DWG, and VRML WRL files for exporting. Additional file formats are supported for input or output through the use of plug-ins. This provides you with practically unlimited file-exchange capabilities with the appropriate plug-ins.

After you have opened, imported, or merged your files into MAX, you can see the data in the MAX viewports. The viewports are powerful tools for viewing your scene from a variety of angles as you create and modify the geometry and generally work with your scene.

Working with XRefs

One of the major new features added to 3D Studio MAX 3 is that of XRefs. *XRefs* (also called external references) are a method of placing objects or entire scenes in your current scene (called the parent scene) by referencing an existing MAX file. If you then make a change to the referenced scene or object, MAX updates all parent scenes to which the changed scene is referenced. If you have worked with programs such as AutoCAD in the past, you will find this concept very familiar. MAX supports two types of XRefs: objects and scenes. You can access both commands through the File menu.

XRef Objects

XRef objects enable you to reference one or more objects from one or more external files into your scene. This saves time and promotes an efficient workflow in a workgroup situation. You can access the XRef object's controls by choosing File, XRef Objects to open the dialog box shown in Figure 2.5.

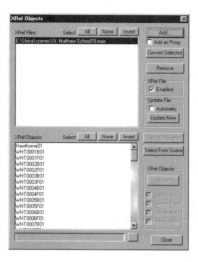

FIGURE 2.5   *The XRef Objects dialog box. Here, you can select a scene and any objects in that scene to be referenced into the current scene. You can also use this dialog box to manage those references.*

Adding XRef objects is a very simple process:

1. Select the Add button in the upper-right corner.
2. Select the MAX file that contains the objects you want to XRef into the current scene.
3. A list appears of objects in that scene. Select the objects you want.
4. Choose Close and the objects are loaded into the scene.

When objects are referenced into the current scene, they are treated as standard MAX objects with a few exceptions. You can scale, rotate, and move the objects around in the scene as you like; you can even change the materials on the object. But, you cannot apply modifiers or change the geometry short of the basic transforms in MAX.

You can return to the XRef Objects dialog box to manage your XRef objects. One thing you might want to do is update the current XRef in your scene. If someone else is working on the object on another machine, you can simply update the XRef to reload it. You can also enable Automatic Updates; that way, if a change is made, it is automatically updated in your scene.

More important, you can select referenced objects in the bottom portion of the dialog box. After you select these objects, you can "bind" them to the scene by clicking the Merge button to merge the object instead of creating a reference to it.

Following are several advantages of XRef objects:

- You can create repositories of objects in individual MAX files. For example, you can create files for trees, cars, people, and more, and then simply XRef the objects into your scenes.

- If you want to change one of the reference objects, changing the repository file updates the object for all scenes that reference it. This, of course, requires good file management on your part to make sure you don't inadvertently update an object that shouldn't be updated.

- You can also use XRefs to manage the parent scene's file size. In the past, if you merged objects into a scene, they became a part of the scene, increasing the size of the scene. Now, only a marker is saved in the scene, telling MAX where and how to load and place the object the next time you load the scene. Hence, the MAX files for parent scenes don't get much larger in size.

- The biggest advantage of XRefs comes when you are working as part of a group on a large scene. Through this system, several people can be working on different objects in the same scene and another person can be collecting these objects and placing them in a scene to see how they work.

One thing to be careful of when working with XRefs is file locations. When an object is referenced into a scene, the location of that file on your system or network becomes important. If you move or rename the referenced file, you will have a broken link in your scene. You can fix this link in the XRef Objects dialog box. To fix the link, you need to remove the XRef and then re-create it by using the Add button. As a rule, if you have sets of files that you will consistently XRef into scenes, place them in a directory or set of directories you will not change.

XRef Scenes

XRef scenes work on a similar principle to XRef objects, but you reference an entire scene rather than just objects out of that scene. If you choose File, XRef Scenes, you receive the dialog box shown in Figure 2.6.

The process for adding XRef scenes to your current scene is the same as for XRef objects, except you don't have to select any objects. When a scene is referenced, you can choose to ignore various parts of the scene, such as cameras, lights, shapes, helpers, or even any animation contained in the scene. You can also bind the scene to another object in your scene so the object becomes a parent of the referenced scene. Then, when the bound object moves, so does the scene.

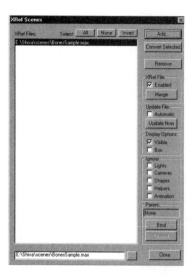

FIGURE 2.6   *The XRef Scenes dialog box, where you can manage entire scenes.*

The most important difference between XRef scenes and objects is the fact that XRef scenes, when loaded into the current scene, cannot be selected, moved, or otherwise modified. You can't even use Move, Transform, or Scale on these scenes unless you bind them to another object. As a result, if you are going to create scenes for referencing into other scenes, you must be careful about the size, scale, and location of all objects in the scenes or they might not match when you import them.

Overall, XRefs are powerful tools for both workgroups and individual animators. By making use of these features, you can create links between files that enable you to make broad changes to large numbers of different scenes without much difficulty or time.

Now that you have a good sense of how files are handled by MAX, it is time to take a look at the MAX viewports.

Working with Viewports

One of the most important user-interface features is the MAX viewports. MAX *viewports* enable you to view your scene from any of a variety of angles. Without the viewports, you cannot select objects, apply materials, or perform any other operation on the scene itself.

Obviously, working with the MAX viewports is very important. MAX comes up with a default setting of four viewports: Top, Front, Left, and Perspective, as shown in Figure 2.1. These views can be changed, manipulated, and controlled in just about every way that you could possibly need. As a result, the capability to configure your viewports becomes important.

Configuring Viewports

MAX viewports support many types of settings and modes, all of which can be configured by you, the user. You can configure MAX viewports in one of two ways. The first method is to right-click the viewport name in the upper-left corner of each viewport window. This pops up a menu where you can adjust the most commonly used viewport settings. Figure 2.7 shows you this pop-up menu.

The second method of controlling viewports is through the Viewport Configuration dialog box, which can be accessed through the pop-up menu, or by selecting Customize, Viewport Configuration (see Figure 2.8). The Viewport Configuration dialog box provides you with more options for the viewports than the pop-up menu. In general, you use this dialog box to set viewport features permanently or to apply the features to more than one viewport at the same time.

FIGURE 2.7

The viewport pop-up menu where you can select the shading level, view, or other viewport options with a right click.

The tabs on the Viewport Configuration dialog box include the following:

■ **Rendering Method:** On this tab, you can set the Rendering Level, Apply To, Rendering Options, Fast View, and Perspective User View options. Figure 2.9 shows you the various rendering methods in MAX viewports.

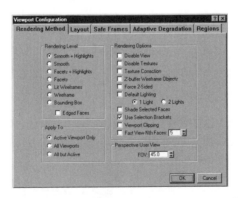

FIGURE 2.8   *The Viewport Configuration Dialog box where you can completely control the viewports in MAX, from the shading level to the layout.*

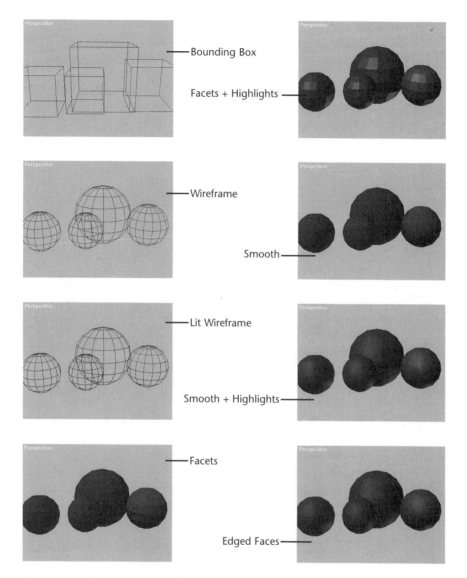

FIGURE 2.9 *The rendering levels available in the Viewport Configuration dialog box. Controlling the rendering level directly affects the performance of your system.*

- ■ **Layout:** At the top of this tab are several predefined layouts from which you can select. You can change the viewports by clicking each shaded area and selecting the view you want from the pop-up menu that appears. You should select the viewport layouts you think will enable you to work with MAX most efficiently.

■ **Safe Frames.** On this tab, you can set the Safe Frame parameters. *Safe frames* create a box in the viewport that indicates the safe area of the view. When you view your animations on a TV, parts of the image are chopped off to fit the TV screen format. Anything that appears within the safe frame will not be cropped on a TV. The default safe frame is 90 percent of the original frame.

■ **Adaptive Degradation.** On this tab, you can set the General Degradation, Active Degradation, Degrade Parameters, and Interrupt Settings options. These control how MAX adjusts the shading level of the viewports to optimize speed.

■ **Regions.** On this tab, you can set up a zoomed region within which to work for camera viewports. In other words, you can temporarily convert a camera view to a blowup of a portion of the camera view so you can work at a higher level of detail. The Virtual Viewport option of the regions is only available when you are using the OpenGL driver.

Working with the Viewport Controls

The viewport controls enable you to maneuver around in the scene. Operations such as zooming, panning, and rotating the view are handled through the viewport controls. Even camera views and others that are created as objects in MAX can be controlled through the viewport controls.

upgrader's note

Previous versions of MAX supported a Swap Layouts feature enabling you to use a hotkey to switch between two different layouts (A and B). That feature is no longer supported in MAX 3 because of changes in the interface.

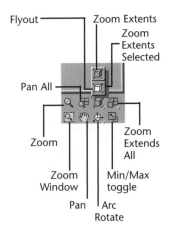

FIGURE 2.10
The MAX Viewport controls, with which you can zoom, pan, or rotate your view of the scene.

The viewport controls are located in the lower-right corner of the MAX interface, as shown in Figure 2.1. Depending on the type of viewport currently active, the buttons shown here will change. For example, a different set of buttons is available for a camera view than for a top view. When you select a viewport control, the button turns green to indicate it is active for the current viewport. Figure 2.10 shows you each of the standard MAX viewport controls.

In addition to the color change on the selected button, the MAX cursor changes to indicate the currently selected viewport control command. Almost all of the viewport controls are based on a click-and-drag methodology. Zoom, which enables you to zoom in and out of your scene, works by clicking and dragging the mouse up and down in the current viewport.

In addition, MAX supports *cursor wrapping*, which occurs when you are using a command such as Zoom. When you are zooming in on a viewport, you are moving the cursor toward the top of the screen. When the cursor reaches the top, it automatically wraps to the bottom of the screen so you can continue to zoom in further.

note

MAX 3 provides full support for the Microsoft Intellimouse. This enables you to use the wheel to perform functions, such as zooming, in any viewport. Three-button mice are also supported, enabling you to pan and zoom with the middle mouse button.

Several of the viewport controls have flyout toolbars (shown previously in Figure 2.10) that provide additional viewport controls. The presence of a flyout toolbar is indicated by a small black triangle in the lower-right corner of the button. To access the flyout, click the button and hold the mouse button down until the flyout appears. For example, the Zoom Extents command has a sister command that performs the Zoom Extents command but limits it to the currently selected object. The Arc Rotate command has two sister commands: one to rotate around the currently selected object and the other to rotate around the currently selected sub-object.

Throughout the course of this book, you will get plenty of practice using the various viewport controls as you work through the exercises.

Selecting Commands

MAX provides several primary methods for selecting commands in its user interface. Commands can be selected from the following:

upgrader's note

The short toolbar that was available in MAX 2.5 and earlier is no longer available in MAX 3. You will need to run your interface at a minimum of 1024×768 to see all of the toolbar when using the small icons. If you are not able to do this, you can click the toolbar and drag it left and right to access commands that are offscreen.

- **Pull-down menus.** MAX has a total of 11 pull-down menus you can use to access certain commands, such as file commands or rendering commands. These pull-down menus work just like pull-downs from other Windows programs.

- **Tab Panel.** A new addition to MAX 3 is the Tab Panel. The Tab Panel is a toolbar that supports a tabbed interface with each tab representing a different toolbar (refer to Figure 2.1).

The Tab Panel is powerful and flexible enough that the Main Toolbar has been moved to the Tab Panel as its own tab. Most of the commands available in MAX are found on the Tab Panel. In addition, you can add your own commands and MAXScript Macros to the Tab Panel as well. The Tab Panel can easily be displayed or hidden bypressing the Y or 2 keys on your keyboard. This hotkey toggle is very useful when you need more screen space to work on your scene.

- **Command panels:** MAX has six command panels (Create, Modify, Hierarchy, Motion, Display, and Utility), each with its own set of commands and functionality. You switch command panels by clicking the appropriate tab to bring that command panel to the front.

- **Floating command palettes:** These palettes are replicas of specific commands found in certain command panels. Because they are floating, they are modeless dialog boxes, meaning you can access them at any time without canceling other commands. An example of such a command panel is the Display floater, which provides you with all of the object display controls on a floating panel.

- **Keyboard shortcuts:** These are simply quick methods of accessing commands by one and two key combinations on the keyboard. To create or adjust your own keyboard shortcuts, select Customize, Preferences from the pulldown menus. Then, select the Keyboard tab in the Preferences dialog box. You may save your own set of keyboard shortcuts to a file if you want to be able to load them into a different MAX session.

In some cases, there are multiple methods for accessing the same command, but most commands are found in only one place in the interface.

When you use MAX plug-ins, they integrate seamlessly into the interface. As such, plug-in commands are accessed in the same way as the standard commands in MAX.

---

note

The first time you load 3D Studio MAX 3, you will notice that the Main Toolbar uses larger icons (24×24 pixels) than it did in previous versions (16×16). The larger icons are intended to be used on systems running at a screen resolution of 1280×1024. If your system is not capable of running that high, you can switch to a smaller set of icons by choosing Customize, Preferences and turning off Use Large Toolbar Buttons on the General tab. You will then need to run your system at 1024×768 to be able to see all of the small icons. All screen shots in this book use the 16×16 pixel icons, so your screen might look different, depending on how it is configured.

tip

MAX 3 supports keyboard shortcuts for both MAX itself and any plug-in that might be running in MAX. At the bottom of the screen, to the left of the Crossing/Window select button, is a Plug-In Keyboard Shortcut toggle. When it is toggled to active, all keyboard shortcuts work with plug-ins. When inactive, they work with MAX itself.

Command Panels

The next method for selecting commands is through the command panels. By far, you will use this method more than any other, especially if you do a lot of work with plug-ins in MAX. Figure 2.11 shows you the Create command panel and its various parts.

3D Studio MAX provides six command panels (Create, Modify, Hierarchy, Motion, Display, and Utility), each with its own set of commands and functionality. You can switch among command panels by clicking the appropriate tab to bring that command panel to the front. Switching command panels cancels the currently selected command.

Take a close look at Figure 2.11 and notice the layout of the Create command panel. Across the top of the command panel are seven buttons, each with a drop-down menu. The seven buttons categorize different types of MAX objects you can create—Geometry, Shapes, Lights, Cameras, Helpers, Space Warps, and Systems.

When you select the Geometry button, for example, a drop-down list appears below the button, categorizing the different types of geometry you can create. Figure 2.12 shows you this drop-down list.

The command panel is hierarchically organized to enable you to quickly and easily find a specific command. After you select a set of commands under the Geometry button, such as Standard Primitives, a rollout appears and lists the types of standard primitives you can create. By selecting any of these buttons, you are actually selecting a command in MAX. When you do so, further rollouts appear below the Name and Color rollouts.

The box command has three rollouts, two of which are open. The Keyboard entry rollout is closed, indicated by the + symbol to the left of the rollout header. Clicking the header once expands the rollout; clicking a rollout header that is already open closes the rollout.

FIGURE 2.11
The Create command panel is where you access most of the commands that generate geometry in your scene.

tip

The entire command panel can be undocked from the right side of the scene and turned into a floating command panel. This makes accessing commands quick and easy. See the section on "Customizing the MAX Interface" later in this chapter.

FIGURE 2.12
The Geometry drop-down list, where you can select the type of geometry you want to create. Selecting a type of geometry changes the buttons listed below in the command panel rollout area.

As you can guess, sometimes the rollouts become much longer than the screen can accommodate. In these instances, you can use the mouse to scroll up and down the rollout by clicking and dragging vertically on any area of the rollout that does not have a spinner or text box.

You can speed up the scrolling of rollouts by holding down the Ctrl key while dragging your mouse. This increases the scrolling speed substantially. You can use this feature in many instances, including zooming or panning in the viewports or browsing in the Material/Map browser.

To make command panel access even easier, you can now right-click the command panel to access a pop-up menu with rollout controls. These controls enable you to maneuver around in the rollouts quickly and easily. Figure 2.13 shows you this pop-up menu.

At the top of the menu shown in Figure 2.13, you can expand or collapse the current rollout or all of the rollouts. In the bottom half of the menu, in a context-sensitive area, you can selectively open and close rollouts specific to the command with which you are working.

FIGURE 2.13
The command panel rollout pop-up menu where you can quickly manipulate a command panel.

The rest of the command panels are similarly configured with command buttons at the top and rollouts at the bottom. Only the Modify and Utility command panels enable you to customize the buttons that appear at the top of the command panel. As you progress through the rest of this book, you will become accustomed to using these command panels.

Keyboard Shortcuts

Another method of accessing commands in MAX is through the use of keyboard shortcuts. Keyboard shortcuts are simply quick methods of accessing commands by a key or a two-key combination on the keyboard. Many people find this is the fastest method of accessing commands.

To create or adjust your own keyboard shortcuts, choose Customize, Preferences from the pull-down menus. Then, select the Keyboard tab in the Preferences dialog box to get the screen shown in Figure 2.14.

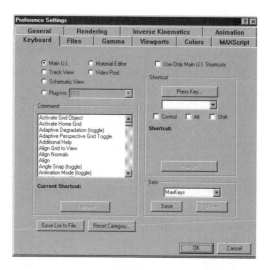

FIGURE 2.14   *The keyboard shortcut controls in the Preferences dialog box. Here, you can create and customize your own keyboard shortcuts to enable quick access to MAX commands.*

At the top of the Preferences dialog box are six categories of keyboard shortcuts to work with: Main UI, Track View, Schematic View, Material Editor, Video Post, and Plug-ins. Any plug-ins you have installed in your system that work with custom keyboard shortcuts will appear in this drop-down list. MAX, by default, supports shortcuts for FFD modifiers, NURBS plug-ins, and Video Post plug-ins in addition to the standard Video Post shortcuts. When you select a category, the commands that can have keyboard shortcuts assigned to them appear in the command window.

To assign a keyboard shortcut, first select the command from the list. Under the shortcut section of the dialog box, select whether you want to use a Control, Alt, or Shift key modifier and then select the Press Key button. When you now press a key on the keyboard, it is assigned to the command. If you select a key modifier (for example, Shift), you need to hold down that key when you select the key to make the command active. After you select a key, it appears in the drop-down list below the Press Key button. Additionally, three checkboxes are available by which you can assign Ctrl, Shift, or Alt modifiers after the fact. If the keyboard shortcut you choose is already assigned to another command, MAX notifies you with a note above the Assign button.

Floating Command Palettes

Another method for accessing commands in MAX is to make use of floating command palettes—replicas of specific commands found in certain command panels. Because they are floating, they are modeless dialog boxes, meaning you can access them at any time without canceling other commands. For the most part, the floating command palettes are intended to be used on machines with a dual screen setup where you can afford the screen real estate. Fortunately, they are handy enough that it also makes sense to use them on small monitors at lower resolutions, where it is difficult to give up even a small amount of screen space.

A good example of such a command palette is the Display palette shown in Figure 2.15. This palette is activated by choosing Display Floater from the pull-down Tools menu. The Display command floating palette provides you with a method of accessing the commands found in the Display command panel without having to leave another command panel.

Another good example is the Object Selection floater, which enables you to perform Select by Name operations at any given time, again without leaving the current command panel.

tip

MAX now supports an Expert mode for working with keyboard shortcuts. In Expert mode, the entire MAX interface (except for viewports) is removed and you work completely with shortcuts. This provides you with much-needed screen real estate. Expert mode is activated by choosing View, Expert mode from the pull-down menus or by pressing Ctrl+X. A Cancel button is provided in the lower-right corner of the screen for returning to normal operation.

FIGURE 2.15   *The Display floater provides you with modeless access to display commands so you do not need to access the Display command panel.*

You might remember from the earlier discussion on command panels that when you switch command panels, the current command is canceled. Using floaters avoids this problem and the associated waste of time. Otherwise, the commands found in the floaters are functionally the same as the commands found in the command panels.

Customizing the MAX Interface

One of the most important new features in MAX 3 is the capability to customize the interface of MAX. In the past, MAX has had a fairly rigid and straightforward interface, with few areas for you to customize. MAX 3 has changed this by enabling you to customize the following areas of the MAX interface:

- Floating toolbars and command panels
- The Tab Panel
- Your own toolbars
- Your own commands

Working with Floating Toolbars

The first customization area to look at is that of toolbars. At the top of the MAX interface you will find the Tab Panel and the pull-down menus. The pull-down menus themselves are actually toolbars, and the Tab Panel is a place where you can put toolbars for quick access. By default, these are in a "docked" position; in other words, they are locked to the top part of the screen.

To undock a toolbar, simply position the cursor near the edge of the toolbar until the cursor changes to an arrow over the top of a white box. When you have this cursor, click and drag to undock the toolbar and place it in a floating position. The Tab Panel cannot be undocked, but you can undock the toolbars on the Tab Panel by right-clicking the Tab Panel and choosing Convert to Toolbar. At this point, the toolbar is removed from the Tab Panel and converted to a floating toolbar. Figure 2.16 shows you the MAX interface with the pull-down menus and command panel floating.

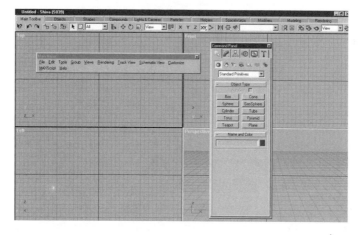

FIGURE 2.16   *The MAX interface with the pull-down menus and command panel floating. These floating toolbars work just like floating toolbars in Microsoft Office. You can resize or reposition them, or even dock them to any part of the screen.*

When a toolbar is undocked, you can dock it in two ways. The first way is to click the toolbar and drag it to the edge of the screen until the outline changes shape. Then, let go and the toolbar docks. You can dock the toolbar on the top, bottom, left, or right edge of the screen. The other way to dock the toolbar is to right-click the title of the toolbar. A pop-up menu appears, as previously shown in Figure 2.17, enabling you to modify the toolbar.

At the top of the pop-up menu are commands to dock or float the selected toolbar. At the bottom of the pop-up menu are commands to enable or disable the display of the toolbars. To conserve more screen real estate, you might turn off certain toolbars you don't that often. Toolbars can also be moved to the Tab Panel, which is discussed in the next section.

FIGURE 2.17

The toolbar customization pop-up menu. Here you can select various options for customizing the toolbars in MAX.

More important, you can customize or even create your own toolbars through this pop-up menu by choosing the Customize option and opening the Customize User Interface dialog box shown in Figure 2.18.

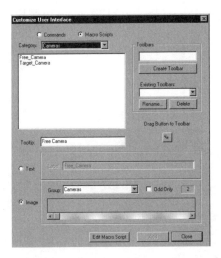

FIGURE 2.18   *The Customize User Interface dialog box, where you can add, delete, or change any commands on any toolbars or the Tab Panel.*

On the left side of the Customize User Interface (UI) dialog box is a list of commands and Macro Scripts you can add to any toolbar. A *Macro Script* is a new form of MAXScript command with which you can quickly and easily create macros and place them on toolbars. This feature is covered in Chapter 18, "Exploring Post Processing Techniques."

The following tutorial shows you how to use the Customize UI dialog box to create your own toolbar of commands.

Creating Your Own Toolbar

1. On any toolbar, right-click the edge of the toolbar to access the pop-up menu. If the toolbar is floating, right-click the title bar.

2. Choose Customize from the pop-up menu to load the Customize User Interface dialog box.

3. In the upper-right corner of the dialog box, find the Toolbars section. In the top blank area, type the name of the toolbar you want to create. In this case, name the toolbar **MAX 3 Fundamentals**.

4. Choose Create Toolbar; a prototype toolbar is created with the specified name. Figure 2.19 shows you the toolbar at this point.

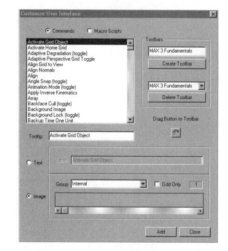

FIGURE 2.19   *The prototype MAX 3 Fundamentals toolbar. Now all you have to do is add commands to it.*

5. Ensure that the Commands radio button is selected. Scroll down the list of commands and find the Quick Render command. Click this command once to select it.

6. In the Tooltip box, enter **MAX 3 Quick Render**. This is the Tooltip that will appear over this button.

7. At the bottom of the dialog box, click the Image radio button, if it is not already selected. This enables you to use any predefined image you want for the image on the button. Under the Group pull-down list box, select Internal and then select any image you want.

8. Click and drag the sample button and drop it on your new toolbar. After you do this, you might need to resize the toolbar to see the button. Figure 2.20 shows you the toolbar at this point.

9. Choose Close to return to MAX. You can now dock the toolbar or use it as you would any other toolbar.

note

The toolbar you just created is already fully functional; it just doesn't have any commands associated with it yet. Be careful not to dock the toolbar at this point—it will appear very small when docked and might be hard to select and undock. Wait until you have added a few commands before docking.

For added practice, you might try creating additional commands on this toolbar or creating your own.

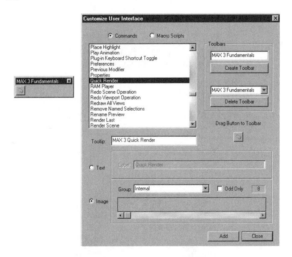

FIGURE 2.20   *The MAX 3 Fundamentals toolbar with a single command added.*

In the previous exercise, the images you used for the buttons were already built into 3D Studio MAX, but you can create your own images for use on buttons. To do so, you must follow a few rules:

1. You might have noticed that when you selected the image for your button in the exercise, you selected an icon image from a predefined group. You may create your own groups by careful naming of the image files you are going to use for the buttons. Image filenames must use the format Groupname_16i.bmp and Groupname_24i.bmp. The numbers 16 and 24 represent the sizes of the images.

You must create both a 16-pixel-square image and a 24-pixel-square image for use on the small- and large-icon toolbars. If both aren't present, the image will not be made available. Image files should be saved in the UI directory of your MAX installation.

2. You may use images that have an alpha channel, but you must tell MAX whether the alpha channel is standard or premultiplied. To do so, the filename should be groupname_16a.bmp for standard images or groupname_16b.bmp if the alpha channel is premultiplied.

3. If a mask channel is present in the image, it is used. If an alpha channel is available in the image, it is used. Otherwise, the color of the pixel in the upper-left corner of the image is used as the transparent color and the mask is generated based on that color.

It is worth mentioning at this point that you do have the option of editing any button you create on a toolbar, after you have created it. Simply right-click the button and choose Edit Button Appearance or Customize to change the button.

Up to this point, only toolbars at the top of the screen have been mentioned. In reality, there is one other toolbar: the entire command panel. The command panel can be pulled off as a floating panel. Unlike the other toolbars, the command panel cannot be moved to the Tab Panel and cannot be docked at the top or bottom of the screen but only on the left or right side of the screen. If you use the command panel in a floating mode, you will probably find you're not using the other floating palettes nearly as much.

Now that you have seen basic toolbars, it is time to take a look at the most flexible area of the MAX interface: the Tab Panel.

Using the Tab Panel

The Tab Panel is another new UI addition to MAX. The Tab Panel is a special toolbar that is designed to be highly customized. By default, the Tab Panel contains 11 separate tabs or toolbars for each of the main categories of MAX commands. The Tab Panel, shown in Figure 2.21, is where you will access many of your commands and most of your custom commands, if you choose to create any.

FIGURE 2.21   *The MAX Tab Panel is a great place to put custom commands or customized toolbars for quick and easy access.*

Unlike other toolbars, the Tab Panel works on a tabbed window basis. Multiple tool-bars are stored on the Tab Panel under different tab names. You can add or delete tabs by right-clicking the Tab Panel tabs and choosing Add Tab, Delete Tab, or Rename Tab. Each tab, in reality, is a small toolbar. As such, any tab can be converted to a toolbar, and vice versa.

To add a toolbar to the Tab Panel as a new tab, right-click the title bar of the toolbar and choose Move to Tab Panel. Now the toolbar appears as the far right tab on the Tab Panel. The only toolbar you can't move to the Tab Panel is the pull-down menu toolbar.

Toolbars that exist on the Tab Panel are just as easy to customize as the regular tool-bars. As a matter of fact, the method is exactly the same, with the only difference being that you must right-click the Tab Panel to access the specific controls. There is one exception—you cannot modify the Main Toolbar on the Tab Panel.

Loading and Saving Custom UIs

Up to this point, you have seen many different ways to customize your system. All of these changes can be saved to custom .cui files you can load into any copy of MAX 3. For example, you might create custom interfaces for different types of tasks, such as modeling, material-editing, and animation. Or, if you have different users who use the same machine at different times, each user can now have a personal user inter-face. To get an idea of how powerful it is to be able to create your own interface, Figures 2.22 and 2.23 show you two different interface layouts that ship as custom UI's for MAX. Figure 2.22 shows you an alternate default layout; Figure 2.23 shows you a games modeling layout.

MAX 3 starts with two different custom UI files, the DefaultUI.cui file and the MAXStart.cui file. The default file contains all the standard MAX interface defaults, enabling you to quickly restore MAX to its factory condition. The MAXStart.cui file is updated with the latest settings every time you end your MAX session to ensure that the interface will be the same the next time you load MAX.

You can save custom interfaces by choosing Customize, Save Custom UI. The default UI is saved at the end of every session. You can also load custom UIs by choosing Customize, Load Custom UI. UI files are saved into your UI directory in your 3dsmax installation. What exactly is saved in the .cui file? Basically, the layout of the inter-face, the toolbars, and the command panels are saved, but many items—such as the preferences—are saved to the 3dsmax.ini file instead and apply to all users.

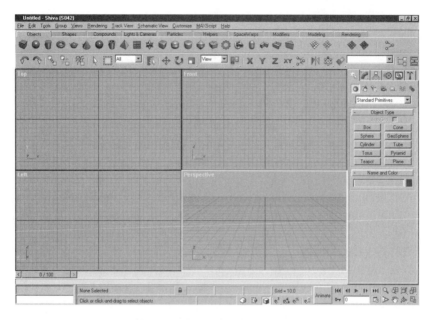

FIGURE 2.22   *An alternate default interface layout.*

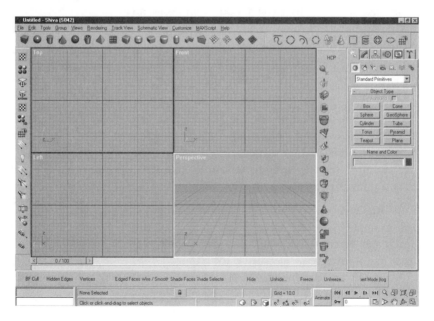

FIGURE 2.23   *A games modeling layout.*

If you happen to make a change to the UI that you didn't mean to do, don't worry about it. By selecting Customize, Revert to Startup UI Layout, you load the UI with which you started the current session. Of course, if you made other changes to the UI, they will also be reset in favor of the original session UI. If you don't want to make any changes to your UI inadvertently, choose Customize, Lock UI Layout to prevent unnecessary changes.

Working with Units, Snaps, and Other Drawing Aids

To accurately work in 3D Studio MAX when you are creating your drawings, you must make use of the several drawing aids in MAX, including *units* and *snaps*. These tools are important for various types of work in MAX, including architectural visualization, forensic animation, and mechanical modeling.

Setting the Units

Units are the basis for understanding length and measurement in MAX. Without the use of units, you would not know the length of one unit as it relates to anything in the real world. To accurately create models in MAX, you must set up a unit system that is appropriate for the type of model with which you are working. For example, a house might be modeled in feet and inches and a piston from an engine might be modeled in centimeters or millimeters.

3D Studio MAX supports several types of units, including metric, U.S. Standard, custom, and generic (the default). *Metric units* enable you to define one unit as a millimeter, centimeter, meter, or kilometer. *U.S. Standard units* are variations of feet and inches and you are able to select whether you want to use decimal or fractional units. For example, you could have a dimension of 6'-5 1/2" or 6'-5.5".

Custom units enable you to define your own unit types. For example, you can set a unit of CS (Column Spacing) to equal 10 feet; MAX then reads coordinates back in CS units. Last, you have the default *generic* units, which are simply decimal units such as 1.100 and are treated as such. You can treat them as inches, feet, or anything you like.

tip

In the world of computers, you can deal with numbers only up to a certain size. Because of this, scenes in MAX become less accurate as they grow larger. For example, at 1-foot resolution, MAX is very accurate, but at a resolution of 671,089 feet, MAX can only be accurate to 0.0625 feet. Although that is still quite accurate, the degree of inaccuracy increases as you get larger. To help compensate for this, an Accuracy Explorer is now included in MAX and appears under the Units settings on the General tab of the Preferences dialog box. Select your units and then adjust the slider to see how accurate you can get.

Units are defined through the use of the Units Setup dialog box. You can access this dialog box, shown in Figure 2.24, by selecting Units Setup from the Customize pull-down menu. When you finish selecting your units and choose OK, the units are immediately put into effect. You can see this by watching your coordinate readout. When the units are selected, the entire MAX interface immediately makes use of them. When you're selecting units, you must take care to type in values with the correct units as well.

After setting your units in your MAX file to the units you want to work with, you can set up your snaps to enable accurate drawing.

Setting Snaps

Snaps force the cursor to jump to a specific place in your scene when you are selecting a point, such as the corner of a box (generally called a vertex). Snaps enable you to precisely position points you select as you are creating or editing an object. For example, if you create a staircase in your scene, you can use snaps to create each step in the correct position so you don't have to move a step after you create it. To accomplish this, set a Vertex snap so you can accurately select the corner vertices of the previous step. You can snap to a wide variety of places, including parts of objects—such as vertices, edges, and pivot points—or parts of the MAX interface—such as the home grid or construction grid.

> **note**
>
> Below the U.S. Standard drop-down list, you will see two radio buttons: Feet and Inches. Use these to determine which unit to use if you type in a value without specifying whether it is feet or inches. For example, if you type in a value of 5, is it five feet or five inches? What you set here determines the result.

> **note**
>
> The coordinate readouts at the bottom of the MAX screen are extremely powerful in helping you to understand what is going on in MAX. They tell you the position of the cursor in the current viewport. They also tell you how far you move an object, when you use the Move command, or how many degrees you have rotated the object. When you work through the exercises, take the opportunity to watch the coordinate readout and make use of it.

Snap commands are accessed through the Grid and Snap Settings dialog box shown in Figure 2.25. To open the dialog box, choose Grid and Snap from the Customize drop-down menu.

As you can see from the Grid and Snap Settings dialog box, there are four areas you can configure through the tabbed sections of the dialog box. The first one is the snaps. MAX has 12 snap types that enable you to control placement or creation of objects. The basic snaps shown here are valid for all objects, but MAX also supports a second set of snaps specifically for use with the NURBS systems. You can access these through the drop-down list in the dialog box.

FIGURE 2.24   *The Units Setup dialog box is where you can select the type of units you are most comfortable working with in MAX.*

Next to each snap you can select is a small symbol. When you activate snaps in MAX and try to pick a point, MAX displays the appropriate symbol for all active snaps. This gives you a clear indication of exactly what you are selecting and where it is in the scene.

Even though you may select one or more snaps in the Grid and Snaps Settings dialog box, snaps are not active until you turn on a snaps toggle, several of which are located at the bottom of the screen, as shown in Figure 2.26. When these are enabled, you can use any combination of Snap modes to create very accurate models inside of 3D Studio MAX.

The Options tab of the Grid and Snap Settings dialog box enables you to define the settings for some of the other snap toggle buttons, including the Angle snap toggle. By setting the Angle spinner under Snap Values, you can determine the degree increments MAX will use when rotating objects while the Angle snap toggle is active. The default is five degrees, forcing you to rotate objects in five-degree increments when it's active.

FIGURE 2.25
The Grid and Snap settings dialog box, where you can define the types of snaps that are active, as well as the grid spacing.

FIGURE 2.26
The snap toggle buttons for MAX. Snaps are not enabled until you enable one or more of the snap toggle buttons.

The Home Grid tab of the Grid and Snap Settings dialog box enables you to set the spacing, in units, of the grid that appears in your viewports. The default is 10 units, with major lines every 10 lines. For example, you might want to change this when you are working in U.S. Standard units. Because you are working in feet and inches, it might be better to set the grid to 12 units so your grid is spaced at 1-foot increments instead of 10 inches.

tip

If you don't want to turn on a snap that is always on, you can enable snaps for single-click selections. To do this, hold down the Shift key and right-click your scene. A pop-up menu appears, where you can select the various snap options.

Along with snaps, construction grids are valuable drawing aids. You can use construction grids to work on completely different planes than with the home grids (XY, YZ, or ZX planes) that are the default construction planes in MAX.

Working with Construction Grids

Construction grids are helper objects that enable you to work on a plane other than the home grid. Working on a different grid can sometimes give you an easier way to work with objects that are rotated in an unusual manner. They are also helpful for creating a group of objects on a plane other than that of the home grid.

For example, you might want to create a sloped table and place objects on the table. You can work in the home grid and rotate and move each object into place on the table. Alternatively, you can create a construction grid on the surface of the sloped table and work directly on the slope as if it were flat.

You can create construction grids by selecting Helpers, Grid from the Create command panel. Then, you create the construction grid by clicking and dragging out a square. After you create the grid, it must be activated before you can use it. In the following exercise, you create a simple box on a construction plane that has been rotated out of alignment with the home grid.

upgrader's note

MAX 3 now supports the use of floating grids in addition to helper grids. Floating grids are temporary grids you use only while you are creating an object. Helper grids are in the scene until you delete them. Floating grids are accessed in the Create command panel. Their properties are defined in the Grid and Snap Settings dialog box on the User Grids tab. See Chapter 4, "Working with Objects," for more information on how to use floating grids.

Working on a Construction Plane

1. Open the file **MF02-02.MAX** from the accompanying CD. This file contains a single construction grid helper that has already been created.

2. Select the grid object and then choose Views, Grids, Activate Grid Object. The home grid disappears and a new, smaller grid appears on the helper object.

3. In the Create command panel, select the Box command and create a box in the Perspective view. Notice how the box is aligned with the new construction grid.

4. Choose Views, Grids, Activate Home Grid to return to the original construction plane.

When put together, units, snaps, and construction grids enable you to work as accurately as you need to when modeling in MAX. Depending on the type of scene, accuracy in your modeling can be very important. With all the accuracy you gain from snaps and grids, however, they do not help when the scene has many objects in it. This is where the capability to control the display of objects comes in.

Controlling the Display of Objects

One of the more important skills that helps speed the work process in MAX is controlling the display of objects in the viewport. In other words, you need to be able to control whether an object is displayed. If, for example, you have a large, complex scene, turning off the display of several objects helps you focus on one particular object.

First, take a look at hiding objects, which you will find very useful when you start creating more complex scenes.

Hiding Objects

MAX provides two methods of controlling the display—using the Display command panel and using the Display floater. The floater is easier to use because you can turn the display of objects on and off without ever leaving the command panel in which you are currently working. (Remember, leaving a command panel cancels the command you are working with in that command panel.) The Display floater is accessed under the Tools pull-down menu.

Here are several display commands you can make use of to hide objects in the scene:

- **Hide Selected:** Hides any selected objects in the scene.

- **Hide Unselected:** Hides any objects that are not selected. This command is particularly useful when you want to work on a single object. You can select that object and then choose Hide Unselected to hide all the other objects in the scene.

■ **Hide by Name:** Makes use of the Select By Name dialog box to help you select objects to hide in a scene. This dialog box, which you will see in many other commands in MAX, enables you to select objects by name. In Figure 2.27, you can see the list of objects in the scene.

FIGURE 2.27   *The Hide Objects dialog box, where you can select objects by name or type and hide them.*

■ **Hide by Color:** All objects have some sort of color assigned to them as they are created. By default, MAX assigns colors randomly, but you can change the color of objects to anything you like. In such circumstances, you can use Hide by Color to hide all objects that are the same color in the scene.

■ **Hide by Category:** All objects exist as a part of one or more categories of geometry. For example, objects are categorized as geometry, lights, helpers, particle systems, or cameras. You can hide all the objects in a particular category in one command.

■ **Hide by Hit:** Enables you to simply click objects to hide them.

After you have hidden objects, you can also unhide them. MAX provides two commands to accomplish this. You can unhide all the objects at once or unhide them by name.

By making use of the display controls in MAX, you can hide and unhide objects at will, making it easier for you to concentrate on specific objects in your scene.

Sometimes, you will want to have an object stay visible in your scene for reference, without being able to make changes to that object. This is where the capability to freeze an object comes in.

tip

When using Hide by Category, the Unhide All button is disabled. To unhide any objects that were hidden with Hide by Category, simply turn off that option.

Freezing Objects

In both the Floater and Command Panel rollouts, you will find a Freeze command. This command works in the same way as the Hide command, but it freezes an object so it cannot be edited or even selected. When an object is frozen, it turns a different color (dark gray for geometry, blue for space warps) to indicate it is frozen. You cannot perform any operations on frozen objects until they are unfrozen.

For example, if you want to model some hair for a human head, you need the head as a reference for the hair, but you do not want to make changes to the head. If you freeze the head, it stays in the scene for reference purposes but cannot be modified as you create the hair.

Hiding and freezing objects are valuable tools for working with objects in MAX. The most valuable tool, however, is still simply giving each object a distinct name.

Object Naming

Regardless of the modeling method you choose, you must develop good work habits to make your life easier—the most important is good object-naming skills. Each individual object in MAX has a name associated with it; for example, when you create boxes, they are named Box01, Box02, and so on. Unfortunately, these object names are not particularly useful in scenes with hundreds of objects.

An extremely helpful approach throughout the project is following a consistent naming convention for all objects, and this is vital when the scene is passed on to others for mapping or animation work. Naming conventions are a matter of personal taste. In MAX, you can name objects just about anything you want, and to practically any length. MAX object names are case sensitive; in other words, *Leftwheel* and *leftwheel* are two different objects.

Objects in MAX can be named when they are created or by renaming them at any time. Whenever you select an object, the object name and color appear on most command rollouts. You can change the name by simply selecting the object name and typing in a new one; there aren't any special commands.

As an example of good object-naming, if you are planning an animation of a single jet fighter, names such as Nose, Right Wing, and Left Wing are okay. But if you are planning a dogfight, you want to distinguish between the right wing objects for each plane, perhaps naming the right wing objects J1Rwing and J2Rwing to indicate Jet 1 and Jet 2 right wings.

tip

Be careful with your naming scheme in MAX. MAX does allow the use of duplicate object names, which can complicate and confuse the scene enormously. Don't use the same name for objects twice in the scene, even if you distinguish the difference with capital or lowercase letter combinations.

Because you can name objects just about anything, be creative with your names so you and others can easily distinguish them when looking at your scene.

Naming conventions become visibly important when you use the Select by Name functions to select objects by name only.

Working with Groups

Even when you have a good naming scheme in place, working in scenes with large numbers of objects can be difficult. Many times, you will want to transform related objects as one object but won't want to go through the hassle of selecting all the objects in question. You can get around this by using the Groups function of MAX.

Groups are collections of objects that are treated as a single object when the group is closed but are accessible as individual objects when the group is open. The following steps show you how to create a group of objects:

1. Select the objects you want in the group.

2. Choose Group, Group. The dialog box appears.

3. In this dialog box, you can name the group. Group names should be treated like object names.

After you have created the group, all of the objects in the group are treated as one unless the group is open. You can also ungroup the objects, explode the group, detach objects from the group, or attach objects to the group.

Groups are very powerful and provide a great way of organizing scenes with many objects. Get into the habit of using groups as early as possible to make your work a little easier.

Groups and object-naming are handy when it comes to manipulating objects in your scene. However, you can't manipulate objects without selecting them first.

Working with Object Selection

One of the most important features of MAX and the MAX interface is object selection. Many commands and operations in MAX require you to select one or more objects beforehand. For example, if you want to move an object from one position to another in the scene, you must be able to select the object to move it.

MAX provides you with many different methods for selecting one or more objects in your scene. These methods include

- Selecting by Object
- Selecting by Region
- Selecting by Name
- Selecting by Color
- Selecting by Named Selection Sets

One of the most common methods of selecting objects in MAX is to use the Select Object button from the Main Toolbar. Select Object is most commonly used to select individual objects but can be used to select groups of objects through the use of regions (which is discussed later in this chapter). Figure 2.28 shows you all of the selection tools on the Main Toolbar tab of the Tab Panel.

Selecting by Object

Selecting by object works by simply choosing the command and selecting a single object. Most of the time, however, you will probably want to select more than one object in your scene to apply materials or perform other operations. In these cases, you can modify the Select Objects command to create additive selections—clicking one object after another and adding each to the current selection. To do this in MAX, hold down

FIGURE 2.28
The selection tools on the Main Toolbar. Each of these tools enables you to select objects in a different way.

the Ctrl key as you select; you will see a small plus sign appear next to the cursor. By the same token, you can hold down the Alt key while using Select Objects to subtract objects from the current selection. In this case, a small minus sign appears next to the cursor.

Select by Objects is good for selecting individual objects or a small number of objects, but you will often want to select a group of objects in an area in the scene quickly and easily. This is where selecting by region comes in.

Selecting by Region

Selecting by region is actually an extension of the Select Object command but makes use of "windowed" selection areas. To create a windowed selection area, define a rectangle (or other shape) around the objects you want to select (the rectangle appears as a dashed black line in MAX). There are two different types of windowed selection areas in MAX: Window and Crossing.

A *windowed* region selects any objects that rest entirely within the region rectangle. If any portion of an object is outside the rectangle, it is not selected. A crossing is the same as a window except that a *crossing* selects any object that is inside of or touches the rectangle. Figure 2.29 shows you an example of a region selection.

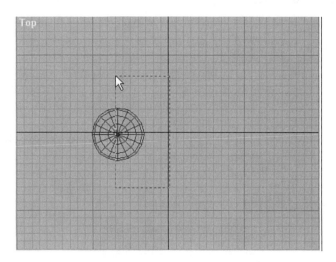

FIGURE 2.29   *A rectangular region selection that crosses the area of a sphere. In this example, a window will not select the sphere, but a crossing will.*

As you can imagine, region select is very powerful, but being limited to a rectangular region can make selecting objects in a complex scene somewhat difficult. Fortunately, MAX enables you to use rectangular, circular, or polygonal shapes for your regions. You can choose the shape by opening the flyout toolbar (click the button to the right of Select Objects on the Main Toolbar). Other than the different shape, these select by region commands all work the same way.

To take region selections a step further, you can even filter the selection set. In other words, you can select only objects of certain types that exist within the selection set. MAX enables you to do this through the Selection Filter drop-down list that is just to the right of the Region Shape control. Figure 2.30 shows you this drop-down list.

FIGURE 2.30

The Selection Filter drop-down list, where you can choose the type of selection filter you want to use.

For example, if you select Warps from the Selection Filter list, you will only be able to select space warps. This filter applies to all select commands except Select by Name. MAX enables you to create "combos" of selection filters, such as warps and shapes instead of just warps. To do this, select the Combos option, which brings up the Filter Combinations dialog box. Each combo you create ends up with a name such as SC (Shapes and Cameras) and appears in the drop-down list.

Although Select by Object is powerful and very intuitive, it can be a difficult way to select a single object you want to work on in a large, complex scene. You always end up selecting an object that is close by. This is where Select by Name comes in.

Selecting by Name

With the Select by Name command, you can select one or more objects based on the name you gave the object when you created it. Select by Name also has the advantage of restricting the list of objects to objects of a particular type, such as geometry or lights. Figure 2.31 shows you the Select Objects dialog box.

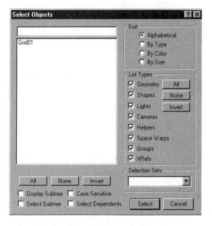

FIGURE 2.31   *The Select Objects dialog box, where you can select one or more objects based on the name of the objects.*

Selecting by Color

In addition to selecting by name, MAX provides you with the capability to select one or more objects by the object color. This can be very handy if you are careful about the colors you select for objects you create. You can access the Select by Color command through the Edit pull-down menu.

Selection Sets

As you can probably guess at this point, you might run across an object—or more appropriately, a group of objects—that you select and unselect quite frequently during the course of creating your scene. There are two ways to handle selecting this group of objects quickly. The first way is to make a group out of them, which is effective but has its limitations. The other way is to make use of named selection sets (which can also include groups). A named selection set is a group of selected objects to which you have given a name. Because you have named it, you can select the same group over and over, quickly and easily.

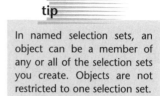

tip

In named selection sets, an object can be a member of any or all of the selection sets you create. Objects are not restricted to one selection set.

Named selection sets are handled in the blank drop-down list on the right side of the Main Toolbar.

Although named selection sets are great, being able to edit the sets is important. For example, you might want to delete a named selection set when you are done with it, or remove objects from the named set, or add to it. For this purpose, MAX provides you with an Edit Named Selection dialog box, shown in Figure 2.32. You can access this dialog box by choosing Edit Named Selections from the Edit pull-down menu.

FIGURE 2.32   *The Edit Named Selections dialog box, where you can edit any named selection sets you have already created.*

You have now seen two floating dialog boxes that are available in MAX: Display and Selection. With the addition of customizable toolbars and a floating command panel, you could easily run out of screen real estate. If you plan on using these dialog boxes or interface features heavily, consider running MAX at 1280×1024 or higher or using a dual monitor setup. (They are excellent production tools, so you probably will make heavy use of them.) As an alternative, consider learning the keyboard shortcuts and running MAX in Expert mode.

Object selection, naming, groups, and drawing aids combine to enable you to work quickly and accurately in your MAX scene. Now it is time to look at how these features and the MAX interface work together to provide you with a truly productive and efficient animation environment.

Bringing It All Together

Now that you have a basic idea of what MAX is and how its interface works, it is time to make use of it. In the following exercise, you get a brief overview of the basic features of MAX, from modeling a simple object all the way through applying materials and animating the object.

Modeling the Letters

In this section, you will model the first part of the elements for the corporate logo.

Creating a Corporate Logo

1. Start by creating some text. In the Create command panel, click the Shapes button. Then click the Text command from the resulting rollout.

2. In the Text field, type the letter **N** instead of "MAX Text." Under the Name and Color rollout.

3. In the Top viewport, click to create the letter. Name the object **N**.

4. Click the Text command to restart it. This time, create a letter **R** and name it **R**. Then, do the same thing to create a letter **P**.

5. On the Main Toolbar tab, choose the Select and Move command. Click the N letter so it is selected. A Transform icon appears.

6. Place the cursor over the Y axis until the axis turns yellow, then, click and drag. You can now move the letter only along the Y axis. Move the letter until the bottom of the letter matches the main X axis line.

7. Repeat steps 5 and 6 for the R and P letters until they are all resting on the X axis line.

8. Now use the Move command along the X axis to position the letters so they are nicely spaced, with approximately half the width of a letter between them. Figure 2.33 shows you how the scene should appear at this point.

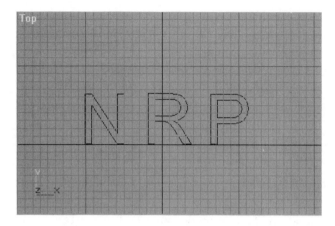

Figure 2.33 *The scene, with the letters N, R, and P on the X axis.*

9. On the Main Toolbar tab, click the Select Objects button. In the Top viewport, click to the lower left of the letters and drag to the upper right, creating a window around the letters. When you let go, all the letters will be selected.

10. Click the Modify command panel tab to access the modifier commands.

11. Click the Extrude command. The extrude modifier is now applied to all three letters, and the rollouts appear in the command panel.

12. Set the Amount of the extrusion to **14.5**.

13. Save the file as **MF02-03a.MAX**.

Animating the Letters

Up to this point, you have created three letters, positioned them in the scene, and extruded them to form 3D objects. Next, you create duplicates of the letters and animate them.

1. All three letters should now be selected and the Top viewport should still be active. Click the Zoom tool. Click in the Top viewport and drag down. This zooms you out.

2. Click Select and Move in the Main Toolbar tab. Hold down the Shift key and then place the cursor over the X axis of the Transform icon until the axis turns yellow.

3. Move the three letters approximately 400 units to the right while holding down the Shift key. Watch your coordinate readouts at the bottom of the screen to see how far you have moved the objects. When you let go of the mouse, a dialog box pops up, prompting you with Clone options.

4. Click Copy and choose OK. The copied objects are automatically named N01, R01, and P01. Now set up a little animation for these objects.

5. Right-click the animation playback button in the lower-right corner of the screen to bring up the Time Configuration dialog box.

6. Under the Animation section, set the length to 900. This creates 900 frames for you to work with, or approximately 30 seconds of animation. Click OK.

7. Choose Select Objects and click the copied N to select it. Right-click the Animation Time slider; a Create Key dialog box opens. Click OK in the dialog box to create animation keys for the three selected letters at frame 0.

8. Left-click the Animation Time slider and drag to the right until you reach frame 30. Click the Animate button.

9. Choose Select and Move from the Main Toolbar and click the copied N01 object. Place the cursor over the X axis until the axis turns yellow and then drag the letter back to its original position (the original N). This creates another animation key. Now, from frame 0 to frame 30, the N moves from right to left.

10. Choose Select Objects again. This time, select the copied R letter. Right-click the Animation Time slider and choose OK to create a key at frame 30.

11. Move the Time slider to frame 60. Choose Select and Move, and move the copied R back into position.

12. Choose Select Object again. This time select the copied P letter. Right-click the Animation Time slider and choose OK to create a key at frame 60.

13. Move the Animation Time slider to frame 90. Choose Select and Move, and move the P back into position.

Modeling and Animating the Words

You have now created some basic animation of having the three letters move from the right to left at different time points. To see this, drag the Animation Time slider back to 0 and then click the Play button. You should see the copied N move into position over the original N, followed by the R, and then followed by the P. Now, you are going to add three words to the scene and give them some animation.

1. Click the Create command panel again. This should place you into the Spline commands. Click Text.

note

You have now played with the Move command a bit. From this point on, you will simply be instructed to move an object along a selected axis at a selected distance. This means to select the command, select the object in question, place the cursor over the correct axis, and then move the object.

2. Set the size of the text to 20.0. In the text field, highlight the existing text and type the word **New**.

3. Click anywhere in the Top viewport to create the text. You will position the text later in the exercise. Name the object **New**. Reactivate the Text command and create the word **Riders**. Repeat again and create **Publishing**.

4. Select the three words you created. In the Top viewport, move them into the area around the copied letters. Make sure you are at frame 0.

5. Click in the Front viewport to activate it. Then, click the Zoom Extents window control. This zooms you out so you can see all of the objects from this view.

6. From the Main Toolbar tab, click Select by Name and select the New, Riders, and Publishing objects.

7. Choose Select and Move, and move the objects approximately –120 units along the Y axis. This places the words physically below the copied NRP letters. Now you are ready to animate each of these words.

8. Select the New object. Move the Animation Time slider to frame 60. Right-click the Time slider and choose OK to create a key. This locks the word New into its current position.

9. Move the Animation Time slider to frame 120. Click the word "Top" in the Top viewport to activate that viewport without deselecting the object. If by chance the word New does get deselected, reselect it.

10. Turn on the Animate button. Move the word New along the X axis until it is just a few units to the right of the original N.

11. Move the Animation time slider to frame 180. In the Front viewport, move the word New along the Y axis (local Z) until it is just below the letter N. In the Top viewport, move the word until it is centered around the N.

12. Move the animation time slider to frame 230. In the Front viewport, move the word New along the Y axis until it is about 120 units above the letter N. Watch your coordinate readouts.

Applying Space Warps to the Letters

At this point, you have created animation for the word New. What now occurs is that the word New comes up from behind the letter N. At frame 180, the word New and the Letter N occupy pretty close to the same position. Later in this exercise, you will explode the letter N at this point so the word New seems to be breaking through. The animation range for the word New is frames 120 to 230. See if you can set up similar animations for the words Riders and Publishing for animation ranges 210 to 320 and 300 to 410, respectively.

Each word should pass through the letter with which it is associated. After you have completed this on your own, continue and create the bombs that will explode the letters.

1. Move the Animation Time slider to frame 0.

2. In the Create command panel, click the Space Warps button. Then, click the Bomb button.

3. In the Top viewport, click in the center of the original N to create the bomb. Set the following parameters for the bomb:

   Strength: 0.75
   Max Size: 6
   Gravity: 0.0
   Detonation: 180 (This is the frame where the bomb goes off.)

4. Click in the center of the R and P letters, as well, to create the other bombs. Set the same settings, except the detonation, which should be set to frames 270 and 360, respectively.

5. From the Main toolbar of the Tab Panel, click the Select and Bind tool. Click one of the space warps and drag to the letter around it. When you do, the cursor will change. Let go of the mouse at this point. You will see the letter change white briefly then back to normally. The space warp is now bound to the letter and will only affect it. Repeat for the other two letters and space warps.

6. Move the Animation Time slider to frame 0 and play back the animation. You should see the letters explode as the words pass through them, as shown in Figure 2.34.

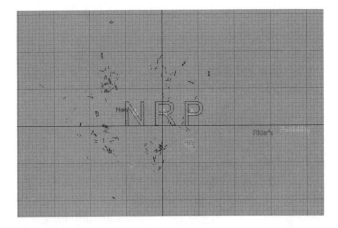

FIGURE 2.34   *The scene as the letters explode when words pass through them.*

Adding Cameras and Lights

At this point, you have some decent animation going. Now, create a camera for viewing the scene and a light for lighting it.

1. Move the Animation Time slider to frame 0. In the Create command panel, click the Cameras button to expand the Cameras rollout. Click the Free Camera command.

2. In the Top viewport, click in the center of the letter R. This creates the camera in the center of the original letters.

3. Activate the Perspective viewport and then press the C key on your keyboard. This converts the Perspective view into the view from the camera you just created.

4. In the Front viewport, move the camera along the Y axis until the Camera view shows you all of the letters NRP with a little extra to spare. Don't move the camera far enough to see the second set of letters or the words.

5. In the Create command panel, click the Lights button to expand the Lights rollouts. Click the Omni light.

6. In the Front viewport, click just to the right of the camera icon and at the same height. This creates the light. Right-click the word Camera01 in the Camera viewport and choose Smooth + Highlights. The lighting appears immediately as a light above the letters.

Adding Visibility Tracks to the Original Letters

Up to this point, you might have been asking, "What about the original letters?" You have been creating all of this animation with those original letters always in the way. Now you are going to take care of them by controlling their visibility. By controlling the visibility of the letters, you can control when they will render. For this logo, you want the original letters to remain invisible until after the words New Riders Publishing have passed by the camera. Then, the letters will appear one by one to spell NRP. You can set that up quickly now.

1. Select the original N. You can use Select by Name to accomplish this quickly. With the N selected, right-click it and choose Properties from the pop-up menu. This launches the object properties for the letter N. Adjust the Visibility spinner to 0.5 and click OK. You haven't really changed anything yet.

2. Right-click the N again and choose TrackView Selected. This launches the TrackView window and displays the animation tracks for the currently selected object. TrackView enables you to fine-tune animation keys. Figure 2.35 shows you TrackView at this point.

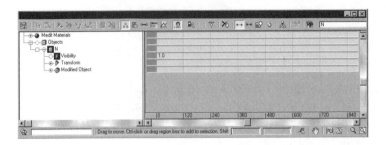

FIGURE 2.35   *TrackView with the N object loaded, ready for you to manually create some keys to control the visibility of the object.*

3. On the TrackView toolbar, find the Add Keys button.

4. Below the N object in TrackView, locate a track named Visibility. Clickce in this Track and a white dot appears. At the bottom of TrackView, a number appears in a box. Highlight this number and set it to 0. This creates a key and places it at frame 0.

5. Click in the track again and place the key at frame 500. Create another key at frame 501. (If you have trouble seeing frames 500 and 501, click the Zoom Horizontal Extents button in the lower right corner of the Track View Window.)

6. Go back to the key at frame 0 and right-click it. This brings up a KeyInfo dialog box with Time and Value spinners; the Time spinner should read frame 0. Set the value to 0.

7. In the upper-left corner, click the right-arrow button and move to the next key, which is at frame 500. Set the value to 0.

8. Click the right arrow again to go to the key at frame 501. Set the value to 1.0. This causes the letter to become fully visible at frame 501. Now close the TrackView window.

9. Repeat steps 53–57 for the R and P letters. Set the appearance time for the letter R to frame 561 and for the letter P to frame 621. Don't forget to create the keys at frame 560 and 620.

10. Save the file.

    If you activate the Camera viewport and play back the animation, you will see the letters start out as a see-through mesh. At the appropriate time, the letters will become solid.

Adding Materials to the Scene

Now, it is time to add some materials to the scene to make it look more realistic. Because there are only letters and words, the materials will be fairly simple, so let's get to it.

1. Click the Material Editor button on the Main toolbar tab of the Tab Panel. This launches the Material editor dialog box where you will see preview windows and controls for editing materials in MAX.

2. The upper left material preview window should be the current. First, click in the Material name drop down list and rename the material to Main Letters.

3. In the Shader rollout, choose Anisotropic from the drop down list.

4. In the Anisotropic rollout, set the following parameters:

   Specular Level: 75
   Glossiness: 50
   Orientation: 90

5. Click the Diffuse color swatch. This launches a color selector where you can choose the color based on RGB or HSV colors. Set the diffuse to 63,50,160 for the Red, Green, and Blue colors respectively. Close the color selector.

6. In the scene, select the N, R, and P objects (the original letters). In the materials editor, choose the Assign Material to Selection button on the Material toolbar. This assigns the material to the letters.

7. In the Materials editor, click the next material preview window. Name this material Words.

8. The default shader type is Blinn, which is fine for this material. In the Blinn Parameters rollout, click the blank button next to the diffuse color swatch. This enables you to use a map instead of a color for the Diffuse color. This also launches the Material/Map browser.

9. In the Material/Map browser, select Bitmap and choose OK. This assigns a bitmap to the Diffuse slot of the material. When you choose OK, you will be prompted with a File open dialog box.

10. Select the file Marbteal.tga and choose OK. The Bitmap parameters rollout appears with the map.

11. Click the Go to Parent button on the Material Editor toolbar. This takes you back up to the main material level.

12. Set the Specular level to 70 and the Glossiness to 40.

13. In the scene, select the New, Riders, and Publishing words.

14. In the Materials Editor, choose Assign Material to Selection.

15. One last material. Click the Main Letters material preview you created earlier. Click and drag this preview and drop it on the third material slot. When you do, a copy is made.

16. Rename this copy to Main Letters After.

17. Set the Diffuse color to 159,50,119 and assign it to the NRP letters that appear at the end of the animation.

Working with Render Effects in the Scene

Now, you have assigned all of the materials to the scene. All that is left is to add one special effect called a Rendering Effect. After the last NRP letters appear, you will make the glow for a few seconds, and then return to normal.

1. Select the NRP letters that appear at the end of the scene.

2. Right-click on the letters and choose Properties. This launches the Object properties dialog box.

3. Set the G-Buffer spinner to 2. This assign a unique ID to these objects that you can key the glow to work off of.

4. Choose Rendering, Effects from the pulldown menus. This launches the effects dialog box where you can add these effects.

5. Click the Add button. Select Lens Effects from the list that appears and choose OK. When you do, the Lens Effects parameters rollout appears.

6. In the list in the left window, click Glow and hit the right arrow button. This adds the glow to the scene. Click the Glow entry in the right window to access it's controls which appear as a Glow Element rollout at the bottom of the dialog box.

7. Under Parameters, set the Size to 50.

8. Click the Options tab. Under Apply Element to, select Image.

9. Under Image Sources, enable Object ID and set the spinner to 2. This matches the G-Buffer setting you created earlier.

10. Set the animation time slider to frame 750. Scroll back up in the Effects dialog box and turn on Interactive in the Effects rollout. The scene will be quickly rendered and the glow will be applied as shown in Figure 2.36.

11. Turn interactive back off. Scroll back down to the Glow Element rollout. Click the Parameters tab. Now, you will animate the intensity to make the glow appear to start slowly, brighten to full, then return back to nothing.

12. Set the Intensity spinner to 0.

13. Set the Animation time slider to frame 550. Turn on the Animate button.

14. Set the Intensity spinner to 1.0. Set the animation time slider to frame 650.

15. Set the Intensity spinner to 2.0. Set the Animation time slider to frame 750.

16. Set the Intensity spinner to 75.0. Set the animation time slider to 850.

17. Set the Intensity spinner to 0. Turn off the Animate button and close the Render Effects dialog box.

18. Save the file. You have now animated the glow. Now, all that is left is to render the scene.

FIGURE 2.36   *The scene after applying a glow. Now, all you have to do is animate the glow.*

19. Click the Render Scene button on the Main Toolbar tab of the Tab Panel. This launches the Render Scene dialog box.

20. Under Time output, select Active Time Segment. Under Output size, choose 320×240.

21. Under Render Output, click the files button. A file save dialog box will appear. Enter the name MF02-03.AVI and choose OK. When you do, a Video Compression dialog box appears. Select Cinepak and choose OK.

22. Click the Render button and kick back and wait. When the animation is done rendering, you will have an AVI file that you can playback with the RAM player or the Windows Media Player. (Note: It may take several hours to render the animation depending upon the speed of your machine.)

This exercise should have given you a good run through of some of the basics of the MAX system. Many of the basic elements you explored here such as modeling, creating and assigning materials, creating cameras, and so on. are used in daily work with MAX. For your use, a copy of this file completed has been provided on the accompanying CD as MF02-03.MAX. The prerendered animation has also been provided as MF02-03.AVI.

As you can see from this exercise, even a simple animation requires heavy use of many features of the MAX interface. Don't worry if some commands you saw in the previous exercise were somewhat confusing. You will understand them better as you progress through the book.

Using the Asset Manager

The last item to take a look at before moving on to modeling is the MAX Asset Manager. This utility program enables you to manage your MAX files, material bitmaps, and so on. You can select the Asset Manager by going to the Utilities command panel and selecting the Asset Manager button. When you launch the manager, you get the dialog box shown in Figure 2.37.

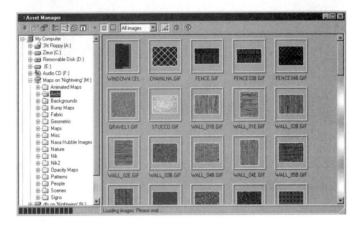

FIGURE 2.37   *The Asset Manager interface, showing you how easy it is to manage files.*

On the left side of the interface is a directory tree of your machine and on the right are bitmap previews of supported files in the current directory. The asset manager supports all bitmaps supported by MAX, as well as MAX files that have previews turned on. From the drop-down list on the toolbar of the Asset Manager, you can select the types of files that will be displayed. Figure 2.38 shows you the Asset manager with MAX files.

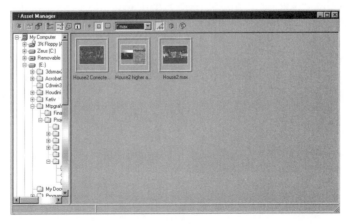

FIGURE 2.38   *The Asset Manager, demonstrating management of all file types supported by MAX.*

You can drag and drop files from the Asset Manager into the scene or into the Material Editor. By double-clicking bitmap files, you can look at a blowup of the file.

Although technically not a user interface feature, the Asset Manager is very handy to know and use early on while you're learning MAX. Future exercises in the book will use it.

Conclusion

This chapter introduced you to the basic concepts behind the MAX 3.0 interface, including:

- The interface layout
- Viewport controls
- Working with files and XRefs
- Command access
- Customizing the interface
- Basic drawing aids, including snaps and grids
- Object display, naming, and grouping
- Creating a project from start to finish (the Corporate Logo)
- The Asset Manager

The tools introduced in this chapter are very important to making efficient use of MAX. By the end of the book, these tools will be second nature to you. The interface might seem awkward at first, but after a few minutes of practice, you will become comfortable very quickly.

The interface is very important for working with MAX commands. Now it is time to start learning how to model. The next chapter covers the principles and theory behind the modeling methods used in MAX 3.

PART II

Modeling Fundamentals

CHAPTER 3

Understanding Modeling Concepts

Before actually exploring the modeling techniques used in 3D Studio MAX, you need to develop a stronger understanding of the underlying terminology and concepts behind the modeling process. In Chapter 1, "3D Graphics and Animation Fundamentals," you explored the overall concepts of 3D graphics. Now, focus in on just the modeling aspects.

When you look at modeling in 3D Studio MAX, you find many different methods you can employ to create the geometry in your scenes. Geometry is handled in MAX as an object that is made up of smaller sub-objects. By manipulating the geometry at an object or a sub-object level, you can create any model you need.

Each modeling method handles objects and sub-objects differently and provides advantages and disadvantages. Some types of objects are easier to model in one method versus another. Over time, you will learn which method to use when. Then again, you might find that one method is your favorite and use that method all the time.

MAX 3 supports the following modeling methods:

- Spline-based modeling
- Polygonal, or mesh-based, modeling
- Parametric modeling
- Patch modeling
- NURBS modeling

Choosing a Modeling Approach

Overall, MAX provides you with many different modeling methods to support the many different uses of MAX. Because of these different approaches to modeling geometry, you might not need to make use of some modeling methods. The following list shows you some examples of where to use specific modeling types:

- **Spline modeling.** Spline modeling is great for creating any type of object that has a profile or shape that can be lofted or extruded. Examples include bananas, bottles, phone handles, wine glasses, and plates. Spline modeling is also sometimes called mesh modeling because the result is usually a mesh model of some sort. It is worth noting that some types of spline-based commands, such as lofts, are now capable of outputting patch surfaces as well as mesh surfaces.

- **Mesh modeling.** Mesh modeling is great for objects that are somewhat planar in nature and not particularly organic. Most of the objects you model will be mesh models. Examples include buildings, simple people, space stations, road intersections, and many others.

- **Parametric modeling.** Parametric modeling involves using objects that have predefined attributes such as width or height, or objects that have modifiers applied to them. An object is considered parametric if you can return to a previous version of it and adjust its attributes. When this is available, you have precise control over the objects.

- **Patch modeling.** Patch modeling is best used when you need to create somewhat organic surfaces that require fairly precise control over the curvature of the surface. Examples include faces, human bodies, and animals.

- **NURBS modeling.** Nonuniform rational B-spline (NURBS) modeling is used when you need to create highly organic surfaces or any type of object that has many curves or difficult curves. Examples include cars, humans, faces, or any other complex surface.

The choice as to which modeling method to use is up to you. For example, you can do architectural modeling with splines just about as easily as with meshes. By the same token, with a little work, you can create a human face with mesh-modeling techniques, but it is probably easier with patches or NURBS.

In any case, the ultimate answer is to become well versed in all modeling methods so you can adequately handle any modeling task that is thrown at you. Throughout this book, all these modeling methods are used in one form or another.

Spline Modeling

Spline modeling takes the approach of creating 3D objects from straight or curved lines called *splines*—lines that are usually defined by vertices and can be straight or curved. These splines can be transformed into 3D objects through a variety of methods or can be rendered directly as renderable splines. The most common purposes for splines are related to modeling, but they can also be used as motion paths for cameras and objects in a scene.

A spline is an object, such as a line, circle, arc, or even text. Like all objects in MAX, a spline is composed of smaller parts (sub-objects) that make the complete spline. Figure 3.1 shows you a spline and the various parts of a spline.

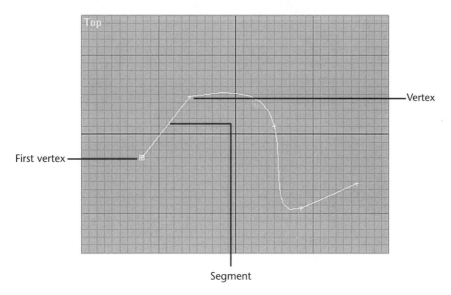

FIGURE 3.1   *A MAX spline and its parts. By understanding how each part of the spline is handled, you can understand how to manipulate the spline to obtain certain effects.*

As you can see in Figure 3.1, the spline is composed of vertices, segments, and an overall spline object. In terms of vertices, each spline has one special vertex, called the *first vertex*. A white box around the vertex indicates the first vertex when you are editing the spline. This vertex indicates the start of the spline and is generally the first vertex you create, unless you are using a prebuilt spline type such as a rectangle, where the location of the first vertex is defined by MAX. The first vertex becomes very important, especially in closed shapes, when you are creating 3D objects from the splines. This problem will be discussed in Chapter 5, "Mesh Modeling Fundamentals."

When you are creating a spline, if you connect the last vertex you draw to the first vertex, you create a closed shape. A *closed shape* is a spline that has no breaks around its perimeter. Many of the spline editing and lofting commands require a closed shape to function correctly.

Vertex Controls

Each vertex in a spline also has a set of tangent controls (called *handles*) associated with it. These handles control how the curvature of the spline is interpreted as the spline enters and leaves the vertex. MAX supports four different types of vertices: Smooth, Corner, Bézier, and Bézier Corner.

Vertex types are applied during the creation process for lines only. Other spline types, such as rectangles and ellipses, have the tangents predefined at creation time. You can edit these tangents anytime after creation.

Corner Vertex

The most basic type of vertex is the corner tangent. *Corner tangents* are angular and do not have any curvature around them. This is the default when you're creating a line. In MAX, you create a line by clicking on two different points in a viewport. If you click and drag when you select a point, you create a type of corner different from the default corner. The type of corner you create is defined in the rollout for the line object. The default is a Bézier corner.

Smooth Vertex

A *smooth vertex* is an interpolated curve before and after the vertex. In other words, a smooth vertex is very similar to an arc and has the same curvature before and after the vertex. Figure 3.2 shows you a spline and Figure 3.3 shows you the same spline with a smooth vertex.

Bézier Vertex

A *Bézier vertex* is similar to a smooth curve but enables you to control the curve of the spline as it enters and leaves the vertex. In a smooth or corner vertex, you cannot do this. Figure 3.4 shows you the same spline with a Bézier vertex applied. Notice the tangent line with the boxes on each end. There are two handles here—one to handle the curvature entering the vertex and one to handle the curvature leaving the vertex. In a Bézier vertex type, the tangents on both sides of the vertex always remain equal.

By adjusting the position of the handles on the tangent line, you can adjust how strong a particular Bézier tangent is. The farther away from the vertex the handle is, the more it pulls the curvature of the spline away from the vertex. The closer the handles are to the vertex, the less they influence the direction of the tangent line.

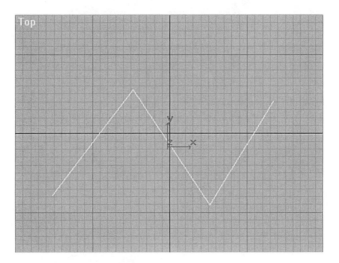

FIGURE 3.2   *A spline with two corner vertices.*

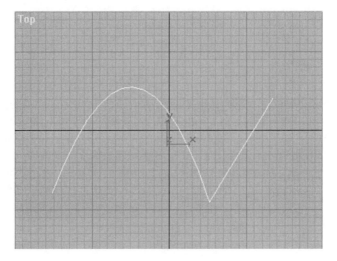

FIGURE 3.3   *The same spline after the corner has been converted to a smooth tangent. Notice how the curvature was interpolated before and after the vertex to create a smooth* **CURVE.**

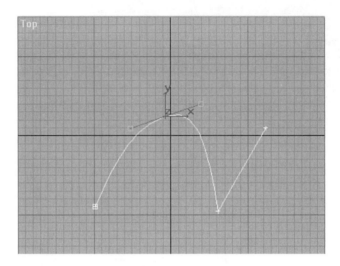

FIGURE 3.4   *The Bézier tangent enables you to define the angle and exaggeration of the spline as it enters and leaves the vertex.*

Bézier Corner Vertex

The last tangent type is a Bézier corner vertex. A *Bézier corner* is the same as a Bézier vertex type, with one difference. In a Bézier vertex, when you adjust the handles, both handles of the line adjust equally. In a Bézier corner vertex, each end of the tangent line is independent of the other and can be adjusted as such, so you can easily create a spline that is almost angular on one side of a vertex and curved on the other. This is shown in Figure 3.5.

Segments and Steps

The next sub-object type in a spline is a *segment*, which is simply the line that exists between two vertices. A segment is composed of smaller straight segments called *steps*. The more steps in a segment, the more accurate the curve but the more memory the spline takes. You can define the number of steps in all MAX splines when you create the spline. Alternatively, you can edit the number of steps after creation. Figure 3.6 shows you a circle with three steps per segment versus a circle with 12 steps per segment.

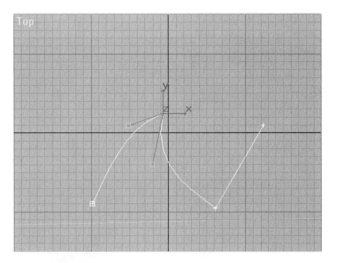

FIGURE 3.5   *A Bézier corner tangent, showing you how the tangents can be adjusted independently of each other.*

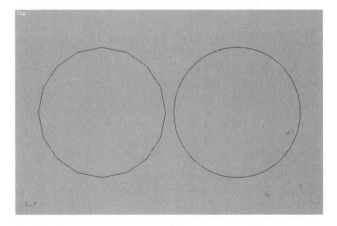

FIGURE 3.6   *Two circles, one using three steps per segment, the other 12. Notice how much smoother the circle is with 12 segments.*

MAX, by default, always tries to optimize the number of steps between vertices and reduce them to a minimum without losing clarity. This helps to make the models smaller without sacrificing detail. For the most part, the number of steps in a spline segment is not important until you try to create a 3D object from the shape. At that point, you might need to adjust the number of steps.

Shapes

When you combine vertices and segments, you get a spline. In MAX, a *shape* is defined as a combination of one or more individual splines that are treated as a single object. For example, if you want to model a wall of a building, one approach is to model the wall as splines and extrude it into a 3D object. If the wall has any windows, they are created as separate splines, but to extrude correctly, the splines must be part of the same shape. When you create splines in MAX, you can set whether you are creating a new shape or adding more splines to the same shape by selecting the Start New Shape button in the Spline rollout.

After you have created shapes, you can convert them to 3D objects. This is called *spline modeling* and is the most commonly used method for creating objects such as bananas, flashlights, or beveled text.

The basic process of spline modeling is fairly simple. First, you create the outline of the object you want to model, as a shape. Then you can extrude, lathe, bevel, or bevel-profile the shape or loft it along another spline to create a more complex 3D object. Figure 3.7 shows you an object that was created by lofting one shape (the star) along a path defined by another shape (the helix).

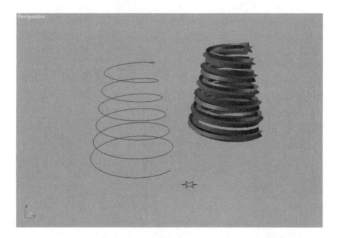

Figure 3.7   *A set of two splines and the resulting 3D lofted object. Here, a star shape has been lofted around a helical spline.*

Renderable Splines

When you create any splines, under the General rollout you will find a section where you can make a spline renderable. In essence, this makes the spline act like a wire object in which you can specify a thickness with which the spline is to be rendered. Figure 3.8 shows you an example of this.

MAX Text

FIGURE 3.8   *A text spline object that has been made renderable. This can be used to create many nice effects, such as neon tubing for signs.*

Mesh, or Polygonal, Modeling

Mesh modeling (also referred to as polygonal modeling) creates 3D objects from three- or four-sided polygons that have been joined together to form a more complex object. Mesh objects are generally created as a series of primitives you can combine, transform, and modify to create the object you need. As a matter of fact, an extruded or lofted spline is a mesh object because it is created out of polygons during the extrusion or lofting process. Figure 3.9 shows you some examples of mesh objects.

FIGURE 3.9   *Several mesh models, including a teapot, a torus knot, a tree, a car, and a person. Total scene size is 62,709 polygons.*

Mesh modeling is the most popular form of modeling in MAX. With mesh modeling, you can combine objects such as boxes and spheres by using a variety of tools to create an almost infinite number of 3D objects.

Mesh Sub-Objects

Much like splines, mesh objects are created out of a series of smaller sub-objects. All mesh objects are composed of vertices, edges, and faces. These sub-objects provide you with a high level of control over the object, especially when you begin to edit the object at sub-object levels. For example, by simply editing a box in various ways, you can create complex objects such as airplanes or hands.

Vertices

At the most basic level of a mesh object is the vertex. Unlike the vertices in a spline, the vertices in a mesh do not have tangent controls and can only be moved, scaled, added, or deleted. Editing a vertex level provides precise control over individual points in the mesh, enabling you to refine your object as you need.

Edges

Between each vertex in a mesh model is an *edge*, the line between two vertices that forms the edge of a quad or tri. (*Quads* and *tris* are small faces that are combined to create a larger object.) For example, a box has six quads and 12 tris, as well as eight vertices. Edges may be visible or invisible. Figure 3.10 shows you the details of a simple box mesh object.

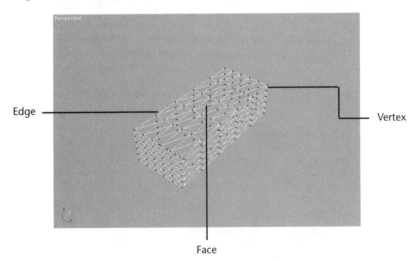

Figure 3.10   *A box object, showing vertices, edges, and faces. By manipulating one or more of these sub-objects, you can transform even a simple box into a more complex object.*

Faces

The edges and vertices of a mesh object combine to form faces. A *face* is the actual triangular surface that is rendered in MAX. Sometimes, a face is also called a polygon—hence the term polygonal modeling. MAX supports two types of faces, as mentioned earlier: quads (four-sided faces) and tris (three-sided faces).

Each face has an associated surface normal, which is a vector perpendicular to the center of the face that determines which side of the face is visible. The normal is also used to handle the smoothing of the object. Because polygons are basically flat surfaces, creating smooth curved surfaces such as spheres requires many polygons unless you use smoothing.

Smoothing is the process by which faceted surfaces are leveled during rendering if the angle of their surface normals is within the defined range for smoothing. MAX automatically applies smoothing to most objects, but you can also apply smoothing to individual groups of faces. You can use the extra smoothing groups to refine the smoothing in areas of objects that are not perfectly smooth. For example, an object with a high degree of curvature—such as a human face—might need extra smoothing groups applied to the transitions between the nose and cheek bones or other areas of the face. You can also apply smoothing to objects that do not yet have smoothing applied to them (usually, these are objects that have been imported from other programs).

Elements

Elements are groups of faces that are treated as a single selection within a larger object. These are most commonly created when you attach one object to another such that both objects become elements of the larger object. All mesh objects have at least one element, which is the object itself. In only certain circumstances, such as when smaller objects are attached together to form a larger object, will you find objects with multiple elements.

This is important to understand, because if you import objects from other programs, you might need to break them apart in MAX to work with them efficiently. Many times, the objects can be broken apart quickly, based on their elements. Elements are also very useful for assigning materials at a sub-object level.

Segments

Mesh models, like splines, have segments that run between vertices. In mesh models, though, segments are used to increase the detail for a variety of purposes. Take a box, for example. If you want to bend the box with the bend modifier, you cannot do so unless you increase the number of segments. There is simply not enough detail in the standard box to bend accurately. Figure 3.11 shows you an example of this. Of course, increasing the number of segments increases the vertices, edges, and faces in the object, making it more complex and time-consuming to work with. You should strive to keep the number of segments in an object as small as possible.

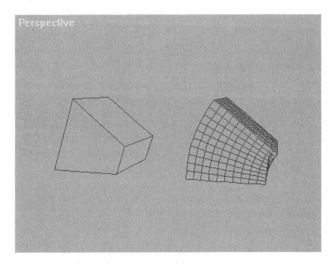

FIGURE 3.11   *A box with one segment versus a box with 10 segments. Both boxes have the bend modifier applied, but notice how the box with ten segments is more accurate. Increasing the segments results in a better bend.*

In general, mesh modeling involves creating one or more objects, whether they are primitives, lofts, or some other type of mesh, and then modifying the mesh to match what you want. For example, a chair can be created out of six boxes. This makes for a fairly plain chair, but with a little sub-object editing and some more detail, you can create a better version of the chair.

Mesh modeling is powerful and easy to use, but it does have its downfalls. Mesh modeling becomes very difficult when you want to create highly organic shapes such as the human face—or just about any living creature, for that matter. When mesh modeling can't handle the job, you must explore other modeling methods to accomplish the same tasks quickly and easily and produce acceptable results.

Parametric Modeling

Parametric modeling is a very powerful modeling method in which all of the parameters for an object can be adjusted or animated at any time. Instead of using a less precise method, such as scaling, you can simply adjust the creation parameters as accurately as you need. Parametric modeling works with splines, meshes, and other types of models. MAX is a parametric modeler through and through, whereas many modeling and animation packages are not.

For example, when you create a box in MAX, you have length, width, and height parameters that can be animated. In addition, you have three segment spinners to control the detail of the box. In many packages, if you want to create a box that changes shape over time, you accomplish this by scaling the box over time. You can do this in MAX, but it is just as easy to animate the length, width, and height parameters.

In addition to modifying the box parameters, you can apply a variety of modifiers to the object to produce different shapes quickly and easily. This creates the *stack*, which is simply a chronological list of modifiers applied to the object. You can go to any modifier entry in the stack and edit the parameters of the modifier. This is another form of parametric modeling, because the modifiers can be individually adjusted or animated, separate from each other. You can even apply different modifiers as tests and remove them from the stack just as easily. Figure 3.12 shows you a box and then the same box after some parametric modifications.

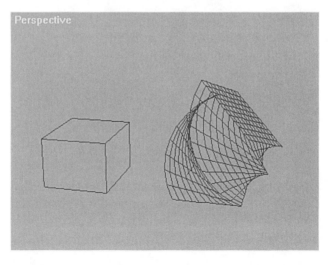

Figure 3.12   *An unmodified box (left) and a box with a modified parametric height value, an increased number of segments, and a parametric twist and parametric bend applied (right). Imagine trying to quickly and easily create such a complex object with standard mesh- or spline-modeling techniques.*

Overall, parametric modeling is extremely powerful if you are animating the creation parameters of the object, including modifiers. In MAX, parametric modeling is not a separate modeling method but rather the underlying methodology for all forms of modeling. However, parametric modeling still does not solve difficult modeling tasks such as human faces. This is where patch and NURBS modeling come into play.

Patch Modeling

Patch modeling makes use of many of the principles found in splines with Bézier tangents. A patch surface has two parts: the surface and a deformation lattice. The *deformation lattice* is a series of connected points along the surface of the patch, with each point of the lattice having control over the associated area of the patch. Adjusting a lattice point adjusts an area of the patch surface, not just a single point as you would see in mesh-editing of a vertex. What is unique here is that the lattice acts as the vertices in a Bézier spline and deforms the surface along a Bézier curve, instead of creating a linear curve. Figure 3.13 shows you an example of this. If you take a section cut of the deformed surface shown in Figure 3.13, it looks like a Bézier spline.

FIGURE 3.13   *A single patch grid that has been adjusted by modifying a single control point. Notice how the surface was adjusted over a large area and how the surface remains smooth.*

Patch Sub-Objects

Like all objects in MAX, patches have objects and sub-objects, including points, edges, and patches. In addition, they have a lattice object that is part of the overall surface. When you edit a patch at a sub-object level, you are editing either the lattice or the surface directly. The points of a patch surface are the control points of the lattice. By adjusting these, you adjust the curvature of the surface. As with splines, the control points of the lattice have independent tangent handles to control the curvature of the surface as it enters and leaves the vertex. Figure 3.14 shows you an example of this.

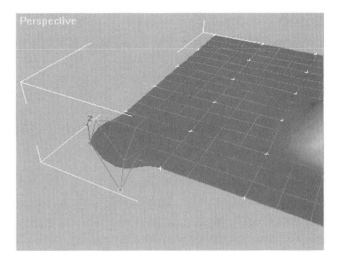

FIGURE 3.14   *A patch-lattice control-point tangent handle. By adjusting these handles, you can control the curvature of the surface around the control point.*

You also can edit the edges of a patch. The only editing that really occurs at this sub-object level is the addition of more patches to the current surface. Any added patches automatically take on the curvature of the selected edge.

Segments

Patches, like splines and mesh objects, have segments that can be used to increase the detail. Segments enable you to precisely control the surface with a more complex lattice or to create a more complex surface that deforms more smoothly. As you increase the number of segments in the surface, the lattice increases correspondingly. Again, you should try to keep the number of segments as small as possible to save memory in MAX.

Doing patch modeling is similar to creating a clay sculpture. You create one or more patch grids that will be used to form the surface of the object. Then, you manipulate the control points to push and pull the surface into the form you want. This might seem tedious and time-consuming, but you can create acceptable results very quickly.

Even with all this flexibility, patch modeling has its limitations. For example, getting the edges of patches to line up correctly to form larger patches can be difficult. You also can't create a blended surface between two patches without help. This is where NURBS comes in.

NURBS Modeling

Nonuniform rational B-spline modeling—just called NURBS—is probably the most powerful modeling method available today for creating complex surfaces. With NURBS, you have two basic approaches to modeling. One is to create NURBS splines and then create surfaces between the splines. The other is to create NURBS surfaces and then adjust the surfaces or create blends between surfaces. MAX provides you with NURBS curves and NURBS surfaces, along with a powerful set of editing tools, to create NURBS objects with either approach.

NURBS Curves

NURBS curves are created out of either points or control vertices. The difference between the two is how the curve is interpreted around the vertices. When points are used, the curve passes directly through the control points. When control vertices (CV) are used, the points act more like a deformation lattice. Figure 3.15 shows you the difference between the two point types when NURBS curves are used.

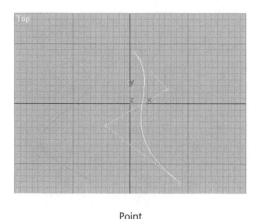
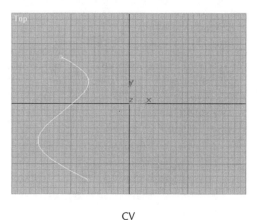

Point   CV

FIGURE 3.15   *Two NURBS curves, one created as a point curve and the other as a CV curve. Notice how the curve is interpreted around the control points.*

CV curves provide several advantages over point curves. A CV curve is interpreted between and around the CVs, making it easier to control the curve. In addition, you can assign weight values to CVs. If you assign a higher weight to a particular CV, the curve is pulled closer to that CV. Weights are relative to the other CVs in the curve, so if each CV has a weight of one and you adjust them all to two, the curve remains the same. But, if you adjust one to a different value from the others, the curve changes.

Like splines, NURBS curves also work as shapes, and you can have multiple NURBS curves under the same NURBS shape. NURBS shapes are then used as the basis for creating NURBS surfaces. This process introduces two key concepts you need to understand when working with NURBS. These concepts are independence and dependence.

Independent and Dependent NURBS Objects

Any NURBS points, curves, or surfaces can be categorized as either independent or dependent. An *independent* NURBS object is a standalone object such as a NURBS curve that does not rely on other geometry to define its shape. A *dependent* NURBS object relies on other NURBS objects to determine its shape and structure. A NURBS surface based on curves is a dependent surface because it depends on the location and orientation of the curves to derive its shape. At any time, dependent curves can be converted to independent curves for various operations. Many of the NURBS commands enable you to create objects as either dependent or independent curves.

NURBS Surfaces

The last type of NURBS object is a NURBS surface. As with NURBS curves, there are two types of surfaces: point and CV. Again, a point curve has control points at each vertex and a CV surface makes use of a lattice, much like a patch model. The difference occurs when you deform the surface by transforming a control point. A patch relies on the principles of Bézier splines to deform the surface. Although this creates a nice smooth surface, it is still an approximation. NURBS surfaces, on the other hand, are extremely accurate and deform better. Figure 3.16 shows you a NURBS surface using CVs.

NURBS objects in MAX are a totally different way of handling surfaces. They are not composed of quads and tris but are true NURBS surfaces. For MAX to render these surfaces, they must be converted to a mesh. This is called *surface approximation* and works by creating as many triangles as necessary to approximate the surface. Fortunately, MAX handles this approximation at rendering time; all you have to do is set the approximation method and values. This enables you to create more accurate approximations of the surface when necessary.

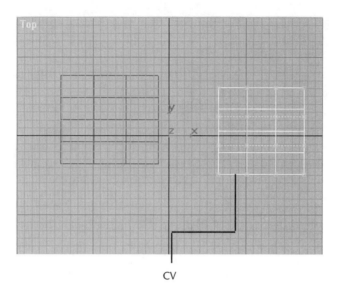

CV

FIGURE 3.16   *A CV NURBS surface that makes use of a lattice. The lattice distributes a smaller number of control points across the NURBS surface when compared to a point surface, where control points exist at every vertex.*

Overall, NURBS takes a different approach to modeling than found in mesh or spline modeling. In mesh and spline modeling, you create objects and deform them into other objects. In NURBS, you create surfaces by blending or by creating surfaces between NURBS splines. It takes a while to get used to this methodology if you are used to mesh modeling, but when you get the hang of it, you will find yourself creating complex models quickly and easily.

Working with Object Properties

All objects in MAX have a standard set of properties associated with them. You have control over some of these properties, but not others. The easiest way to access an object's properties is to select the object, right-click it, and choose Properties from the pop-up menu. Figure 3.17 shows you the Properties dialog box.

Object Information

The Object Information section of the Object Properties dialog box provides you with information about the currently selected object. When more than one object is selected before you access the Object Properties dialog box, the Object Information section is grayed out and unavailable. Each of the Object Information options is listed below and briefly described:

tip

When modeling in MAX, strive to keep the number of vertices, faces, and polygons as low as possible. The more vertices and faces you have, the larger the object is and the longer it takes to manipulate, display, and render.

- **Name.** This text box displays the name of the object. If you wish, you can change the name of the object here or in the command panels. To the right of the Name box is a color swatch showing you the current color of the object. Clicking the color swatch enables you to change the color.

- **Hide.** Enables you to hide the object from the display.

- **Freeze.** Enables you to freeze or unfreeze an object. A frozen object is visible in the scene but cannot be selected or edited.

- **Dimensions.** These are the X, Y, and Z dimensions of the object in world space units.

- **Vertices.** This is the number of vertices in the object.

- **Faces.** This is the number of faces in the object.

- **Shape Vertices.** This is the total number of vertices in the current shape. This value appears only when you select a spline for displaying its properties.

- **Shape Curves.** This is the number of individual splines with the shape. This value appears only when you select a spline for displaying its properties.

- **Parent.** All objects in the scene are linked to a parent object of some sort. In most cases, this is the root of the scene, but objects can be linked as children to other objects. You will see more on this in Chapter 15, "Understanding Animation Concepts."

- **Material Name.** This is the name of the material currently assigned to the object.

- **Num. Children.** When the selected object is a parent, this displays the number of objects that are children of the selected object.

- **In Group.** If the object is a member of a group, the group name appears here.

- **G-Buffer.** This is the object channel of the object for use with special-effects packages found in video post, the Material Editor, or the render effects.

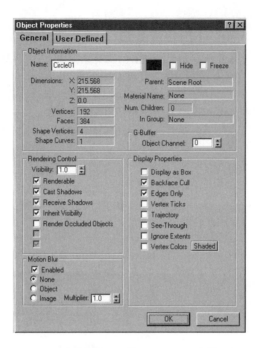

FIGURE 3.17   *The Object Properties dialog box, where you can define features that are common to all objects in MAX.*

Rendering Control

The Rendering Control section of the Object Properties dialog box controls various properties of the object at render time. Each option is listed below and briefly described:

- **Renderable.** When this is checked, the object is processed and rendered by MAX's rendering engine. When unchecked, the object is ignored by the rendering engine. You can use this feature to create objects that are markers, spacers, or others that do not need to be rendered but help you with the modeling or animation.

- **Cast Shadows.** When checked, the object casts shadows if it is lit by a shadow-casting light. When unchecked, the object does not cast shadows. When used in combination with exclude lists, you can accurately control when and where shadows appear in your scene.

- **Receive Shadows.** When checked, the object shows a shadow if a shadow is cast on it. When unchecked, the object does not display shadows that are cast on it.

- **Inherit Visibility.** If this object is a child of another object, this checkmark defines the visibility of the object to be inherited from the parent object. If you hide the parent object, this object hides.

- **Render Occluded Objects.** When this checkmark is active, objects that are occluded, or hidden, by this object are rendered. This is used mostly for effects, such as lens flares behind transparent objects.

Motion Blur

The Motion Blur section of the Object Properties dialog box enables you to define which method, if any, MAX will use to blur an object that is moving quickly through the scene. See Chapter 12, "Fundamentals of Materials," for more on motion blur. There are three types available:

- **None.** No motion blur is applied to the object. This is the default.

- **Object.** The object is blurred by rendering it repeatedly and compositing the renderings together into the scene. This method is rather time-intensive.

- **Image.** This is the fastest motion blur available and produces fairly good results. It blurs the object by blurring the pixels of the final rendering. The Multiplier spinner defines how much blurring occurs. Higher multipliers result in more blurring, giving the object the appearance of moving faster.

Display Properties

The last section of the Object Properties dialog box to look at is the Display Properties section. These control how the object appears in the scene and are very similar to the controls found in the Display command panel. Each option is listed below and briefly described:

- **Display as Box.** Enables you to display the object as a bounding box. This is independent of the shading mode you select in the scene.

- **Backface Cull.** When objects are drawn in wireframe, all edges are drawn. Backface cull removes the edges that would normally be hidden in real life. This is on by default.

- **Edges Only.** This controls the display of edges. When unchecked, any edges that are shared but hidden are shown as a dotted line.

- **Vertex Ticks.** Shows the vertices in the object, regardless of the display mode or sub-object selection.

- **Trajectory.** When the position of an object is animated, it creates a motion path called a *trajectory*. This checkbox enables the display of the motion path when one is present.

- **See-Through.** Forces the object to display itself in an x-ray mode so you can see other objects, such as bones, inside of it.
- **Ignore Extents.** When this option is enabled, commands such as Zoom Extents ignore this object in their calculations.
- **Vertex Colors.** Displays the object in the viewport according to the colors assigned to the vertices.

The controls found in the Object Properties dialog box are rarely needed, but they are very handy on occasion. By far, the rendering controls and information readouts are the most important.

Conclusion

This chapter introduced you to several topics related to modeling in MAX. These topics included

- Spline-based modeling
- Polygonal or mesh-based modeling
- Working with sub-objects and level editing
- Parametric modeling
- Patch modeling
- NURBS modeling

Modeling is sometimes difficult, even in a program such as MAX. This is especially true when you try to model an object with a method that is not ideally suited to that type of modeling. Fortunately, MAX provides you with many different types of modeling methods. Each modeling method creates objects out of various sub-objects, such as vertices, faces, and edges.

As you progress through this book, you will learn how to manipulate objects and sub-objects by using various modeling methods to create the objects you need. The next chapter introduces you to the basic modeling methods available to you in MAX.

CHAPTER 4

Working with Objects

Before learning how to create objects in 3D Studio MAX, it is important to understand how to manipulate and work with those objects in 3D space. These skills are important because you will rarely, if ever, be able to create the exact object you want in exactly the correct place. Many times you will create your object somewhere else in the scene or in a different file completely. Then, you must manipulate the object to correctly place it in the scene.

This chapter focuses on how to manipulate and control objects through the 3D Studio MAX interface. In particular, this chapter focuses on the following topics:

- Moving, Scaling, and Rotating Objects
- Copying (Cloning) Objects
- Working with Align, Array, and Mirror
- Working with the Spacing Tool

Moving, Scaling, and Rotating Objects

The most basic type of editing in MAX is transforming objects. You can apply three types of transforms to objects in MAX: Move, Scale, and Rotate. Obviously, you will use these commands over and over again, so you need to become very familiar with them. Each transform is accessible in a variety of ways—most commonly by selecting the command from the Main Toolbar or from the right-click menu. The transform commands are shown on the Main Toolbar in Figure 4.1.

You can also access the transform commands by right-clicking any selected object or group of selected objects. In the pop-up menu that appears, you will see the three transforms. Figure 4.2 shows an example of the pop-up menu.

A small difference exists between the toolbar and pop-up menu commands. The transform commands on the toolbar enable you to select one or more objects, whereas the pop-up menu relies on an existing object selection. Because of this, the toolbar commands are selection and transformation commands at the same time.

The most common transform is the Move command. This command enables you to reposition any selected object or group of objects anywhere in the scene. This works by choosing the command and then clicking the selected object and dragging it to its new location. When you're using the Move command in this manner, the object snap system in MAX becomes very handy for helping you quickly and accurately place objects.

The Rotate command works by the same method as the Move command, except that you end up rotating the selection set. By default, rotations are handled in a view reference coordinate system and around the Z axis. This enables you to rotate the object in the same way in any orthographic viewport. If you rotate a box in the Top viewport and then in the Front viewport, it appears to be the same, but the rotation is applied along two different axes. Rotate is commonly used in conjunction with the Angle snap toggle, enabling you to restrict the rotation of objects to specific increments, such as five degrees or one degree.

The Scale command, on the other hand, is a little more complicated because there are three Scale commands you can use in MAX:

FIGURE 4.1
The Move, Scale, and Rotate transform tools on the Main Toolbar. These commands are also found in the right-click menu.

FIGURE 4.2
The right-click menu, where you can find access to the transform commands, as well as a variety of other commands, depending on the type of object you have selected.

tip

The right-click menu in 3D Studio MAX 3 has been significantly enhanced since R2.5 and earlier. Not only do you have access to the transform commands, you also have access to many of the basic editing commands found in editable mesh, editable patch, and NURBS surfaces. Practice with these commands and you will find them very useful.

- **Scale.** Performs uniform scaling along all three axes of the selected object. Axis restriction has no effect on this command. You can scale objects in terms of percentages; for example, 200% is twice as large and 50% is half size. Scale is commonly used in conjunction with the Percent snap toggle to restrict the scale to percentage increments such as 10%.

- **Non Uniform Scale.** This version of scale enables you to scale the object nonuniformly along an axis or plane. The application of the scale is controlled by the axis restriction. Most of the time, when you select this particular Scale command, you will receive a warning message about applying nonuniform scales to objects. This warning will be explained in Chapter 5, "Mesh Modeling Fundamentals." Until then, simply ignore the warning.

- **Select and Squash.** This is another axis-independent command that essentially squashes the object in multiple axes.

All of the Scale commands rely heavily on the location of the center, or pivot point. If you have an object that has a center five units away from the actual pivot point, and you scale that object 200%, the object ends up 10 units away from its pivot point. In other words, all parts of the object are scaled, including the distance to the pivot point. In general, it is best to have the pivot point in the center or at the bottom of the object when scaling.

tip

When using any transform command (Move, Rotate, or Scale), you can use the lock selection feature of MAX to speed up workflow. You can lock or unlock the selection set by pressing the spacebar (the Lock icon at the bottom of the screen turns yellow). When lock is active, you cannot select anything else. This enables you to click anywhere on the screen and drag to perform the transformation. Locking selections is also helpful in crowded scenes or with cloning.

note

At the bottom of the MAX screen, just to the right of the Lock icon, you will find a set of coordinate readouts. Whenever you apply a transform to one or more objects, these readouts will tell you, in MAX units, how much transform you have applied in each axis. This readout is very handy, especially for rotations.

Using the Transform Gizmo

MAX 3 makes it very easy to see and restrict transforms through the use of a new Transform gizmo. Whenever you select an object and activate one of the transform commands, this gizmo appears at the center point (also known as the pivot point) of the object. Figure 4.3 shows you the Transform gizmo for the Move command.

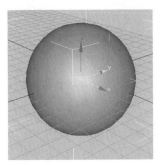

FIGURE 4.3   *The Transform gizmo, which enables you to control how you transform objects without enabling an axis lock.*

When you move the mouse over the Transform gizmo, various parts of the gizmo become active (and turn yellow). These areas indicate how you can restrict the transform. For example, if you choose the Move command and place the cursor over the X axis, only the X axis becomes yellow. If you click and drag at this point, you are able to move the object only along the X axis.

If you look out a little way from both the X and Y arrows on the Transform gizmo, you will notice two small lines forming a corner. By clicking on these lines and dragging, you can restrict the transformation to a plane—in this case, the XY plane. This enables you to move the object anywhere in the X or Y directions, but not Z. You will also find planar corners for YZ and ZX restrictions.

The importance of this Transform gizmo comes in the form of a smooth workflow. In the past, if you wanted to have this type of axis restriction, you had to enable the axis restriction by selecting it from the Main Toolbar or the right-click menu. This was not difficult (and you can still do it in MAX 3), but it required an extra click or two that is no longer necessary. Take a moment and try transforming a basic box or sphere, first by using the Transform gizmo and second by using the axis restrictions located on the Main Toolbar or the right-click menu. You will find that the Transform gizmo is much faster.

note

The display of the Transform gizmo is easily turned off by choosing Views, Show Transform Gizmo. You can also turn it off by pressing the X key. If you load a scene and the Transform icon is not there, check these settings. More than likely, you have accidentally pressed the X key and turned the gizmo off.

note

When you view the transform gizmo in an orthogonal viewport such as the top or front viewports, the axis that points toward the viewport is not visible. For example, in the Top viewport, the gizmo will display the X and Y axes, but not the Z. This is because you cannot move the object along the Z axis in the top viewport.

Most exercises in this book make use of the Transform gizmo to perform transforms along a specific axis, plane, or coordinate system. You will get plenty of practice using it. If, for some reason, you decide you don't like it, you can disable the Transform gizmo in the Preferences dialog box on the Viewports tab.

The following exercise introduces you to using transforms in conjunction with the Transform gizmo.

Using Transforms to Manipulate Objects

1. Load the file **MF04-01.MAX** from the accompanying CD. Figure 4.4 shows you the scene at this point, which is a table and a few objects to place on that table.

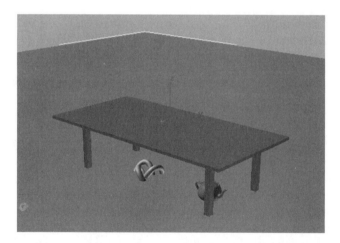

FIGURE 4.4   *A scene with a table and a few other objects. You will use the transform commands to move these objects from the ground onto the table.*

2. On the Main Toolbar, choose Select and Move. In the Top viewport, click the teapot.

3. Move the cursor over the Y axis so the axis turns yellow. Drag the teapot up under the table.

4. With the teapot still selected, right-click the Front viewport to make it active. Move the cursor over the Y axis again and move the teapot until it sits on top of the table, as shown in Figure 4.5.

FIGURE 4.5   *The scene with the teapot sitting on top of the table instead of on the ground.*

Up to this point, you have seen how to transform an object by using the Transform gizmo in different viewports. Now use the Transform gizmo to do the same thing, but in the Perspective view only.

5. Activate the Perspective view. Choose the Min/Max toggle button to maximize the viewport.

6. With Select and Move still active, click the torus knot to select it.

7. Move the cursor over the Y axis until the axis turns yellow. Drag the torus knot until you think it is under the table.

8. Move the cursor over the Z axis until the axis turns yellow. Drag the torus knot vertically until it is on top of the table. (This might be much easier to visualize with the Perspective view in shaded mode. If it is not already shaded, turn on Smooth + Highlights for this viewport).

9. Repeat the Move process for the hedron that still exists on the floor.

As this exercise has shown you, the transform commands are very easy to use. In some circumstances, you will find it easier to use them in different viewports for different operations, as with the teapot. In other cases, you might be able to get away with just using the Perspective view, as with the torus knot. Most of these decisions boil down to personal preference, but you will run into instances where you will need to work in different viewports.

Now that you have seen how easy transforms are to use, it's time to take a look at how transforms work in relation to the coordinate systems in MAX.

Working with Coordinate Systems

All the transforms—such as Move, Rotate, and Scale—base the transformation of the selected object on the currently selected coordinate system. The coordinate system determines how the object is actually transformed. The ability to use alternate coordinate systems in MAX (called reference coordinate systems) gives you the flexibility you need to transform objects under just about any condition.

The type of coordinate system is so important because of axis restriction. It is possible to restrict the transformation of an object to a single axis. The best example of this is the Rotate command. By default, when you rotate an object, you are rotating it around the Z axis, thus restricting the transform. But, the reference coordinate system determines the orientation of the Z axis within the object.

When you select an object to which you want to apply a transform, a Transform gizmo appears, indicating the X, Y, and Z axes for the currently selected coordinate system. This gizmo is your key to determining the location and orientation of the coordinate system and how the object will react when you transform it.

The default coordinate system for transforms, for example, is a view coordinate system that places the transform tripod in alignment with the current viewport. In this orientation, the X axis is always horizontal, Y is always vertical, and Z always comes out of the viewport toward you. This is true of most viewports. Camera, Perspective, and User views make use of the world coordinate system for transforms instead of screen coordinates. You can select coordinate systems from the Main Toolbar by selecting the reference coordinate system drop-down list shown in Figure 4.6. Here, you can select the type of coordinate system you want to use when you transform an object.

MAX provides seven different reference coordinate systems you can use to control the transformation of objects. Each is listed here and briefly described:

- **View.** The default transform coordinate system that relies on the view to set the X, Y, and Z axes. This coordinate system is used in any planar view, such as the Top, Right, Back, or Left views of the scene. In these views, the axis tripod always appears with X to the right, Y to the top, and Z coming out of the screen toward you.

- **Screen.** Aligns the transform tripod to the screen. This appears best when viewing the scene from a Perspective view. Normally, in a Perspective view, the coordinates are aligned along the world coordinate system. Switching to Screen forces the coordinates to align to the screen.

FIGURE 4.6

The Coordinate Systems drop-down list. From this list, you can select the type of coordinate system MAX will use when performing transforms on an object.

- **World.** The standard world space coordinate system. This is an absolute setting, in which the X, Y, and Z axes are always aligned in the same direction. The world space coordinates are always indicated by the Home grid, which is the grid that appears in the MAX viewports by default. The grids appear along the XY, YZ, and ZX planes, depending on your viewport.

- **Parent.** When you have a child object that is attached to a parent, the coordinate system derives itself from the parent object. Later in this book, you will see how to link one object to another, creating a Parent-Child hierarchy.

- **Local.** The local coordinate system for the object. When you rotate an object, you rotate its coordinate system as well. This is the most popular reference coordinate system to use when you are rotating objects.

- **Grid.** The Grid coordinate system aligns the axis tripod to the current construction grid helper object.

- **Pick.** A user coordinate system in which you can pick an object to which to align the coordinate system. Doing so adds the selected object's name to the bottom of the drop-down list, so you can pick it again later in the same session.

You will find that when you are working on a scene in MAX, you will routinely switch between reference coordinate systems to better control the transforms you apply to objects. You will probably most commonly use the View, World, and Local coordinates to perform your work.

The following exercise enables you to see how to make use of the Transform gizmo in conjunction with a reference coordinate system.

Working with Alternate Coordinate Systems

1. Load the file **MF04-02.MAX** from the accompanying CD.

2. Choose Select and Rotate. In the Top viewport, click the box and drag it vertically to rotate it. Watch your coordinate readouts and rotate the box 45 degrees.

3. Activate the Perspective view.

4. Move the cursor over the X axis of the Transform gizmo and rotate the box 45 degrees around this axis. This box should be oriented much like the box shown in Figure 4.7.

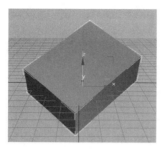

FIGURE 4.7   *The box after applying two sets of transforms. At this point, it is difficult to rotate the box around its long axis without changing coordinate systems.*

At this point, the box has been rotated around two axes. Now, assume you want to rotate the box around the long axis. How would you do that? No matter how hard you try, you cannot successfully accomplish this without using a reference coordinate system, because you won't be able to lock the rotation to the long axis otherwise.

5. Click the reference coordinate system drop-down list and select Local. (Watch the tripod change in the Perspective viewport.)

6. Move the cursor over the X axis until the axis turns yellow. Then click and drag and rotate the box another 45 degrees.

This exercise clearly illustrates the importance of using axis restriction in combination with the reference coordinate systems. This exercise also demonstrates just how easy it is to use the Transform gizmo to perform transforms with an axis restriction.

Controlling the Transform Center

As you have just seen, the Transform gizmo is always located at the transform center of the object. The transform center is usually called the center point or, more commonly, the pivot point of the object. All objects are transformed in relation to this pivot point. The pivot point is especially important when you're doing rotations.

The pivot point controls are located on the Main Toolbar between the reference coordinate system drop-down list and the axis restriction buttons on the Main Toolbar. Figure 4.8 shows this flyout toolbar. These commands enable you to set the location of the center point of the reference coordinate system.

tip

In most cases, selecting a particular axis on the gizmo will not be a problem. But in some cases, you might need to rotate the view before you will be able to select the axis you want.

MAX provides three types of center point controls you can use:

FIGURE 4.8
The pivot point center controls, with which you can define where the pivot point is when applying transforms to one or more objects.

- **Use Pivot Point Center.** Each object in MAX has its own local coordinate system. The origin of the local coordinate system, called the pivot point, is generally at the center bottom of the object. This is the default location for the center point of the coordinate system. When you select different reference coordinate systems, they will always be located at the pivot point, but oriented differently.

- **Use Selection Center.** When you select more than one object, the pivot point option is not easy to use. This option sets the center point to the geometric center of the selection set. In this case, the center point might be located anywhere in 3D space and is not always restricted to the bottom of the geometry as with the pivot center.

- **Use Transform Coordinate Center.** When you select a reference coordinate system, it might have its own center. For example, the world space option has a center at 0,0,0, or the origin of world space. Selecting this center enables you to transform objects around that point.

By selecting the appropriate center point, you can further refine how the transform is applied to the object.

The pivot point center option brings up another interesting feature. As mentioned, all objects have a pivot point. When you select a different transform center point, you are doing so on a temporary basis. It is possible to permanently change the location of the pivot point of an object.

FIGURE 4.9
The Hierarchy command panel, where you can access the controls to manipulate the pivot point of one or more selected objects.

Changing the Pivot Point

To change the pivot point of an object permanently, select the object and go to the Hierarchy command panel, where you will find the pivot point controls shown in Figure 4.9.

Six buttons are worth exploring at this point. Each is listed here and briefly described:

- **Affect Pivot Only.** This option enables you to transform the pivot point only. You cannot transform the geometry when this is active. When you select the Affect Pivot Only button, you can move, scale, or rotate the pivot point. A special icon appears in MAX, on which you can perform the transform. Figure 4.9 shows you this icon, which also appears with Affect Object Only.

- **Affect Object Only.** The opposite of Affect Pivot Only. Here the pivot point is static, and you transform the object to adjust the pivot point.

- **Center to Object.** Aligns the pivot point to the center of the object. If you remember from earlier discussion, the default is centered but at the bottom of the geometry. The Center to Object option centers the pivot point completely.

- **Align to Object.** Aligns the X, Y, and Z axes of the pivot point with the local coordinate system of the selected object.

- **Align to World.** Aligns the pivot point with the world coordinate system.

- **Reset Pivot.** Resets the pivot point to its original setting. Be careful when using this with Affect Object Only. If you select Affect Object Only and move the object, the object does not return to its original position when you reset the pivot point. Instead, the pivot point returns to its original location in the object but at the object's new position in the scene.

There are many instances in MAX when it is practical to adjust the pivot point of an object. The most common is when you import an object from another program. The pivot point might not be in the center of the imported object. You can correct this with Center to Object. Another common use includes moving the pivot point to affect how the object is rotated. When you get more into animation, you will see the importance of this feature.

Working with the Transform Type-In Dialog Box

Up to this point, you have been applying transforms by using the mouse in combination with axis restrictions, snaps, and reference coordinate systems. These are all handy tools for quickly placing objects; however, with the exception of the snaps, they are not very accurate. To help with this, MAX has a Type-In dialog box where you can precisely type in the transforms you want (see Figure 4.10).

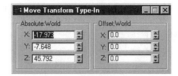

FIGURE 4.10   *The Transform Type-In dialog box, where you can type in specific values for the currently selected transform. This gives you precise control over the transform.*

Type-in dialog boxes are very handy, especially when you want to move an object a specific distance or scale the object a percentage along one axis. Typing is much more accurate and quicker than using the standard click-and-drag mouse methods.

You can access the Move Transform Type-In dialog box through Tools, Transform Type in the pull-down menu or by right-clicking the Transform gizmo on the Main Toolbar. This dialog box is used in conjunction with the Move, Scale, and Rotate commands exclusively. You select the object, activate one of the transform commands, and then open the Type-In dialog box if it is not already open. At this point, you can use the mouse to move objects, or simply type the desired transforms in the dialog box.

The Transform Type-In dialog box changes to match the type of transform you are working with. Figure 4.10 shows the dialog box for the Move command. If you select Scale, the dialog box shown in Figure 4.11 appears.

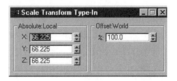

FIGURE 4.11   *The Transform Type-In dialog box for the Scale command.*

The Scale Transform Type-In dialog box enables you to work with transforms in two different ways: Absolute or Offset. With the Absolute type-ins, all transforms are applied in the world coordinate system. If you select an object and apply a Move transform with a Z value of three, the object moves three units in the Z axis. If you exit the transform and come back, the Z axis value will still be three.

With Offset, on the other hand, you are applying the transform relative to the current position of the object. Offset makes use of the current reference coordinate system (explained in the next section) in the context of the current viewport to define the direction in which the transform will be applied.

Using the Transform Type-In for Object Manipulation

1. Load the file **MF4-03.MAX** from the accompanying CD. Figure 4.12 shows you the scene, which is the table scene from the first exercise, with the torus knot and teapot on the ground.

FIGURE 4.12   *The table scene with the teapot and torus knot located under the table, on the ground. A precise transform will place them on top of the table.*

2. Choose Select by Name from the Main Toolbar. Select both the torus knot and the teapot (hold down the Ctrl key for multiple selections) and choose the Select button.

3. Click the Select and Move button to activate it. Then right-click the same button to bring up the Type-In dialog box.

4. Under the Offset:World section, type in **38** for the Z axis spinner. When you press Enter, notice that the selected objects move 38 units vertically.

After the transform, the teapot is correctly positioned but the torus knot isn't. The reason for this is that the torus knot has a different pivot point, which is in the center of the knot. The pivot point for the teapot is at the base of the teapot. You need to do an additional transform on the torus knot only.

5. Select the torus knot and use the Transform gizmo to move it into the correct position.

The previous exercise illustrates the importance of understanding the location of the pivot point when it comes to transforms. The torus knot is an excellent example of what happens when you have different pivot points. The problem is easily enough remedied by moving the torus knot more than the teapot.

Now that you have seen how transforms work, it is time to explore how they work with different coordinate systems.

Copying (Cloning) Objects

Even as simple as transforms are in MAX, you can begin to see just how flexible and powerful they are. Now, you can take this one step further by using the transforms to create new objects. You accomplish this by using the MAX reference or cloning system.

The reference system is a general method of handling how an object is copied in MAX. Making a copy of an object in MAX is easy enough—simply hold down the Shift key when you perform a Move, Rotate, or Scale. When you select the new location for the object, you will be prompted for an object name and type. (Figure 4.13 shows this dialog box.) Copying an object in MAX is called *cloning*, and you can create three types of clones: copies, instances, and references.

FIGURE 4.13   *The Clone Options dialog box, where you can define the name and type of clone you will create out of the currently selected object.*

- **Copy.** A copy is an exact duplicate of the object in every manner, except for the name. A copy takes up just as much memory as the original object. As you create clones, MAX automatically renames the cloned objects by numbering them, unless you give the new object a new name every time. If you run across objects named tree01, tree02, and so on, they might have been cloned.

- **Instance.** An instanced object does not take up additional memory in the scene except at render time, thus making your files much smaller. An instance is an exact duplicate of the original object, but it is still related to the original.

If you apply a modifier, it will be applied to all instances of the object in the same way, so it's easy to create effects such as a set of flowers blowing in the wind. Each flower can be an instance. Then simply apply the Bend modifier to one instance, and all the flowers will bend at the same time. By animating one instance of the Bend modifier, you animate all.

- **Reference.** A referenced object is similar to an instance but is considered a one-way instance. In other words, if you apply a modifier to the original object, the reference is affected as well, but if you apply the modifier to the reference, the original is not affected. The reference maintains its own modifier hierarchy.

Throughout MAX, you will find places where you can use references and, more commonly, instances. You can, for example, instance bitmaps in the Material Editor or animation controllers in TrackView. In all cases, the copied objects are the same as the original, and any changes made to one affects all instances of the object. As you progress through the many areas where you can use instances, you will see how and why this is a very powerful tool.

In addition to the transform commands, you'll find a Clone command in the Edit pull-down list. You use this to make a clone of any selected object, in exactly the same position. When this is done, the original object is deselected and the clone is selected so you can immediately transform it.

Using Move, Scale, and Rotate, with their associated functionality, is a common task you will perform in everyday work with MAX. But there are still a few other, less often used transform commands to look at.

Working with Align, Array, and Mirror

Three other types of transform commands exist in MAX that you should be aware of: Align, Array, and Mirror. These commands are transforms because they change the positions of objects and, in some cases, create one or more copies of the objects as the position is changed. You can find these commands in the Main Toolbar, as shown in Figure 4.14, as well as in the Tools pull-down menu.

Working with Align

The Align command is used to align one object to another. The alignment can occur as a position, rotation, or scale. To perform this operation, you simply select the object you want to align. Choose the Align command and then select the object to which you want to align. At this point, the dialog box shown in Figure 4.15 appears.

FIGURE 4.14

The Align, Array, and Mirror commands on the Main Toolbar tab of the shelf.

FIGURE 4.15   *The Align dialog box, where you can define how the selected object is aligned to another in the scene.*

As shown in Figure 4.15, the Align command includes several very powerful options. Each is listed here and briefly described:

- **Align Position (Reference Coordinate System).** These controls define which coordinates of the selected object are aligned to the destination objects. You simply select each check box and the transformation is applied. In addition, you can define which center point of the objects are aligned by choosing Minimum, Center, Pivot, or Maximum. This alignment occurs in the selected reference coordinate system, which is read back in the parentheses. This means alignment is also specific to the coordinate system.

- **Align Orientation (Reference Coordinate System).** These check boxes control which axes are also aligned to the destination object. This occurs in the local coordinate space at all times.

- **Match Scale.** Last, you can match the scale of the aligned object at the X, Y, and Z axes, regardless of the coordinate system.

As you can see, the Align command provides you with plenty of detail, but several other Align commands are available in the Align toolbar flyout, which is shown in Figure 4.16.

The Align command is a quick, yet powerful way to manipulate an object quickly and accurately. Take the teapot in the last exercise as an example. To perform that transform with the Type-In dialog box,

FIGURE 4.16

The Align toolbar flyout, where you will find commands to align objects to objects, object normals, highlights, cameras, and views.

you needed to know how tall the table was, and that information was provided for you. If you don't know the information, the Transform Type-In dialog box is not very helpful, but you could use Align to perform the same operation. The following steps are all that would be necessary:

1. Select the teapot.
2. Choose the Align command from the toolbar.
3. Select the tabletop.
4. Select Z axis as the align position, Minimum for current object and Maximum for Target object. Choose OK and the teapot is placed on top of the table.

The Align to View command aligns objects to the current viewport. There is also an Align Camera command that can align objects to a camera view. These are specialty commands that are only used in certain circumstances. Coverage of these commands is beyond the scope of this book.

Working with Array

The next transform command is the Array command. The Array command enables you to create multiple copies of an object in either a circular or grid-like fashion. Arrays can occur in one dimension, two dimensions, or even three dimensions. You can even set the array to create copies, instances, or references of the original object. To array an object, select the object and then select the Array command. The Array dialog box shown in Figure 4.17 appears.

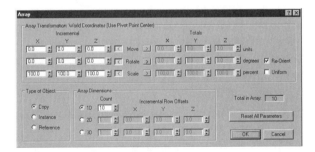

Figure 4.17   *The Array dialog box, where you can control exactly how objects are arrayed.*

The Array dialog box includes several controls you can use to define how the array works. These controls are listed and briefly described here:

- **Array Transformation.** These controls define the spacing of the array components. This can be done either incrementally or totally. Incremental sets a defined spacing between objects, and Total defines an overall length within which the objects are created. You can select which control is active by clicking the arrows between Incremental and Total. This can be applied to the Move, Rotate, and Scale aspects of the array.

- **Type of Object.** These controls enable you to define whether the array is created as a copy, an instance, or a reference.

- **Array Dimensions.** These control the overall dimensions of the array and whether it is one-, two-, or three-dimensional.

Figure 4.18 shows an example of an arrayed set of teapots on the tabletop.

FIGURE 4.18   *A set of teapots that have been copied by using the Array command. The pivot point of the original teapot is located at the center of the circle. This is a quick way of making many copies of an object.*

Working with Mirror

Probably the most used special transform command is the Mirror command. This command creates an exact mirror duplicate of a selected object and enables you to mirror an object about a single axis. Simply select the object and choose Mirror. When you do this, the Mirror dialog box shown in Figure 4.19 appears.

The Mirror command provides you with two sets of controls. The first control is the Mirror axis, which you can define just as you define the axis restriction controls.

tip

Under certain circumstances, using the Mirror command might be inadvisable. If you are going to use the mirrored object in a Boolean operation later on, this might cause the Boolean to fail. Make sure you keep a copy of the original object in case the mirrored object causes problems.

The Offset spinner shown in Figure 4.19 enables you to set the mirrored object a specified distance from the mirror line. Like the other transformation commands, the Mirror command makes use of the selected reference coordinate system to perform the mirror operations.

FIGURE 4.19   *The Mirror dialog box, where you can define how the selected object is mirrored.*

The second control enables you to define the clone options. By default, the Mirror command does not create a clone, but you can set it to create a copy, an instance, or a reference.

Working with the Spacing Tool

The Spacing tool is a new addition to MAX 3. It provides you with the capability to make multiple copies of an object relative to another object. The best example of this would be making copies of one object along a spline. You can see the use for a tool such as this when you might want to create a bunch of telephone poles along the edge of a road.

The Spacing tool is available by selecting Tools, Spacing Tool from the pull-down menus. When you do, you receive the dialog box shown in Figure 4.20.

The Spacing tool works by dividing the selected spline into lengths you specify and then placing copies of the selected object at those points.

The following exercise gives you a brief example of how to use the Spacing tool to create a series of telephone poles along a road.

FIGURE 4.20   *The Spacing Tool dialog box, where you can select the spline and the object to copy along that spline.*

Using the Spacing Tool to Copy Objects Along a Spline

1. Load the file **MF4-04.MAX** from the accompanying CD. Figure 4.21 shows you the scene at this point, which contains a ground plane, road, telephone pole, and spline.

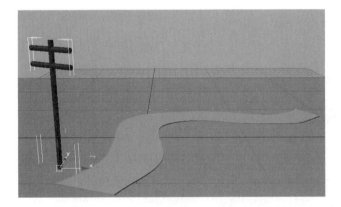

FIGURE 4.21   *The telephone pole scene before using the Spacing tool. You will use this tool to quickly make copies of the telephone pole along the edge of the road.*

2. Select the Telephone Pole object.
3. Choose Tools, Spacing Tool from the pull-down menu. This launches the Spacing Tool dialog box.
4. Choose Pick Path and click the spline to the left of the road.

5. Set the Count spinner to 4 and see the copied telephone poles quickly appear in the scene.

6. Set the Type of Object to instance and choose Apply.

7. The telephone poles are created at this point. Choose Close. Then, delete the original telephone pole. Figure 4.22 shows you the final version of the scene.

As you can see from the last exercise, the Spacing tool can be very useful, but it does have limitations. You might have noticed that the poles are copied correctly but are not oriented correctly. You can quickly correct this by rotating each pole. There are many options to the Spacing Tool dialog box. Take a few minutes and explore some of the ways in which you might make use of this tool. Use the original telephone scene as a basis for exploration. Other ways you might make use of this tool include placing lights on a string to create Christmas lights or placing railroad ties along a railroad track.

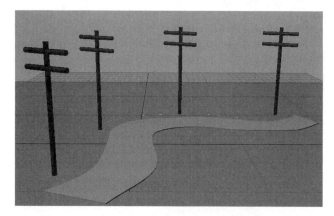

Figure 4.22   *The scene after using the Spacing tool. The telephone poles were quickly copied and correctly positioned.*

Conclusion

This chapter focused on basic object-manipulation skills, using some of the most commonly used commands in 3D Studio MAX. Overall, skills such as transforms and cloning are vital to working with the MAX system. You will use these skills every day you work with MAX to create your scenes, manipulate objects, assign materials, or perform hundreds of other tasks in MAX.

- **Transforms.** The Move, Scale, and Rotate commands, which are used to position objects correctly in the scene.

- **The MAX Reference System.** Provides three different methods (copy, instance, and reference) for creating copies of objects in the MAX scene. By controlling the type of copy, you can control how the copied objects are related to other objects in the scene.

- **Reference Coordinate Systems.** Objects are always transformed around a specific point and a specific coordinate system. The reference coordinate system enables you to define the position and orientation of a coordinate system that MAX will use when transforming objects.

- **Align, Mirror, and Array.** These advanced transform commands provide automated methods of transforming objects.

- **The Spacing Tool.** Another advanced transform command that gives you the capability of copying objects along a path.

Now that you have seen how to do some basic object manipulation, it is time to look at mesh modeling, including the use of the stack and modifiers. The next chapter introduces you to the first of several different methods of creating geometry in 3D Studio MAX.

CHAPTER 5

Mesh Modeling Fundamentals

Mesh modeling is the most common form of modeling in 3D Studio MAX 3. It involves creating 3D objects out of mesh triangles by using a variety of methods. The most fundamental aspect of mesh modeling is the creation and editing of splines and primitives, by which you can create many types of objects. You can also set up mesh objects for transformation by methods discussed in Chapter 6, "Mesh Modeling Tools."

This chapter discusses several of the most commonly used methods for modeling mesh objects, starting with spline modeling. In particular, this chapter covers the following topics:

- Spline Modeling
- Editing Spline Objects
- Creating Primitives
- Working with Editable Mesh

Spline Modeling

To learn how to begin creating objects in 3D Studio MAX 3, start with the most basic object: the spline. Splines in MAX 3 are created out of vertices and segments, which form the splines. Each vertex can be a different type, enabling you to control the curvature, or tangent, of the spline as it enters and leaves the selected vertex.

By combining and modifying splines in MAX 3, you can create many types of objects. Examples of such objects include phone cords, wine glasses, and ground surfaces. The trick is in how you create the spline and then transform it into a 3D object.

Creating Splines

MAX 3 supports a variety of spline types, the most basic of which is the Line command. The Line command enables you to create almost any shape or form you want and is the most flexible of the splines. Other spline types include circles, arcs, text, and others. By creating and combining one or more of the spline types, you can create many shapes necessary for your modeling tasks. Much of the work that is done with splines is used as a framework for the creation of 3D objects based on those splines.

All of the spline commands in MAX 3 are found in the Create command panel, under the Shapes button. Figure 5.1 shows the Splines rollout and all of the spline commands. Of course, when you select a particular spline, you get the associated rollouts and controls for that command.

In MAX 3, you can create 11 different types of basic shapes through the spline commands. By editing these shapes, you can create a limitless variety of other shapes. Figure 5.2 shows you some of the spline shapes you can create in MAX 3.

FIGURE 5.1
The Splines rollout in the Create Command Panel. Here, you can select which type of spline you want to create.

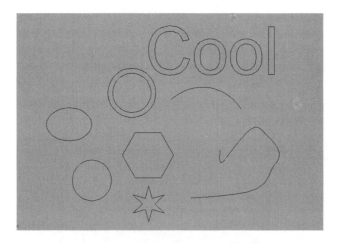

FIGURE 5.2   *Various spline shapes you can create in 3D Studio MAX.*

MAX handles splines as shapes. One or more splines can be combined to create more complex shapes for you to use. The Start New Shape button shown at the top of Figure 5.1 enables you to create new shapes or add splines to the currently selected shape. In this manner, you can refine and build all of the shapes you might need.

The Line Command

The Line command and its rollouts are shown in Figure 5.3. Before you create a line, you can adjust settings—such as the initial corner type or the drag corner type—to match the type of line you want to draw.

To create a line, you select the Line command and then choose the locations of the vertices of the line. The line is drawn according to the order in which you select the vertices. When you click to place a vertex, you generally create a corner vertex, but if you click and drag while placing the line, you create a Bézier vertex. The Bézier vertex enables you to control the curvature of the spline as it enters and leaves the vertex. Obviously, clicking and dragging to create the curvature of a spline is not an exact method, and creating the exact curve you need can be difficult. Many times you will need to modify the spline and its vertices after you have created it.

When you are creating a line, a white box appears around the first vertex you create to mark it as the first one you drew. The location of the first vertex is important for many 3D operations involving splines. If, while you are still creating the shape, you place another vertex over the first vertex, MAX asks if you want to close the shape. This creates a shape without any breaks in its boundaries, called a *closed shape*, which is also important for many 3D operations. Many of the other spline commands, such as Rectangle and Circle, automatically create closed shapes and create a first vertex in a predefined location on the spline.

FIGURE 5.3
The Line rollout, where you can define the type of line you want to create.

As you create the line, MAX automatically creates the minimum number of steps per segment to accurately portray any curve you define. Remember that a segment is the section of a spline between vertices. The default setting is six steps per segment, with MAX set to *optimize* this number. Optimization is the process by which MAX removes as many steps as possible without compromising the curvature of the line. For example, a straight segment has one step,

tip

When creating a line, you can restrict the creation of the spline to 90-degree angles by holding down the Shift key. This enables you to easily create orthogonal shapes.

but a curved segment might have up to six or more steps. By reducing the steps, you reduce the amount of memory the line takes, as well as the complexity of the line and any geometry generated from that line.

Optimization can also be set to *adaptive*, which means MAX adaptively adds or removes steps from the spline as the curvature changes. Obviously, the more curvature that exists in the spline, the more steps are needed to accurately represent the curve. Of course, you can override the optimization settings and set your own number of steps as well.

The Text Command

Another commonly used spline command is the Text command. (In later chapters, you will get more practice with other spline commands.) The Text command is used to create 2D text that can then be converted to 3D. MAX enables you to use any TrueType font that is installed on the system to create text.

If you open the Text command in the Create command panel of MAX, you will see a variety of controls. If you have done any word processing, these controls should look familiar. At the top of the rollout, you can select the font. Then, you can select bold or italic and the type of justification you want to use. Below that are three spinners to set the size, kerning, and leading. And finally, there is a large white box where you can type the text you want.

As you can see, the Text command is not quite like other spline commands. It has many more options and is used for the specific task of creating text. Figure 5.4 shows you an example of the word Cool created with MAX text.

tip

If you are not familiar with text and typography, here are a few useful definitions:

Font. Determines the shape, size, orientation, and position of the letters. Different fonts provide you with different looks for your text.

Justification. Enables you to set how the text is placed in multiline text objects.

Kerning. Enables you to control the spacing between letters.

Leading. Adjusts the amount of space between text lines.

FIGURE 5.4 *The word "Cool" created as a spline in MAX by using the Text command. This word can now be converted to 3D, if necessary.*

In the following exercise, you use the Text command along with the Line, Circle, and Star spline commands to create a logo for a fictitious corporation.

Creating a Text Logo

1. In the Create command panel, click the Shapes button. In the drop-down list, make sure you have Splines selected and not NURBS curves. This expands the Splines rollout.

2. Click the Donut command. In the Top viewport, click and drag from approximately 0,0 out to a radius of approximately 140. (Watch your command panel readouts to see where you are.)

3. Move the mouse inward and create the interior of the donut approximately 20 units inward.

4. After creating the donut, go to the command panel and change radius 1 to 140 and radius 2 to 120. Name the object Border.

5. Expand the General rollout and turn on Renderable. Set the Thickness to 2.0. This enables the spline to render as a 3D object without having to create a 3D object.

6. From the Main Toolbar tab on the shelf, choose Select and Move to activate the Move tool. Right-click the Select and Move tool. Enter 0 for the X, Y, and Z spinners under the Absolute:World section of the dialog box. This moves the donut to exactly 0,0,0 in the Top viewport.

note

The Shapes commands are also available on the Shapes tab of the shelf. Feel free to select the commands from there instead of the command panel, if that is your preference. Most exercises in this book make use of one or the other.

7. In the Create command panel, choose the Star spline type. Again, in the Top viewport, click at 0,0,0 and drag out to about 130 units. Move the mouse inward until you are fairly close to 0,0,0 again and click.

8. In the command panel, set radius 1 to 130 and radius 2 to 10. This creates a nice star effect. Name the object **Star**.

9. Expand the General rollout and turn on Renderable again. Set the thickness to 1.5.

10. As with the circle, use the Move command and the type-in dialog box to position the star at 0,0,0 precisely.

11. Select the Text command from the Splines menu. Set the font to Arial, the size to 60, and the Kerning to –3.0. Click the Italics button to italicize the text. In the text field, highlight MAX Text and replace it with **XYZ Corp**.

12. In the Top viewport, click where you want to create the text.

13. From the Main Toolbar tab on the shelf, choose Select and Move and position the text so it is roughly in the center of the circle.

14. On the Main Toolbar, choose Quick Render to render the scene using the default lighting and colors of the splines. (If the colors come out dark, change the colors of the spline objects. You don't need to assign a material at this point.) Figure 5.5 shows you what the resulting image should look like.

The previous exercise begins to show you just how powerful the splines are in MAX. You might have noticed in the rendering that the splines did not render smoothly. If this is the case, select each spline and go to the Modify command panel. In the general parameters, turn off the Optimize check box and change the Steps spinner to a higher value to generate a more accurate spline.

The other spline commands available in MAX 3 vary in how they work when compared to the Line and Text commands. Some make use of click-and-drag techniques to create the spline object, such as Circle and Ellipse. Others work more like the Line command by accepting simple clicks without dragging the cursor; arcs are created in this way. Still, others require both techniques, such as the Helix command.

Now that you have seen how to quickly create splines, take a look at how to edit the splines. In the previous exercise, you had to do very little editing, but you will edit most splines extensively.

FIGURE 5.5   *The scene after a quick render. This scene shows how easy it is to begin creating in MAX, even with just splines.*

Editing Splines

The true power of working with splines is the capability to edit and refine the shape. Without this, you cannot create many of the shapes you will need for your projects.

Any line shape is automatically created as an editable mesh; however, other splines, such as circles and arcs, must be converted to editable splines. You can convert a spline to an editable spline either by right-clicking the spline and choosing Convert to Editable Spline or by going to the Modify command panel, clicking the Edit Stack button, and choosing Convert to Editable Spline. After you convert the spline to editable, you have access to all of the component parts of the spline, such as segments and vertices. You can edit splines at four different levels: shape (called the object level), vertex, segment, and spline.

Editing Splines at the Object Level

Object-level editing of splines is the default method when you enter the Modify command panel with a spline selected. Figure 5.6 shows the rollout that appears.

upgrader's note

In previous versions of MAX, when you accessed the editable spline controls, you received different rollouts for different sub-objects. In MAX 3, all commands are visible, but commands that do not work with the current sub-object level are grayed out and unavailable. Changing sub-object levels changes which commands are available.

Editing splines at an object level enables you to perform three basic functions. First, you can attach one or more splines to the current shape. Object-level spline-editing enables you to combine separate splines into a single shape after you have created them. In addition to adding splines to a shape, your lines can be added to the shape as you create them.

Under the General rollout of the Editable Spline command panel, you can control the interpolation options (otherwise known as the detail settings) of the splines in the current shape. These settings will override any settings you applied when you created the splines and are applied to all splines in the shape. You can also set the rendering options of the splines by giving the splines a rendering thickness. This enables you to make all of the splines in the shape-renderable entities that can have materials assigned to them.

Almost all of the commands you can use with editable splines are quickly accessible if you right-click the selected spline. Figure 5.7 shows you the menu that appears. You can select a particular sub-object level to work at, or directly access a particular command. This menu changes and is available for editable mesh, editable patch, and NURBS surfaces as well.

By far, most of the object-editing you will do with splines involves attaching one or more splines to the current shape.

Editing Splines at the Vertex Level

The first, and most important, sub-object level you can work with in splines is the vertex level. You can access the commands for this level through the right-click menu or by clicking Sub-Object in the Modify command panel and selecting Vertex from the drop-down list. When the vertex sub-object controls are active, you can access any of the commands present in the command panel rollout, or you can use any of the standard MAX transforms to position and adjust the vertices of a spline.

FIGURE 5.6

The Editable Spline rollout, where you find all of the controls available for editing splines at various sub-object levels.

When the vertex sub-object selection is active, the only objects you can select in the scene are the vertices on the currently selected spline. This means if you choose Select Object, you can select one or more vertices to edit. When you select the vertex, it turns red and an axis tripod appears. Depending on the type of tangents this particular vertex is using, you might also get a set of green tangent handles. Figure 5.8 shows a selected vertex with tangent handles.

If you right-click the selected vertex, you can change the type of tangents being used by the vertex. A spline vertex can have four different types of tangents. You can set these corner types while creating the spline if you are using the Line command, but for the other spline commands, the only way to set the tangents is to use sub-object editing.

After you have set the tangent types, you can transform the vertex or the tangent handles with the Move and Rotate commands. The Scale command affects only the tangent handles. When you scale a vertex, the distance of the tangent handles away from the vertex is scaled. As such, the Scale command does not affect the Corner or Smooth tangent types.

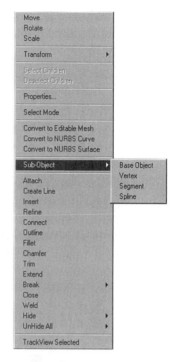

FIGURE 5.7

The right-click menu, where you have quick access to a wide variety of commands—in this case, the editable spline commands.

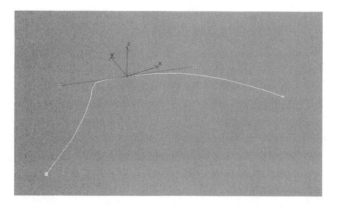

FIGURE 5.8   *A selected Bézier vertex, showing its tangent handles. By adjusting the handles, you can adjust the curvature of the spline.*

Editable spline contains several different types of commands, outside of the transform commands, that are very useful in creating and editing splines. These commands include

- **CrossInsert.** In cases where you have two splines in the same shape that cross, you can use the CrossInsert command to insert a vertex at the location where they cross. The threshold spinner enables you to define the maximum distance between the splines in which the vertex will be created.

- **Fillet.** This command enables you to select a particular vertex and create a *fillet*, or curve. The spinner defines the size of the curve. Select the vertex and then drag the spinner to create the fillet.

- **Chamfer.** The Chamfer command is the same as fillet, except it creates a flat, straight edge to the corner instead of a rounded edge.

- **Bind/Unbind.** In some cases, you will want to connect the endpoint of one spline to the midpoint of another in the same shape. The Bind/Unbind commands enable you to do this. When you bind a vertex, it turns black to indicate this state. The vertex then reacts to changes in the spline to which it is bound and cannot be transformed by using the standard transform commands.

- **Refine.** The Refine command enables you to refine a spline by adding vertices to the spline. It has a Connect option that enables you to add vertices and connect those vertices as you go. It also has options to bind the vertices and create linear or closed versions.

By making use of the transform commands in combination with the rollout commands, you can take a spline such as a rectangle and adjust it to practically any other shape.

Editing Splines at the Segment Level

The next level at which you can edit a spline is the segment level. As with vertices, you can select and transform segments at will. Also as with vertices, a pop-up menu appears when you right-click any selected segment. This menu is the same as the vertex menu except for the last two entries, which enable you to select whether the segment will be a curve or a straight line. Choosing one or the other will have no effect on the vertices themselves, only on how the segment between the two is interpreted.

tip

These vertex level commands—especially Bind/Unbind, CrossInsert, and Refine—are important for many types of spline editing. They are especially useful if you are going to use Surface tools, which are covered in Chapter 7, "Patch Modeling Methods." Surface tools enable you to surface a spline cage with patches.

Many of the commands found here in the command panel are the same as those found under the vertex-level editing commands, but they work on a segment instead. There are two differences: the Detach command, with which you can detach selected segments and create a new shape or create a copy of a segment as a new shape, and the Divide command, with which you can equally divide any segment into smaller segments by placing equally spaced vertices along the spline.

Editing Splines at the Spline Level

The last level of spline editing occurs at the spline level. Overall, most of the editing you do to a spline will occur at a vertex or spline level. Vertex editing is used to refine the shape of a spline, whereas spline editing is used to combine two or more splines or create new splines. With spline-level editing, you will find a set of commands that enable you to combine open and closed splines in a variety of methods. Editing at a spline level also involves manipulating individual splines that exist within the larger, more complex shape. Finally, you can create a mirror of a spline (using the Editable Spline mirror tool), and the resulting copy is still a member of the current shape.

The most basic command at the spline level is the Close command, which connects the first vertex to the last vertex and creates a closed spline within the shape. You can also use the Outline command to create parallel copies of the spline. Creating an outline of a circle, for example, creates a donut shape. The distance between the original spline and the offset copy is defined by a spinner or a drag of the mouse.

The Reverse command is very similar to the First Vertex command. The Reverse command simply reverses the order of the vertices of a spline and is extremely useful when you're using the spline as an animation path or as an edge for a surfacing operation. You also have Trim and Extend commands you can use to trim splines back to match other splines or extend them.

Through the use of sub-object editing, you can modify and control a spline or shape all you want. The following exercise shows how to use some simple spline editing to refine a spline into a 3D cage that resembles the outline of a nose. In the next chapter, you will use this cage to create a 3D nose.

Creating a 3D Nose Cage out of Splines

1. Load the file **MF05-01.MAX** from the accompanying CD. This file has the outline of the nose drawn as a line, as shown in Figure 5.9.

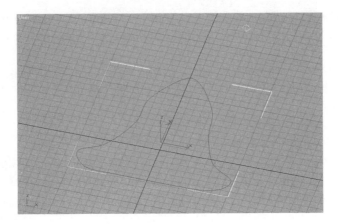

FIGURE 5.9   *The outline of the nose. Using Editable Spline, you will create a 3D outline of the nose.*

2. Select the spline and go to the Modify command panel. Because this was originally created as a line, it is already an editable spline. Select the Vertex sub-object mode.

3. To make the editing easier, turn on a vertex snap. Choose Customize, Grid and Snap Settings. Turn off Grid Points and turn on Vertex. Close the dialog box.

4. At the bottom of the screen, click the 3D Snap button.

5. On the Geometry rollout, choose Create Line. Click a vertex and then click the same vertex on the opposite side of the nose. Right-click to end the Line command.

6. Repeat for the rest of the vertices. Figure 5.10 shows you the nose at this point.

7. With Create line still active, click the vertex at the top of the nose. Create the line down the center of the nose, but place the second vertex just short of the bottom of the nose. Right-click to end the Line command.

8. Turn off 3D snapping.

9. In the command panel, choose Bind. Click the last vertex you drew and drag down to the bottom of the nose. When the cursor changes, let go. You should see the vertex snap to the bottom segment and turn black, as shown in Figure 5.11.

   Up to this point, you have created all the necessary splines for the nose shape. Notice how all of the splines form 3- or 4-sided shapes; this is important for use in Chapter 7. Now you need to refine the model a little further by adding some vertices and then moving them. To do this, you use the new CrossInsert feature.

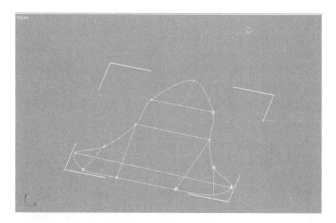

FIGURE 5.10   *The nose cage after the first set of additions.*

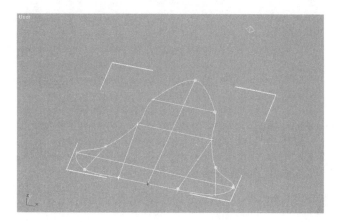

FIGURE 5.11   *The nose shape with the bound vertex in place at the bottom of the nose.*

10. In the Modify command panel, choose CrossInsert and set the spinner to 1.0. This determines that if the crossing splines are within 1 unit of each other, the CrossInsert vertex will be created.

11. For each point where the splines cross in the center of the nose, click the intersection once. A vertex should appear each time.

12. From the Main Toolbar tab, choose Select and Move. Select all of the vertices in the nose model. Right-click one of the selected vertices and choose Smooth from the right-click menu. This converts all of the vertices to smooth vertices.

13. With Select and Move still active, window-select around each vertex in the center part of the nose and move it along the Z axis to give the nose some depth. You need to window-select because CrossInsert actually inserts two different vertices, one on each crossing spline. Window selecting selects both.

14. Move each vertex vertically until you have a nose shape similar to the one shown in Figure 5.12. You might wish to use Rotate View to look at the nose from different angles to make sure you moved the vertices correctly.

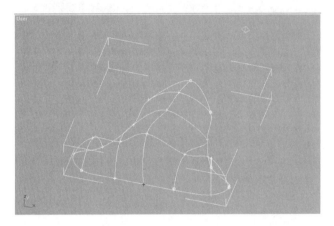

FIGURE 5.12   *The nose cage after adding vertices and moving them into the correct position. It is now ready for surfacing.*

15. Save the model as **MF05-01a.MAX** for use in Chapter 7.

The nose you just created will be completed in Chapter 7, where you will surface the nose with the new Surface modifier. You might take some time at this point to see how easy it is to create different noses by adjusting the frame you just created.

From the last exercise, the power of sub-object editing—whether it is used on splines or other types of objects—should be obvious. You took a simple outline and modified it into a much more complex shape with very little effort.

Most of the methods for converting splines into 3D objects involve using Modifiers (discussed later in this chapter), so converting splines to 3D objects will be covered after you have a good understanding of how modifiers work. In the interim, take a look at how to deal with 3D mesh objects, starting with primitives.

Creating Primitives

3D primitives are the basis of many modeling packages and provide you with a method for creating many simple objects. Many times, these objects are combined or modified to form other objects. MAX 3 provides you with two sets of primitive objects: standard and extended. The standard primitives include Box, Sphere, Geosphere, Cone, Cylinder, Tube, Torus, Pyramid, Teapot, and Plane. The extended primitives include objects such as Hedra, Torus Knot, Chamfer Box, Chamfer Cylinder, Oil Tank, Capsule, Spindle, L Extrusion, C Extrusion, Gengon, Ringwave, and Prism.

When you model with primitives, you will almost always end up transforming or modifying the primitives to create other objects. You can create walls in a building with a series of long thin boxes, for example. You can place door and window openings by adding more boxes and creating compound objects out of them. Rarely will you ever use single primitives by themselves.

Using AutoGrid to Create Primitives

MAX 3 now supports the use of a new method of creating primitives called AutoGrid. Normally, when you create a primitive, it is created on the home grid in the viewport in which you are currently working. You can also create primitives on special helper grid objects after you activate those objects. Creating primitives on helper grids enables you to work on a plane other than the home plane.

AutoGrid takes this analogy a step further. Whenever you create a primitive with AutoGrid enabled, a temporary grid is created wherever you place the mouse. If the mouse is over another object, the grid is aligned perpendicular to the normal of the face the cursor is over. (The normal is an imaginary vector coming out of the center of each face, used to determine the visible side of the face.) To see more clearly how AutoGrid works, perform the following steps:

1. Create a sphere in the Perspective viewport. Switch the viewport to Shaded mode so you can more easily see what you're doing.

2. In the Create command panel, turn off Smoothing so you can see each individual face.

3. Choose the Box command.

4. At the top of the command panel, turn on AutoGrid. Now move the mouse over the surface of the sphere, but don't click yet. As you move the mouse over the surface of the sphere, notice that the Transform gizmo aligns the Z axis with the normal of the face.

5. With the cursor over a face, click and drag and create a box as usual. As you do, watch for a grid to appear. The creation of the box is aligned to this grid. When you have finished creating the box, the grid disappears and AutoGrid waits for you to select the next orientation. Figure 5.13 shows you AutoGrid at work.

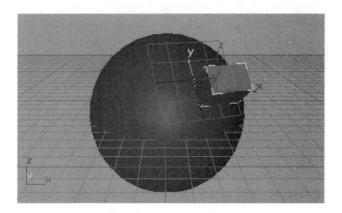

FIGURE 5.13   *Using AutoGrid on a sphere. This tool enables you to create primitives directly on the surface of other objects.*

AutoGrid works with primitives and with any other creation tool, such as splines, helpers, cameras, and even lights. This productivity tool can save you an enormous amount of time if you consistently work on planes other than the home grid. AutoGrid is extremely useful when you're working on sloped surfaces, creating detail objects on the exterior of a ship, and in many other situations.

In the following exercise, you use primitives to build a simple chair for use in the bowling alley scene.

Building a Chair with AutoGrid

1. Start a new file in MAX. In the Create command panel, select the Box object.
2. Click at 0,0 in the Top viewport, drag out to around 10,10, and let go. Move the mouse toward the top of the viewport and click to give the box a height.
3. With the box selected, go to the Create command panel and set the width and length to 1 and the height to 18. Name the object Chair Leg1.
4. Select Region Zoom and zoom in on an area surrounding the Box object. Create three other boxes exactly the same but approximately 18 inches apart, forming a square. Name the objects Chair Leg2 through Chair Leg4.

5. Select the Box command again. Create a box that is slightly larger than the four chair legs and one inch thick. Name the object Chair Seat.

6. Choose Zoom Extents All; then, choose Select and Move. In the Front viewport, click the box you just created and move it vertically in the viewport until it rests on top of the chair legs. Figure 5.14 shows the chair at this point.

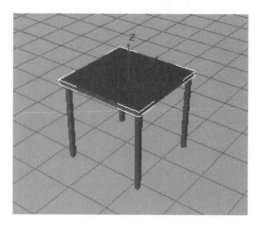

Figure 5.14   *The chair after creating the legs and the seat. Now all you have to do is create the back of the chair.*

7. In the Perspective viewport, zoom until you are close to the seat of the chair.

8. Select the Cylinder command from the Create command panel and turn on AutoGrid. Place the cursor on the top of the chair seat and click and drag to create the first cylinder, with a radius of 0.5 and a height of 18. Create five more cylinders in the same manner but spaced evenly across the back of the seat. Name the objects Chair Back1 through Chair Back6.

9. Use Select and Move again to make any adjustments that are necessary to the cylinders.

10. Turn off AutoGrid and select the Box command again. In the Top viewport, create a box that outlines the top of the cylinders, with a height of 1. Name the object Chair Back7.

11. Use Select and Move and position the last box at the top of the cylinders in the Front viewport. Figure 5.15 shows the finished chair.

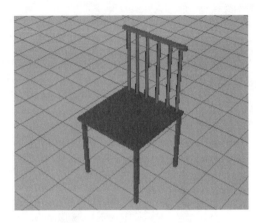

FIGURE 5.15   *The completed chair. Now it is ready to be merged into other scenes.*

12. Select all of the chair objects and choose Group, Group from the pull-down menus. Name the group Chair.

13. Save the file as **MF3CH502A.MAX**.

For the most part, the primitives in MAX are straightforward and easy to generate. By combining one or more primitives, you can quickly and easily create more complex objects. The other primitives (not explored here) are just as easy to create and easy to combine to create other objects. A more powerful method of using primitives, however, is converting them to editable meshes and then editing those meshes to produce objects that would otherwise be more difficult to create.

Working with Editable Mesh

When you create an object such as a primitive, the object is considered a primitive and not an editable mesh. In other words, when you go to the Modify command panel with a primitive selected, you can still adjust its creation parameters such as width or height. As with splines other than a line, you must convert primitives over to an editable mesh to be able to edit them at different levels. Just as with splines, you can do this through the right-click menu or in the Modify command panel by using the Edit Stack button. Almost all mesh objects can be converted to an editable mesh. When they can't be converted, you can apply an Edit Mesh modifier to access the same controls.

Editable mesh works like editable spline. All of the controls are visible in the rollout, but they are activated depending on the type of sub-object level with which you are working. Many of the functions you saw in the editable spline controls are available in editable mesh. For example, in editable spline, you had a Chamfer control for vertices.

Editable mesh has Chamfer for both vertices and edges. The main difference is that editable mesh has five different sub-object levels instead of three. Figure 5.16 shows you the Editable Mesh rollout.

Working with Vertices

Vertex-level editing provides you with a high degree of control over the editing of mesh objects, but adjusting the vertices of an object can also be very tedious. To enter Vertex mode, click the Vertex button in the Modify command panel or select it from the right-click menu. With Vertex mode selected, the object shows a bunch of small blue dots, representing the vertices. Figure 5.17 shows the vertices of a sphere. If you select one or more vertices, they turn red to indicate their new state. You can then apply standard MAX transforms to the vertices to adjust your object.

Beyond the basic transforms, you also have several vertex commands in the Command rollout. Some of these commands are the same as their spline cousins, such as Weld Vertices or Create, Delete, and Detach. Others perform new functions. You can, for example, use the Soft Selection command to transform a single vertex and have the transform also affect surrounding vertices. This makes it easier for you to create bulges in objects and control how those bulges appear.

FIGURE 5.16
The Editable Mesh rollout, where you will find all of the controls necessary to edit every aspect of a mesh object.

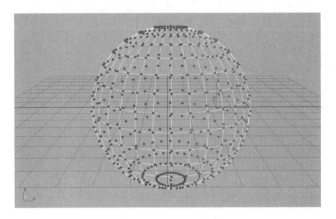

FIGURE 5.17   *A sphere when you're working at the vertex level. Blue dots represent vertices; red represent selected vertices.*

Vertex-level editing now includes the capability to chamfer corners of objects by selecting the vertex at the corner and applying the chamfer in editable mesh. In addition, you can also select to remove any isolated vertices, which are common wherever you have deleted faces from an object. A neat addition to editable mesh is the Slice Plane control. When you enable this button, a yellow plane appears in the viewport. Use the transform commands to position this plane somewhere in the object. When you press the Slice or Cut buttons, the mesh object now splits where it intersects the plane and a new set of vertices is created. This is a quick and easy way to add detail to an object in places where it would otherwise be difficult.

The only other different feature for vertex-level editing of a mesh object is Vertex Colors, with which you can assign different colors to different vertices. Using colors this way makes selecting a group of vertices easier. In general, this feature is for game developers and programmers, but it is handy for selections.

The following exercise shows an example of how to use vertex editing to create a pear out of a sphere.

tip

By default, vertices in MAX 3 are displayed as small blue dots. If you want to make them more visible, you can set them to display as larger blue dots. To do this, choose Customize, Preferences. On the Viewports tab, select the Show Vertices As Dots option and set it to Large Dots. Changes appear in the scene immediately.

upgrader's note

If you are used to using Affect Region from MAX 1, 2, or 2.5, you'll want to know it has been renamed Soft Selection wherever you can use that function. Functionality of the command is the same, with a few additional controls to better define how Soft Selection works.

Using Vertex Editing to Create a Pear

1. Create a basic sphere in MAX with a radius of 40.

2. While the sphere is selected, right-click the sphere and choose Convert to Editable Mesh.

3. Right-click again and choose Sub-Object, Vertex to enter vertex-level editing.

4. Choose Select Object from the Main Toolbar and select the vertex that is the north pole of the sphere.

5. Expand the Soft Selection rollout and turn on Soft Selection.

6. Set the Falloff to 40. When you do, notice that the vertices around the selected vertex change color. This indicates how much influence you are setting with the falloff value. The closer the color is to red, the more it moves with the selected vertices.

7. Set the Pinch value to –1.5 and Bubble to 0.90.

8. In the Perspective viewport, choose Select and Move. Click the Z axis and drag the vertex along it. As you move the vertex along the axis, you are creating a shape resembling that of a pear, as shown in Figure 5.18.

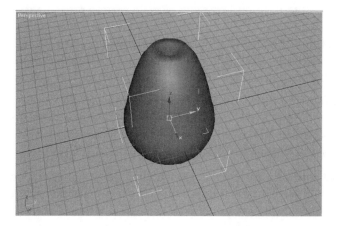

FIGURE 5.18   *A sphere, using Soft Selection to adjust a vertex. With only one vertex move, you can create a basic pear.*

Vertex-level editing is always a good way to make fine adjustments to a model. The previous exercise illustrates how powerful a modeling tool it really is.

Working with Edges

The next sub-object type is Edge. Here, you can control the edges of the faces. As with vertices, you can select individual edges and transform them. Also as with vertices, you can chamfer edges if you wish. Most of the time, edge-level editing is used to control the visibility of edges. A nice feature is AutoEdge, which enables you to change the visibility of edges based on the angle between their surface normals.

tip

If you are running OpenGL and have enabled Draw Wireframe Using Triangle Strips, all edges in the model will appear visible, including hidden edges. By default, Triangle Strips are turned off, resulting in slightly slower wireframe performance.

One of the more interesting edge-level controls is the ability to create a shape based on the edges you select. In other words, you can create a spline that matches the surface edges of an object. This makes it easy to loft an object along the surface of another or perform other interesting modeling chores that require you to work on the edge of an object.

Working with Faces and Polygons

MAX 3 supports two different levels of face editing. A basic face is a three-sided face within an object; a polygon can be one or more faces that are treated as a group. (For example, when you create a box, it is built out of 12 faces, with two faces to each side, but these two faces are treated as one polygon.) Hence, MAX supports working with faces or polygons. The commands you can execute on the two are the same; just the selection is different.

As with vertices, when you're working at face level, you can select faces and transform them with the standard MAX transform commands. Also as with vertices, when you select a face, MAX gives you a clear indication of the selection set by highlighting the entire surface of the face in red, as shown in Figure 5.19.

Editable mesh enables you to perform many different operations on all faces or a selection of faces in an object. Some of the more important operations you can perform include the following:

- **Attach and Detach Faces.** These operations enable you to add faces to or detach faces from the current object. When detaching, you can choose to detach to an element or to a separate object that you can name.

- **Surface Normals.** A normal is a vector used to define the visible side of a face. Faces that have normals pointing away from the camera will not render unless Two-Sided is enabled. These utilities enable you to view the normals of selected faces, as well as flip or unify those normals.

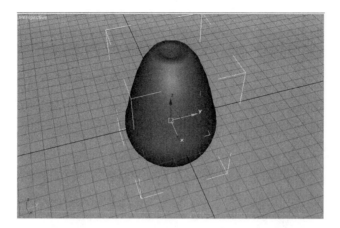

FIGURE 5.19   *A mesh object with a random set of faces selected. Notice how the entire face is highlighted instead of just the edges, making it clear what you are working on.*

- **Assign Material IDs.** Material IDs are identifier numbers assigned to individual faces for material purposes. This enables you to assign different materials to different faces within the same object. Many times, when you attach objects to other objects with different materials, you end up with faces that have different IDs.

- **Smoothing Groups.** Most curved objects—even spheres—are created out of flat faces. They appear curved thanks to smoothing between these faces, which you accomplish by assigning the faces to smoothing groups. Selected faces can be assigned to one of 32 smoothing groups for smoothing. You also have options for selecting by smoothing group and Auto-Smoothing the selected faces.

- **Tessellate.** Tessellation is a fancy way of subdividing a face into more faces and increasing the complexity of the object. Tessellation is sometimes necessary for certain transforms and modifiers, but it should be used with care because it increases the complexity of your model.

- **Extrude and Bevel.** These two controls work together to enable you to extrude faces and then optionally bevel them. This makes it easy to create complex objects such as hands from simple objects such as boxes.

- **Explode.** This command enables you to explode a group of selected faces into separate objects—very handy if you have a set of faces selected that are not connected to each other. This command detaches each face and creates it as a separate object in the scene.

Many of these functions are available as separate modifiers in MAX, enabling you to apply them through Edit Mesh or individually. If you apply them individually, you should use MeshSelect first to select the faces to which you want to apply the modifiers.

Working with Elements

The last sub-object level supported by editable mesh is the element level. Whenever you attach one object to another with editable mesh, both objects become elements of the larger object. You can also select groups of faces and detach them as elements of the larger object so they are much easier to select. Elements support the same set of editing tools that faces and polygons do. Again, the only difference is how easy it is to select the faces.

Most of the editing you will do to a mesh object will occur at a vertex or face level. At the vertex level, you can reposition, add, or delete vertices to change the shape of an object. At the face level, you can add or remove surfaces from the object, as well as increase the detail, assign Material IDs, or perform many other operations. Face-level editing is powerful when you work with geometry that was imported from another modeling program. The import process does not always work perfectly, so some editing must be done to correct the errors. This is generally done at the face level.

Overall, the ability to edit objects—whether they are meshes or splines—at any level of detail is important to creating crisp, accurate models that use as little detail as possible while creating stunning imagery. As you grow with your modeling experience, you will see more and more where sub-object editing and modeling are important.

The following exercise shows you how to use sub-object editing to create the basic form of a wing-type airplane. To do this, you will take a simple box and modify it. In Chapter 6, you will take the plane you create here and give it a smooth, curved look.

Modeling a Jet from a Box

1. In the Top viewport, create a box that is 80 units by 80 and 10 units tall. Set the length segments to 4 and the width segments to 2.

2. Right-click the box and choose Convert to Editable Mesh. This converts the box to an editable mesh and places you in the Modify command panel.

3. Activate Vertex sub-object mode either by using the right-click menu or by selecting Vertex in the Modify command panel.

4. From the Main Toolbar tab, choose Select and Move. In the Top viewport, select the bottom row of vertices. Move these vertices down and to the right, creating a swept wing.

5. Move the second row of vertices down and to the right but keep them closer to the center of the plane. Figure 5.20 shows you how the wing should look at this point.

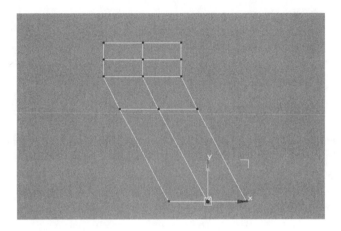

Figure 5.20   *The box after modifying two sets of vertices. At this point, you have created the basic shape of one wing.*

6. Repeat steps 4 and 5 for the top two rows of vertices, but move them up and to the left to create the opposite wing.

7. Rotate the view to a user view where you can see the ends of the wings.

8. Select the six vertices at the end of the wing. On the Main Toolbar tab, choose Non-uniform Scale.

9. Place the cursor over the Z axis so it highlights and restricts the motion. Click and drag and scale the vertices along the Z axis until they almost touch. This makes the wing thinner. Repeat for the opposite wing.

10. Select the vertex that is in the center of the plane but on top. Move this vertex along the Z axis approximately 20 units. Figure 5.21 shows you the plane at this point.

11. Rotate the view so you can see the bottom of the plane. Switch to Polygon mode and select the four polygons in the center of the plane.

12. In the Modify command panel, click the Extrude button. In the viewport, click the selected faces and drag down. Extrude the faces approximately eight units. You can watch the spinner in the modify command panel to see the results of the extrusion.

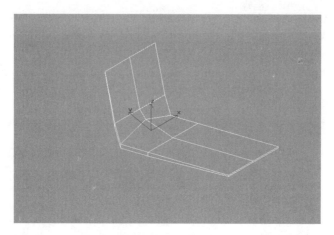

FIGURE 5.21   *The plane after modifying the center vertex. This modification created the pilot canopy. Now, all that's left is a few minor modifications to create the engines.*

13. Rotate the view so you can see the back of the plane.

14. Select the four polygons in the center back of the plane and extrude them 18 units to form the engine exhausts.

15. With the faces still selected, choose the Scale command from the Main Toolbar tab. This time, make sure you don't select Non-uniform Scale. Scale the faces down approximately 70% of their original size. Figure 5.22 shows you the plane at this point.

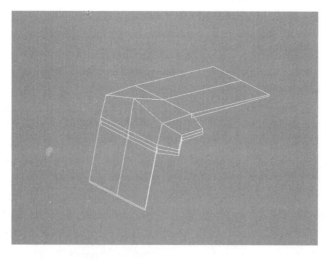

FIGURE 5.22   *The plane after using the extrude command to create the engines.*

16. Click on Extrude again and extrude the selected faces into the plane to make the exhaust ports.

17. Save the files as **MF05-03a.MAX**.

As the last exercise shows, it is relatively easy to create quite complex objects out of simple objects such as a box. In this case, by using the editable mesh controls, you were able to work with the box at different levels to manipulate it into the form that was needed.

Mesh editing is a powerful method of modeling, simply because of the level of control you have. As you learn MAX and other ways of modeling in MAX, you will find yourself time and time again returning to these methods for one reason or another. It is a good idea to get plenty of practice with editable mesh and editable spline and fully explore all of the commands associated with them. In later chapters, you will take the models you created in this chapter and further refine them, using other tools.

Conclusion

Splines and primitives are the beginning of the modeling process, working toward creating more complex objects. Almost all scenes make use of some primitives and most make use of some splines. This chapter introduced you to creating and editing both splines and primitives. In particular, this chapter focused on the following topics:

- Creation of splines
- Editing of splines
- Creation of primitives
- Editing of primitives

In the next chapter, you will take editing a step further by exploring the uses of modifiers and how they can be used to create much more complex objects quickly. You will also explore the use of compound objects where you combine two or more objects to form a new one.

CHAPTER 6

Mesh Modeling Tools

In the last chapter, you saw how to create both splines and primitives. You also learned how to convert these objects to their editable form for further editing. Now it is time to learn how to edit the objects even further through the use of modifiers and compound objects. This chapter introduces you to the following topics:

- Working with Modifiers
- Using the Stack
- Creating 3D Objects from Splines
- Advanced Mesh Modeling

Working with Modifiers

One of the most powerful and useful features of 3D Studio MAX is the ability to use modifiers. *Modifiers* are routines that change and transform objects in specific ways. For example, you might want to create an ice cream object to go on top of an ice cream cone. The easiest way to do this is to create an object and then apply a Twist modifier and twist it around the world coordinate system Z axis.

Modifiers work by adjusting all or part of the geometry. A Twist modifier, for example, works by adjusting the location of the vertices of an object. Other modifiers work at various sub-object levels, such as vertex, edge, or even face level. As such, modifiers are useful modeling tools, as well as powerful tweaking tools.

Modifiers are parametric in nature, which means each modifier has an associated set of controls you can set and adjust at any time. The parameters of a modifier can even be animated, providing you with many powerful animation tools.

To apply a modifier to an object, select the object and then go to the Modify command panel. At the top of the command panel are the most commonly used modifiers. The More button enables you to access a dialog box list of all of the modifiers available in the system. Figure 6.1 shows you the Modifiers dialog box. You can apply modifiers to more than one object at a time, but it is recommended that you apply them on an object-by-object basis.

FIGURE 6.1   *The Modifiers dialog box, where you will find a complete listing of all modifiers available in MAX.*

Modifiers that appear in the command panel are "smart" enough to recognize the type of geometry selected. In other words, modifiers only work on certain types of geometry (patches versus NURBS versus meshes versus splines). If you select a spline, only modifiers that can work on the spline will be active; the others will be grayed out. Some modifiers, such as Edit Patch, can be used to convert one object type to another—such as a mesh over to a patch—which can then be edited. In such cases, you might see a different type of modifier available, indicating that the selected object can be converted if you so desire.

MAX 3 has many modifiers already built into it. As you add plug-ins, you will get more and more modifiers to use. Obviously, not all of these modifiers will fit in the Modify command panel; therefore, the Modify command panel is fully configurable and customizable.

As you work with MAX 3, you will find you use some modifiers more than others. You will probably want to add these modifiers to the Modify command panel so you do not have to use the More button every time you want to apply the modifier. You can accomplish this by choosing Configure Button Sets in the Modify command panel. This displays the Configure Button Sets dialog box, where you can change buttons in the Modify command panel (see Figure 6.2).

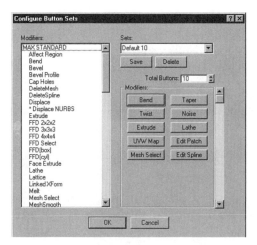

FIGURE 6.2   *The Configure Button Sets dialog box, where you can define the set of buttons that appears at the top of the Modify command panel.*

The Modify command panel supports up to 32 modifier buttons at any given time. If you want to run this many modifier buttons, run MAX 3 at 1280×1024 or higher. When you increase the number of modifiers, blank buttons appear in the dialog box. To assign a modifier to one of these buttons, first select the button. Then, double-click the modifier you want that button to represent from the list on the left side of the dialog box. You may assign modifiers to blank buttons or change existing buttons.

Applying Modifiers to Objects and Sub-Objects

All objects in MAX 3 are composed of objects and of smaller sub-objects. Modifiers can be applied to entire objects or to a selection of sub-objects. For example, you can create a box, convert it to editable mesh, go to vertex sub-object, select a set of vertices, and then apply a modifier while still in sub-object mode. The modifier will now appear in the stack with an asterisk next to it, indicating it is working on a sub-object selection set instead of the entire object. Hence, the modifier only affects the selected sub-objects.

There are several types of modifiers, such as MeshSelect, whose only purpose is to create a selection of sub-objects for use by the next modifier applied to the object. Hence, you have full control over how modifiers are applied to objects.

Using a Modifier Gizmo

Most modifiers also have their own sub-objects called gizmos. The gizmo sub-object is available in many modifiers, such as Bend, Twist, or UVW Map. The gizmo is a helper object that tells MAX how to apply the selected modifier to the object. Figure 6.3 shows an object with a Twist modifier applied to it. The cage that surrounds the object is the gizmo and usually appears yellow in the MAX viewports.

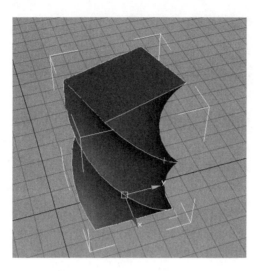

FIGURE 6.3   *A box with a Twist modifier applied to it. The object surrounding the box is the gizmo that defines how the twist is applied.*

When the Sub-Object gizmo selection option is active in the Modifiers command panel, you can apply standard MAX 3 transforms such as Move, Copy, and Rotate to the gizmo to determine how the twist effect is applied.

In addition to the standard gizmo, the Twist modifier also has a center point sub-object gizmo, which determines the location of the center point of the twisting effect. By adjusting either the gizmo or the center point, you can create a wide variety of effects with just the one modifier. Some other modifiers in MAX 3 make use of one or more gizmos.

When you are creating objects, you might need to apply only one modifier to create the effect you want. Many times, however, you will apply more than one modifier to a single object. The list of modifiers applied to the object is called the history, or the *stack*.

Using the Stack

The stack is a linear history of modifiers that have been applied to the selected object. The stack is what enables you to return to any modifier assigned earlier and make adjustments. This makes the stack one of the most important parametric tools in MAX 3, because you can essentially edit the history of an object with it.

For example, you can create a box and apply Bend, Twist, and Taper modifiers to it. At any point, you can return to the original box and make it taller or wider but still see the effect of the applied modifiers, providing practically unlimited opportunities to explore, modify, and change your objects.

The capability to modify any portion of an object or its history is possible through the MAX geometry pipeline, which enables you to work parametrically with modified objects.

Understanding the MAX 3 Geometry Pipeline

The geometry pipeline in MAX 3 is important because it helps you understand how modifiers work and how they are applied to the geometry. To demonstrate the geometry pipeline, consider an object that has five modifiers applied to it. While you work on the object, you can see the end result as if you had built the object without modifiers.

When you come in the next morning, restart MAX, and reload the file, MAX rebuilds the object by recreating the original object and then reapplying each of the modifiers (with their saved settings) to the object. Without the rebuilding process of the geometry pipeline, the stack could not be possible. The only downfall to this is that sometimes the application of a modifier can take a few minutes to process, depending on the complexity of the object. When this occurs, the object has to be rebuilt every time you load it and you have to wait. This is part of the price of a truly parametric system. Fortunately, because of how optimized MAX is, you will rarely run across this problem.

As you apply various modifiers, they pass the geometry up to the next modifier in the stack list. If you have applied a twist to an object and then decide to apply a bend, the bend will operate on the geometry in the state it is in after the Twist modifiers. In other words, the Twist modifier passes the object geometry to the Bend modifiers after applying its effect.

Working with the Stack

The stack is an extremely powerful and—fortunately—easy-to-use tool in MAX 3. When you select a newly created object, the stack is already active with just one entry in it. As you apply modifiers to the object, they appear in the Stack drop-down list, shown in Figure 6.4.

Through the Stack drop-down list, you can select a particular modifier. You can even go back as far as the original object, adjust its parameters, and immediately see the result of your changes in the viewports. Below the Stack drop-down list are five Stack control buttons (see Figure 6.5) that further enable you to work with the stack.

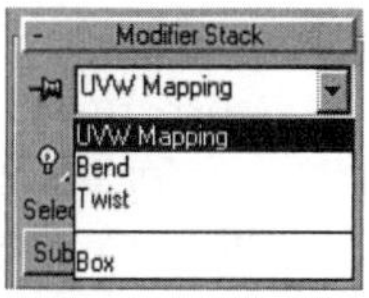

FIGURE 6.4
The Modifier Stack drop-down list, showing a box with Twist, Bend, and UVW Mapping modifiers applied to it.

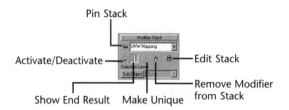

FIGURE 6.5   *The Stack control buttons, with which you can control how the stack works.*

Each button shown in Figure 6.5 is listed here and briefly described:

- **Pin Stack**: When this button is active, the Modifier stack—and the Modifier command panel, for that matter—are locked to the current object. If you select another object, the stack and modifier panel will not change.

- **Active/Inactive**: Activates or deactivates the current modifier.

- **Show End Result**: Toggles the display of the end result. When this is active, you see the object after all the modifiers in the stack have been applied. When it's inactive, you see the object with all modifiers up to and including the current modifier applied.

- **Make Unique**: Turns an instanced modifier into a unique one. Instanced modifiers most commonly occur when you apply a modifier to more than one object at the same time. This results in the modifier's being instanced for each object.

- **Remove Modifier from Stack**: Deletes the current modifier from the object and the object's stack.

- **Edit Stack**: Accesses the Edit Stack dialog box, where you can perform operations such as reordering or collapsing the stack.

You can access many of the important stack functions through the Edit Modifier Stack dialog box. The most important functions are the capability to reorder the stack by using Cut, Copy, and Paste, and the capability to collapse the stack.

Reordering the stack enables you to move modifiers to different locations in the stack. This can result in quite different objects because the modifiers are applied to the result of the last modifier. You can reorder by selecting a modifier in the stack and choosing either Cut or Copy. Then, select a new location and choose Paste. MAX 3 places the new modifier above the selected position in the stack.

If you click the Edit Stack button without any modifier applied to the object, you get a pop-up menu that asks whether you want to convert the geometry to an editable mesh, editable patch, or NURBS surface. Also on this menu is an option to access the Edit Stack dialog box. This is the easiest way to convert an object from mesh to a NURBS surface or a patch.

Obviously, the more modifiers you apply to an object, the more memory that particular object will take. At some point, you will decide that the object you have created is correct and no longer needs any changes. At that point, the parametric aspects of the object are also no longer needed. To conserve memory, you can collapse the stack, which removes all of the modifiers from the object and leaves the final result as an editable mesh object. Thus, it takes up much less memory.

The following exercise shows you how to make use of the stack to create the ice cream on an ice cream cone. During this exercise, you will see how to apply and work with modifiers, as well as the stack.

tip

If you decide to collapse the stack on an object, make sure you want to do so because the Collapse Stack command cannot be undone. Collapsing the stack removes any animated parameters that might have been a part of any modifier and it also removes the parametric capabilities of the object. If you want to keep the animated or parametric parameters of the object, do not collapse the stack.

Working with Modifiers to Create an Ice Cream Cone

1. Load the file **MF06-01.MAX** from the accompanying CD. This file is an ice cream cone with a block of chocolate ice cream that you will modify. Figure 6.6 shows this file.

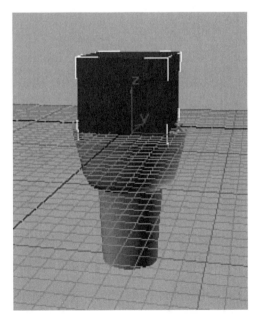

FIGURE 6.6   *The ice cream cone and ice cream block before using modifiers.*

2. Choose Select Objects and select the box on top of the cone.

3. From the Modify command panel, select the Taper modifier. When its controls appear in the command rollout, set the amount to –0.50.

4. Click on the Twist modifier to apply it to the block. Set the angle to –360.

5. At this point, the twisted box looks very bad. The reason for this is the lack of detail in the box itself for the Twist modifier to work on. Now go back into the stack and adjust the detail in the box so it will correctly deform.

6. Click on the Stack drop-down list and select Box. Set the Length, Width, and Height segment spinners each to 20. This immediately corrects the problem, but the ice cream is still not correct.

7. Click on the drop-down list again and select Taper. Adjust the taper amount to –0.75.

8. The last thing to do is adjust the size of the ice cream to more approximately match that of the cone. Select the Stack drop-down list and choose Box again.

9. Set the Width and Length spinners each to 83.

10. Now that the ice cream looks good, it is time to collapse the stack because you will not be changing it anymore. Choose Edit Stack, Collapse All.

11. Choose Yes at the warning message about the consequences of collapsing the stack.

12. Choose OK. Figure 6.7 shows the completed ice cream cone.

13. Save this file as **MF05-02a.MAX**.

    The previous exercise clearly illustrates how flexible and easy to use the stack is, opening a whole world of possibilities for you as a modeler. You will constantly find new ways to make use of the stack as you gain more experience with MAX 3.

    As mentioned earlier, modifiers work not only on mesh objects but on other types of objects in MAX 3. One of the most common uses of modifiers is to convert splines into 3D objects.

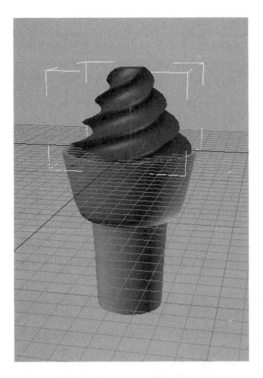

FIGURE 6.7   *The ice cream block after applying Twist and Taper modifiers to create a more realistic look.*

Creating 3D Objects from Splines

Now that you have seen how to make use of the stack in MAX, it's time to get back to the splines covered in Chapter 3, "Understanding Modeling Concepts." Most of the methods for converting the splines to 3D objects make use of modifiers. Several methods for converting splines into 3D objects exist in MAX 3, with the most common being extrusion, lathing, beveling, and lofting. (Beveling is very similar to extrusion and is not covered in this book.)

Extruding Splines

An *extruded* spline has been given a thickness in a particular direction. You can also think of extruding as making an exact copy of a spline at a certain distance away from the original and then creating a surface between the two.

Take, for example, a case where you want to create a wall for a house. You can easily do this in MAX by drawing the elevation of the wall in splines (or importing the splines from another drawing package, such as AutoCAD or Adobe Illustrator) and then extruding the wall to a particular thickness. In many cases, this is easier than using 3D primitives and Boolean operations or other methods of creating the same object.

You can find hundreds of examples in which extrusions can be helpful in the modeling process. For example, you can extrude text to create 3D text. You can extrude many shapes to create complex objects such as walls, CDs, cookie cutters, and even simple tires. In general, extrusion works great if the object has one profile and a consistent height.

Extrusion of a shape is handled by applying an Extrude modifier to the selected shape. After extrusion is applied in the Modify command panel, you can adjust the height, as well as the axis along which the shape is extruded. The Z axis is the default axis for most extrusions.

Extruding a spline is a powerful method for creating 3D objects out of 2D shapes. In many instances, however, you cannot create a specific object by using extrusions. In those cases, you must use other techniques, such as lathing.

Lathing Splines

A *lathed* spline has been rotated around a point in space, usually the center, left (minimum), or right (maximum) edge of the spline. As the spline is rotated, a surface is generated to create the 3D object.

When creating a lathed spline, you can control the number of degrees around which the object is created, as well as the number of segments to create smoother objects. In addition to controlling the amount of lathing, you can control in which world space axis the lathe will occur. The amount of detail in the resulting object is a combination of the detail in the original spline and the settings in the lathe process.

note

When you extrude text, you might find that the letters do not always extrude correctly. This is usually font-dependent. Not all TrueType fonts extrude correctly. If you run across this problem, try a different font.

An example of a lathed spline is a wine glass. This would be impossible to create as an extrusion because of how the glass is shaped. It is an excellent candidate, however, for a revolved surface. All you need to do is create a profile or section cut of half of the glass. Figure 6.8 shows you an example of a wine glass profile and the resulting lathed object.

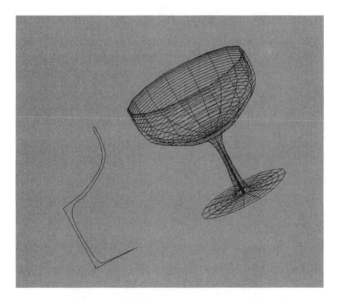

Figure 6.8   *A spline profile and the resulting 3D lathed wine glass object.*

As with the Extrude command, a spline is lathed by applying a Lathe modifier and then adjusting the number of degrees, the number of segments, and the center axis location. You can also set the type of geometry for the Lathe command to output, such as mesh, patch, or NURBS geometry.

In the following exercise, you take a bowling pin and create a 3D version of it using the Lathe command.

Lathing the Bowling Pin

1. Load the file **MF06-02.MAX** from the accompanying CD.
2. Choose Select Object and select the spline.
3. Go to the Modify command panel and choose the Lathe button. Figure 6.9 shows you the bowling pin at this point.

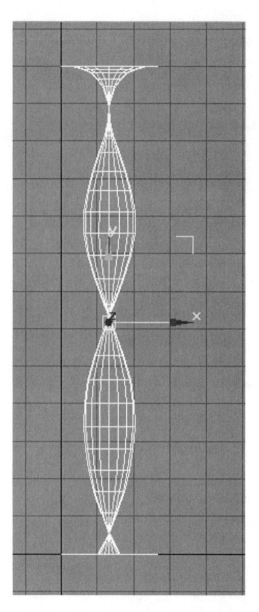

FIGURE 6.9   *The bowling pin after applying the Lathe modifier. The defaults of the modifier do not produce the correct result, so you must adjust them.*

As you can see from Figure 6.9, the pin is wrong. This occurs from incorrect alignment of the center point of the lathe. The spline is lathed around a center point, which can be defined as the minimum, center, or maximum point of the spline shape. The default is the center point, which is the geometric center of the bowling pin shape. What is needed here is to lathe the object around the left edge of the shape—its minimum point.

4. Click the Min button under Align to set the center point of the lathe to the correct edge of the bowling pin shape. The bowling pin is now correctly lathed. Figure 6.10 shows you the resulting pin.

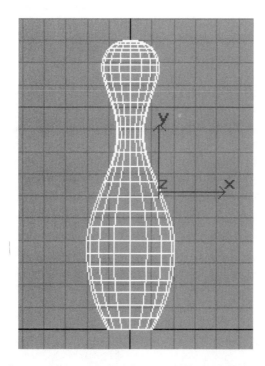

FIGURE 6.10   *The bowling pin after correctly adjusting the lathe modifier.*

5. Name the object **Bowling Pin1**.

6. Save the file as **MF06-02a.MAX**.

When you're using the Lathe command, the center point around which the spline is lathed is critical. MAX 3 provides three choices: Min, Center, and Max, with Center being the default. The center point is the geometric center of the shape to be lathed. The Min, or minimum, point is the farthest left point of the shape, whereas the Max, or maximum, point is the farthest right point in the shape. In addition to selecting the center of rotation under Direction, you can also select the axis about which the lathe occurs. The default is the Y axis.

Lathing is helpful for creating many types of objects that are circular in nature but have varying profiles. Wine glasses, plates, simple clocks, or even footballs are great examples of when to use the Lathe command. You can probably think of many more objects you might like to create with this command.

The Lathe command is very powerful, but it is limited to objects that can be revolved around a center point. The last method for converting splines to 3D objects is the loft method, by which you create a compound object instead of using modifiers. It is discussed in the "Compound Objects" section later in this chapter. Now take a look at a few specific mesh-modeling techniques.

Advanced Mesh Modeling

Before wrapping up this chapter, there are several more mesh-modeling techniques worth taking a look at. In Chapter 5, "Mesh Modeling Fundamentals," you spent some time setting up models that could be further refined through other techniques. Now it is time to take a look at those techniques. The first involves using the MeshSmooth modifier and the rest are based on compound objects that combine two or more objects to make a third. We'll start with MeshSmooth modeling.

Applying MeshSmooth Modeling

MeshSmooth modeling is an important modeling method because it takes a regular mesh object, such as a box, and smoothes its sharp edges, making it more like a sphere. Figure 6.11 shows you an example of a box before and after applying MeshSmooth.

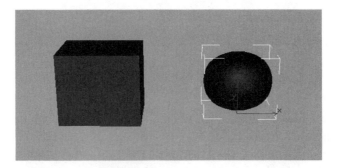

Figure 6.11   *A box before and after applying MeshSmooth. Notice how nice and smooth the box surface ended up.*

Through the use of MeshSmooth, you can create basic mesh cages and smooth them into organic 3D objects that look very good. This modifier is an example of where mesh editing techniques discussed earlier in this chapter become very handy. For example, you can take a box and modify it into the basic shape of a hand or a jet plane. Applying a MeshSmooth modifier smooths out the hard edges to make a more organic object.

MeshSmooth now supports a smoothing type called nonuniform rational mesh smoothing (NURMS) that results in much smoother objects than in earlier versions of MAX. NURMS also supports the use of cages to influence the smoothing. As an object is smoothed by MeshSmooth, an approximation of the original object is created. MeshSmooth uses two sub-object methods—Vertex and Edge—that appear as a cage around the MeshSmoothed object. When you select an edge or vertex, you can apply a weight value, forcing the mesh to more closely or less closely approximate that point in 3D space. In other words, MeshSmooth with vertex and edge weighting provides you with a fine degree of control over how the mesh object appears.

The following exercise shows you how to make use of MeshSmooth to create a hand from an existing box that has already been edited into the necessary basic shape.

Creating a MeshSmoothed Hand

1. Load the file **MF06-03.MAX** from the accompanying CD. This file contains a box object that has been modified into the rough form of a hand. Figure 6.12 shows you the scene at this point.

FIGURE 6.12   *A simple roughed-out hand, created by modifying a box. Now you will apply a MeshSmooth modifier to create a more realistic look.*

2. Select the hand.

3. In the Modify command panel, choose the More button to launch the Modifiers dialog box.

4. Select MeshSmooth and choose OK. The hand immediately receives some smoothing.

5. Set the Iterations spinner to 2 to add more smoothing and create a more complex hand.

6. Set the smoothness to 0.75. Figure 6.13 shows you the resulting hand.

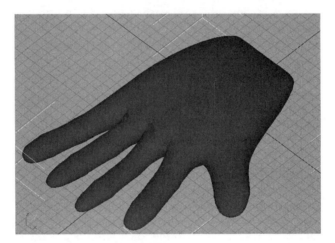

FIGURE 6.13   *The hand after applying and adjusting the MeshSmooth modifier. By adjusting the parameters, you can get different-looking hands quickly.*

As you can see from the previous exercise, MeshSmooth provides a quick, powerful method for creating organic-looking objects from very basic objects. Take a moment to load up the plane object (file **MF05-03a.MAX**) you created in the last chapter and see how it works when you apply MeshSmooth to it. You might take some time to experiment and see if you can create a better-looking hand or even a face with MeshSmooth.

Working with Compound Objects

A compound object is created by combining two or more objects. You can find eight types of compound objects in the Create command panel by clicking on the Geometry button and selecting Compound Objects from the drop-down list. For the purposes of this book, you'll explore four of these: Booleans, Scatter, Loft objects, and Terrain. The last two make use of splines, and the first two make use of mesh objects.

Booleans

Boolean objects work on the principle of Boolean algebra and are used to create compound objects by combining two or more primitives. You can create three types of Boolean objects: a Union, an Intersection, and a Subtraction. Figure 6.14 shows you an example of two primitives and the results of creating the three different types of Boolean with them.

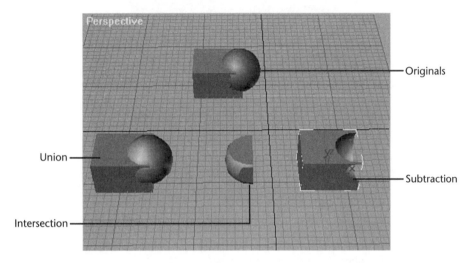

FIGURE 6.14   *Two primitives and what happens to them when they are combined as Boolean objects.*

Booleans provide a powerful method of modeling in MAX 3. You can easily create many types of objects by using Booleans. Most commonly, you can use Booleans to subtract the volume of one object from another. When you create the third object, the original two objects are considered *operands*. You can manipulate these operands and even animate them over time in MAX, resulting in the capability to parametrically change your final Boolean objects.

The following exercise shows you how to create a bowling ball with finger holes.

Using Booleans to Create a Bowling Ball

1. Load the file **MF06-04.MAX** from the accompanying CD. This file contains a sphere and three cylinders and is shown in Figure 6.15.

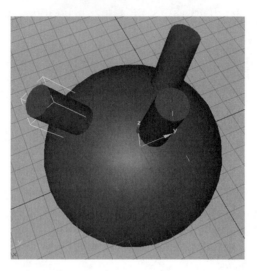

Figure 6.15   *A sphere and three cylinders. You will subtract the volume of the cylinders from the sphere to create the bowling ball.*

2. Select the sphere.
3. In the Create command panel, select Compound Objects from the drop-down list.
4. In the rollout that appears, select Boolean.
5. Choose Pick Operand B and click on one of the cylinders. The cylinder disappears and a hole is left in the sphere.
6. Click on Boolean again to restart the command.
7. Choose Pick Operand B and select the next cylinder.
8. Repeat steps 6 and 7 for the last cylinder. Figure 6.16 shows you the resulting bowling ball.

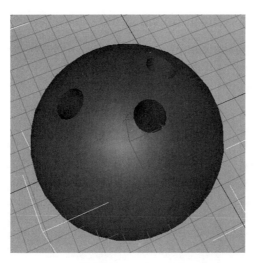

FIGURE 6.16   *The ball after subtracting the cylinders out of it to create the finger holes.*

Booleans represent one kind of compound object that performs a specific, yet powerful, function for modeling complex objects. Now take a look at the Scatter compound object.

Scatter

The Scatter compound object enables you to make copies of one object across the surface of another. Some good examples of this type of compound object include hair on a head, grass on a lawn, or trees on a landscape.

To make use of Scatter, you simply need a source object and a distribution object. You select the source object, go to the Scatter command, and then choose the Select distribution object button. Scatter contains a variety of controls to manage the spacing, orientation, and size of the objects that are distributed across the surface. You can save your scatter settings and apply them to other source and distribution objects.

In the following exercise, you use the Scatter compound object to create a mine with proximity sensors.

tip

The Boolean compound object creates the compound object with adaptive optimization turned on. Adaptive optimization reduces the number of polygons in the final shape. Unfortunately, this can create problems with the final Boolean. If you see problems such as missing faces, try turning off the Optimize Result check box at the bottom of the Boolean rollout.

Creating an Underwater Mine by Using Scatter

1. Load the file **MF06-05.MAX** from the accompanying CD. This file contains two spheres, one large and one small.

2. Choose Select Object and select the smaller sphere.

3. Select Compound Object from the Create command panel drop-down list. Then select Scatter from the rollout that appears.

4. Choose the Pick Distribution Object button and select the larger sphere.

5. Under Source Object parameters, set the number of Duplicates to 100 and the Vertex Chaos to 0.25. (The Vertex Chaos adds a little randomness to the vertices of the small sphere, making them look rough.)

6. Set the Distribution Object parameters to Perpendicular and Even. The result, shown in Figure 6.17, is what an underwater mine looks like.

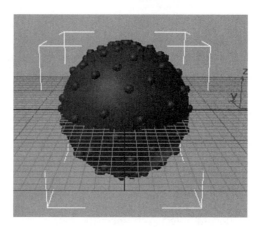

FIGURE 6.17   *The sphere after scattering the smaller sphere across its surface. Now it looks like an underwater mine.*

The Scatter compound object is an extremely powerful modeling tool. At this point, take a few moments to try different settings in the command panel to achieve different results. Just be aware that, depending on the parameters you choose, the screen might take a few minutes to update. The next compound object type to look at is Loft objects.

Loft Objects

The last method for converting splines to 3D objects is lofting. Lofts are very similar to extrusions except for three key differences:

- Whereas an extrusion is straight and at a defined distance, a loft extrudes a shape along a loft path.

- As the shape is lofted along the path, you can deform it by using one or more of the five deformation tools available in MAX 3.

- You can loft an object along a path and also change profile shapes along the path as the loft is created.

These three items make lofting extremely powerful but a little confusing sometimes.

An example of a Loft object might be a banana. A banana could not really be created as an extrusion, lathe, or bevel, but it can be created as a loft. Many other objects can be created as loft objects, such as phone cords and handsets; even the bowling pin you created as a lathe can easily be created as a loft.

You create Loft objects by first creating the profile shape and then the loft path, which is a separate shape. Then, you select either shape, go to the Create command panel, and select Loft from the Compound Objects menu. Figure 6.18 shows you the resulting rollout.

Many times, when you create a Loft object, you will need to deform it in one way or another to create the object you want. To do this, go to the Modify command panel while the Loft object is selected and find the standard loft rollouts. At the bottom of the rollouts, find the Deformations rollout shown in Figure 6.19.

FIGURE 6.18

The Loft rollout, where you can set the initial creation parameters for your Loft object.

FIGURE 6.19   *The Deformations rollout, where you can select the deformations you want to apply to the Loft object.*

MAX 3 provides five different deformations you can apply to a Loft object. Each can be activated or deactivated by clicking the button to the right of the deformation type. You may enable as many deformations of the same type as you like. Each deformation is listed here and briefly described:

- **Scale**: Applies a scale to the loft shape as it travels along the path. This is the most often used deformation.

- **Twist**: Twists the loft shape, using the loft path as the center point of rotation. Objects such as twisted metal gates are easily created with this deformation.

- **Teeter**: In a normal deformation, the loft shape is always kept perpendicular to the loft path. With this deformation, you can rotate the loft shape off of perpendicular for subtle changes in the Loft object. For example, if you used Teeter, you can make a circular lofted shape appear as if it has been cut at an angle with a knife.

- **Bevel**: Enables you to apply a bevel to the loft shape as it is extruded along the loft path. This is similar to the scale deformation but is much more exaggerated and difficult to control.

- **Fit**: The most difficult of the set to use. In a Fit deformation, you make use of two additional spline shapes: a top view of the object and a side view of the object. When the loft shape is lofted, it is forced to conform to the two profiles. An example of this type of lofting is the creation of a telephone handset.

Deformations are applied through the use of a Deformation grid. This grid provides you with a graphical representation of exactly how much deformation you are applying to specific points of the Loft object. Figure 6.20 shows you the Scale Deformation grid and all of its parts.

tip

If you are going to create a loft with more than one loft shape, make sure you line up the first vertex of each shape along the path, or the object will appear twisted. A white box indicates the location of the first vertex.

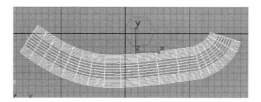

FIGURE 6.20   *The Scale Deformation grid and its interface.*

The horizontal axis of the Deformation grid represents the length of the Loft object. The vertical axis represents the strength of the deformation. By adding vertices to the deformation line and then repositioning them, you can apply the deformation precisely at any point. The deformation line is essentially a spline and can make use of corner points as well as Bézier tangent points to create and apply curvature to the line. You can also apply and control the deformation in the X or Y axis, or both, through the Deformation dialog box.

The following exercise shows you how to create a banana as a Loft object.

Lofting a Banana

1. Load the file **MF06-06.MAX** from the accompanying CD. This file contains two shapes: a six-sided polygon representing the cross section of a banana and a spline representing the length and curvature of the banana.
2. Choose Select Object and select the Line object.
3. In the Create command panel, click on the drop-down list and select Compound Objects.
4. Select the Loft button to access the Loft controls.
5. Choose Get Shape in the Command panel rollout and click the six-sided polygon. Immediately, a shape appears in the Perspective viewport, as shown in Figure 6.21.

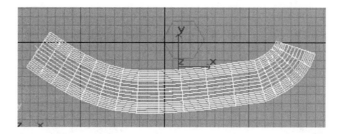

FIGURE 6.21   *The loft shape after adding the polygon as the shape to be lofted along the line.*

Before proceeding, you should note that the Loft object will only appear in a shaded viewport unless you change the Skin Parameter display options.

6. With the banana still selected, go to the Modify command panel.

7. Scroll down to the bottom of the rollout and access the Deformations rollout. Here, you can apply a deformation to finish the banana. Select Scale; the Scale Deformation dialog box appears.

8. Click and hold the Insert Corner Point button until you get a flyout. Choose the bottom button on the flyout; this is the Bézier Corner point button.

9. Click at 20, 70, and 90 percent on the red line to create three new points.

10. Select the Move point button.

11. Click and drag and move the point at 0 to a positive 20 percent value.

12. Move the point at 20 vertically to 90.

13. Move the point at 70 vertically to 90.

14. Move the point at 90 vertically to 30.

15. Move the point at 100 vertically to 25. You should get a deformation chart similar to the one shown in Figure 6.22. Figure 6.23 shows the resulting banana.

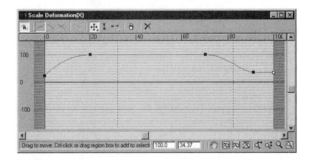

FIGURE 6.22   *The Scale deformation grid after applying the necessary changes to make the banana. Notice how the graph looks like the profile of a banana.*

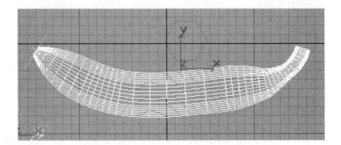

FIGURE 6.23   *The banana mesh after applying the scale deformation.*

16. Name the object **Banana**.

17. Save the file as **MF06-06a.MAX** for use in a later chapter.

Overall, creating splines and converting them to 3D objects is a very intuitive and powerful method of modeling. After you have created your shapes (composed of one or more individual splines), you can convert the shapes to 3D objects by beveling, extruding, lathing, or lofting them. Because many of these operations are implemented as modifiers, you can adjust the parameters of the final 3D objects at any time.

Conclusion

This chapter introduced you to the concepts behind mesh modeling. This popular modeling method enables you to create a wide variety of 3D objects with ease by using a large number of techniques. This chapter showed you how to deal with the following topics:

- Modeling splines
- Editing splines
- Editing meshes
- Working with the stack
- Working with compound objects

This chapter showed how powerful the MAX 3 modifier system and the stack are for creating parametric models. By creating an object and then applying modifiers to it, you can change the object into totally different objects. As this occurs, MAX 3 tracks a history of changes to the objects with the Stack feature. Working with modifiers and the stack were the two key points covered in this chapter.

In the next chapter, you will learn about another modeling system in MAX 3, called the patch modeling system. This system makes use of a modeling method that is better suited to producing certain types of organic objects.

CHAPTER 7

Patch Modeling Methods

Up to this point, you have explored the mesh modeling tools available in MAX. Now it is time to explore a different method of modeling called patch modeling. Patch modeling works with Bézier patches to create objects. Patch modeling is more powerful than mesh modeling for creating curved surfaces, but not as powerful as NURBS modeling. This chapter introduces you to the methods and techniques necessary for modeling by using patches in MAX 3. In particular, this chapter covers the following topics:

- Understanding Patch Modeling
- Working with Editable Patch
- Working with Surface Tools

Understanding Patch Modeling

Patches are used to model surfaces that are curvilinear in nature, such as the human head, mountains, or a wide variety of other objects. Patches are naturally suited to these tasks—patches are based on Bézier splines, adjustments to patches result in smooth curves instead of the straight lines you find in mesh modeling.

Patch modeling makes use of surfaces that are controlled and deformed through the use of vertices (often called control points). By adjusting a simple vertex, you can affect an area of the surface of a patch. Figure 7.1 shows a simple patch (on the left) and the same patch after adjusting one control point (on the right).

When you adjust a patch surface by moving a control point, it is deformed as a Bézier curve. In other words, the deformations are smooth, not angular like you might find when you adjust a vertex on a mesh. Like a Bézier tangent on a spline, the control points of a patch surface also have tangent controls you can adjust to give a different look to the curvature of the surface. Figure 7.2 shows the surface from Figure 7.1, with tangent adjustments to one corner.

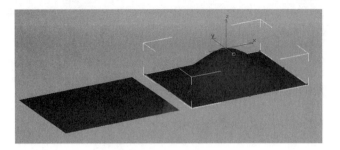

FIGURE 7.1   *A patch before and after adjusting a single vertex. Notice how the change results in a smooth curved surface as opposed to the sharp surfaces of mesh modeling.*

MAX supports two types of patches: quad patches and tri patches (see Figure 7.3). The basic difference between the two is the underlying geometry and the use of quads versus triangles. The quad patches are more commonly used because they generally deform more smoothly than tri patches.

Creating and editing patches is fairly easy. You create a patch surface in the Create command panel. To find the patch commands, click on the Geometry button and choose Patch Grids from the pull-down menu. When you create a quad patch, you can define the length and width as well as the number of segments, very much like a plane primitive. Tris, on the other hand, only allow you to define a width and height. To increase the density of a tri mesh, you must convert it to an editable patch.

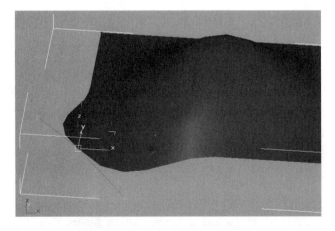

FIGURE 7.2   *The surface shown in Figure 7.1, after adjusting the tangents of a corner vertex.*

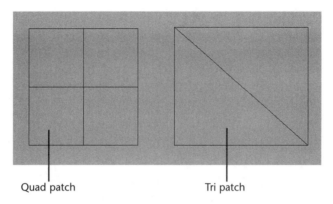

Quad patch   Tri patch

FIGURE 7.3   *The quad patch versus the tri patch. Quads are more common because they deform better than tri patches.*

Converting Objects to Patches

Basic patches can be created as quads and tris, but dealing with these is somewhat limiting and tedious. For example, modeling a mountain from a quad patch will result in a fair amount of editing. Fortunately, most objects can now be converted to editable patch at will. All of the primitives and extended primitives can be converted to patch surfaces, and vice versa.

Most of the time, converting to patches is fine, but you won't always want to convert primitives to patches. Take the RingWave extended primitive as an example. This primitive is the only one that automatically generates animation when created. Converting the RingWave primitive to a patch surface removes the animation from the object, so you might want to experiment a little before actually converting primitives to patch objects.

Conversion to a patch surface can be handled in three different ways. The easiest way is to right-click the object in question and choose Convert to Editable Patch from the pop-up menu. The second way is to select the object, go to the Modify command panel, and click the Edit Stack button. A pop-up menu appears, where you can select Convert to Editable Patch. The last method is to apply an Edit Patch modifier to the top of the stack.

In the RingWave example, applying an Edit Patch to the top of the stack preserves the animation inherent in the RingWave object. The downside is that the object will take up more memory from the conversion than as a mesh object. The same is true of any object where you have previously applied modifiers.

upgrader's note

In earlier versions of MAX, patches made use of a lattice to handle deformations of the patch surface. Now you can work directly on the surface, much as with a mesh object.

After you have applied modifiers to a mesh object, the only two ways to convert it to an editable patch are to collapse the stack or to apply the Edit Patch modifier. In most cases, the Edit Patch modifier will be the way to go. As a basic rule, don't convert an object to a patch surface or apply an Edit Patch modifier unless you have a reason.

Patch Output from Lofts

Other commands in MAX have been modified to support patches as well. Take the Loft compound object. In previous versions of MAX, Loft was strictly a mesh-based tool. In MAX 3, the lofter can now be configured to output a patch surface instead of a mesh surface. The option to output a patch instead of a mesh can be found on the Surface rollout for a Loft object, as shown in Figure 7.4.

FIGURE 7.4
The Surface rollout of the Loft compound object, where you can set the output of the lofter to be a patch instead of a mesh.

It should be noted that not all possible outputs from the loft compound object can be created as patch objects. Most Loft objects that use a Fit deformation, for example, will probably not convert to a patch. In such cases, you will be forced to use a mesh output instead.

After you have created a patch surface or converted another object into a patch surface, you can begin the process of editing that surface. Patch modeling is a push-pull type of modeling system in which you push and pull on the control points of the patch surfaces to create the object you want. You accomplish all of this through editable patch or the Edit Patch modifier.

Working with Editable Patch

As with splines and primitives, you can convert quad and tri patches to an editable patch state and edit the sub-objects of the patch surface. Any objects converted to patch surfaces are created as editable patches unless they have the Edit Patch modifier applied (this modifier performs the same functions as editable patch).

When you go to the Modify command panel after you have converted a patch to editable patch, you see the rollouts shown in Figure 7.5. As with the Editable Spline and Editable Mesh rollouts, one of the Editable Patch rollouts has buttons that activate or deactivate based on the type of sub-object you have selected.

Editable patch enables you to work with patches at four different levels:

- Objects
- Vertices
- Edges
- Patch sub-objects

Object-Level Patch Editing

Object-level patch editing is available through the Editable Patch modifier when Sub-Object Selection is disabled. The main controls available to you at an object level include the Attach command and the Tessellation controls.

The Attach command enables you to attach any other object to the current patch surface. If the object is not already a patch surface, it is converted to a patch surface before it is attached to the current surface. A Reorient check box enables you to reorient the coordinate system of the attached object to match that of the new object.

Working with Vertices

The most basic level of patch editing is at the vertex level. You can access the vertex level controls either by right-clicking the patch surface and choosing Sub-object, Vertex from the pop-up menu or by clicking the Vertex button in the Modify command panel.

FIGURE 7.5

The Editable Patch rollout, where you can quickly access all of the sub-object editing controls for patch surfaces.

The most important aspect of vertex-level editing is the capability to select a vertex and transform it with the standard MAX transform commands. This is how you push and pull on the patch surface to create the shape you want. As with Bézier splines, when you select a vertex, you get two or more handles you can use to control the tangents of the surfaces as they enter and leave the vertex. Just as with spline Bézier tangents, the vertex tangents work completely in 3D. Figure 7.6 shows a selected vertex and the associated tangent handles.

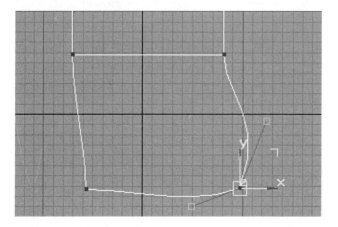

FIGURE 7.6   *A patch with a vertex selected, showing the vertex tangents. By adjusting the tangents, you can control the curvature of the surface around the selected vertex.*

You can adjust the tangent handles independently, or you can select Lock Handles in the Command Panel rollout to lock the handles together so that when you adjust one, the other adjusts as well.

In Chapter 5, "Mesh Modeling Fundamentals," you learned that MAX 3 splines support the binding of vertices. Later in this chapter, you will see how to use the Surface modifier to create patch surfaces from splines that can use the bind vertices. In such cases, the Editable Patch vertex controls also provide you with the capability to bind patch vertices to the center point of splines that are a part of the patch surface. This condition is usually only present when you're using Surface tools, which are discussed later in this chapter.

Beyond these basic capabilities, the only other feature of Vertex editing is the capability to weld vertices together. This becomes important when you attach other objects to the current surface. Their vertices will not be welded together, even if they overlap, and you must manually weld them.

Working with Edges

The next level at which you can edit a patch is edge level. Like vertices, edges can be transformed by using the standard MAX transform commands, but the most common use for edge-level editing is to add more quad or tri patches to the current surface.

To add a patch, select an edge and then click the Add Tri or Add Quad button to add that type of patch to the surface. Patches that are added to the surface automatically take on the shape of the current edge. Figure 7.7 shows you a surface before and after adding a patch. Notice how the added patch automatically takes on the shape of the selected edge.

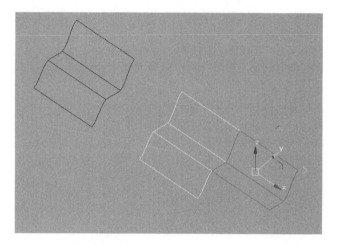

FIGURE 7.7   *A patch surface before and after adding an additional quad surface by using the edge tools. Notice how the added surface takes on the shape of the original surface.*

As patch surfaces are added to the original surfaces, the overlapping vertices are automatically welded. Thus, you can begin to transform the vertices immediately, without having to do any further editing.

Working with Patch Sub-Objects

The last level for editing a patch is at the patch level. In cases where you have added patches or attached objects, you will have multiple sub-patches as part of the overall patch surface. The sub-object level enables you to deal with these. You can select individual patches and detach them from the surface or delete them altogether.

After you select a patch surface, you can assign material IDs to individually selected patches. This enables you to control the material assignments across the surface of the patch. Figure 7.8 shows you the Surface rollout, where you can apply material IDs and even smoothing groups.

One of the more important controls available in the patch-level editing controls is the Subdivide control, with which you can subdivide the current patch into smaller patches. If the Propagate option is turned on, the subdivisions propagate to any patches that share an edge with the selected patch. Figure 7.9 shows you a patch surface before and after subdividing one of its smaller patches.

Now that you have seen how to model with patches, it is time to put that knowledge to practical use. The following exercise shows how to create the basic topology of an island by using patches.

FIGURE 7.8

The Surface Properties rollout for patch sub-objects. Here, you can assign Material IDs and smoothing to individual patches in the patch surface.

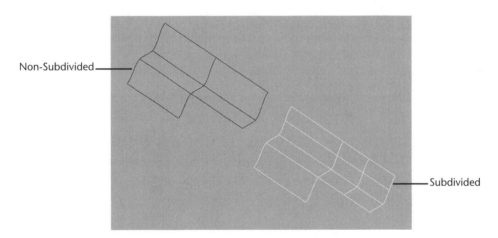

Non-Subdivided

Subdivided

FIGURE 7.9   *A patch surface before and after using the Subdivide command with Propagate turned on.*

Creating Island Topology

1. Select Patch Grids under the Create command panel and create a quad patch that is 50 units by 50 units.

2. Right-click the patch and select Convert to Editable Patch.

3. Set the sub-object type to Edge.

4. Choose Select Objects from the Main Toolbar tab and select the right edge of the patch. Under the Topology section, choose Add Quad.

5. Continue adding quads until you have created a 4×4 grid of quad patches. (You can simplify the process by selecting more than one edge at a time with a region window.)

6. Under sub-object selection, choose Vertex. Select each vertex around the edge of the patch, and move or adjust the vertex to create a random shoreline. Figure 7.10 shows one possible island shoreline, created by moving the vertices and tangent handles.

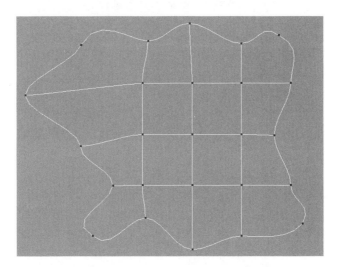

FIGURE 7.10   *One possible island configuration, created by moving the vertices and their tangents to create a curved shoreline.*

7. Rotate the view to a User view where you can see the entire island.

8. Select the center vertex and move it along the Z axis approximately 100 units.

9. What's left over at this point is a set of vertices between the center vertex and the outer vertices. Using Select and Move, place these vertices at random heights and positions to create the rest of the island. (Try experimenting with the tangent handles in the Z axis to further control the slopes.) Figure 7.11 shows one possible island at this point.

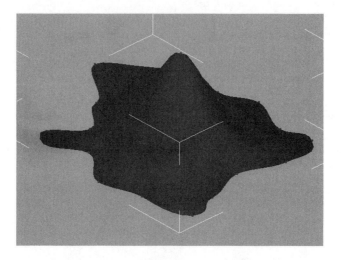

Figure 7.11   *The island after moving the inner vertices vertically to create 3D depth. This figure represents one possible configuration of the island.*

10. Save the file as **MF07-01A.MAX**.

From the previous exercise, you can begin to see the power of modeling with patches in MAX and the ability of patches to create organic forms quickly and easily. However, sub-object editing is a tedious way to go about patch modeling. MAX 3 introduces a more elegant method called Surface tools that provides you with a higher degree of control.

Working with Surface Tools

Surface tools are a set of modifiers designed to enable you to create spline frameworks that can be surfaced with patches. This is a nice solution because of how powerful the spline modeling tools are in MAX. Basically, you create a spline shape that represents the basic shape of the object you want to create. In Chapter 5, you created a nose spline cage. Now, you will see how to convert that cage to a patch surface quickly and easily.

Surface tools include two modifiers: Cross Section and Surface. In addition, there are a series of enhancements to both editable spline and editable patch, most notably, the Bind Vertices, CrossInsert, and Reverse tools that were added to editable spline. These tools are designed to make working with Surface tools even easier.

Before jumping into creating the patch surfaces, take a look at some tips for creating splines that will work with Surface tools:

- Make sure the splines form a closed shape.
- Make sure the splines form 3- or 4-sided closed areas; otherwise, the surface will not generate correctly. For example, if you create a 6-sided NGon, it will not surface correctly because it is 6-sided. However, if you use the Create Line tool in editable spline and connect two opposite vertices, you can correct this problem. Figure 7.12 shows you an example of this.

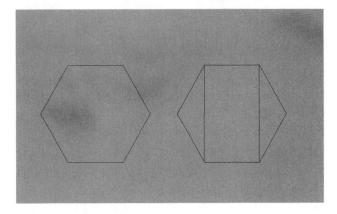

FIGURE 7.12   *A NGon that will not work with Surface tools versus a modified NGon that forms 3- and 4-sided areas.*

- If you have crossing splines in the shape, use CrossInsert to create a vertex at that point.
- If you are trying to duplicate a known object or face and you have a picture of this object, scan the picture in and load it as a background in a viewport. Then, use the picture as a template for creating your splines.

Generating Patches by Using Surface

After you build the spline cage, you can create the patch surface. You accomplish this by applying the Surface modifier to the spline. After you apply the modifier, you get the rollout shown in Figure 7.13.

The two most important controls in the Surface modifier are Threshold and Steps. The Threshold spinner defines a distance; if two vertices in the spline are within that distance, they are treated as one by the modifier and, as a result, the generated patch surface has a single vertex at that point. Otherwise, you would end up with a discontinuous or broken surface. The Steps spinner simply defines the overall number of steps in the patch surface. This affects the amount of detail in the resulting object. Higher step values result in more accurate patches that take up more memory.

The following exercise shows you how to make use of the Surface modifier to create a 3D object from a spline cage.

Using Surface Tools to Model a Nose

1. Load the nose cage you created in Chapter 5. If you did not complete this file, load the file **MF07-01.MAX** from the accompanying CD. Figure 7.14 shows you the scene at this point.

FIGURE 7.13
The Surface Modifier rollout, where you can control how the surface is created.

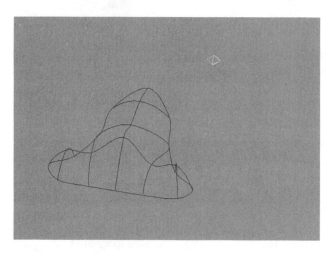

FIGURE 7.14   *The nose cage that is ready to be surfaced by using Surface tools.*

2. Select the nose cage and choose Select and Move from the Main Toolbar. Hold down the Shift key and move the nose to the right to make a copy of it.

3. When prompted, select Reference as the type of copy. This makes a copy that is a duplicate of the original but can have different modifiers applied to it without affecting the original. Choose OK.

4. Select the second copy of the nose cage. In the Modify command panel, click the More button.

5. From the Modifiers list, choose Surface and click OK.

6. Adjust the Threshold spinner until the entire cage is surfaced. This should occur somewhere between 2.0 and 18. Figure 7.15 shows you the nose at this point.

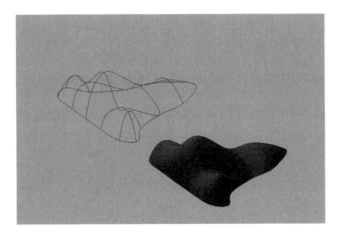

FIGURE 7.15   *The surfaced nose after applying the Surface modifier.*

7. Save the nose as **MF07-01a.MAX**.

The previous exercise illustrates just how easily you can use Surface tools in the creation of organic surfaces. The exercise also illustrates a powerful use of the MAX reference system. Because you made a reference copy and applied the Surface modifier to it, you are now able to go back to the original nose cage, make adjustments, and see the results on the surfaced nose in real time. This same technique works very well with MeshSmooth, as well. Take a moment to play with the nose cage. See how many different types of noses you can create simply by editing the nose in this setup.

Surface tools and editable patch both illustrate the power and flexibility inherent in the patch modeling system. It's a great way to create basic organic objects, but it is even more powerful when you consider the Tessellation tools.

Conclusion

Patch modeling is a powerful method of creating organic surfaces. Whether you choose to create these surfaces by creating quads and tris and editing them or by using Surface tools, you can create amazingly detailed models in a short amount of time. This chapter showed you the following topics related to patches:

- Creating quads and tris
- Editing any patch surface
- Converting objects to patch surfaces
- Using surface tools

As powerful as patch modeling is, it is not the most powerful organic modeling system in MAX. That title goes to the NURBS system, which you will explore in the next chapter.

CHAPTER 8

Exploring NURBS

NURBS (Nonuniform Rational B-Splines) are a powerful and commonly used modeling method for creating organic shapes or any objects that require accurately curved surfaces. NURBS are used to model everything from cars to dinosaurs to bicycles. If the object has a lot of complex curves and curved surfaces in it, it is a perfect candidate to be modeled by using NURBS.

Unlike patch modeling, NURBS comes in two forms: curves and surfaces. NURBS curves are similar to regular splines in MAX but produce much smoother curves and can be easier to create and control. This chapter introduces you to the following topics involving NURBS:

- Overview of the NURBS System in MAX
- Creating NURBS Curves
- Creating NURBS Surfaces
- Editing NURBS Objects
- Editing NURBS Sub-Objects
- Trimming NURBS Surfaces
- Render Time Considerations

Overview of the NURBS System in MAX

NURBS, like other modeling methods, are totally integrated into MAX. The most basic form of NURBS appears as a NURBS curve. The controls for NURBS are found in the Create command panel under the Shapes button. There you will find a drop-down list with the NURBS curves on it. MAX supports two types of NURBS curves: Point and Control Vertices (CV). Surfaces appear as their own entry under the Geometry drop-down list. There are also two types of surfaces: Point and CV. In addition to creating basic NURBS shapes, you can also convert many primitives and objects in MAX to NURBS surfaces.

There are two approaches to working with NURBS in MAX. The first method is to create NURBS curves and generate surfaces based on those curves. The second method is to go straight to creating the surfaces, much as in patch modeling. The more flexible of the two methods is working with curves first, so take a look a NURBS curves.

Creating NURBS Curves

NURBS curves are very similar to MAX splines but are based on a different mathematical formula. Thanks to the different mathematics behind the scenes, you can use NURBS curves to create very smooth curved lines. These, in turn, can be used to create organic shapes that you can loft, extrude, lathe, or otherwise form into complex curved 3D objects.

NURBS curves in MAX are located under the Shapes button in the Create command panel. To access the NURBS curves, click the Splines drop-down list and select NURBS curves. The NURBS Curves command rollout appears (see Figure 8.1).

Like regular splines, NURBS curves are treated as shapes and you can form multiple curves together to create a single curve. You control this through the Start New Shape button, which works exactly like the spline version. Many of the NURBS surface commands that require two or more curves to operate correctly require the curves to be part of the same shape.

Point Curves Versus CV Curves

Two types of curves are available in NURBS modeling in MAX 3: Point and CV (standing for control vertices). A point curve draws the NURBS curve through each point you choose in the scene. CV curves, however, work much like a lattice by providing control points on which the curve is based. Figure 8.2 shows you both types of NURBS curves. CV curves and point curves can both exist in the same larger NURBS curve.

FIGURE 8.1

The NURBS Curves rollout, where you can select the type of NURBS curve you want to create.

Point curves A are easier to draw with because they produce more accurate representations than CV curves. Controlling the curvature of a NURBS CV curve is sometimes easier; however, when you adjust the position of a CV curve, it affects the curvature of the line but not to the same degree as the equivalent change in a point curve. CV curves also have the advantage that you can apply weights to the individual points to make the curve adhere more closely to certain points. Point curves don't allow this functionality.

When you compare NURBS curves to standard MAX splines, you will find creating curved splines much easier than using the Line command and adjusting in and out tangents. On the other hand, because of their capability to create smooth curved lines, creating a straight line with a NURBS curve can be difficult. If you need a straight line segment, regular MAX splines can be imported into NURBS curves through Attach or Import in the Modify command panel.

upgrader's note

In MAX 2 and 2.5, if you wanted to use a NURBS curve to create a surface, you had to convert the curve over to a surface, much like converting a box to an editable mesh. MAX 3 automatically converts the curve when necessary, so the conversion you had to do in MAX 2 and 2.5 is no longer necessary.

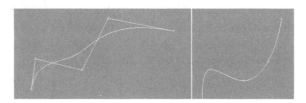

FIGURE 8.2   *A point curve and a CV curve. Notice the difference in how the curve is interpreted between the points.*

The Attach command works like the Mesh attach commands and converts the selected spline to a NURBS curve, but Import maintains the edit history and base parameters of the imported object. Use the Import command when you want to go back and edit the original object at any time. You also have Import Multiple and Attach Multiple commands that provide a Select by Name dialog box where you can select the objects you want to use in your NURBS curve.

NURBS curves share some of the same functionality found in splines. When you select a particular curve type, such as a point curve, you see the rollout of commands shown in Figure 8.3.

As with splines, NURBS curves support step settings and optimization for the segments between vertices. But unlike splines, NURBS curves default to using adaptive stepping to provide the best results. Unless you really need to change them, you should probably leave these settings alone. In addition, NURBS curves support the Renderable feature, which turns the curve into an object that will render correctly. As with splines, you can set a thickness and have the curve generate mapping coordinates.

NURBS curves also support a new drawing mode in MAX 3. If you take a close look at the rollout for either the point or CV curve, you will see an option called Draw in All Viewports. When you create a curve in MAX, you can normally draw in only the viewport where you started the curve. With MAX 3, you can draw in any viewport by simply moving the mouse to that viewport and continuing to draw. This functionality makes creating NURBS curves much easier. If you don't like this functionality, simply turn off the option and you can create NURBS curves in the same manner as you do with splines—one viewport at a time.

The following exercise illustrates how easy it is to create curved shapes with NURBS curves.

FIGURE 8.3
The Point Curve rollout, where you can define the options of the curve before creating it.

Creating a Wineglass Profile by Using NURBS Curves

1. Go to the Shapes section of the Create command panel and access the NURBS curve controls.
2. Select CV curve. (This type of curve is used because approximating the wine glass shape is easy with it.)

3. In the Top viewport, zoom out a little. Turn on 2D Snaps and then click once each at approximately the following coordinates:

   0,0
   60,0
   60,10
   10,10
   10,100
   10,120
   80,150
   80,250
   70,250

4. At this point, select coordinates on your own to approximate the interior curve of the shape. When you're finished, click the start point to close the shape. When asked if you want to close the curve, choose Yes. You should get a curve similar to the one shown in Figure 8.4.

5. Turn off 2D Snaps. Now that the basic curve is complete, right-click the curve and choose Modify mode. Then right-click again and choose Curve CV level, where you can edit the CVs of the curve.

6. Manually edit each CV, using Select and Move from the Main Toolbar tab, until you have a shape you like.

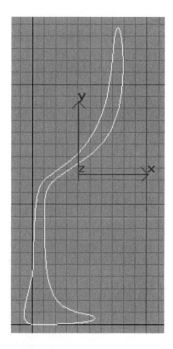

Figure 8.4
The wineglass outline after creating the basic shape. Now a little editing is required to more closely match the shape of the glass.

7. When you have the CVs positioned, select the two CVs at the bottom of the glass and adjust their weight in the Modify command panel. As you adjust the weight, notice how the curve more closely approximates the position of the CVs. Repeat this process wherever you need to bring the curve closer to the CVs. Figure 8.5 shows an example of one possible glass shape.

8. Save the file as **MF08-01a.MAX**.

As you can see from this exercise, working with NURBS curves is not much more difficult than working with splines, but they are much easier to use for creating highly curved shapes and forms such as the wineglass you just created. Of course, curves are only part of the NURBS tools in MAX; now take a look at surfaces.

Creating Basic NURBS Surfaces

NURBS surfaces can be based on either standard surfaces—much as patches are—or NURBS curves. You create standard NURBS surfaces in the Create command panel under the Geometry button, with NURBS Surface selected in the drop-down list. As with NURBS curves, there are two types of surfaces: Point and CV. Figure 8.6 shows an example of each.

Point and CV NURBS surfaces are created just like the MAX primitive plane—they produce a flat surface that you must manipulate through sub-object editing into other forms. In that respect, the NURBS surface primitives are fairly limiting. More complicated surfaces can be generated quickly by converting mesh or patch objects over to NURBS surfaces. You do this by right-clicking the object you want to convert and choosing Convert to NURBS Object. In most cases, this works just fine, but not always.

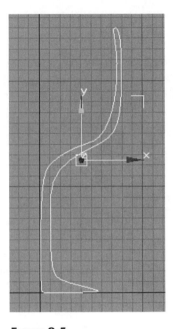

FIGURE 8.5
The wineglass shape after adjusting the curves. The glass shape is now ready to be converted to a 3D NURBS surface.

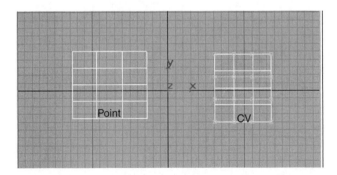

FIGURE 8.6   *A point surface versus a CV surface. Notice similarities between the surfaces and the same types of NURBS curves.*

Since creating NURBS surfaces is not difficult, you can jump into editing NURBS objects. Because curves and surfaces make use of the same interface, they are treated here as the same type of object.

Editing NURBS Objects

You can edit NURBS curves and surfaces after creation, just as you can other MAX objects; however, you do not need to apply a modifier to the object or convert it into an editable form. All you have to do is access the Modify command panel, and the NURBS controls are immediately made available to you.

You can work with NURBS objects on two levels in MAX. You can edit the object as a whole or you can edit the sub-objects of the object, which can include curves, individual surfaces, points, and CVs. The easiest way to edit the object as a whole is to use the NURBS floater, which you access by choosing the NURBS Creation Toolbox button. This button is found in the General rollout of the Modify command panel when you have a NURBS object selected. Figure 8.7 shows the resulting dialog box.

FIGURE 8.7   *The NURBS toolbox with commands subdivided by point, curve, and surface. Almost all NURBS commands can be accessed through this box.*

The NURBS toolbox is interactive with the command panel rollout. In other words, because the commands appear in both places, when you select a command in the toolbox, the command panel version becomes active and the rollouts appear for that command. You will not often need the command panel rollouts, but occasionally they are nice to have when you want to type in specific values for a command (such as a Transform).

The commands in the NURBS toolbox are divided into three sections—Points, Curves, and Surfaces—which you can look at in more depth in the following sections.

NURBS Point Commands

The Points commands provide various methods of adding points to the currently selected NURBS object. The most common of these buttons is the Create Point command, which enables you to add independent points to the curve—points you can later connect with other curves.

The other point commands include the following:

> **note**
>
> Many of the NURBS commands are based on the concepts of independence and dependence. An *independent* NURBS object does not rely on other NURBS objects for its shape; a *dependent* NURBS object relies on other NURBS objects to define it. A blended surface, for example, is a surface that is formed between two separate surfaces—the two separate surfaces are independent objects, but the blend surface is dependent. It is possible to convert a dependent surface to an independent surface, but not the other way around.

- **Create Offset Point.** Enables you to create a point that is related to another point and offset from it. If you move the base point, the offset point moves as well.

- **Create Curve Point.** Enables you to create a point that lies on an existing curve. When you move the cursor over a curve, the curve turns blue and a box appears. Click to place the point.

- **Create Curve-Curve Point.** Enables you to create a point at the intersection of two curves. Select one curve and then the other to create the point. After you create the point, you can trim either curve back to the inserted point.

- **Create Surface Point.** Enables you to create a point that lies on an existing surface. Works like Create Curve Point, but on surfaces.

- **Create Surface-Curve Point.** Enables you to place a point at the intersection of a curve and a surface. You can alternately trim the curve, if you like.

Most of the point commands are used to create points that you will later connect with curves—or possibly surfaces. Remember to watch the Command Panel as you select each type of point you want to create. A different rollout pops up for each point type and provides you with the options for that point, such as trimming.

NURBS Curve Commands

In addition to the regular NURBS curve commands, you also have a complete set of curve tools you can use to create additional NURBS curves based on existing curves. These tools enable you to create and modify the NURBS curves in many different ways. Many of these tools create copies of selected curves. When this occurs, all curves are considered part of the same larger NURBS curve, which you can later convert into a surface. There are a total of 18 curve controls in the NURBS toolbox. Some of the more interesting controls are listed here:

- **Create Transform Curve.** This command enables you to perform Move, Scale, and Rotate commands to create a new curve from an existing curve.

- **Create Blend Curve.** This Enables you to create a curve that is a blend between the endpoints of two existing curves.

- **Create Surface-Surface Intersection Curve.** Enables you to create a This curve that defines the intersection line between two NURBS surfaces. You must have two intersecting NURBS surfaces to use this option.

- **Create U/V Iso Curve.** NURBS This surfaces make use of U and V iso lines to define the surfaces. This command replicates either U or V lines as a curve.

- **Create Normal/Vector Projected Curve.** These two commands enable you This to project a NURBS curve onto a NURBS surface. The first uses the normal of the surface; the second uses a vector such as the Z axis to perform the projection. These handy commands enable you to draw on a plane and then project onto a surface for operations such as trimming.

- **Create CV/Point Curve on Surface.** Enables you to draw either a CV or a point This curve directly on a NURBS surface. You must have an existing surface to be able to use this command.

- **Create Surface Edge Curve.** This command enables you to duplicate This the edge of an existing NURBS surface and create that edge as a curve.

The curve commands are used to create additional NURBS curves that will eventually form the basis for creating a surface. For example, you might create a NURBS surface you like. You can then use the Create Surface Edge curve command to duplicate the edge of the surface. Finally, by simply extruding that curve, you can create a 3D apron for the surface.

NURBS Surface Commands

The last set of commands available in the NURBS toolbox—a total of 17—deal directly with the creation and manipulation of surfaces. Most of what you do in NURBS leads up to using these commands. Many of these commands duplicate their Curve counterparts and work the same way, except they only work on surfaces. Here are some interesting surface commands that are not duplicated by curve commands:

- **Create Extrude Surface**. Takes a NURBS curve and enables you to extrude it along the X, Y, or Z axis to create a surface. This is similar to the Spline Extrude command.

- **Create Lathe Surface.** Enables a you to create a lathed object from a spline. Works very much like the Spline Lathe command.

- **Create Ruled Surface.** Enables you to connect a series of splines a with a surface. Connections are made as linear surfaces, resulting in hard edges at the curves.

- **Create Cap Surface.** Enables a you to cap any NURBS surfaces with open holes. Will not work in all cases.

- **Create U and U/V Loft Surfaces.** These two commands are similar to Create Ruled Surface, but they don't create hard edges at the curves. a Instead, the curves are treated as smoothed points on the surface. The U command takes curves in a single direction, and U/V uses curves in both the U and V directions. This is similar to creating a 3- or 4-sided patch from three or four connected curves.

- **Create 1- and 2-Rail Sweeps.** These two commands are very similar a to the Loft command. Both take a shape and a path and extrude the shape along the path. The difference is that the a 2-rail version has two paths along which the shape is extruded and stretched.

- **Create a Multisided Blend Surface.** Enables you to create a surface a between three or more adjacent surfaces.

- **Create a Fillet Surface.** Enables you to create a filleted surface a between the edges of two existing surfaces.

Now that you have some idea of what the basic toolbox commands can do, take a minute to explore them. In the following exercise, you use the NURBS toolbox to create a wineglass like the one you created earlier in this chapter—as a NURBS surface, this time.

Creating a NURBS Wineglass

1. Load the file **MF08-01a.MAX** that you created earlier in this chapter. If you did not complete the exercise, you can find the file on the accompanying CD. Figure 8.8 shows you the scene at this point.

2. Select the curve.

3. Go to the Modify command panel. Click the NURBS toolbox button.

4. Choose Create Lathe Surface.

5. Click the NURBS curve. The surface is immediately created.

6. Switch your view to Shaded mode. Notice that the surface is incorrect. With the command still active, click Flip Normals in the Modify command panel. This flips the normals so the surface is generated correctly. Figure 8.9 shows you the resulting surface.

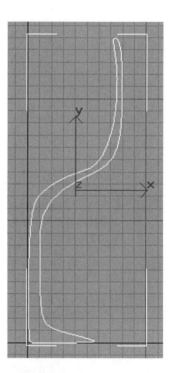

FIGURE 8.8
The NURBS curve representing the profile of a wineglass.

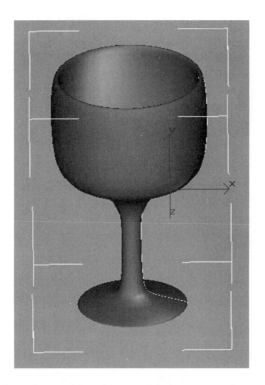

FIGURE 8.9 *The wineglass after applying the NURBS lathe command.*

7. NURBS are relational, so the shape of the wineglass is dependent on the original curve. To illustrate this, go to the Curve CV sub-object mode in the Modify command panel.

8. Select the CV that is about in the middle of the glass on the right side. Move this CV to the right to make the bottom of the glass wider. As you do, notice that the surface updates immediately. Figure 8.10 shows you the wineglass at this point.

The previous exercise illustrates how easy it is to take a NURBS curve and create a 3D surface out of that curve. It also illustrates the interdependence of curves and surfaces in NURBS, which enables you to adjust the original curve and immediately see the results in the surface.

Now that you have seen how to create surfaces in a variety of ways, it is time to explore how to edit surfaces at a sub-object level.

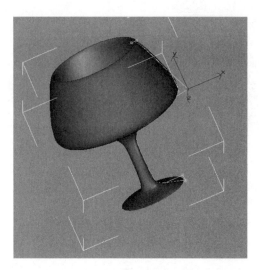

Figure 8.10   *The wineglass after adjusting a CV on the original curve. Thanks to the dependence of the surface on the curve, the surface is automatically updated.*

Editing NURBS Sub-Objects

Beyond editing the NURBS objects at the object level, you can also edit them at a
sub-object level, much as you can a spline. NURBS objects can contain up to five different types of sub-objects—Point, Curve Point, Curve CV, Curve, and Surface.

Editing Points

NURBS objects support editing three kinds of points that appear as two kinds of sub-
objects. The basic point is available when you have created points by using the commands in the NURBS toolbox or have a point curve in the object. Curve CV is
available whenever the NURBS object has a CV curve attached to it. These two sub-
object types enable you to work with any individual point on these curve types.

When point sub-objects are active, the points on a NURBS curve appear as green
boxes. You can select one or more of these boxes and edit them by using the standard MAX transform commands. In general, the Scale and Rotate commands have
no effect on a point in a point curve—only the Move command is useful here. The
moving of points can be animated over time.

When you select a point, the Modify command panel changes to reflect the type of
point you chose. For example, at the top of the rollout, a set of selection commands
appears as dotted buttons, enabling you to select individual points, rows or columns
of points, or both. Figure 8.11 shows you the rollout for a standard point.

Aside from the standard transform controls, the Modify command panel includes several controls you can use to edit points. Many of these commands are similar to the commands used for editing splines in MAX and include the following:

- **Name.** Individual points can have their own names assigned to them, making them easier to distinguish from other points in the same surface.

- **Hide/Unhide All.** Enables you to hide selected points or unhide all points in the object.

- **Fuse/Unfuse.** Enables you to fuse (join) one point to another. This is similar to the Weld operation in a spline. Unfuse divides a point into two.

- **Extend.** Enables you to add a point to a curve and extend the curve to meet that point. This is often used to add points to the ends of curves to make them longer.

- **Delete.** Enables you to delete selected points.

- **Refine.** Enables you to add more points to the existing curve to make it more complex. For a point curve, you can add curve points. For a surface, you can add Rows, Columns, and Rows&Columns of points all at once.

- **Make Independent.** Enables you to disassociate the selected points from the curve or surface on which they exist.

- **Remove Animation.** Removes all animation keys from the selected points.

- **Soft Selection.** Enables you to create a soft selection of points for transform commands. Same as the Soft Selection from editable mesh.

FIGURE 8.11

The Point Editing rollout, where you can adjust settings for any points you have added to the NURBS object.

CV points have many of these same attributes but are different in several key ways. For example, a CV point cannot have a unique name, but can have a weight assigned to it through the Weight spinner. CV points also have an Insert option that enables you to insert points on the CV curve without altering the shape of the curve.

By working at a Point sub-object level, you have all of the controls for point curves that you have for splines, plus some additional controls that are specific to NURBS curves.

Editing Curves

Just as you can edit NURBS curves at a Point or Vertex level, you can also edit them at a Curve level. This is important because a NURBS curve can be formed from smaller NURBS lines. This is very similar to the shape-spline relationship you find when modeling with splines. When you select the Curve sub-object type, you get the rollout shown in Figure 8.12.

As with point or CV editing, you can select any individual curve and transform it with the standard MAX transform commands. With curves, however, you can use Scale and Rotate in addition to the Move command. MAX also provides you with two different selection methods, just as with points. The first method selects individual curves; the second selects a curve and any connected curves (curves that share endpoints but are still different curves).

In addition to the transform commands, there are several specific curve-related commands you can use to modify the selected curve. Many of these are the same as those found in the Point and CV rollouts, but they work at a Curve level. The others are listed here:

- **Reverse.** Reverses the order of the points in the curve. When you select a curve, a green circle appears at one end, indicating the first point. Reversing is sometimes necessary when you create a surface based on the curve. Both curves that form the edges of the surface must have the first point on the same side, or the surface will twist.

- **Make Fit.** Creates a fit curve from the selected point curve. A fit curve has many more points in it and is much higher in detail. This commands spawns a dialog box where you can set the number of points in the fit curve. Figure 8.13 shows the Make Point Curve dialog box and a curve that has been transformed from a four-point curve to a fit curve.

FIGURE 8.12
The Curve Editing rollout. You will find a common rollout and a curve-specific rollout, depending on the type of curve you select.

FIGURE 8.13   *The Make Point Curve dialog box, where you can specify the number of points for the curve.*

■ **Convert Curve.** This command launches a dialog box where you can convert point curves to CV curves and vice versa (see Figure 8.14).

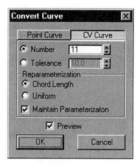

FIGURE 8.14   *The Convert Curve dialog box, where you can select the type of curve to which you want to convert and then select the parameters for that conversion.*

■ **Detach.** Enables you to detach the currently selected curve as a separate curve element. By choosing the Copy check box, you can opt to copy the curve instead of performing a straight detach.

■ **Break.** Breaks the selected curve into two separate curves at the point you select.

■ **Join.** Enables you to join the endpoints of two curves. This is done with a click-and-drag operation from one endpoint to another. A blended curve is then created between the two.

■ **Material ID.** Enables you to assign a Material ID to individual curves in the NURBS object. You can also select curves based on their ID.

In addition, some controls are related to the specific type of curve selected (point or CV). These include the following:

■ **Close.** Connects the first and last vertices of a curve with a blended curve, resulting in a closed curve. This is available for both CV and point curves.

■ **Degree.** On a CV curve, you have a lattice. The Degree spinner affects the overall strength of the lattice. The higher the degree, the less influence the lattice has over the shape of the curve. You can set the Degree spinner to 2, 3, or 4.

■ **Reparameterize.** For CV curves, you will find options to reset the parameters of the curve by using either Chord Length or Uniform methods.

The last sub-object level to take a look at is the Surface sub-object level. If you select the Surface sub-object, you can work with individual surfaces in the object. Then, you can use either MAX transforms, as usual, or change the parameters in the command panel shown in Figure 8.15.

Many of the commands here are the same as those found when editing NURBS curves. The different commands are:

- **Make Loft.** Converts the selected surface to a loft surface. In this case, a NURBS surface is generated by U and V lines, which define how the surface appears. A loft surface enables you to control the number of U or V lines in the surface so you can create highly detailed surfaces.

- **Convert Surface.** As with curves, individual surfaces can be converted from one type to another. This button launches the Convert Surface dialog box, where you can choose the type of surface you want to convert to and the parameters surrounding that conversion. Figure 8.16 shows you the dialog box.

- **Make Rigid.** Enables you to make selected surfaces rigid. When a surface is rigid, you can only transform the surface with the Move, Scale, or Rotate commands. You cannot move the CVs of the surface or change the number of points. Rigid surfaces take up less memory than standard surfaces.

- **Make Point.** Enables you to change the number of points in a point surface. Clicking this button launches the dialog box shown in Figure 8.17. This is a quick way to increase the complexity of a point surface.

FIGURE 8.15

The Surface rollout, where you can control the various properties for each individual surface in the NURBS object. At the bottom of the rollout are commands specific to each type of Surface.

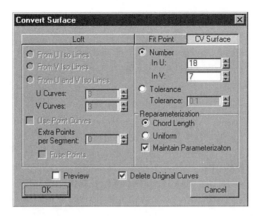

FIGURE 8.16   *The Convert Surface dialog box, where you can convert surfaces from one type to another.*

FIGURE 8.17   *The Make Point Surface dialog box, where you can specify the number of points to create in the surface.*

- **Renderable.** Defines whether the selected surface will appear when rendered.
- **Display Normals.** Displays the surface normals for the surface.
- **Flip Normals.** Enables you to flip the normals for the entire surface. Many commands, such as Lathe, require this operation to correct flipped face normals, because the normals in these commands rely on curves. The order of the points in the curves determines the direction of the face normals.
- **Materials.** Includes various controls for working with materials on NURBS surfaces. These controls are covered in Chapter 13, "More On Materials."
- **Break Row.** Enables you to break the surface along a U row. This physically splits the surface into two separate surfaces.
- **Break Col.** Enables you to break the surface along a V column. Again, this breaks the surface into two separate surfaces.
- **Break Both.** Enables you to break the surface along both the U and V contour lines. This breaks the surface into four separate surfaces.

All other commands you might find in the Surface sub-object rollouts have functions similar to those found in the NURBS Curve rollouts. The only difference is that they work on surfaces instead of curves.

By making use of the Curve and Surface object and sub-object controls for NURBS objects, you can create a wide variety of complex objects in MAX. The following exercise shows how to create a ball-return carriage for a bowling alley.

Creating a Return Carriage for a Bowling Alley

1. Load the file **MF07-02.MAX** from the accompanying CD. This file contains two sets of NURBS curves that you will use to create a ball-return carriage for use in the bowling alley scene. Figure 8.18 shows the initial scene.

2. Select the return carriage curves (in dark red), which were created as NURBS curves. Go to the Modify command panel.

3. In the NURBS toolbox, choose Create Uloft Surface.

tip

MAX 3 supports a new NURBS feature called Relational Stack, provided as a check box in the NURBS General rollout. If you have a NURBS surface where you did NOT animate any part of it, disabling Relational Stack saves memory and render time. When Relational Stack is enabled, the animated parameters are passed up the stack and the NURBS surfaces contain more information, making for longer render and processing times. If you didn't animate any part of the NURBS object, you can leave this off (with animation, you need to turn it on).

FIGURE 8.18   *A set of NURBS curves representing the general outline of the ball-return carriage.*

4. Select the bottom curve and then the next three curves, working your way up the outside of the object. As you do, a NURBS surface is generated. Continue working your way up and in to the center of the return. When you are finished, right-click to end the command. Figure 8.19 shows the object at this point.

FIGURE 8.19   *The NURBS carriage after the first surface command.*

5. Choose the Create Cap Surface command from the NURBS toolbox and select the center ring. You might need to adjust the view to select the correct area. In the Modify command panel, click Flip Normals to correctly orient the surface. Figure 8.20 shows the completed return carriage.

6. Hide the Return Carriage object.

7. Select the other NURBS curves in the scene. In the NURBS toolbox, choose Uloft.

tip

Loft and Ruled surfaces were not used here because of the resulting curvature of the surfaces. You would get unusual results if you continue to surface the interior of the object with Uloft.

FIGURE 8.20   *The return carriage after capping the center surface.*

8. In the Top viewport, select the lines in order from left to right to create the surface. In the Modify command panel, go to Surface sub-object editing. Select the curve and then turn on Flip Normals to correctly orient the normals. (If you render the object without doing this, it will appear incorrect.) Figure 8.21 shows you the surface at this point.

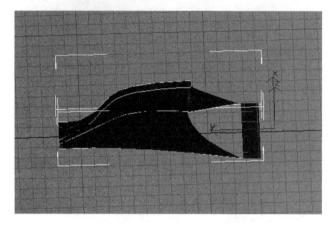

FIGURE 8.21   *The Return Carriage object after applying a Uloft surface to it.*

9. Choose the Blended Surface tool from the toolbox.

10. Select the Open edge of the surface you just created; then, drag down to the ground and select the inner edge of the square surface at the bottom. A basic surface is created.

11. Activate the Sub-Object selection and choose Surface as your sub-object.

12. Select the surface you just created. In the Modify command panel, scroll down until you see the Blend Surf parameters. Turn on Flip End 1; set Tension 1 to 0 and Tension 2 to 3.0.

13. Unhide the Return Carriage object. Save the file as **MF08-02a.MAX**. Figure 8.22 shows the final object.

FIGURE 8.22   *The Return Carriage object after applying and adjusting all the NURBS Surfaces.*

As you can see from this exercise, creating organic objects by using NURBS is easy. There is still one feature of NURBS to explore: trimming.

Trimming NURBS Surfaces

A *trimmed* NURBS surface is a surface that has a hole cut out of it. That hole is defined by a NURBS curve. To create a trimmed surface, you must do several things, all listed here:

1. Create at least one surface for trimming and at least one curve with which to trim.

2. Project the curve onto the NURBS surface.

3. Enable trimming.

4. Define the trimming parameters so that the trim is executed correctly. Options including flipping the side of the trim.

Outside of these items, trimmed NURBS are simply surfaces with curves attached to them. The surfaces are then trimmed back to the curves if you enable Trimming.

Using NURBS requires a slightly different way of thinking, compared to other modeling methods in MAX, but when you get used to working with NURBS, you'll find all sorts of uses for them. Now that you know how to model, take a look at what happens with NURBS at render time.

Render Time Considerations

When it comes to rendering, there are a few items to consider about NURBS surfaces—the most important is using the Approximation controls. NURBS surfaces cannot be rendered directly by the MAX rendering engine but must first be converted to polygons by a process called *tessellation*. Normally, tessellation just occurs behind the scenes, but MAX 3 provides a set of controls for defining exactly how the tessellation of the patch surfaces will occur.

Using Surface Approximation Controls

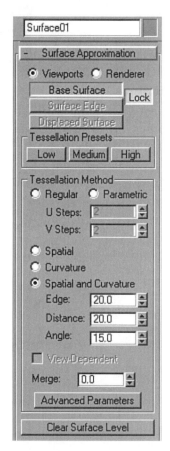

Figure 8.23 shows the tessellation controls for NURBS surfaces, found at the bottom of the NURBS rollouts in the Modify command panel. Tessellation of a NURBS surface occurs at two levels: Viewport and Renderer. Most of the time, you will set the Viewport levels lower than the Renderer levels to get better display performance and more accurate renderings. Only when Viewport is active will you see the tessellation of NURBS surfaces.

The Surface Properties rollout where you will find the controls necessary to control the tessellation of patch surfaces.

Under the Tessellation section of the rollout, you have a set of controls you can use to override the default patch settings. After you select where you want to apply the tessellation, you can select the type, of which you have six choices: Fixed, Regular, Parametric, Spatial, Curvature, and Spatial and Curvature.

- **Fixed.** Provides no tessellation of the surface. The detail in the patch surface is derived from the Steps setting under Topology. You can set the Steps value to as high as 100 per patch surface. In all other tessellation cases, the Steps setting is ignored.

- **Regular.** Provides no a simple, evenly distributed tessellation method that results in fairly low polygon renderings and retains the form of the patch surface.

FIGURE 8.23

The NURBS tessellation controls, where you can set up how the surface will be converted to polygons for rendering.

- **Parametric.** Enables no you to subdivide the surface into even numbers of U and V steps. For each U or V step, one row of faces appears between each vertex. Figure 8.24 shows a normal patch versus a parametrically tessellated patch.

- **Spatial.** Sets no the tessellation of the object based on the spatial distances within the patch. Spatial tessellation uses an analytical routine to correctly tessellate the surface.

- **Curvature.** Sets no the tessellation of the patch surface based on the amount of curvature in the surface. In areas where the curvature is higher, the tessellation is higher. This is another analytical method and produces the best results when the lowest number of polygons possible is important.

- **Spatial and Curvature.** A combination of both the spatial and curvature no methods and provides the best results on highly complex models. Whenever you choose any of the spatial or curvature methods, the Advance Parameters button becomes available. When you click on this button, you receive the dialog box shown in Figure 8.25, where you can further control the tessellation parameters.

In advanced parameters, you can choose from three methods of creating spatial- or curvature-based tessellations. The most basic and default form is the Grid method, which simply divides the object into a grid and tessellates accordingly.

The Tree method enables you to define a minimum and maximum number of subdivision levels to use. For example, a highly curved section of a NURBS object might get subdivided up to five times, whereas a flat section won't get subdivided. It's worth noting that any settings above 5 might cause problems because the tessellation could become extremely dense.

The last method is the Delaunay method, which converts the surface to a network of triangles. The spinner enables you to define the maximum number of triangles that will appear in the patch. Figure 8.26 is the nose surface from previous chapters, tessellated by using the Delaunay method.

tip

When experimenting with the Tessellation parameters, a good idea is to convert your viewport to a Wireframe view. Then, when you adjust the Viewport settings of the tessellation controls, you will see the updates in the viewport clearly. You might try this when exploring the options described in this section.

tip

Mesh objects can also be tessellated when you apply the Displace Mesh space warp. When you do this, you will find a set of controls for approximating meshes, similar to those for patch surfaces. These controls are intended for use in conjunction with the Displace Map in the Material Editor.

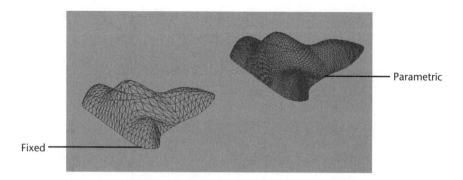

FIGURE 8.24   *A surface tessellated by using Fixed versus Parametric tessellation. Notice how much more accurate the parametric version is.*

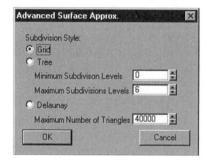

FIGURE 8.25   *The Advanced Surface Approx. dialog box, where you can set advanced methods for tessellating patch surfaces.*

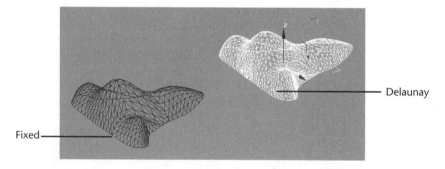

FIGURE 8.26   *The nose tessellated by using the Delaunay method. Notice that the surface triangles are all equilateral triangles.*

After you have set the tessellation methods for the viewport and the renderer, you should receive a smooth surface when you render the patch surface. Remember, the higher the tessellation settings, the longer the rendering will take, so try to use the lowest settings that produce satisfactory results.

NURBS surfaces can also be tessellated differently on a per-surface basis. In other words, different surfaces within the same NURBS objects can use different tessellation techniques. Under the Tessellation methods section of Figure 8.??, you will find a Lock to Top Level check box. This locks the tessellation controls to the top-level NURBS object, ensuring that all surfaces within the object use the same tessellation methods.

At the top of Figure 8.27, you will see three buttons. These buttons enable you to define different parameters for different parts of the NURBS surface. Options are Base Surface, Surface Edge, and Displaced Surface.

Base Surface and Surface Edge enable you to have different settings for the surfaces versus the edges of the surface. Most of the time, you will set these to be the same so that the edge and surface have continuity. You should not change them unless you are having a problem with the rendering of an edge or surface. The Displacement option is used when the material assigned to the surface is using a displacement map, which physically deforms the surface by using the colors of the map. Brighter colors (those closer to white) result in higher peaks. You will learn more about displacement mapping in Chapter 13.

The last option for NURBS tessellation is the View Dependent check box. Normally, when you set up the tessellation controls, the same tessellation settings are used throughout the entire animation. View Dependent changes the settings based on how close or how far away the object is from the camera. The farther away it is, the less detail is needed, so less tessellation is generated. This is great when you have objects that move close to and far away from the camera in your scenes, but it can also result in longer object setup times at the beginning of each frame. Use the View Dependent option with caution, because the increase in setup time might not offset the decrease in memory use and render time.

FIGURE 8.27

The Surface Approximation rollout, where you can set parameters defining NURBS tesselation.

Conclusion

NURBS surfaces are the most powerful method for creating complex organic shapes, but learning to use the system properly—so you can create objects quickly and efficiently—takes time. This chapter introduced you to the basics of NURBS modeling; it's up to you to explore more on your own. This chapter discussed the following topics:

- Working with curves and surfaces
- Editing curves and surfaces
- Creating new surfaces
- Trimming surfaces
- Handling render time problems

Now that you have seen the major modeling techniques in MAX, it is time to explore another way of creating geometry that is so much fun: Particle Systems.

CHAPTER 9

Working with Particle Systems

The last modeling tools to look at in MAX are some of the more interesting ones: Particles. Particles are used to create various effects any time you need lots of small pieces of geometry. Examples of uses of particles include dust clouds, smoke, mist, waterfalls, and many others. This chapter introduces you to using the built-in particle systems for MAX. In particular, you learn about the following topics:

- Uses for Particles
- Types of Particle Systems
- Working with Particle Systems
- Controlling Particles
- Other Particle Features

Uses for Particles

By their nature, particle systems create large numbers of objects, ranging from very small objects, such as dust, all the way up to just about any object you can imagine. Particle systems are also time based, meaning they almost always occur over a period of time. (In some cases, however, time does not matter, such as when you're using a Particle Cloud system with static particles.) Particle systems also have many parameters for controlling how the particle system reacts over time. Through the use of these features, particle systems can create a wide variety of effects. Some of the more interesting items you can create with particle systems include

- **Rain, snow, hail, or sleet.** These can be easily created by using a Spray, Snow, SuperSpray, or Blizzard particle system. They are excellent candidates for particle systems because of the large numbers of objects that are all animated.

- **Smoke, steam, and other transparent effects.** These are usually created by using the Spray or SuperSpray particle systems and almost always involve some inventive use of materials. (See Chapter 12, "Fundamentals of Materials," for more information on how to create these types of materials.)

- **Water, waterfalls, and such.** These types of effects are created with the built-in MAX particle systems. In some cases, they look good; in other cases, they don't, due to limitations in all particle systems. (Imagine trying to create a stream of water flowing into a bowl and having the bowl fill with particles.)

- **Dynamics.** Particle systems in MAX 3 can be used in dynamic simulations that you will explore in Chapter 16, "Exploring Basic Animation Methods." For example, you can use particles to knock over boxes.

- **Starfields and clouds.** Particles can be used to create diverse static effects such as starfields or clouds, using the Particle Cloud system.

- **Tornadoes, hurricanes, and other wind effects.** Particles can be used to create and simulate tornadoes and hurricanes. Many of these effects rely on the Path Follow space warp.

- **Flocks, schools, and swarms.** In many cases, you can replace the particles of a system with instances of animated objects. This makes it easy to simulate flocks of birds, swarms of bugs, and even schools of fish. With a little work, you can also simulate objects moving across the surface of another object.

- **Basis.** Particles can also be used as the basis of many types of effects. For example, the plug-ins UltraShock and Afterburn create highly realistic smoke and volumetric effects, but all of these effects are based on and use particle systems.

This list represents a small fraction of the effects you can create by using particle systems. At the end of this chapter, you should return to this list and see what other types of effects you think you could add to this list.

Types of Particle Systems

Of course, for different types of effects, you have different types of particle systems. MAX supports several built-in particle systems, and there are quite a few third-party plug-in particle systems such as Sandblaster and Particle Studio from Digimation. MAX supports six different types of particle systems:

- **Spray.** Creates basic sprays such as water fountains or rain. Use this system when you want simple particle effects.

- **Snow.** Creates a simple snow effect and has a few more parameters related to the particle shape, size, and tumble. Again, this system is great for simple snow effects.

- **Pcloud.** Creates a static cloud of particles and can be used to create effects such as 3D starfields or a flock of birds. Particles can be restricted to a variety of object shapes.

- **Parray.** Great for creating particles that emit from any type of object or for advanced explosion effects.

- **SuperSpray.** A much-enhanced version of the standard spray system and will probably be the most-used particle system. You can create most, if not all, of the particle effects you will need with this system.

- **Blizzard.** A much-enhanced version of snow.

The last four particle system types have literally hundreds of configurable parameters. Fortunately, outside of the basic parameters, all four systems share the same parameters. Even so, there are many more particle parameters covered in this book, so you will get an overview of the more important particle functions from SuperSpray.

Working with Particle Systems

Particle systems are created by selecting the object type (available in the Create command panel under Particle Systems) and clicking and dragging in any viewport to create the particle dummy object or particle system emitter. The emitter is not a enderable object and is only used to control the location and orientation of the emitter system. Figure 9.1 shows the Particle System icon and emitter for a SuperSpray particle system.

Adjusting the Parameters

After you create the particle system, you must go to the Modify command panel to adjust the parameters. You cannot immediately edit the parameters in the Create command panel; they will not have any affect until you edit them in the Modify command panel.

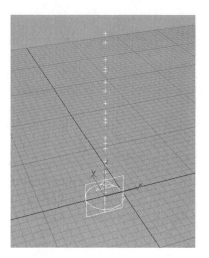

Figure 9.1   *The SuperSpray emitter with a particle stream active.*

When you enter the Modify command panel, notice that there are eight parameter rollouts for the SuperSpray particle system. Of these eight, seven of them are shared by the SuperSpray, Blizzard, Particle Cloud, and Particle Array particle systems. The only one that is different is the Basic Parameters rollout. Each of these rollouts provides a specific set of controls for the specific particle system. The eight parameter rollouts start with the following:

- **Basic parameters.** These parameters vary from particle system to particle system and define how the system appears. In the SuperSpray particle system, for example, you can control the formation of particles, such as their axis and spread, as well as what type of geometry appears in the viewports while you work on the system.

- **Particle generation.** These parameters define the number of particles in the system, as well as their life and size. Because particles occur over time, each particle has a life that is defined by a certain number of frames. If a particle has a life of 60 frames, for example, the particle appears in the scene for 60 frames. If that particle appears at frame 30, it shows in the scene until frame 90. In addition to controlling the life parameters, you have precise control over the size of the particles, including variations.

- **Particle type.** Particle type parameters enable you to define the type of particle that appears when you render the scene. The viewports generally use ticks to represent the particle system, but in the final rendering, you will probably have more particles of specific shapes or types. These are the three types of particles you can use:

- **Standard Particles.** Includes standard particle types such as triangles, cubes, facing, spheres, tetrahedrons, sixpoint, constant, and special. These options provide various shapes of renderable surfaces that are substituted for each particle in the system.

- **MetaParticles.** Replaces each particle with metaballs. Metaball modeling works by creating surface tension between spheres to create an organic surface. You can use MetaParticles to create flowing liquids and other types of effects. Be careful when using this particle type because it can take large amounts of time to prepare and render.

- **Instanced Geometry.** Replaces each particle in the system with an instance of a selected piece of geometry. This can be great for creating effects such as flying flocks of birds. You can create a single bird with animation and then substitute it into the particle system to create the flock.

After you select the particle type, various parameters associated with that type become available.

- **Particle Rotation.** Particle Rotation parameters enable you to control the rotation of an object over its life. You can control the speed and axis around which the particles rotate (regardless of the type of particles you use).

- **Object Motion Inheritance.** The particle emitter, like many objects in MAX, can be fully animated. When it is, Object Motion Inheritance parameters control how the motion of the emitter (whether an object or a helper) affects the motion of the particles as they are emitted.

- **Bubble Motion.** Bubble Motion parameters enable you to add a little wobble to the particles such as you might see in a bubble stream under water. Generally, you will use these parameters on thin, directed particle streams. The Bubble Motion parameters are not affected by space warps.

- **Particle Spawn.** Particle Spawn parameters control the spawning of secondary particle systems from, for example, particle collisions, making it easy to create effects such as drops landing in water or colliding in space.

- **Load/Save Presets.** The Load/Save Presets parameters enable you to load and save preset particle system settings. With so many parameters to deal with, the capability to load and save the settings is very important.

By combining the parameters found in these eight rollouts, you can create almost any kind of particle system effect you will possibly want. Only a few highly specialized effects (such as breaking an object down into particles and reassembling it into another object) cannot be created with these systems.

Now that you have an idea of how the particle systems work and some of the parameters associated with them, it is time to create one. The following exercise shows how to create a simple water fountain.

Creating a Water Fountain with a SuperSpray Particle System

1. Load the file **MF09-01.MAX** from the accompanying CD. Figure 9.2 shows you the scene at this point.

FIGURE 9.2   *The water fountain scene before the addition of the particle system.*

2. Open the Particle Systems rollout under the Create command panel and select SuperSpray.

3. In the Top viewport, click and drag to create the system at the center of the fountain.

4. In the Front or Left viewport, use the Move command to position the system at the top of the fountain, as shown in Figure 9.3.

   To actually create the correct fountain effect, you need to make use of a Gravity space warp, which applies a gravity effect to the particles. Space warps are fully covered later in this chapter. You will use only the one space warp at this time.

5. Select the Space Warps button from the Create command panel. In the drop-down list, select Particles & Dynamics and then select the Gravity space warp from the accompanying rollout.

6. Click and drag in the Top viewport to create the space warp. Then use Move to position the space warp in the center of the fountain and about 40 or 50 units above the fountain.

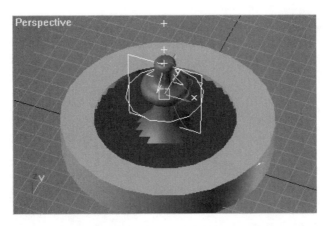

FIGURE 9.3   *The scene with the particle system emitter correctly placed. Now all you have to do is set up the system.*

7. From the Main Toolbar, choose Bind to Space Warp. Click the space warp and drag over to the SuperSpray emitter; let go when you see the cursor change. This binds the particles to the gravity effect and makes them active.

8. Go to the Modify command panel while the space warp is still selected and set the strength to 0.25.

9. Select the SuperSpray emitter and set the Animation Time slider to 50. This sets the current time to frame 50, where you can better see the particle effect.

10. In the Modify command panel, under the Modifier Stack drop-down list, select SuperSpray (it will be below the Gravity Binding entry in the stack). Set the following parameters:

    Under Basic Parameters:
    1st Spread 20
    2nd Spread 75

    Under Particle Generation:
    Set the Use Rate spinner to 20
    Speed 5
    Emit Stop 100
    Life 50

    Under Particle Type:
    Select Sphere

11. Choose the Play Animation button in the lower-right corner of the scene to see the particle effect. Click again on the same button to stop the playback. Figure 9.4 shows the completed water effect.

FIGURE 9.4   *The water fountain after setting up the particle system.*

12. Save the file as **MF09-01a.MAX** for use in a later chapter.

As you can see, the particle systems require a decent understanding of the animation system in MAX, which you will learn about in later chapters. This exercise also demonstrated how powerful particles are for creating effects like the water fountain.

Now that you have been introduced to the basics of how a particle system works, explore each of the systems in a little more detail.

Particle Systems in Depth

The spray system is the most simple particle system of all. Figure 9.5 shows you the command rollout for a spray particle system. In this rollout, you will find only the most basic controls.

Because this type of system is so simple, it makes a great example for explaining some of the most basic points of all particle systems. This section breaks down a particle system to see what it is made of. The important sections of the system follow:

■ **Viewport/Render Counts.** Because particle systems deal with many small objects, rendering 5,000, 10,000, or more particles is often necessary to achieve the effect you want. Obviously, such high particle numbers result in dramatic slowdowns of the viewports; hence, you have settings for both Viewport and Render counts. The Render counts are only used at render time and are generally set to a higher value than the viewports. SuperSpray and other particles handle this setting with a percent spinner.

- **Drop Size.** The size of the individual particles in MAX units.

- **Speed.** The speed at which the particles are emitted from the particle emitter. Animation of the emitter does not affect the particles for a spray particle system; particles are simply emitted from whatever orientation the emitter has at a particular frame.

- **Variation.** In the spray particle system, this spinner enables you to add variation to the direction in which particles are emitted. Figure 9.6 shows you a system using a variation of 0 versus one using a variation of 10.

The next set of controls enable you to define the shape of the particles both for the viewport display and for final rendering. Viewports can display drops, dots, and ticks for a Spray particle system. For rendering, Spray can only render tetrahedron or four-sided facing polygons. Facing polygons are simply flat surfaces oriented toward the camera; they are most commonly used in creating systems that use materials with opacity, such as smoke.

All particle systems must abide by timing controls as well. As mentioned earlier, all systems except the Particle Cloud system work over time. The timing controls are as follows:

- **Start.** This spinner is also known as the birth time of a particle; in other words, it's the first frame at which a particle is released from the emitter. Some systems also have an End spinner that defines the frame where the last particle is emitted (Spray does not have an End setting). You can set negative Start frames so that the particles are already emitting in the system at frame 0.

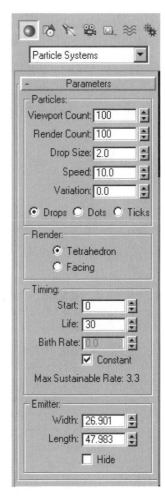

FIGURE 9.5

The Spray Particle System command panel rollout. Here, you can control the various aspects of a spray particle system.

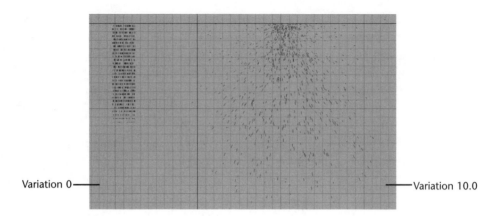

Variation 0 ————   ————Variation 10.0

FIGURE 9.6   *A spray particle system with no variation versus a spray system with a variation of 10. Notice how much more natural the system with variation looks.*

- **Life.** This spinner defines how long a particle is alive, in terms of frames. If this spinner is set to 30, an individual particle remains on the screen for 30 frames. For example, if a particle is born at frame 12, it dies or disappears at frame 42. Longer life settings result in longer particle streams.

- **Birth Rate.** This spinner is active only when Constant is turned off. When active, this spinner defines the number of particles emitted per frame. This number of particles are emitted continuously until the Count limit has been reached, at which point the particle system stops emitting.

The last controls available in the Spray system enable you to control the size of the emitter, which is also controllable at creation time. The particle system is directly affected by the size of the emitter.

The Snow particle system has basically the same parameters, but adds a Tumble spinner that enables you to force the particles to rotate over their life. This fully simulates falling snowflakes—hence, the system name Snow.

Particle Generation

Spray and Snow are the simple particle systems. The others are considered the full-featured or advanced systems. Now take a look at some of their controls. Many are the same as those found in Spray and Snow but just have different names, so they will not be covered. We start with the Particle Generation rollout shown in Figure 9.7.

The first set of controls that are new are the Subframe Sampling controls. Because particles work over time, it is possible to calculate their positions at subframe intervals, making for a smoother particle system. You can enable this feature for Creation Time, Emitter Translation, and Emitter Rotation. These do increase the amount of time necessary to create the system, but they are generally well worth it.

SuperSpray adds Grow From and Fade For controls to the particle size controls, which enable you to create particles that are emitted with a very small size, grow to their full size over a set number of frames, and then fade back to a small size over a set number of frames at the end of the animation. This has a tendency to make the particle system look a little more natural.

One of the most interesting controls is the Seed spinner. In many scenes, you will make multiple copies of the same system. With Spray and Snow, these copies will all be exactly the same. With the advanced particle systems, however, you can set a seed number so the particles all execute with the same parameters but don't look exactly the same.

Particle Types

Of course, one of the most important aspects of a particle system is the type of particles visible within the system. For example, a system looks very different when you use spheres versus stars. Snow and Spray have limited particle types, but SuperSpray and the other systems have an almost unlimited variety of

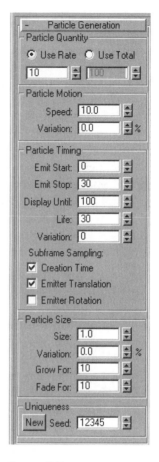

FIGURE 9.7
The Particle Generation rollout. Here, you can control how particles are formed in the system.

particles. Figure 9.8 shows you the Particle Type rollout for a SuperSpray particle system.

SuperSpray supports three basic types of particles: Standard, MetaParticles, and Instanced Geometry. Each type has its own section of settings in the rollout. Standard particles are simple geometric objects that can be used as particles. The particle system can only support use of one type of standard particles at a time, so if you want to have mixed particles, you need to create separate particle systems and overlap their particle streams. MAX provides a total of eight different types of standard particles. The type of standard particle can dramatically change the size of the geometry in the system. For example, if you choose a facing particle, each particle contains two faces, but if you choose a sphere, each particle contains considerably more faces.

The next type of particle is a MetaParticle. MetaParticles are essentially spheres. What makes them unique is that the spheres form metasurfaces or "blobby" surfaces, so you can easily create particle systems that appear as solid fluids, such as flowing paint. When you select the MetaParticles option, the controls in the MetaParticles parameters section become available. The most important control is the tension spinner. Consider MetaParticles to be like drops of liquid mercury. When those drops get close enough together, they form one continuous surface. The same thing happens with MetaParticles. The Tension spinner controls the amount of surface tension between the spheres. Figure 9.9 shows you a particle system using a MetaParticle particle type.

The last type of particle you can use in one of the advanced particle systems is the Instanced Geometry particle type. This type enables you to take any existing object and use it as a particle in your particle system to create any particle type you like. When you select Instanced Geometry, a Pick Objects button becomes available that enables you to select objects in the scene. Be careful when using instanced geometry particles, however, because they can drive up the face count in your renderings very quickly.

Any type of object from mesh objects to NURBS objects can be used as a particle in the particle system. Objects that have children can also be used. When you pick such an option, you can select to use the entire subtree as well. If you want to use multiple objects as a single particle, simply group those objects together before selecting them. These objects can also contain their own animation. For example, you can create a bird with wings flapping. Then, when the geometry is used in the particle system, the system controls the position and orientation of the system, but the original object animation controls the flapping of the wings. You can even offset the animation for the individual particles so the birds in the system don't all flap their wings at the same time. Figure 9.10 shows you a particle system that uses an animated fish as the particle.

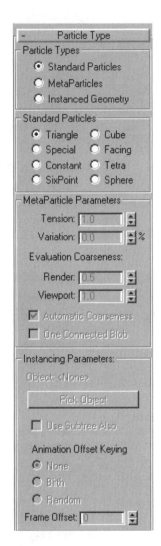

FIGURE 9.8

The Particle Type rollout, where you can define the shape of the particles in the system.

FIGURE 9.9   *A particle system that uses MetaParticles. Notice how the system appears to be a thick fluid.*

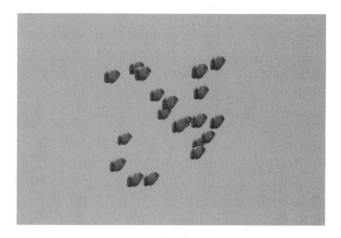

FIGURE 9.10   *A particle system using an animated fish as a particle.*

The following exercise shows you how to use the Instanced Geometry option to create a school of fish.

Creating an Animated School of Fish with Particle Cloud

1. Load the file **MF09-02.MAX** from the accompanying CD. This file contains a simple animated fish. Figure 9.11 shows you the scene at this point.

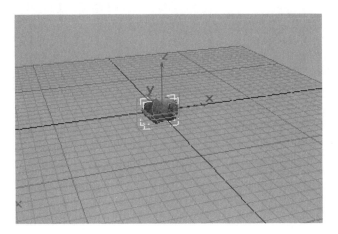

Figure 9.11   *The fish you will use to create a school of fish.*

2. In the Create command panel, select Particle Systems from the Geometry drop-down list.

3. Click on Particle Cloud. In the Top viewport, click and drag to create the Particle Cloud system. It's created just like a box—watch the readouts in the command panel and create a box that is roughly 500 units square.

4. Click on Zoom Extents and then go to the Modify command panel.

5. Under Viewport Display, turn on the Mesh option. This forces the viewport to display the geometry of the particles instead of just ticks. Note: This might slow down your display performance.

6. In the Particle Generation rollout, set the Use Rate spinner to 20. This increases the number of particles.

7. Turn on the Direction Vector radio button and set the Speed to 10.0. This forces the particles to move at a rate of 10 along the X axis. Notice the vector coordinates.

8. Under the Particle Type rollout, select Instanced Geometry.

9. Under Instancing Parameters, choose Pick Objects and then click on the fish. Turn on Random under Animation Offset Keying. This gives each fish a different starting point for its animation.

upgrader's note

MAX 3 contains a new setting for MetaParticles called One Connected Blob, which appears as a check box in the rollout. When this setting is enabled, all particles are treated as one large metasurface. This increases rendering speed, but you must make sure your particles are large enough. Otherwise, the setting uses up a tremendous amount of resources trying to create the surface. If this happens, simply increase the number of particles or the size of the particles (or both).

10. Under Particle Generation, set the particle size to 0.25 to scale the particles down.

    At this point, the particle system is almost completely set up, but you might notice that the fish are swimming backwards. This is because the particles pick up their orientation from the original fish object. Also, if you are viewing this system in a shaded viewport, you will notice that the particles don't have any materials. You can fix these problems quickly.

11. Select the original fish object and rotate it 180 degrees around its Z axis. This corrects the orientation of the fish.

12. Select the Particle System again. In the Modify command panel, scroll down to the Particle Type rollout. At the bottom of this rollout is a Material Mapping and Source section. Click on Get Material From. This updates the material of the particle system to use the Fish's material.

13. Select the original fish object again. In the display command panel, choose Hide Selected. This hides the fish object (it does not need to be visible for use in the particle system).

14. Activate the Perspective viewport and play back the animation. As the animation progresses, notice that each fish is animated at a different time.

    The previous exercise shows you just how easy it is to use custom particles in a particle system. It also shows how flexible the systems are in dealing with custom particles.

    Now that you have seen the basic parts of a particle system, take a look at how to control particles in your animation.

Controlling Particles

Even though you probably haven't explored too much on the animation side of MAX, you will get a little practice now. Controlling most objects over time is relatively simple. Particle systems are slightly different from general animation and modeling, partly because of the number of objects in the system. You can control and animate many of the parameters in the Modify command panel, but particles are most commonly controlled through the use of space warps. Space warps are special objects that apply various forces to particles (and to other objects) when the system is bound to the space warp.

Using Space Warps

Space warps are found in the Create command panel. Click on the Space Warps button to find a drop-down list where you can access the different types of space warps.

Three types of space warps can be used with particle systems—Particles & Dynamics, Particles Only, and Dynamics Interface. Figure 9.12 shows the rollout for the Particles & Dynamics space warps. All of these space warps can be applied to particle systems. The Gravity, Wind, Push, Motor, and PBomb can also be used with the Dynamics utility. Figure 9.13 shows you the Particles Only rollout, which has a selection of space warps that work only on particle systems.

FIGURE 9.12
The Particles & Dynamics Space Warps rollout, where you will find the most commonly used particle space warps.

Wind

The Wind space warp is used in a particle system to create the appearance of blowing wind. To create wind, click in the viewport to create the center of the space warp and drag out to define the outer edge. The actual size of the Wind icon does not change its effect. The orientation of the icon does matter if the Planar option is chosen: the wind blows in the direction the arrow on the icon is pointing. To bind the Wind space warp to a particle system, use the Select and Bind tool.

Gravity

The Gravity space warp is a subset of Wind, containing only the Force area parameters, with the same definitions as for Wind.

Push

The Push space warp imposes a force on particles perpendicular to the Push icon. Unlike Gravity, a Push incorporates a feedback mechanism from the velocities of particles. As the particles approach the target speed, the force acting on them decreases until there is no force applied at the target speed.

FIGURE 9.13
The Particles Only Space Warps rollout, where you find a set of warps you can use to control the motion of particles in your scene.

Motor

The Motor space warp functions nearly the same as the Push space warp, but applies a rotational force rather than a linear force. All of the Motor parameters are identical to those in Push, except in the Strength Control area. In this area, instead of specifying a linear force and a target velocity, you specify a torque and target revolutions.

UDeflector, SDeflector, Deflector

The UDeflector, SDeflector, and Deflector space warps are used to detect collisions with deflectors and to bounce the particles off of the deflectors. The deflector in a UDeflector space warp is any geometric object you select. The deflector in an SDeflector is the spherical icon of the space warp. The deflector in a Deflector is the planar icon of the space warp. The parameters in Deflector are a subset of those in SDeflector, which in turn are a subset of those in UDeflector.

MAX 3 also provides a second set of deflectors: SomniFlect, PomniFlect, and UomniFlect. These are very similar to the original deflectors, but provide enhanced capabilities such as the following:

- **Refraction.** The ability to have particles pass through the deflector helper and change their motion path. Much like sunlight passing through glass or water.

- **Spawn particles.** Enables the particles to spawn upon interaction with the space warp.

- **Full control over time.** You can set start and end points for where these types of space warps are used.

Displace

When the Displace space warp (located under Geometric, Deformable Space Warps) is applied to particle systems, it applies variable forces on the particles, based on the bitmap or map applied to the Displace icon. From areas of the icon where the bitmap or map has a low luminance value (the dark areas), no or low force is applied to the particle system. From areas of the icon where the bitmap or map has a high luminance value (the light areas), a high force is applied to the particle system. The parameters associated with the Displace space warp are the same as those for the Displace modifier.

Path Follow

The Path Follow space warp is used to force particles to follow a spline. You can use the Taper parameters to control how fast the particles converge or diverge from the spline path as they move along it. You can use the Swirl parameters to control how fast the particles rotate around the path as they move along it. You can also control how fast the particles move along the path and whether they move at a constant speed. The following exercise shows you how to use Path Follow to create a tornado.

Creating a Tornado by Using Path Follow

1. Start a new scene in MAX. Right-click the Animation playback button to access the Time Configuration.

2. Set the Length of the animation to 900 and choose OK.

3. In the Create command panel, go to the Spline commands and choose Helix.

4. In the Top viewport, click and drag to create the helix. Create the helix with the following settings:

   Radius 1: 20
   Radius 2: 60
   Height: 200
   Turns: 10

   Figure 9.14 shows you what the helix should look like at this point.

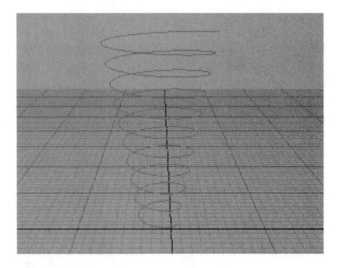

FIGURE 9.14   *A helix that forms the base shape of the tornado.*

5. In the Create command panel, go to the Geometry button and select Particle Systems from the drop-down list. Select a Spray particle system.

6. In the Left viewport, create the Spray icon. Set the dimensions to be 15 wide and 20 high.

7. Set the Animation time slider to frame 50 so you can see some particles. Then, move and rotate the spray emitter so it is at the bottom of the helix with the spray pointing toward the beginning of the helix, as shown in Figure 9.15.

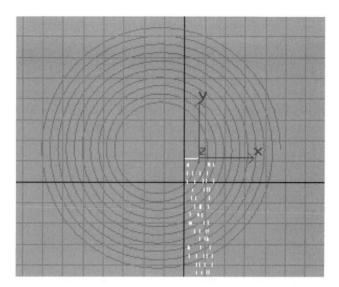

FIGURE 9.15 *The scene with the Spray particle system correctly placed at the bottom of the helix.*

8. From the Main Toolbar tab of the shelf, click the Select and Link button.

9. Click the particle system. Hold down the mouse key and drag to the helix. Notice that the cursor changes when you move the mouse over the helix. Let go and the helix blinks to indicate it has been selected. This step links the particle system to the helix so that when the helix moves, so does the particle system.

10. In the Create command panel, click the Space Warps button and choose Particles Only from the drop-down list.

11. Click Path Follow. In the Top viewport, click and drag to create the Path Follow icon. The size doesn't matter.

12. In the command panel, click Pick Shape Object and select the helix. Now, you must bind the space warp to the particle system.

13. From the Main Toolbar tab of the shelf, click the Bind to Space Warp button.

14. Click the Space Warp icon and drag over to the particle system. Again, when you place the cursor over the particle system, it changes. Let go when the cursor changes and the particle system highlights to indicate that it has been bound. The particles immediately begin to follow the path.

    The basics of setting up the particle system and the space warp are now complete. All that is left is to make some adjustments to each so that the system looks more like a real tornado.

15. With the Space Warp still selected, go to the Modify command panel and set the

following parameters:

Start Frame: –450
Travel Time: 450
Last Frame: 900
Constant Speed: On

16. Select the Particle system. In the stack, locate the Path Follow Binding entry. Open the stack and choose Spray. Set the following parameters:

Viewport Count: 2,000
Render Count: 5,000
Speed: 10.0
Variation: 10.0
Start: –450
Life: 450

17. The particle system immediately fills the helix. Click the Playback button to see the animation. Figure 9.16 shows you the completed tornado.

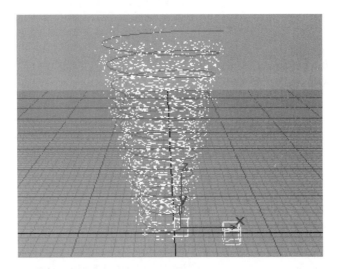

FIGURE 9.16   *The completed tornado, using both a spray particle system and a Path Follow space warp.*

18. Save the file as **MF09-03a.MAX** for use in a later chapter.

The beauty of the setup in the previous exercise is its flexibility. By applying a Bend modifier to the helix, you can make the tornado bend and twist. By animating the position of the helix, you can make the tornado move across the ground.

PBomb

The PBomb space warp is used to blow particle systems apart. In the Blast Symmetry area of the PBomb parameters rollout, you can set the blast force to be Spherical, Cylindrical, or Planar. With the Chaos parameter, you can add random forces to each particle. (The Chaos parameter value is used only if the Duration value is 0.)

The following exercise shows how to use the PBomb space warp to create a unique effect. In this exercise, you use PArray and PBomb to blow up the same object.

Using the PBomb Space Warp

1. Load file **MF09-04.MAX** from the accompanying CD. The scene is a set of pins in a bowling alley, as shown in Figure 9.17.

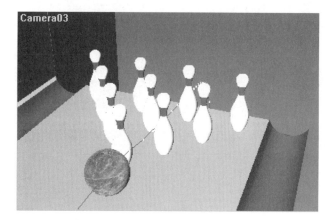

FIGURE 9.17   *The bowling alley scene, where you will use the PBomb space warp to blow up some pins.*

2. Advance to frame 0:0.21, just before the bowling ball hits the lead pin.

3. Create a PArray particle system in the Top view near the lead pin. In the PArray panel's Basic Parameters rollout, click Pick Object and select the lead pin as the object-based emitter. In the Viewport display area, turn on Mesh and set Percentage of Particles to 100.

4. In the Particle Generation rollout, set Speed to 0 and Life to 0:2.0.

5. In the Particle Type rollout, turn on Object Fragments in the Particle Types area. In the Object Fragment Controls area, turn on Number of Chunks. In the Mat'l Mapping and Source area, turn on Picked Emitter and then click Get Material From. In the Fragment Materials area, set Outside ID to 1 and Backside ID to 2.

6. Using Select by Name, select object Lane 2 Pin 0 (the lead pin) and hide it.

7. Create a PBomb space warp in the Top viewport, with the PBomb space warp centered next to the lead pin on the side where the bowling ball is located. Set Start Time to 0:0.22 and Duration to 0:0.0. Set Strength to 0.75 and Chaos to 25.

8. In the Left viewport, move the center of the PBomb space warp up about one-quarter the height of the bowling ball.

9. Using Bind to Space Warp, bind the PArray particle system to the PBomb space warp.

10. In the Top viewport, create a Gravity space warp. Set Strength to 0 and turn on Animate. Then, go to frame 0:0.20 and Shift + right-click the Strength spinner to set a key for Strength at the current key. Go to frame 0:0.21 and again Shift + right-click the Strength spinner. Go to Frame 0:0.22 and set Strength to 0.75. Turn off Animate and bind the Gravity space warp to the PArray particle system.

11. Create a UDeflector space warp. Click Pick Object and use Select by Name to select Lane 2 as the object-based deflector. Set Bounce to 0.5 and bind the PArray particle system to UDeflector space warp.

12. Play back the animation in the Camera viewport.

The resulting MAX file is stored as **MF09-04a.MAX** on the accompanying CD for comparison.

As seen in the previous example, you can apply multiple, cumulative space warps to the particle systems. You can use the Path Follow space warp to route particles through your scene and use the deflector space warps to have the particles interact with objects in your scene.

Other Particle Features

Before wrapping up this discussion of particles, three more areas of control for particles are worth looking at briefly:

- Particle Rotation and Collision
- Spawning
- Bubble Motion

As you might suspect, you can control the rotation of particles in the particle system. You can find these controls in the Rotation and Collision rollout (Figure 9.18) of any of the advanced particle systems.

With Particle Rotation, you can define a Spin Time, which defines how quickly the particles are rotating. You can also define a direction of rotation. This direction can be random, in the direction of the travel of the particles, or in a user-defined direction.

In addition to the rotation, you can control Interparticle Collision. This feature, which is new to MAX 3, enables you to have particles bounce into each other and react naturally. Much like a deflector, choosing this option enables you to define a bounce parameter that defines how quickly particles move away from each other after colliding.

Particle Spawning is a fun tool that enables you to create many types of effects. With Spawning, each particle in the particle system creates or spawns a new particle system. You can use Spawning to create effects from trails to fireworks. You can have particles spawn on death or collision, or you can have them spawn trails. When you set up the spawn, you are setting up another, simpler particle system.

The last particle effect to look at is Bubble Motion. This simple set of controls enables you to force the particles to move like bubbles. This effect is very much like a sine wave, and has amplitude, period, and phase controls much like those of a sine wave. This effect is usually limited to making bubbles rise in water or other similar effects.

Particles are a powerful and fun way of creating effects such as dust clouds, schools of fish, or any of hundreds of others. This chapter just touched on the basics of

FIGURE 9.18
The Particle Rotation and Collision rollout, where you can define rotations and control interparticle collisions.

particle systems. There are many parameters associated with particle systems, as well as a large variety of space warps to use to control the systems. Learning how to use these systems to achieve the effects you want can take a long time.

Conclusion

MAX provides you with six types of built-in particle systems. These six systems enable you to create most of the particle effects you will ever need in MAX. This chapter focuses on how to create and use these systems. In particular, you learned about

- Types and uses of particle systems
- How to create particles
- How to control particles

This chapter concludes the sections on modeling in this book. Now it is time to look at how to create those fantastic images you see in books, magazines, on TV, and on the Big Screen. To start learning how to create images, you need to learn about scene composition, which is the subject of the next chapter.

PART III

Scene Composition Fundamentals

CHAPTER 10

Understanding Composition Concepts

Now that you have a basic sense of how to model in 3D Studio MAX, it is time to look at the aspects of MAX that enable you to create photorealistic, or near photorealistic, renderings. To create these renderings, you need to have a good understanding of scene composition—the application of cameras, lighting, and materials to a scene to make it render well.

Before looking at specific techniques, you need to become more familiar with the terminology you will run across. This chapter focuses on the concepts and terminology behind scene composition and includes the following topics:

- Understanding Cameras
- Understanding Light
- Understanding Materials
- Understanding Rendering
- Working with Colors in MAX

Understanding Cameras

The first concept in MAX that you need to understand is cameras. A camera is an object in MAX that lets you view the scene as you would see it in a real-world sense: in perspective. Most of the views in MAX viewports are orthographic, providing you with parallel projections of the scene. These are often handy, but they are not realistic. MAX's Perspective view is a much more realistic look at the scene; however, it does not provide the precise controls for accurately viewing a scene. Cameras enable you to have this control.

In 3D Studio MAX, the camera is a virtual camera that duplicates many of the controls and settings found on a real camera, while adding some special features that real world cameras do not have. If you are familiar with 35mm photography, many of the terms discussed here will be familiar.

The camera concepts covered in the following sections include

- Lens length and field of vision
- Focus and aperture
- Camera movement

Lens Length and Field of Vision (FOV)

In a real camera, the lens length (also called focal length) is the distance from the center of the lens to the image it forms of the subject on the camera's film (assumed to be an infinite distance in front of the lens). The normal lens length of a camera is considered to be 50mm, which is similar to that of the human eye. This is why the 50mm lens is also referred to as the "normal" lens.

There is a direct relationship between the lens length and the field of vision (FOV), which is the angle that encompasses everything you can see through a lens with a given focal length. The typical FOV for a 50mm lens is 40 degrees. Figure 10.1 shows you an example of several lens lengths and their associated FOVs.

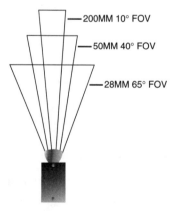

FIGURE 10.1   *Lens length has a direct effect on the field of view. As the focal length is reduced, the FOV is widened.*

When the length of a lens is changed, the field of view changes in inverse proportion. For example, if you reduce the lens length of a lens to 28mm, the FOV widens to 65 degrees. This is why lenses from 20mm to 35mm are considered wide-angle lenses. By the same token, if the focal length is increased to 200mm, the field of view drops to 10 degrees. Lenses with 85mm and longer lens lengths are known as long lenses or telephoto lenses.

note

As you learn about cameras and millimeters, keep in mind that film sizes such as 35mm are a related but separate subject that has to do with image output. This will be discussed later in this chapter.

At one time, photographers had to have many different lenses available for their cameras to shoot a wide variety of subjects, from broad vistas to distant objects. As optics became more sophisticated, however, the zoom lens was developed. This lens enabled photographers to adjust their lens lengths over a broad range of settings. These days, a photographer can generally get away with just two lenses: a 35–80mm zoom and an 80–200 zoom. These modern lenses often have a macro lens setting that enables users to take extreme close-ups as though they were using a low-powered microscope.

In MAX, the lens length of a camera is calculated by mathematical formulas, so you can define just about any lens length you need for a given camera. However, real-world cameras are used as a reference, so MAX provides you with a set of standard lens lengths from which to choose. You can also type in any specific lens length you like. Figure 10.2 shows you examples of several different lens lengths. Note that there is not a need to include the equivalent of a macro setting, because virtual cameras can be placed very close to the subject to achieve that effect.

Figure 10.2   *Sample lens lengths: (a) 15mm, (b) 20mm, (c) 24mm, (d) 28mm, (e) 35mm, (f) 50mm, (g) 85mm, (h) 135mm, (i) 200mm.*

As you can see, in addition to adjusting the size of the subject, the wide lens settings have a tendency to exaggerate the perspective in a scene, and the longer lenses reduce it. As a result, wide lens angles often impart a feeling of massiveness to a subject, while telephoto lenses are used to flatten (compress) scenes so that distant objects seem closer together.

Focus and Aperture

Of course, lens length isn't the only part of a real camera lens. One of the most commonly used controls on a manual camera is the focus adjustment. Focus adjusts the optics in the camera so that the subject is sharp and clear. However, focus is not object-specific; it is a range—a set of near and far distance settings called depth of field. Figure 10.3 shows you an example of depth of field. Depending on the lens settings, the depth of field might be narrow—with only a few objects within a few inches of the focus point being clear—or wide (like many fixed-focus cameras)—with everything from a few feet away to infinity in focus.

(a)   (b)

FIGURE 10.3   *Depth of field effects: (a) MAX does not create a depth of field, so everything is in focus. (b) Variable depth of field enables you to select a portion of the image to be in focus, while the rest is out of focus.*

Real-world camera effects, such as depth of field, are not directly supported by the cameras available in MAX. Fortunately, many camera- and lens-based effects are handled by the Lens Effects package included with 3D Studio MAX. In the past, this package was implemented as a Video Post routine, and you will find other lens effect plug-ins that are Video Post-based. In MAX 3, lens effects are created in the Rendering Effects Post process, where they not only render faster than a Video Post effect, but you have more control over the effect. Chapter 17, "Exploring Other Animation Methods," discusses rendering effects and Video Post.

Camera Movement

When it comes to movement, cameras in MAX hold a massive advantage over their real-world counterparts. In 3D space, cameras are free to move anywhere in the scene, even inside of objects. In addition, multiple cameras can be defined, allowing the action to be viewed from several angles at the same time.

In addition to mimicking 35mm cameras, MAX can imitate their motion picture and video counterparts. While most of the following moves require a real camera to be mounted on a tripod or dolly (wheeled platform), there are no such restrictions for virtual cameras, even though they can behave in the same manner. Many of the camera moves discussed here are implemented as viewport controls when you are working in a camera viewport.

Pan and Tilt

Two of the most common moves in film-making are pan and tilt. A *pan* is a horizontal rotation of the camera from right to left, or vice versa (as shown in Figure 10.4). A pan is often used to move the camera from one subject to another or to see more of a landscape than will fit in the frame.

A *tilt* is the vertical equivalent of a pan, rotating the camera up or down. Tilts are often used to showcase tall objects, such as buildings, but also might be used on a character to give the impression that the viewer is "sizing him up."

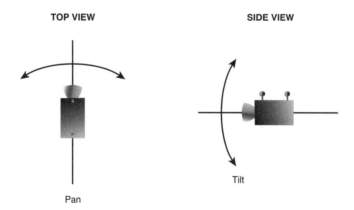

FIGURE 10.4   *Pan and tilt camera movements: A pan is a horizontal rotation of the camera. A tilt is a vertical rotation of the camera.*

Tracking and Dollying

A *dolly* is a wheeled platform on which a camera can be mounted. The term dolly, or *truck*, is also used as a verb to refer to moving the camera around on the floor during the shot to get closer to or farther away from the action, or to view it from a different side, as shown in Figure 10.5. In MAX, the Dolly command moves the camera closer to or farther away from the subject without changing the lens length.

In film-making, a dolly is sometimes mounted onto a steel track, allowing the camera to move smoothly along a predefined path. Therefore, "truck" usually refers to the movement of the camera along a single axis, either horizontal or vertical.

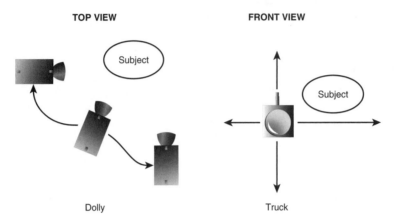

FIGURE 10.5   *Dolly and Truck camera movements. Dolly moves the camera around, usually on the same "floor plane" as the subject. Truck moves the camera horizontally or vertically.*

Bank and Roll

In the real world, banks and rolls are difficult to do unless the camera is hand-held or mounted in a motion control rig, but MAX cameras handle them with ease. *Roll* means to rotate the camera around its viewing axis, making the scene appear to spin (see Figure 10.6). *Bank* is simply an automatic roll that occurs when a camera moves through a curve in a path. Creating the illusion that you are flying in a plane or tumbling out of control are two of the most popular uses for roll.

Clipping Planes and Targets

Another unique feature of MAX cameras is clipping planes. A *clipping plane* is perpendicular to the camera view at a specific distance away from the camera. MAX supports two types of clipping: near and far. With a near clipping plane, any objects between the camera and the clipping plane are not rendered. Near clipping planes are excellent for making section perspectives through buildings. Far clipping planes remove all objects beyond the clipping plane, thus reducing the geometry in the endering pipeline and, in most cases, speeding up rendering.

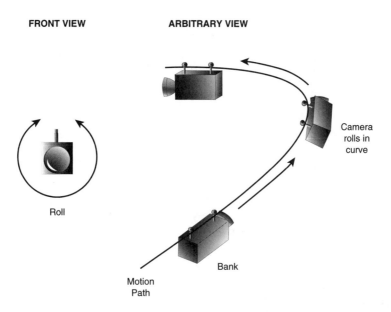

FRONT VIEW

ARBITRARY VIEW

Camera
rolls in
curve

Roll

Bank

Motion
Path

FIGURE 10.6   *Roll and bank camera movements: Roll is the rotation of the camera around the viewing
axis. Bank is an automatic roll applied to cameras moving along a curved path.*

MAX supports two types of cameras: target and free. A target camera has a camera
location and a defined target at which it always points. This is represented in MAX by
a camera icon with a line drawn to a box "target." The
camera and target can be moved independently of
each other, providing easier control. The target
enables you to see exactly where the camera is pointed from any other viewpoint, making positioning
faster and easier. A free camera does not have a target
and is used in special circumstances, such as path-
based animation, when you want the camera to follow a path and always look in the direction of the
path. Both types of cameras are shown in Figure 10.7.

Cameras enable you to set up any true view of your
scene that you want. While you are doing this, MAX
lights the scene with two default lights so you can see
what is going on, but to create a realistic scene, you
must create and add your own lights.

tip

MAX 3 now supports viewport
clipping planes, which enable
you to preview, in the viewport,
what a camera clipping plane
might look like. To access this
feature, right-click the viewport
label and enable Viewport
Clipping. A red bar appears on
the right side, with two arrows
on it. The top arrow is the back
clipping plane and the bottom
is the front. Simply slide the
arrows up and down to clip the
scene.

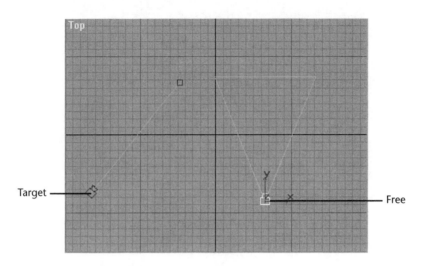

FIGURE 10.7   *The MAX camera icons: Target camera and Free camera.*

Understanding Light

Visible light is composed of a spectrum of colors running from red to violet. When light rays strike an object, some of these colors are absorbed by the material while others are reflected. The amount and color of the light reflected from objects enables us to see them as red, or lime green, or any other color in the spectrum.

Computer displays, because they are generally viewed by producing light rather than reflecting it, use the additive color model, in which white light consists of equal amounts of red, green, and blue light. If the level of one of these three colors drops slightly below the others, the result is something other than white.

Color *temperature* is a scale used to differentiate between these near-white spectrums of light. Color temperature is measured in kelvins, which refers to the temperature to which a black object must be heated to have it radiate that particular spectrum of colors. This has nothing to do with the operating temperature of light sources, however—it's just a scientific scale.

What color temperature does from a practical standpoint is indicate the warmth or coolness of the light in terms of color. Note that the scale is counterintuitive, however. For example, cool (meaning bluish) fluorescent lights are rated at 4000K, while typical warm (yellowish) incandescent lamps are 290K. Quantifying color temperatures can be helpful when you want maximum color accuracy because our eyes tend to consider the main source of light illumination to be white regardless of whether it is noon sunlight

(5000K) or a halogen desk lamp (3300K). When the image is output, however, the color differences might become more noticeable. MAX does not let you specify a particular color temperature, but you can adjust the colors of a light to match. Some plug-in renderers, such as RadioRay, do let you specify every aspect of a real-world light that it will simulate when rendering.

Another important element of light is *intensity*—the brightness of the source or reflection. The angle at which a light ray strikes a surface and is reflected into our eyes (called the *angle of incidence*) has an effect on how brightly the object appears to be illuminated from our perspective. For example, if you hold a flashlight in front of your face and point it along your line of sight at a very smooth, flat surface, most of the light is reflected back into your eyes and the surface seems brightly lit. If, however, you stand at a 45-degree angle to the surface, it appears darker because much of the light is being reflected away from you. Figure 10.8 shows you an example of this.

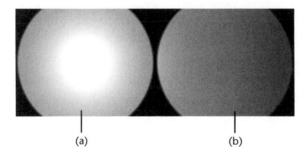

(a)   (b)

FIGURE 10.8   *The effect of angle of incidence on apparent brightness: (a) A surface lit and viewed at a 90-degree angle. (b) The same surface lit and viewed at a 45-degree angle.*

Light reflecting off an object goes on to illuminate other objects as well—an effect called *radiosity*. The cumulative effect of all the light bouncing off all the objects in an area is called *ambient light*. This ambient light has no discernible source or direction, but acts to illuminate everything in the scene. In MAX, ambient lighting is a very subtle control that affects the overall brightness of objects in a scene, regardless of the lighting. Radiosity can be simulated through the use of other programs, such as Lightscape, or plug-in renderers, such as RadioRay.

Another property of light is that it becomes weaker with distance, which is called *attenuation*. This occurs because the atmosphere is full of tiny particles that block and reflect the light rays. Larger particles, such as those in smoke and fog, dramatically increase the effect, while attenuation occurs to a much lesser extent in space, because there are far fewer particles to block the light rays.

Types of Lights

MAX supports five kinds of light sources that you can make use of to illuminate your scenes. These include omni (or point) lights, directional (or distant) lights, spotlights (both target and free), and the global ambient light. Figure 10.9 diagrams these types of lights.

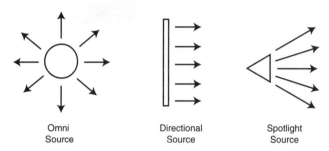

Omni
Source

Directional
Source

Spotlight
Source

FIGURE 10.9   *3D light sources: An omni or point light casts light in all directions, a directional light casts parallel light along a single axis, and a spotlight casts a cone or pyramid of light.*

An omni (omni-directional) light source casts light in all directions. It is also known as a point light. This type of light is usually ideal for simulating any kind of nondirectional light source, from bare-bulb fixtures hanging in an attic to the sun in an outer space scene. Figure 10.10 shows you an example of an omni light.

FIGURE 10.10   *The omni-directional light source (white diamond) positioned in the center of the scene casts light in all directions.*

Directional lights, also called distant lights, project light along one axis only, and all the beams are parallel, not unlike a laser beam. Directional lights are good for simulating sources that are very far away, such as the sun in a terrestrial scene. Because the source is so distant, the light rays appear parallel and all shadows cast by the light are also parallel, (see Figure 10.11).

The shadow controls in MAX 3 have been completely rewritten to give you more control. You now have control over the shadow density and color and can apply mapping to the shadows. Also, the lights now support plug-in shadows so you can change the shadow-casting algorithms with ease.

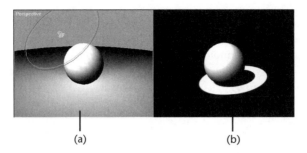

(a)   (b)

FIGURE 10.11   *Directional light characteristics: (a) A directional light source, which casts parallel light rays, aimed down a sphere. (b) The resulting shadows are also parallel.*

Spotlights are very similar to directional lights but cast light from a single point in a cone fashion, much like the light from a flashlight. Although directional lights have parallel beams, spotlights do not. Spotlights are heavily used in MAX to create general lighting, special highlighting, light coloring, and many other uses.

Lighting Controls and Effects

MAX offers a standard set of controls for light sources, including intensity, color, and shadow settings. MAX also provides include and exclude lists as well as projection mapping and attenuation controls.

Brightness and Color

Intensity sets the brightness level of the source. In general terms, this is considered to be a color of 255—pure white. In MAX, however, you can also use a multiplier setting to increase or decrease brightness. By adjusting the multiplier of a light, you can easily "blow out" the highlights of an object, giving it an overexposed appearance. MAX actually tracks colors that are brighter than 255,255,255. These are called unclamped colors and can be accessed by other routines, such as the lens effects package.

Color is controlled by RGB and HSV color sliders and simulates the use of colored plastic gels over photography lights. The use of colored lights can give a scene a theatrical flair, complementing the material colors and adding extra interest to lighted surfaces. Colored lights can also be used to create some interesting effects by blending different colored light sources.

Colored lighting doesn't have to be showy to be effective. By making subtle adjustments to the color balance of a light source, you can simulate the color temperature of an incandescent bulb, a fluorescent tube, or the sun on a hazy day.

Shadows

Lights in MAX are capable of casting shadows when they shine on objects. This is an option that must be enabled in the MAX lights and is not on by default. When you enable shadows on a light, there are two types of shadows you can use: shadow maps and raytraced shadows. Each type of map has its own set of features and controls. You can freely mix shadow map and raytraced shadows in your scene, but in general you should try to stick to one or the other. Figure 10.12 shows you examples of both.

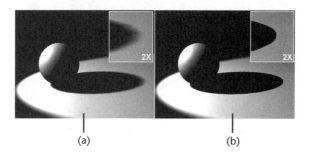

(a)   (b)

FIGURE 10.12   *Shadow types: (a) Shadow mapping produces natural-looking, soft-edged shadows. (b) Raytraced shadows are sharper and more precise.*

Shadow mapping is a scanline rendering technique for creating shadows. It creates a grayscale texture map based on the lighting and mesh objects in the scene and then applies it to the objects at render time. Mapped shadows are soft-edged and more natural looking than raytraced, but become blocky and inaccurate in some situations.

The blockiness can be reduced by increasing the shadow map size, which adjusts the amount of memory the system can use to create the map. Increasing the size to 1024 or 2048 (the default is 512) can go a long way toward smoother shadows but obviously has an impact on render times as well, especially if more than a few shadow maps need this kind of resolution. Shadow maps also support a sampling feature. The more times a map is sampled, the softer and more realistic the shadows are, but with slightly longer rendering times. For final renderings, you should increase the number of samples along with the shadow map size. Figure 10.13 shows you an example of using shadow maps.

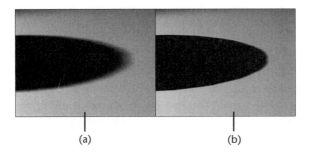

(a)   (b)

FIGURE 10.13   *Effects of shadow map size: (a) Blockiness and smearing with a 256K map size. (b) Increasing the map size to 1024K reduces the problem but increases render time.*

The other problem with shadow maps is that they might not be properly positioned in the scene. This most often occurs at the intersection of two objects, where the shadow of one is being cast on the other. In some cases, the shadow might be offset from the mesh intersection. Adjusting the map bias setting moves the shadow closer to or farther away from the casting object, enabling you to correct this situation.

Raytraced shadows are defined by using raytracing renderer techniques. Unlike the results of the soft-edged shadow mapping technique, raytraced shadows have a hard edge but are very accurate and precise. This is good for the sharp, dramatic shadows you would find in space or on airless worlds, such as the moon. Because raytraced shadows make use of raytracing techniques, they can dramatically increase rendering times based on the geometry that is casting shadows.

For both types of shadows, you can also control the density, color, and mapping of the shadows. Density control is important because it enables you to control how dark a shadow really is. Color control is important for unusual lighting situations where you are using strongly colored lights and want to have colored shadows. Last, you can even apply maps to shadows now so you can be creative in your shadow effects.

Attenuation

Another important aspect of lights in 3D Studio MAX is *attenuation*. In the real world, lights do not travel forever. For example, if you point a flashlight at the ground, it creates a fairly bright spot, but if you move the bright spot away from yourself on the ground, the light becomes less intense in the bright areas. This is called attenuation.

It is important to use attenuation in lighting situations to control how much light you have in a scene. In MAX, it is very easy to create many lights that have the effect of washing out the scene.

Attenuation of lights in MAX works very much like clipping planes for a camera in that you have both near and far ranges to determine where the light falls off to nothing. Additionally, however, you can control how quickly the light dissipates by setting a Decay parameter. Proper setting of attenuation parameters can easily make the difference between a well-lighted scene and a mediocre scene.

Hotspot and Falloff

Spotlights and directional lights have controls that enable you to define the concentration of light in the beam they project. The adjustments are given in degrees and are represented on screen by two cones that show how wide the beams are set (see Figure 10.14).

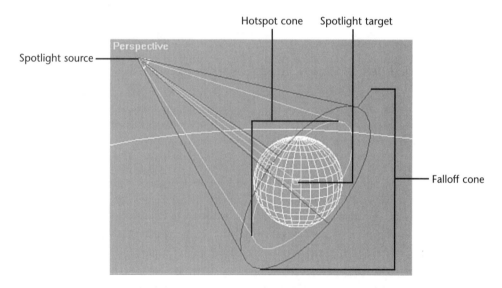

FIGURE 10.14   *Hotspot and falloff settings are visually represented by cones. This aids in the positioning of the lights without doing excessive test renders.*

The hotspot adjustment defines the angle of the inner portion of the beam of light that is projected at the current intensity setting for that source. The falloff setting sets the perimeter of the outer portion of the beam, indicating where the intensity has dropped all the way down to zero. In other words, the light is constant across the hotspot area and then falls off linearly between the hotspot and falloff cones.

When the hotspot and falloff settings are within a few degrees of each other, the light appears to be sharply focused, with very little transition between full intensity and none at all. When the differences in angles are much larger, the beam looks softer and tapers off gradually from the bright hotspot to the edges of the beam, as shown in Figure 10.15.

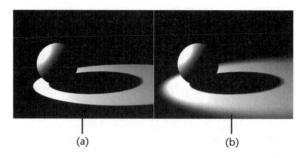

(a)   (b)

Figure 10.15   *Effects of hotspot and falloff sizes: (a) When hotspot and falloff settings are close together, the beam appears focused. (b) Widening the difference between settings makes the beam softer and more diffuse.*

Include and Exclude

MAX also enables you to set up your lights so they affect only certain objects that you identify. There are two ways to do this: Include enables you to pick a list of objects that the specified light affects, while you can use Exclude when you want most of the objects in the scene to be affected but want to select a few objects that should be left out. MAX also enables you to set the type of include or exclude that the light will use—you can include an object in or exclude it from illumination, shadow casting, or both.

Include and Exclude are something of cheats because you can't control light that way in the real world; however, because lighting is such a time-consuming process, features like this are great for fine-tuning and achieving difficult effects easily. For example, say that you've set up a spotlight that creates a perfect highlight on one of the objects in your scene. Unfortunately, the spill from that spot is shining on many other objects that you don't want illuminated that way. The solution is to add the desired object to the Include list for that light so that it is the only object affected.

MAX lights and cameras are used to compose and illuminate your scene. You can create literally hundreds of techniques and effects and use them to set the mood of your scene. This is an art called digital cinematography and will be explored in more detail in Chapter 11,"Working with Lights and Cameras".

After you have set up lights and cameras, you will want to start adding materials to your objects to give them a lifelike appearance.

Understanding Materials

A *material* is a set of attributes assigned to the surface of an object. When these settings are rendered, MAX interprets them to generate the appropriate colors based on the lighting and the camera position. MAX comes with a variety of materials that have many settings you can control to create just about any type of surface for your scene. Before looking closely at materials, this is a good time to take a look at how colors are interpreted by MAX.

Working with Colors

MAX interprets colors in the same way a computer does, by using the RGB color model. The RGB color model works by combining different saturation values of red, green, and blue to create an array of colors, sometimes called color channels. The number of shades you have in each color channel defines how many possible colors you might have. For example, if you have eight 2^8-bit color channels, you have 256 shades of red, green, or blue, resulting in a total of 16.7 million possible colors. (This is calculated by multiplying $2^8 \times 2^8 \times 2^8$.) 16.7 million colors is often referred to as 24-bit color space (3×8-bit channels).

MAX actually renders images in 48-bit color space and reduces the number of colors down to 24-bit for output in most cases. Sometimes, you can use higher colors, depending on your hardware and software configuration. Most video work is done in 24-bit color and most film work is done in 24- and sometimes 48-bit color.

When working with MAX, you will find various places to make use of color, including materials and lights. When you need to adjust a color, you often see a color swatch. Clicking that color swatch launches the MAX color selector, shown in Figure 10.16.

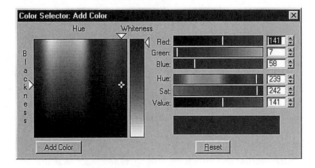

FIGURE 10.16   *The MAX color selector, where you can select the color you want to use.*

In the MAX color selector, all colors are treated as RGB, but you have three methods of selecting colors: RGB, HSV, and Blackness and Whiteness. In the RGB method, you simply adjust the RGB spinners or sliders for each color channel. In HSV, a slightly different approach is taken. HSV stands for Hue, Saturation, and Value. Adjusting the Hue gives you the general color, which you can then fine-tune by using the Saturation and Value spinners.

The last and most intuitive method for selecting colors is to use the Blackness, Hue, and Whiteness sliders found to the left of the color selector. Here, you see a color gradient. Clicking and dragging around in the color gradient quickly selects a rough color that you can then refine with the Blackness or Whiteness spinners. You can further refine the color with the RGB or HSV spinners. In any case, adjusting colors by using one method adjusts the settings of the other methods to provide the same color.

tip

If you don't like the MAX color selector, MAX 3 now supports plug-in color selectors that enable you to select colors in a variety of different ways. MAX ships only with the default selector, but if you have a third-party plug-in color selector, you can choose it in the Preferences on the General tab.

Now that you have an idea of how colors are interpreted by MAX, it is time to take a look at how colors are used in materials.

Material Colors

A basic material in MAX provides a plastic or flat look, much like paint on a flat surface. The colors on this surface are defined in three different ways: Ambient, Diffuse, and Specular, as shown in Figure 10.17.

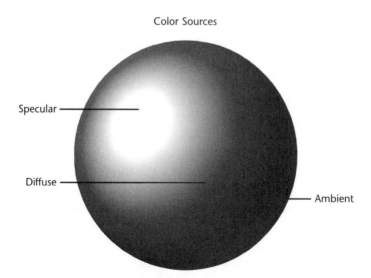

Color Sources

Specular

Diffuse

Ambient

FIGURE 10.17 *An object's rendered appearance is influenced by three different sources of color and value. Ambient is the color of the object in shadow, Diffuse is the color of the object's material, and Specular is the color of the highlight.*

- **Ambient color.** The hue an object reflects if it's not directly illuminated by a light source (its color in shadow). This is rarely black because the ambient light in the scene usually guarantees at least some illumination on every surface. Generally, the ambient color is a very dark shade of the diffuse color, but it can be set to whatever you desire.

- **Diffuse color.** The hue assigned to the object. This is the color that's reflected when the object is illuminated by a direct lighting source.

- **Specular color.** The hue of any highlights that appear on the object.

Shading Models

MAX enables you to render objects at different levels by using different shading models. A shading model is how the MAX rendering engine interprets the colors and highlights assigned to the material. In MAX, you determine the shading mode in the material. MAX 3 supports nine shading models (plus raytracing, for a total of 10) in addition to a wireframe mode that renders the object as a wireframe, using the current shading model. Each shading model is listed below and briefly described:

- **Wireframe.** This is the fastest and most basic rendering mode. It is very similar to a wireframe display in a viewport. Any material in MAX can be converted to Wireframe by enabling the Wire check box in the Shader rollout of the material.

- **Constant.** This mode is also called a flat, shaded mode. MAX calculates the color and value of a polygon face based on the normal at the center of the face. The resulting image is a collection of sharply defined polygon surfaces, each with one solid color. This is a quick way to render a scene and is often used for test animations. This mode is available to all materials by enabling the Faceted check box in the Shader rollout of the material.

- **Phong.** In this mode, MAX calculates the color at each vertex of the face and then interpolates the result across the polygon face. The effect is smoothly blended object surfaces that are much more realistic than a flat rendering's surface. In addition, *specular highlights* (the bright reflections of light seen on glossy objects) are added for more realism.

- **Blinn.** This mode is similar to Phong, but produces a more subtle highlight that tends to look a little more realistic.

- **Metal.** This mode provides enhanced highlights and deep rich colors with the material itself, giving the material a deep metallic appearance.

- **Oren-Nayer Blinn.** This mode is very similar to the Blinn mode; the difference is in the highlights. Oren-Nayer has a very subtle highlight, making this type of shading excellent for fabrics and other nonreflective surfaces.

- **Anisotropic.** This is the first shading mode that supports anisotropic shading. Anisotropic shading occurs when you have a bright highlight on a curved surface. In real life, this highlight has a tendency to get stretched in one direction or another. This shading mode enables you to create basic anisotropic effects in the context of a Blinn- or Phong-like rendering mode.

- **Strauss.** This shader is used to create enhanced metal effects and generally is better than the older metal shader.

- **Multilayer.** This shader is the last anisotropic shader. It is called a multilayer shader because it enables you to layer specular highlights on top of each other. If the highlights are different, you can create an anisotropic effect.

- **Raytracing.** In the raytracing method, the color and value of each pixel on the screen is calculated by casting an imaginary ray backward from the viewer's perspective into the model, to determine what light and surface factors are influencing it. The difference between raytracing and the other methods mentioned earlier (collectively called *scanline rendering* techniques) is that the ray can be bounced off of surfaces and bent—just like real light—producing excellent shadows, reflections, and refractive effects. MAX actually implements raytracing as a material instead of as a completely different rendering mode. This gives you the advantage of selectively raytracing objects in the scene, as well as just pure speed.

Figure 10.18 shows you examples of each type of shading level.

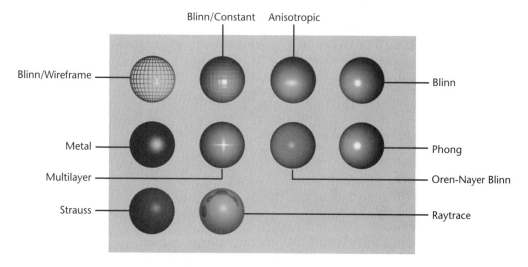

FIGURE 10.18 *The various rendering modes available in MAX 3.*

By correctly choosing the rendering level for each material, you can mix and combine different rendering methods within the same scene. This provides you with the ultimate in flexibility for controlling the materials and producing realistic scenes.

Material Properties

After you have set the rendering mode for the material, you set the material properties to define how the material looks. Material properties (sometimes called surface attributes) include color (which was covered earlier), but more often involve additional settings such as shininess or reflection.

Shininess and Shininess Strength

Shininess is the overall reflective nature of the objects—in other words, the glossiness. Shininess has an effect on the size of the specular highlight, with matte objects having larger highlights and shiny objects having smaller ones, as shown in Figure 10.19.

Shininess

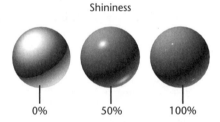

0%   50%   100%

FIGURE 10.19   *Shininess is a measure of an object's surface gloss. At 0% the material is matte, while 100% produces maximum glossiness. Note how the specular highlight shrinks as the object is made glossier.*

Shininess works together with Shininess Strength (sometimes called Specularity) to give the viewer information about the reflectivity and characteristics of the material, so pay attention to how the two affect a material's appearance.

Shininess Strength adjusts the intensity of the object's highlight, if it has one (see Figure 10.20). By adjusting the Shininess in combination with the Shininess Strength, you can create a wide range of glossy to matte materials.

Anisotropy

MAX 3 now supports Anisotropic rendering in three of its material shaders. Anisotropy is what happens to the specular highlight of a curved object when the light strikes the object at an angle. Anisotropic highlights are most notable when viewed through a camera lens and appear as horizontally or vertically stretched highlights, as shown in Figure 10.21.

Specularity

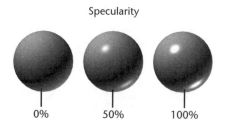

0%   50%   100%

Figure 10.20   *Shininess Strength sets the intensity of a material's highlight. Shininess and Shininess Strength work together to define an object's glossiness. It also plays a major role in simulating metallic materials.*

The amount of anisotropy in the material is fully controllable in MAX 3. You can create vertically squeezed highlights just as easily as horizontally squeezed.

Opacity

Opacity is a material attribute that controls the amount of light that can pass through an object. If opacity is set to 0%, the object is virtually invisible; if set to 100%, the object is opaque. Any other settings make the object more or less translucent, as shown in Figure 10.22.

In addition to setting a general opacity to the material, you can control exactly how the opacity is interpreted through extended material parameters. These options will be covered in Chapter 11, "Working with Lights and Cameras," and Chapter 12, "Fundamentals of Materials" where necessary.

Figure 10.21
A sphere rendered with Anisotropic shading. This type of highlight might appear on such objects as the glass canopy of a jet fighter.

Self-Illumination

Self-illumination adjusts how much an object appears to be lit from within. As the percentage of self-illumination increases, it flattens out the effects of the ambient and diffuse lighting sources until the object appears to be one solid value (see Figure 10.23). Self-illumination has no effect on specular highlights, however. Self-illumination is used in a variety of situations, most commonly when you have a bright light source such as the lights on a car. By making the lights self-illuminated, they appear brighter and more realistic.

Transparency

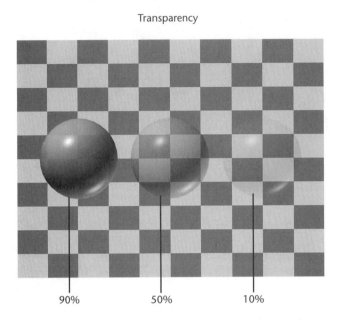

90%   50%   10%

FIGURE 10.22   *Opacity controls the amount of background imagery that can be seen through an object.*

Luminosity

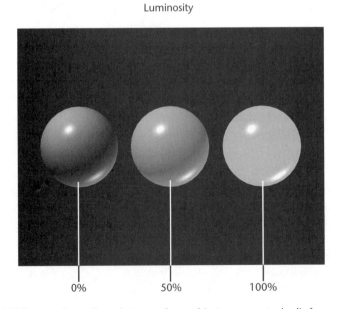

0%   50%   100%

FIGURE 10.23   *Self-illumination adjusts how much an object appears to be lit from within. 0% is completely unlit, while 100% is totally self-illuminated.*

Using Mapped Materials

Beyond the basic material properties, MAX can also make use of mapped material properties. Mapped materials (sometimes called Texture Maps) use either scanned-in bitmaps or procedural (mathematically defined) maps in place of such aspects of a material as the diffuse color. For example, to create a wood material, you can replace the diffuse color with an image of a real piece of wood. You can then adjust shininess and other parameters to make the wood appear more or less polished.

MAX provides you with many channels where you can make use of mapping in materials. Each is listed below and briefly described:

- **Ambient.** Replaces the ambient color of a material with a map. This is rarely used.

- **Diffuse.** Replaces the general color of a material with a map. This is the most common use of mapping. Materials generated this way rely on mapping coordinates on the objects themselves to correctly place the map on the surface of the object.

- **Specular.** The specular highlight of an object can be perturbed (distorted) with a map to give the appearance of a less smooth but still shiny surface. In this case, the intensity of the colors of the map determines where the highlight appears and where it doesn't. This helps to create materials that are less plastic-looking and more realistic.

- **Shininess.** Similar to a specular highlight but affects the shape of the highlight instead of just the colors.

- **Shininess Strength.** Enables you to use a map to vary the shininess strength.

- **Self-Illumination.** Enables you to use a map to control where an object is self-illuminated and where it is not.

- **Opacity.** Enables you to use a map to control where an object is opaque and where it is not.

- **Filter Color.** Enables you to adjust the colors of an object by using a map. This is generally only used with transparent objects, where you can see the background behind the object. The filter color is used to tint the transparent colors.

- **Bump.** Enables you to apply a 3D look to an object through the use of a map. This is the second most commonly used map and is used to give a surface the appearance of 3D geometry without ever having to create the geometry.

- **Reflection.** The property of a material to reflect its surroundings. Usually, you see reflection in highly polished or waxed surfaces such as new cars, silver goblets, or even water. MAX implements reflection as a procedural map that can be either raytraced or environmentally generated.

- **Refraction.** Refraction is the bending of light as it passes through an object such as water or glass. Refraction can be handled as a map or as a procedural map and can be raytraced.

- **Displacement.** Since MAX 2.5, materials have also had a displacement mapping channel. This channel is meant to be used on materials that are applied to NURBS objects to physically displace them. Unlike a Bump map, this type of mapping actually generates the NURBS geometry at render time.

note

The mapping channels listed here are the most common. Some materials, such as the raytrace material, have more mapping channels than those shown here.

Figure 10.24 shows you an example of each of these types of maps and their effects on a material.

FIGURE 10.24   *A wide array of material characteristics can be altered by using bitmaps in the different types of mapping available.*

Because mapped materials make use of a bitmap image, such as a GIF, Targa, TIF, or JPEG, they require mapping coordinates. Mapping coordinates are simply a method of telling MAX how and where to apply the bitmap to the surface of an object. You will see how to create and use mapping coordinates in Chapter 12.

Mapped materials also make use of procedural materials—materials that are defined by mathematical formulas instead of scanned images or colors. MAX provides you with several procedural materials, and many more are available as plug-ins from various developers. With this capability, you can create or have access to almost any kind of material property you might ever need.

After you have created and applied lights, cameras, and materials to your scene, you render the scene. *Rendering* is simply the process by which MAX takes into account all of the geometry, lights, materials, and cameras and produces an image. Rendering can take anywhere from a couple of seconds to minutes or even hours, depending on a wide variety of factors. Rendering is covered in Chapter 14, "Rendering".

Conclusion

In this chapter, you learned about the basic theories behind composition. In particular, you learned about the following:

- Cameras and how they are handled by MAX
- Lights and the variety of lights you can use in MAX
- Materials and how you can apply them to objects in a MAX scene

Lights, cameras, and materials all work together to take the geometry you have created and produce a photorealistic rendering of the scene, based on those settings. Actually, creating lights and materials is not a cut-and-dried process but more of "Try one setting and see if it produces the result you are looking for; if not, try again."

Now that you have a basic understanding of lights, cameras, and materials, it's time to see how to put them together to create a photorealistic scene. The next chapter covers how to create and use lights and cameras in a scene.

CHAPTER 11

Working with Lights and Cameras

Lights and cameras are key elements in producing a good rendering or animation. First, there is the camera. This provides a method for viewing your scene realistically. By carefully placing your camera, you compose the scene for the viewer. After it is composed, you light the scene by strategically placing one or more lights to achieve a variety of effects.

This chapter focuses on the techniques necessary to quickly yet accurately compose a scene. In particular, this chapter covers the following topics:

- Creating a Camera
- Manipulating Cameras
- Camera Perspective Matching
- Working with Lights
- Controlling Shadows
- Creating Basic Lighting Special Effects

Creating a Camera

3D Studio MAX provides two types of cameras: target and free. A target camera has an eye position (the location of the camera) and a target point (a 3D point in space) where the camera is looking. A free camera does not have a target but is otherwise the same.

The camera controls are located in the Create command panel under the Cameras button. Choosing this button reveals the two camera commands. If you click the Target button, you get the Target Camera rollout, where you can create a target camera. Figure 11.1 shows the rollout.

Creating a target camera is most easily done in the Top viewport, where you can easily select the camera and target locations and then simply move the camera and target vertically along the Z axis into the position you want. Of course, you can create cameras in any view, including the Perspective view.

To create the camera, click in the Top viewport at approximately the location where you want the camera to be. Drag toward the area of the scene where you want the camera to look, and then let go. A camera icon appears, as shown in Figure 11.2. This icon is representative of the camera and is not considered geometry; as such, it will not render in the scene.

FIGURE 11.1
The Cameras rollout where you can select and create the type of camera with which you want to view your scene.

Creating a Camera View

After you create the camera, you can transform the camera or the target independently or together to correctly position the camera. Of course, to make transforming the camera a little easier, it is a good idea to view what the camera is seeing. This means you need to convert one of the viewports to a Camera view, which you can accomplish by selecting the viewport and pressing the C key. The view switches to the currently selected camera. If no camera is selected and more than one exists in the scene, you get a dialog box that enables you to select the camera you want to use.

In this chapter, cameras are created before the lighting. You do not necessarily have to work in this order. You may create lights at any time. Because MAX creates default lighting of two omni lights for the scene, setting up cameras and a lot of other work can be done before lights are created. You might even want to create materials before you add lighting. The actual order of creating the scene is up to you.

Alternatively, you can switch the view through the Viewport Configuration dialog box or by right-clicking the name of the viewport and selecting the Camera view you want from the resulting pop-up menu. Cameras appear in the Views section of the menu under their own names.

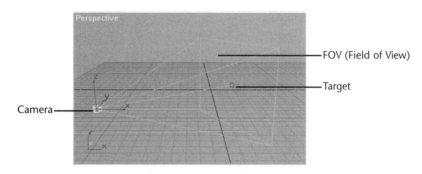

Camera

FOV (Field of View)

Target

FIGURE 11.2   *A typical Target Camera icon, showing you the camera, the target, and the field of view.*

After you create a Camera view, you can either use the MAX transform commands (except Scale) on the camera icons in the other viewports or use the Camera viewport controls to manipulate the Camera view, as described in the following section. Either way, you adjust the Camera view.

When you are happy with the view from the Camera viewport, you can select the camera and then adjust the camera parameters in the Modify command panel.

Working with Camera Parameters

After you create the camera, you can fine-tune it to match the view you are looking for. MAX has three sets of controls you can use to fine-tune a camera: Lens Length, Environment Ranges, and Clipping Planes.

Lens Length

The lens length is the most important camera parameter. If you remember from Chapter 10, "Understanding Composition Concepts," the lens length works in conjunction with the field of vision (FOV) to determine how much you can see in your Camera view. MAX 3 comes with nine presets that match 35mm camera lenses, such as 35mm, 50mm, and 200mm. Selecting one of these presets sets the Lens and FOV spinners. Alternatively, you can type in any value you might need for either spinner.

tip

A free camera is the same as a target camera but with one difference: A free camera does not have a target. Free cameras are intended for use in animation in which the camera is attached to a motion path or a trajectory. You can control the direction of the free camera by using any standard transform on the Free Camera icon. When you create and place a free camera, it appears perpendicular to the current construction plane and must be transformed to the correct position.

tip

Like all other objects in a scene, cameras can have individual names. If you are going to have more than one camera in your scene, giving them unique names makes it easy for you to pick the camera from a list, if necessary.

The FOV spinner in MAX is exceptionally flexible, enabling you to specify the FOV horizontally, vertically, or diagonally through the flyout toolbar to the left of the FOV spinner. These adjustments enable you to match almost any real camera you might run across. Adjusting the FOV in a different axis does not alter the aspect ratio of the camera—only the relative size in that particular direction. The other directions and the lens length adjust to match. As an option, you can also set your camera to an orthographic projection, but this is generally not used because it is the same as a User view, which nullifies the use of the camera.

Below the lens length presets are two noteworthy check boxes. First is Show Cone. A cone is a visible representation of the viewing area of a camera and is visible when the camera is selected. When this check box is active, the cone is visible even when the camera is not selected. This can be very useful when you are positioning objects in your scene and you do not have a Camera view visible. The other check box is the Show Horizon check box, which causes a black line (which does not show in the final rendering) to be drawn across the Camera viewport to represent the horizon. This line moves as you move the camera. Horizon lines are used in camera matching.

tip

When you are transforming a camera with MAX transforms, you need to select the camera, the target, or both. You can easily choose both by selecting the camera axis line that runs from the camera to the target.

upgrader's note

A new feature in MAX 3 is the capability to switch camera types in the Modify command panel. If you create a target camera and decide later that you want the camera to be a free camera, simply choose the correct type in the Modify command panel.

Environment Ranges

The next parameters are the Environment Ranges, which you use in conjunction with environmental effects, such as fog. You can set two types of ranges: Near and Far. By default, these are set to 0 and 1,000 units, respectively, and the near range can never be set larger than the far range. If you check the Show check box, you can visibly see the ranges on the Camera icon, as shown in Figure 11.3.

By adjusting the near and far settings, you can control where camera-dependent effects, such as fog, appear. Fog is an environmental effect that you can apply by selecting Render, Environment from the pull-down menus. Fog and other environmental effects are covered in Chapter 14, "Rendering."

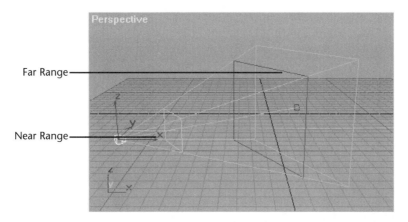

FIGURE 11.3   *The near and far camera ranges, used to control environmental elements, such as fog.*

Clipping Planes

Clipping planes are settings you can use to clip off either the front or rear of a Camera view. Clipping off the front removes all objects between the camera and the front clipping plane. You can use this to create such effects as cutting a hole in the side of a building to view into it. The far clipping plane removes any objects beyond that plane, which removes objects that would be too small to render. You can also use this feature to make objects disappear or appear in the distance.

Like environmental ranges, clipping planes have both near and far settings and show in the Camera icon when you activate Clip Manually. Figure 11.4 shows the resulting Camera icon.

After you have fine-tuned your camera, you will probably not need to make any further adjustments unless you animate the camera, which is covered in Chapter 16, "Exploring Basic Animation Methods."

The following exercise shows you how to create a few Camera views for a bowling alley scene.

Creating a Camera View

1. Load the file **MF11-01.MAX** from the accompanying CD. This is a simple bowling alley, as shown in Figure 11.5.

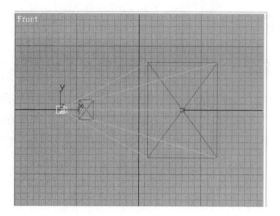

Figure 11.4   *The near and far ranges of a camera when viewed in a MAX viewport. You can use these to control certain camera-based effects, such as fog.*

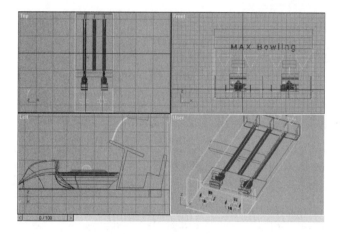

Figure 11.5   *The bowling alley scene before adding any cameras.*

2. In the Create command panel, select the Cameras button. Then, select Target in the rollout that appears.

3. In the Top viewport, click around the right side of the eating area and drag toward the other end of the bowling alley.

4. In either the Front view or the Side view, move the camera vertically 72 units.

5. Select the camera target and move it up 48 units so you are looking at a slightly downward angle along the length of the alley.

6. Activate the User view and press the C key on your keyboard to set it to the current Camera view. Figure 11.6 shows this view.

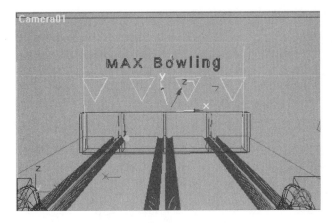

FIGURE 11.6   *The bowling alley viewed through the first camera.*

7. The view is a little too narrow in the Camera viewport. Select the camera and go to the Modify command panel.

8. Set the lens length to 35mm. This widens the view and makes it look better.

9. Save the file as **MF11-01a.MAX**.

10. Repeat steps 2–8 and create a camera that looks from the other end of the alley toward the eating area. Figure 11.7 shows you this Camera view.

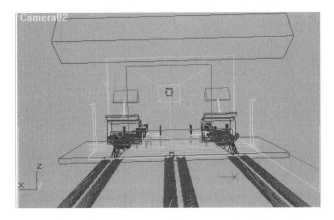

FIGURE 11.7   *The view of the bowling alley through the second camera.*

11. Save the file again.

The previous exercise illustrates how easy it is to create cameras inside of MAX, but cameras aren't particularly useful unless you light the scene so you can see what's going on.

Working with Lights

One of the most important—if not the most important—aspects of a high-quality rendering or animation is lighting. Lighting provides the illumination for the scene, as well as a sense of depth and realism through the use of shadow. A well-lighted scene always looks better than a scene with the greatest camera angles and materials but poor lighting. Lighting lends itself to experimentation and trial and error; even minor adjustments to the lighting of a scene can make the difference between a good scene and a great scene.

MAX provides you with four types of light to work with—ambient light, spotlights, omni lights, and directional lights. Ambient light is present in every scene, but you must create the others. Take a look at ambient lighting first, because it is always there.

Controlling Ambient Lighting

The most basic type of lighting in a scene is the ambient lighting, which gives the scene an overall brightness. If you remember from Chapter 10, ambient lighting is a general lighting applied to all objects in the scene. It is analogous to the lighting you see after the sun has set but before it gets dark, when everything is lit but there aren't any shadows. Ambient lighting is present in all scenes in MAX by default. In most cases, you never need to adjust the ambient lighting, but occasionally you will. A daytime scene works just fine with the default ambient lighting, for example, but a nighttime scene might require reducing the ambient light so that objects do not appear to almost glow in the reduced lighting.

You control the ambient light of a scene through the Environment dialog box, shown in Figure 11.8, which you access through the Render pull-down menu.

Ambient light is controlled through the color swatch under Global Lighting. By clicking on this swatch, you can access the color selector. Ambient light is interpreted as a shade of gray, with darker colors resulting in less ambient light. In general, then, all you have to do is adjust the Whiteness slider to adjust the ambient lighting. The default is 11,11,11 when interpreted as RGB.

FIGURE 11.8   *The Ambient controls in the Environment dialog box.*

Creating Lights

Creating a light in MAX is very similar to creating a camera. Some lights are created with sources and targets, like a target camera, whereas others are simple points, like a free camera. Beyond this similarity, working with lights is totally different. In addition to ambient lighting, the basic lights are Target Spot, Free Spot, Target Direct, Free Direct, and Omni, with the most common being Target Spot and Omni.

To create a target spotlight, you select the Target Spot command in the Create command panel for Lights. Then, you click at the location where you want the light. Drag out until you reach the target and then let go. Like a camera, the spotlight and target are individual objects you can transform individually by using the standard MAX transform commands. You can even set one of the viewports to be a Spotlight viewport, showing you the view from the selected spotlight. Figure 11.9 shows Target Spotlight and Omni Light icons and their parts.

An omni light is even easier to create. Simply selecting the Omni command and selecting a point in 3D space creates the omni light at that point.

tip

Many users choose to turn off the Ambient light completely (set the color to 0,0,0) and then set up additional lights in the scene to simulate reflected light. In general, this approach looks better but requires extra setup time and additional lights.

upgrader's note

The lights in MAX 3 support a new check box called Affect Ambient. This enables individual lights to affect only the ambient lighting and color of objects in a scene. You can use this if you need to fine-tune ambient lighting problems.

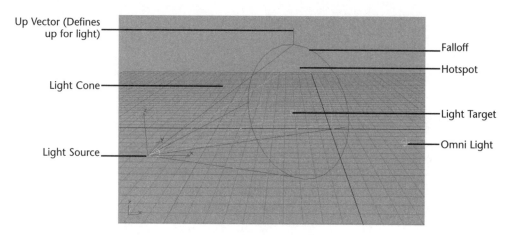

Up Vector (Defines up for light)

Falloff

Hotspot

Light Cone

Light Target

Omni Light

Light Source

FIGURE 11.9   *A spotlight, an omni light, and their parts.*

Also, as with cameras, after you create a light, you need to go back and fine-tune the light settings to create the effects you want. This is generally accomplished by selecting the light and going to the Modify command panel. Figure 11.10 shows you the rollout for a spotlight. Omni and direct lights have similar rollouts.

At the top of the Light rollout, notice two very handy check boxes: On and Cast Shadows. With the On check box, you can enable or disable a light without having to delete it from a scene—very handy for testing the influence of a light on a scene. Cast Shadows simply forces the light to cast shadows into the scene.

After you have created the light, you can go back to adjust and fine-tune its parameters to match the various aspects of your scene. One of the more important properties of a light is its color.

Setting the Light Color

To the right of the On check box in the Modify command panel rollout is the color swatch for the light, indicating the color of the light that is cast from this source. Below the color swatch are the RGB and HSV spinners for the light color. You can adjust these spinners to set the color of the light, or you can double-click the color swatch to use the MAX color selector.

FIGURE 11.10
The Spotlight rollout, where you can change the light parameters. Notice that different types of parameters are clearly defined by different rollouts.

The default color is 255,255,255—pure white. The light color you choose should reflect the light source type you are trying to simulate. For example, an incandescent light is a warm yellow when compared to the cold white of a fluorescent light.

All lights in MAX 3 also have a Multiplier spinner, which defines just how intense the light is. By adjusting the Multiplier, you can create low-intensity lights that have subtle effects on the scene, or completely blow out portions of the scene with highly intense lights. You can even set negative intensity values to remove light from the scene, if necessary.

upgrader's note

A new feature of MAX 3 lights is the capability to change the light type on the fly. In previous versions of MAX, you had to delete the light and then create the new one. Now you can simply select the light, go to the Modify command panel, and choose the light type you want from the Type drop-down list.

MAX 3 also provides a set of controls designed to affect the surfaces of objects. These controls include Contrast, Soften Diff. Edge, Diffuse, Specular, and Ambient Only and provide you with precise control over the lights and their effect on the ambient and diffuse color of a material. The Contrast spinner sets the amount of contrast between the ambient and diffuse material colors on a lighted surface. The default is a contrast of zero; by setting a higher contrast value, you can create harsh lights such as those that might be found in outer space.

The Soften Diff. Edge spinner enables you to soften the edge between diffuse and ambient lighting. This is most effective when you have two lights shining on the same surface such that a crossing pattern appears in the lighted area. Setting a value of 100 here eliminates that crossing but also results in slightly less light on the surface.

tip

The only useful way to test the effect of a light is to render the scene. Because these are test renders, you should use only the necessary geometry to minimize the amount of time necessary. Rendering is covered in Chapter 14, but you will be introduced to the basics of rendering during the exercises in the next three chapters.

Last, you can control which portion of the material color the light is affecting. For this, there are three check boxes: Diffuse, Specular, and Ambient Only. By default, both Diffuse and Specular are on and Ambient Only is off. With these controls, you can use one light to affect the diffuse color and another to affect the specular color differently. Of course, you might not want the light from a particular light source to affect every object in the scene, so MAX supports light includes and excludes.

Light Includes and Excludes

You can find the Exclude button to the right of the Light color swatch in the Light rollout. This button is actually the Include/Exclude button, depending on the type of operation you decide to use. Selecting this button displays a dialog box where you can select objects to be either included or excluded from the influence of the currently selected light (see Figure 11.11).

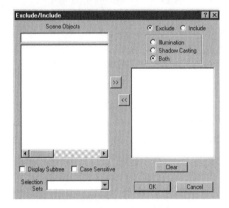

FIGURE 11.11   *The Light Include/Exclude dialog box, where you can select objects in the scene and include or exclude them from the influence of the light.*

You can select one or more objects from the left side of the dialog box and copy them to the list on the right. Then, depending on your settings at the top of the dialog box, the selected objects will be either excluded or included in the illumination, shadow casting, or both properties of the selected light.

Includes and excludes are very important for controlling light in a scene, especially when you want to illuminate only a single surface with a little extra light. Unfortunately, a single light can only exclude or include objects, but not both. If you need to do both, clone the light and use one light for excludes and the other for includes.

Light Attenuation

Lights can also be attenuated; in other words, you can control where they are in effect. In real life, the intensity of light dies off as you get farther away from the source. This is similar to attenuation. Attenuation also works like the ranges on a camera—you can set near and far ranges and where they start and end. Figure 11.12 shows a Light icon with near and far ranges.

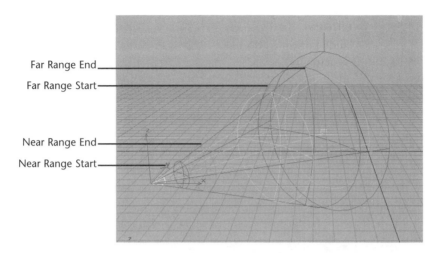

Far Range End

Far Range Start

Near Range End

Near Range Start

FIGURE 11.12   *A spotlight, showing the near and far ranges. You have both a start and end setting for both types of ranges.*

Another method of attenuation you can use is *decay*. Decay does not make use of the attenuation settings and forces a more realistic decrease of light over distance. There are three choices: None, Inverse, and Inverse Square. When set to None, the light has full intensity from start to end. With Inverse, the light is not reduced quickly, as shown in Figure 11.13. Figure 11.14 shows the Inverse Square option, which is considered to be fairly close to the way light decays in real life.

FIGURE 11.13   *A spotlight using an Inverse falloff. Notice how the light does not fall off very quickly.*

FIGURE 11.14   *A spotlight using an Inverse Square falloff. Notice how quickly and how much more realistically the light disappears.*

After the attenuation of lights, you can control specific parameters related to each type of light. A spotlight has the most parameters, such as shadow control, cone size, shape control, and others. These parameters are explored here. Other lights, such as omni lights, have a subset of spotlight parameters. An omni light has all of the shadow controls, for example, but does not have cone control because omni lights do not have light cones.

Hotspot and Falloff Controls

First, you can set the hotspot and falloff settings for the spotlight. These are given in degrees and represent the angle of the cone of light. In the hotspot (shown as a light blue in the Light icon), the light is constant at full intensity. Between the hotspot and falloff (shown as a darker blue line), the light reduces from full intensity to none. By adjusting these two parameters, you can create spotlights with crisp, sharp-edged shadows to very soft, very diffuse shadows, when shadows are enabled for the light.

No light will show outside of the hotspot and falloff ranges unless you turn on Overshoot, which forces the spotlight to become a point light that casts shadows only in the hotspot and falloff ranges but does cast light in all directions.

tip

Attenuation of lights is an important aspect of creating realistic renderings. Without attenuation, it is very easy to add too much light to a scene. Make sure you use attenuation whenever possible.

Of course, the basic spotlight uses a circular projection, but you can set the light to be rectangular by selecting the Rectangular radio button. When you do this, you can control the aspect ratio of the light, which is its ratio of width to height. Thus, you can create and control circular and rectangular shapes of light in MAX 3.

In addition, you can assign a bitmap to the rectangular light to turn it into a projector. This enables you to project the bitmap, as you would out of a film projector—great for creating effects such as a drive-in movie theater.

Working with Shadows

All of the basic light types in MAX 3 are capable of casting shadows, including omni lights. Shadows are very important to the realism of a scene. Without shadows, the scene does not have the 3D depth to make it look real. It can also be hard to tell where objects exist in the scene without shadows.

Look at Figure 11.15, which shows a box with a teapot on the surface. Without shadows, it is difficult to tell how high the object is above the box, but if you add shadows, as shown in Figure 11.16, the teapot is clearly sitting on the surface of the box below. Shadow control is very important.

FIGURE 11.15   *A teapot scene without shadow casting. It's hard to tell exactly where the teapot is in the scene.*

FIGURE 11.16   *The same teapot scene with shadow casting turned on. Notice how much more realistic the scene looks.*

MAX 3 provides two methods of creating shadows with lights: shadow maps and ray-tracing. By default, all lights created in MAX have shadow casting turned off. You can turn on shadows in two different places: in the General Parameters rollout or under the Shadow parameters of the Light rollout. You must turn on Cast Shadows for the light to have shadows. Once it is on, you select the type of shadows from the drop-down list in Shadow Parameters. The settings for the type of shadows you choose appear in a separate rollout.

You can select to use either shadow maps or raytraced shadows. Shadow maps make use of generated grayscale bitmaps to create the shadows, whereas raytracing physi-cally traces each shadow with rays. In general, shadow maps are used for speed and for soft shadows and raytracing is used for accurate, hard shadows.

Shadow maps are generally used when you do not need crisp, clear, hard shadows or highly detailed shadows. If you create a 3D tree, for example, and set a spotlight to cause the tree to cast shadows, the type of shadow to use depends on the type of lighting you want. On a crisp clear fall or spring day, you might use raytracing to get crisp shadows, but on a slightly over-cast or hazy day, a shadow map will do. Figure 11.17 shows a Douglas fir with shadow maps; the same fir is shown in Figure 11.18 with raytraced shadows.

note

MAX 3 now supports plug-in shadow engines. This means that in the future, you might see plug-ins for different meth-ods of generating shadows. One example might be a high-ly accelerated raytrace shadow plug-in.

Figure 11.17   *A tree casting shadows, using shadow maps. Notice how soft the shadows are.*

Figure 11.18   *The same tree, using raytraced shadows. Notice how crisp the shadows are.*

For shadow maps, there are three sets of controls: Bias, Map Size, and Sample Range.

- **Bias:** Controls how far away from the shadow-casting object the shadow will appear. The default is 4 units. For tight, accurate shadows, you might set this to 1 or even 0.

- **Map Size:** Determines the overall size of the shadow map. A default size of 256 creates a map 256×256 pixels in size. Larger maps are more accurate but use more memory exponentially. A map that is 2048×2048 will take a considerable amount of RAM. You should use the smallest map size possible and never use a map larger than 2048. If you need more accuracy than that, use a raytraced light.

- **Sample Range:** Determines how many times the shadow is sampled. Larger values are used here to prevent aliasing in the shadow, but at the cost of increased render time. Higher sample ranges also have the effect of softening the shadows even further. In MAX 3, this spinner can be set from 0 to 50, but you will rarely need to go above 20 or so. Raytracing has only a single Bias setting.

Both shadow maps and raytraced shadows support shadow color and shadow density controls that enable you to control exactly how the shadows appear in your scene. For example, if you want to create a brightly lit outside scene, you might have a dark-shadow color and density. If, instead, you want to simulate an overcast day, you can reduce the density significantly to quickly achieve this effect. The color can also have maps applied to it to define different types of effects, such as caustics.

After you create your lights and set the settings, you are ready to test-render the scene and make any adjustments that are necessary. The following exercise shows how to create several different lights, including omni and spotlights, for a typical kitchen scene.

Lighting a Kitchen

1. Load the file **MF11-02.MAX** from the accompanying CD. Figure 11.19 shows you the scene before adding any lighting.

2. In the Create command panel, click the Lights button and select Omni light.

3. In the Top viewport, click approximately in the center of the light in the middle of the room. In the Front viewport, move the light up until it is just below the light.

4. Go to the Modify command panel and set the following omni light parameters:

   Color: 255,253,226
   Cast Shadows: On
   Near Attenuation Use: On
   Near Attenuation End: 37.0

Far Attenuation Use: On
Far Attenuation Start: 94.0
Decay: Inverse Square

5. Activate the Camera view and click the Quick Render button on the Main Toolbar tab of the shelf. Figure 11.20 shows you the resulting rendering.

FIGURE 11.19   *The kitchen scene before adding any lighting.*

FIGURE 11.20   *The kitchen after creation of the first main light.*

6. Go back to the Create command panel. Lights should still be active. Click on the Free Spot button.

7. In the Top viewport, click above the sink in the center of the geometry representing the light. In the Front viewport, move the light up until it is just below the light again.

8. Go to the Modify command panel and set the following parameters for the free spot:

   Color: 255,253,236
   Cast Shadows: On
   Hotspot: 45
   Falloff: 75

9. Again, render the camera viewport by using Quick Render. Figure 11.21 shows you the resulting rendering.

FIGURE 11.21   *The kitchen after adding the second light, over the kitchen sink.*

Up to this point, you have created two of the main lights for illuminating the scene. Now you will create three additional lights—one for general lighting and two for special highlights.

10. Go back to the Create command panel and click Omni again.

11. In the Top viewport, click the center of the room, but on the camera side of the center island. In the Front viewport, move the light up until it is in the center of the room.

12. Go to the Modify command panel and set the following parameters:

    Color: 255,253,236
    Multiplier: 0.75

13. Activate the Camera viewport and choose Quick Render again. Figure 11.22 shows you the resulting rendering.

FIGURE 11.22   *The kitchen after adding a general illumination light.*

14. Now create two more omni lights. Place them above the kitchen countertops but below the upper cabinets. Place one on each side of the sink. Go to the Modify command panel and set the following parameters:

    Color: 255,253,236
    Cast Shadows: On
    Multiplier: 0.3
    Far Attenuation Use: On
    Far Attenuation Start: 34
    Far Attenuation End: 53

15. Render the scene again. You will now see subtle highlights on the countertops, indicating lights are present under the upper cabinets. Figure 11.23 shows you the final rendering.

16. Save the file as **MF11-02a.MAX**.

FIGURE 11.23   *The kitchen after adding the last set of lights.*

The last exercise demonstrates the importance of good lighting in a scene. It also shows that you need to do a lot of test-rendering to make sure the lighting is correct. You might take some time and try to create different lighting situations for the kitchen, such as special lighting for the stove.

Special-Purpose Lighting

You can use lights to create certain basic special effects that evoke a mood or are necessary for accurate lighting. With MAX 3, for example, you can use volumetric lights to create fog-filled lights or lights shining through misting water. As a matter of fact, most bright light sources that shine at night—such as searchlights—have some sort of volumetric quality about them.

Another type of special effect is the creation of a projector light that projects an image or sequence of images from a spotlight source. You can use this to create effects such as movie projectors or drive-in theaters.

Atmospheric Options

A volumetric light is a light that appears to have a foggy aspect to it wherever the light actually appears. Figure 11.13, earlier in this chapter, shows you an example of a volumetric light.

Volumetric lights are actually modifications of existing shadow-casting lights in your scene. To turn a light into a volumetric light, it must cast shadows and must use shadow maps. A raytraced shadow will not work. The only other requirement is that the scene must be rendered in a Camera viewport to see the volumetric light.

Volumetric lights are added and set up through the Environment dialog box, which you can access by selecting Rendering, Environment from the pull-down menus. They can also be set up by selecting the light and going to the Modify command panel. There you will find an Atmosphere and Effects rollout where you can add atmospheric and lens effects directly to the light. This is the quickest and easiest way to create volumetric lights.

To add a volumetric light, choose the Add button and select Volumetric light from the list of Environmental Effects. After you select the volumetric light type, the roll-outs for a volumetric light appear. Figure 11.24 shows you these rollouts.

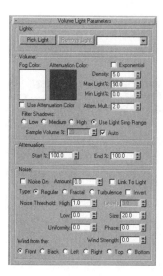

FIGURE 11.24   *The Volumetric Lights rollout, where you can define how the volumetric light appears in the scene.*

To add one or more lights to the volumetric effect, choose the Pick Light button and select various lights in the scene. When this is active, you can select only light objects, making the selection easier. As you select lights, their names are added to the drop-down list on the right.

After you have selected the lights to which you want to apply the same volumetric effect, set all of the volumetric parameters and then close the Environment dialog box. When you render the scene, MAX will automatically process the volumetric information. Volumetric light controls are broken down into three categories: Volume, Attenuation, and Noise.

The Volume controls enable you to set the color of the fog, as well as the density, minimum and maximum light percentages and the filtering of shadows. Most of the time, you will vary the Density, Color, and Min and Max spinners to control the effect.

You can use Attenuation to cause the volumetric effect to decay, along with the light source, if the light is making use of attenuation.

Last, you can apply various types of Noise to the volumetric light to make it appear less constant. Through the use of the Noise parameter, you can make the volumetric fog look like smoke or very subtle fog.

The following exercise shows how to add volumetric lights to a parking lot light to simulate a foggy evening.

Experimenting with Volumetric Lighting

1. Load the file **MF11-03.MAX** from the accompanying CD. Figure 11.25 shows you the scene at this point.

FIGURE 11.25   *The parking lot light with the basic lighting already set up.*

2. Using Select by Name, select FSPOT01.

3. Go to the Modify command panel and scroll down to the Atmospheres & Effects rollout.

4. Click on the Add button. Choose Volume Light and click OK in the dialog box that appears.

5. In the command panel, select the Volume Light entry and choose Setup. This opens the Environment dialog box. Set the following parameters:

Density: 1
MAX Light %: 75

6. On the Main Toolbar, choose Quick Render. Figure 11.26 shows you the resulting scene.

FIGURE 11.26   *The scene after adding a single volumetric light. Now the parking lot light seems to be shining through a fog.*

7. Repeat steps 2 through 6 for FSPOT02 to complete the scene.

As you can see, volumetric lights are powerful in the effects they can create, but they do come with the cost of longer rendering times. The more volumetric lights you have in a scene, the longer it will take to render. Use them only when necessary.

Working with Lighting Utilities

MAX 3 now supports two lighting utilities that were added to make working with lights easier. These utilities are actually MAXScript commands, which shows just how powerful MAXScript is (see Chapter 19, "A Brief Introduction to MAXScript," for more on MAXScript). The first utility to look at is the Light Lister.

Light Lister

The Light Lister is found on the Lights & Cameras tab of the shelf. When you click this button, a dialog box pops up and lists all of the lights that exist in the scene (see Figure 11.27). If no lights exist, it gives you an error message stating so and then exits.

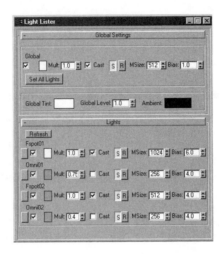

FIGURE 11.27   *The Light Lister dialog box, which provides simultaneous access to multiple light settings.*

This dialog box has two rollouts, one for global light settings and the other for individual lights. If you look at the individual lights listed in Figure 11.27, you will see a row of buttons, spinners, and color swatches for each one. The first blank button enables you to actually select the light. Then, you can turn the light on or off, change the color, set the multiplier, turn on or off shadow casting, and set the shadow parameters.

These controls represent 80 percent of the things you will most likely adjust in a light. With this Lister, you can now adjust multiple lights simultaneously. This prevents you from having to select each light, make the change, and then move to the next light.

Light Include/Exclude

The last lighting utility is an include/exclude utility also found on the Lights & Cameras toolbar. When you click this button on the toolbar, you get the dialog box shown in Figure 11.28.

FIGURE 11.28   *The Light Include/Exclude utility, which enables you to select one or more objects in the scene and then set include/exclude settings for each light.*

To make use of this utility, first select the objects in the scene you want to either include or exclude. Then launch the utility. Choose Assign to Light and click the light to which you want to assign the objects. If you want to see what objects are assigned to a particular light, click Choose Light and then select the light in the scene to display the object list at the bottom of the dialog box.

These utilities, along with all of the other lighting controls in MAX 3, provide you with a tremendous amount of control over the lighting you can create in MAX. Now all you need is practice setting up lights. Don't worry if you don't get the hang of it immediately—even experienced users are always experimenting with new ways to handle the lighting in their scenes.

Conclusion

This chapter showed you how to create lights and cameras for use in your scenes. In particular, you learned the following:

- How to create cameras
- How to adjust cameras
- How to create lights
- How to adjust lights
- How to create some basic lighting effects

You need cameras to view the scene in a way that looks correct. Cameras in MAX match the cameras used in the real world, so there is a nice correlation. After you have a view of the scene, you need to provide a greater sense of realism by illuminating the scene with various light types that are available in MAX.

After you have illuminated the scene, you are ready to apply materials. The next chapter focuses on how to create and apply basic materials to your scenes.

Fundamentals of Materials

Up to this point, you have seen how to model, illuminate, and view your scenes, but for the most part, no thought has been given to the objects in the scene, other than their shape. All objects in real life are made up of some sort of material, whether that material is plastic, wood, or plasma.

Materials are part of what brings a scene to life. With the correct creation and application of materials to objects, your scenes become more real. Just as there are many types of materials in the world, there are many types of materials you can work with in MAX.

This chapter focuses on working with the fundamental aspects of all materials, such as colors, and the next chapter focuses on texture-mapped materials. In particular, this chapter covers the following topics:

- Working with the Material Editor
- Working with Material Libraries
- Understanding Material Types
- Creating a Standard Material
- Assigning Materials to Objects
- Working with Materials Other than Standard

Working with the Material Editor

The key to working with materials in MAX is the Material Editor—a single dialog box through which you create, manipulate, and assign materials. You have three ways to access the Material Editor: by choosing the Material Editor button on the Main Toolbar tab of the shelf; by selecting Tools, Material Editor from the pull-down menus; or by pressing the M key. Figure 12.1 shows the Material Editor.

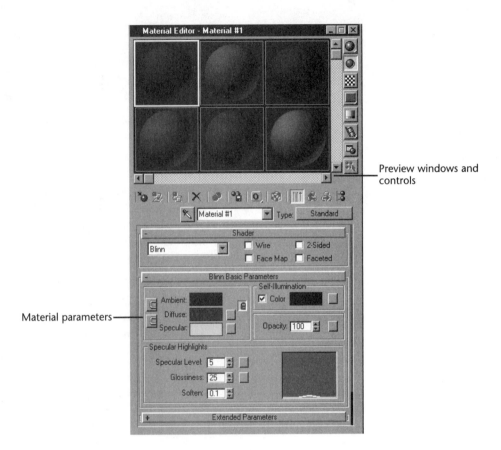

FIGURE 12.1   *The MAX Material Editor, where you can load, create, save, and assign materials in your scene.*

The Material Editor is broken down into two basic sections: the preview windows and the material controls. The preview windows provide a sample of what the material would look like on a sample object. The material controls enable you to actually manipulate and change the currently selected material. First, take a look at how to use the Material preview windows.

Manipulating the Previews

When you first open the Material Editor in a new scene in MAX, there are six material preview windows, representing materials 1 through 6. (Later in this chapter, you will see how to open 15, or even 24, preview windows.) Like objects, MAX materials can have (and should have) individual material names. Until you change the names, MAX names the basic materials Material #1 and so forth.

The preview windows make use of the default MAX scanline renderer, which means that the preview of the material is just as accurate as the final rendering will be. You can configure the preview windows to use any plug-in rendering engine you have installed in MAX, and you should configure the Material Editor to use the engine with which you are going to render the scene. This helps give you an accurate preview of what the material will look like when you load it into the scene. Run Windows 95/98 or NT at 24-bit color for best viewing of the material previews.

A white box surrounding the material preview indicates the currently selected material. When a material is selected, its parameters appear in the rollouts below the preview windows. As with the MAX viewports, you can make any material preview window and the material associated with that window active simply by clicking it.

On the right side of the preview windows is a column of buttons. These are the Material Editor Preview Window controls, which enable you to control some of the basic features of the material previews. Figure 12.2 shows these buttons and their names.

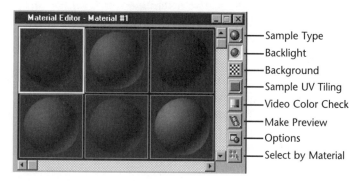

FIGURE 12.2   *The Material Editor preview window controls, with which you can define how the material previews look in the sample windows.*

Each of the Material Editor preview window controls provides you with control over a specific aspect of the Material Editor preview window. For example, the Sample Type button enables you to select the type of geometry that appears in the preview window. You can select box, cylinder, or sphere. You can also configure MAX to use any custom object as a sample type.

The Material Editor previews are lit by two omni lights, one in front and one in the rear to provide backlighting. The Backlight button enables or disables the backlighting. Because most objects have some sort of backlighting to bring out the details in the shadows, this is usually left on.

Some materials that are somewhat transparent—such as glass or water—are difficult to see in the default material preview window. You can use the Background button to set the background of the preview window to either gray or a colored checkerboard. For materials that use maps, the Sample UV Tiling button sets the number of times the sample bitmap is repeated over the surface of the object, so you can preview the material as it would look tiled.

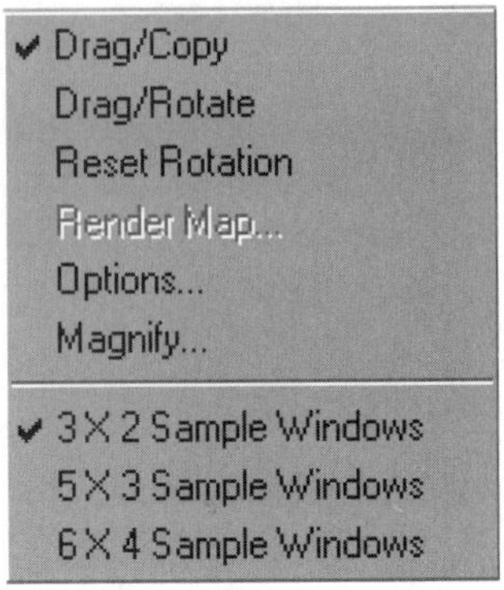

For output to video tape, you can use the Video Color Check button to check the colors of the material versus a video output color palette, such as the NTSC or PAL video formats. This enables you to check your material for colors that are illegal or unreadable under those video formats. Video Color Check relies on the Rendering Preferences to determine which format to use. Along the same lines, you can use the Make Preview button for quick previews of any materials that have animated material properties.

FIGURE 12.3
The preview window pop-up menu, where you can access various controls and settings for the preview windows.

The last two buttons don't affect the material previews but are still very useful. Options enables you to set the various options for the Material Editor previews, such as lighting, custom objects, and antialiasing. The Select by Material button enables you to select one or more objects in the scene that have the current material assigned to them. This command makes use of the Select by Name dialog box, but only objects with the current material show in the list.

Beyond these basic material preview controls, you can also set different preview settings by right-clicking any preview window to bring up the pop-up menu shown in Figure 12.3. You can quickly configure the preview windows, such as setting the number of visible material preview slots or loading a custom object into the preview through the Options entry on the menu.

Through the Preview Window pop-up menu, you can set and control several features. First, you can set the mouse state for the preview window. The default is Drag/Copy, which enables you to drag the current material preview and drop it on another preview window to make a copy of the material. You can also use this feature to assign materials to objects in the scene by dragging the material preview and dropping it on the object.

You can also set the mouse type to Drag/Rotate. This essentially gives you the viewport command Arc Rotate in the material preview. When Drag/Rotate is active, the mouse cursor changes to the same cursor as Arc Rotate. All clicks and drags end up rotating the sample object. You can reset the rotation when you have finished.

tip

If you have a three-button mouse, such as a Logitech MouseMan, the middle button enables the Drag/Rotate feature without a need to choose it from the right-click menu.

At the bottom of the preview window pop-up list, you can select from three viewport configurations. The default six windows are actually a 2×3 grid of preview windows. You can select 5×3 and 6×4 to work with more materials at once. Figure 12.4 shows the Material Editor with 6×4 loaded.

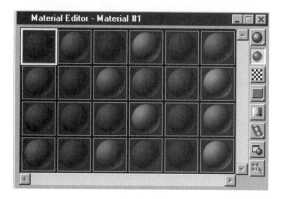

FIGURE 12.4   *The Material Editor, showing a 6¥4 material preview sample setup. This is the maximum number of previews that can be visible at one time.*

With the 5×3 or 6×4 Material Editor preview options, the preview windows have a tendency to get fairly small, even on large displays. Fortunately, the pop-up menu has a Magnify option that creates a resizable dialog box to give you a larger preview. Magnify is also available when you simply double-click on the preview window itself. Because this dialog box uses the scanline renderer, updates to the Magnify preview window might take a few seconds when you're using maps or procedural materials, especially if you made the window fairly large. Figure 12.5 shows the Magnify window.

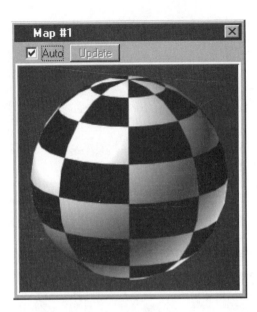

FIGURE 12.5   *The Magnify window, where you can generate larger previews of the material with which you are working.*

The last option of the pop-up menu is the Options button, which enables you to configure the rest of the Material Editor options. The resulting dialog box is shown in Figure 12.6.

As mentioned earlier, the material previews make use of two omni lights to illuminate the sample object. In the Material Editor Options dialog box, you can set the light color and multiplier values for each light so you can more closely approximate the lighting in your scene. You can also set the Material Editor to use a custom sample object by selecting the blank button to the right of File Name. If you elect to use this option, you should try to use relatively simple custom objects; using more complex objects results in longer preview times. Use custom objects to see what the material will look like on an object that is more complex than a cube, cylinder, or sphere. This way, you can make use of the preview windows instead of having to render the entire scene or portion of a scene to see the material on the object.

If you use plug-in renderers, such as RayMAX or Comicshop, you can set the Material Editor to use that rendering engine instead of the default MAX scanline rendering engine to create the material previews. This requires the plug-in rendering engine to be set as the current rendering engine in the MAX Preferences. You can do this by choosing File, Preferences, and going to the Rendering tab in the Preferences dialog box. There you will find the buttons that enable you to select both the production and draft rendering engines.

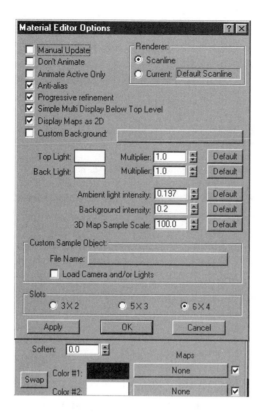

FIGURE 12.6   *The Material Editor Options dialog box, where you can change how the Material Editor looks and works.*

The material preview controls are very powerful in helping you see what the material will look like under just about any condition, before you ever apply it to an object. But they are only part of the Material Editor; the rest is the actual material controls themselves

Loading Materials

The material controls enable you to load, save, assign, and manipulate materials in the Material Editor. The material controls include everything below the material previews, including the buttons and the material rollouts. Figure 12.7 shows these controls.

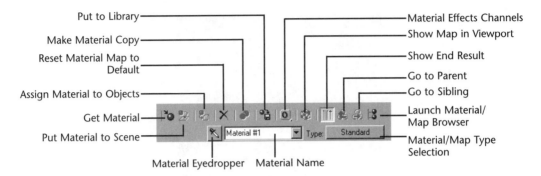

FIGURE 12.7   *The material controls in the Material Editor. Here, you can load, save, and edit the materials directly.*

Above the rollouts and below the preview windows in the Material Editor is a set of buttons that enable you to load and assign materials in MAX. You can use the Get Material button to start the material/map browser, where you can load new materials or maps or previously created materials from a library into the current material slot. If you make a copy of a material with the same name as a material already in the scene, you can use Put Material to Scene to replace the material properties of the existing material with the new material.

Use the Assign Material to Selection button to assign the material in the current active slot to the current active object selection. This works very well for both single object selections and multiple object selections. If you want to reset a material to its default settings, you can use the Reset Map/Mtl to Default Settings button. Then, you can start the material from scratch if you want. Another method for creating a new material is to use the Make Material Copy button, which makes a copy of the current material, with all the parameters the same, including the name. Then, you can simply change the name and the parameters as you want, to create a new material.

Of course, after you create a new material or set of materials, you should save it to a library so you don't have to create it again. The Put to Library button saves the material in the active slot to the currently loaded material library.

The Material Effects Channel button assigns the material a channel effect number, which is used in Video Post to apply special effects (such as a glow) to objects or parts of objects, based on their materials. You can assign a total of 16 material effects channels to various materials. These are covered in Chapter 18, "Exploring Post Processing Techniques."

When working with materials that have a bitmap or procedural map applied to them, you can use the Show Map in Viewport button to make the current bitmap visible in the interactive renderer when the viewport shading level is set to Smooth + Highlights.

Like an object with a long modifier stack, materials can have multiple levels of effects. You can use the Show End Result button to isolate a specific section of the material you are working on or to enable you to see the material with all sections active. Along a similar line, in complex materials with many levels of effects, you can use the Go to Parent button to navigate from one level to another. For example, multi-sub-object materials have several levels of material controls. In a multi-sub-object, more than one material is assigned, and each is assigned to different material IDs. The overall material is the parent. The Go to Sibling button enables you to move sideways in the material hierarchy, rather than vertically.

The last button spawns the Material/Map Navigator dialog box, which you can use to navigate through the materials and maps of the currently selected material. This is a convenient way to drag part of a material back into the same material, such as copying a bitmap into the bump channel. This dialog box is different from the browser and is used only for information purposes. Figure 12.8 shows the Material/Map Navigator dialog box.

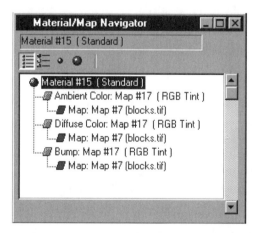

FIGURE 12.8   *The Material/Map Navigator, where you see which maps you are using in a particular material.*

Like the MAX commands and modifiers in the command panels, the Material Editor makes use of rollouts. Each material has six basic rollouts: Shader, Shader Basic Parameters, Extended Parameters, SuperSampling, Maps, and Dynamic Properties.

The Shader rollout enables you to select the type of shading algorithm to be used in the material. MAX supports seven shading methods, which will be explored later in this chapter. You can also set four specific rendering features, such as faceted or wire rendering.

The Shader Basic Parameters rollout changes, depending on the type of shader you select in the Shader rollout. For example, if you select the Blinn shader, this rollout is titled the Blinn Basic Parameters rollout. These Basic Parameters include such features as color, shininess, and opacity. Many simple materials, such as plastic, make use of only basic parameters. With the Extended Parameters rollout, you have greater control over material properties such as opacity, wireframe rendering, and reflection dimming.

The Maps rollout provides you with the capability to assign bitmaps or procedural maps to various material properties. For example, instead of assigning a color to the overall color of the material, you can assign a map. Some map controls are also located in other rollouts—for example, the Diffuse map slot. If you look in the Shader Basic Parameters rollout, you will find a blank button next to the Diffuse color swatch. You can use this button to assign the map if you don't want to go through the Maps rollout. The Dynamic Properties rollout provides you with a set of commands to set the properties when you use the MAX dynamics system. These properties are covered in Chapter 17, "Exploring Other Animation Methods."

As you can see, the Material Editor is a powerful interface you can use to create just about any type of material you want. Now that you are familiar with the interface, it is time to look at how to create some simple materials, such as paints, plastics, and metals.

Assigning Materials to Objects

One of the more important aspects of working with a material is the ability to assign the material to objects in the scene. MAX provides two primary methods for accomplishing this. First, you can click and drag the material preview and drop it on the object to which you want to assign the material. As you place the cursor over the object, a Tooltip appears, telling you the name of the object so you know exactly which object it is. This works well for individual material assignments.

The other method involves selecting one or more objects in the scene. Then, with the objects selected, choose the Assign to Selected button in the Material Editor to assign the current material to the objects. This is the best method to use when you need to assign the same material to more than one object at a time. Of course, you should choose the method that is easiest and makes the most sense for you.

Eventually, you will assign a material to an object and then want to edit the material; however, because of the large number of materials in your scene, the material might no longer be loaded in a preview window and you might not remember the name you assigned to it. This presents a problem that is easily solved in several ways. First, in the Material Editor, next to the Material Name drop-down list, find the Eyedropper button. Selecting this and then clicking an object in the scene loads the material on that object into the current material slot. This is the easiest method.

You can also opt to choose Get Material and then set the Browse From options to Scene, which displays all of the materials in the scene. To the right of each material, MAX lists the objects that have the material assigned to them. Furthermore, you can use object properties to find out the name of a material assigned to an object, or you can use MAX's Summary Info to see what materials are assigned to objects.

Assigning materials to objects is relatively easy, as is retrieving materials from the scene into the Material Editor, even when you have forgotten the name of the material.

Working with Material Libraries

The Material/Map Browser, shown in Figure 12.9, is your only method for browsing and managing the materials with which you are currently working. Because you are working with a browser, you can browse materials and maps from a variety of sources. As a matter of fact, there are six sources you can select from the Browse From section of the dialog box: Mtl Library, Mtl Editor, Active Slot, Selected, Scene, and New.

The Mtl Library button enables the display of materials that are contained in the current material library. When this is enabled, the library file functions appear at the bottom left of the Material/Map Browser so you can open, merge, and save library files. Library files have a .MAT extension and are generally saved in a Matlibs directory under your 3D Studio MAX installation, but they can be saved and loaded from anywhere on the system.

The Merge function enables you to merge the material library from a specific MAX file so you can use materials that were used in that file.

The Mtl Editor button displays materials that are currently in the Material Editor. Because there are 24 slots in the Material Editor, a list of 24 materials appears when active, regardless of the number of materials you have created.

You can also display new materials or materials that are in the active slot, assigned to the currently selected object, or assigned in the current scene, by selecting the appropriate option.

FIGURE 12.9   *The Material/Map Browser, where you can select materials and maps for use in your scene.*

At the top of the Material/Map Browser dialog box are seven buttons that enable you to further control the display of the materials in the browser. The four buttons on the left define whether or not a material preview is active, and if so, how large the preview is. Figure 12.10 shows the library material list with material previews active.

FIGURE 12.10   *The Material/Map Browser with material previews enabled.*

The three buttons on the right provide additional library functions. The first button is Update Scene Materials from Library. This updates all of the materials in the scene with the materials of the same name from the current library. Next is Delete from Library, which deletes the selected material from the current library. Last is the Clear Library button, which deletes all of the materials in the current library. This is essentially how you create a new material library. Delete all the materials in the current one, add new materials to the library, and then use Save As to save the library under a different name.

The following exercise shows you how to add some materials to a material library.

Creating a Material Library

1. Load the file **MF12-01.MAX** from the accompanying CD. The file doesn't have any geometry. After you have opened the file, open the Material Editor, if it isn't already open.

2. In the Material Editor, click on the Get Material button.

3. Set Browse From to Mtl Library.

4. Choose Clear Library. Click on the Material Editor to return to it.

5. The first four material preview slots at the top of the editor contain materials defined in the MAX file. You want to save these to a material library. To do this, select each new material in the Material Editor and choose the Put to Library button. When you do so, you will be asked to give the material a name. Each material already has a name, so choose OK. As you add them, they appear in the Material/Map Browser.

6. In the Material/Map Browser, choose Save As.

7. Name the file **MF12.MAT** and save it to your Matlibs directory.

   As you can see from this exercise, creating and saving a material library is very easy. Now see how easy it is to load materials from a library and assign them to objects in a scene. The following exercise shows you how to assign predefined materials to the table scene from Chapter 4.

Loading and Assigning Materials

1. Load the file **MF12-02.MAX** from the accompanying CD. This is the table scene from Chapter 4 with a torus knot and a teapot on the table, as shown in Figure 12.11.

2. Open the Material Editor in MAX.

3. Choose Get Material. In the Material/Map Browser, select Browse From, Mtl Library and then choose File, Open.

4. Select the file **MF12.MAT** from the accompanying CD (or the file you created earlier in this chapter). This loads four materials.

5. Double-click the Red Metal material. This assigns it to material slot #1.

6. Click on the Material Editor to make it active, but leave the Material/Map Browser open.

FIGURE 12.11   *The table scene before adding any materials. Now you will select each object and add a material to it.*

7. In the MAX scene, select the torus knot that is on the table.

8. Choose Assign Material to Selection to assign the materials. Notice that when you do this, the material preview window has four white triangles in the corners to indicate that the material is active and assigned in the scene.

9. Click in slot #2 to activate that slot. Click on the Material/Map Browser window. Double-click on the Blue Glass material to assign it to the slot.

10. Select the teapot and assign the Blue Glass material to it.

11. Activate another material slot and assign the Green Metal material from the library to it.

12. Select the table and assign the material to it.

13. Activate another material slot and assign the Beige Floor material to it.

14. Assign the Beige Floor material to the floor plane object.

15. Close the Material Editor and the Material/Map Browser. Activate the Perspective viewport and click on the Quick Render button on the Main Toolbar tab of the shelf. The results are shown in Figure 12.12.

FIGURE 12.12   *The scene after applying four basic materials to it.*

16. Save the file as **MF12-01a.MAX**.

This exercise shows you how easy it is to load predefined materials, assign the materials to objects, and then quickly generate a rendering of a scene. As you build material libraries over time, you will find yourself repeating these steps many times over. Now that you have seen how to handle materials, take a closer look at the types of materials available to you in MAX 3.

Understanding Material Types

When you look at the Material/Map browser in the Material Editor, you can see the materials available to you, but if you set the Browse From option to New, you get a list of material types (shown in blue dots) or material maps (shown in green parallelograms) When you load a material, you essentially create a new material with basic parameters. MAX provides several material types you can make use of that are extremely powerful. In addition, you can purchase plug-in material types to add even more material types to MAX.

MAX provides 10 material types, including Standard, Blend, Composite, Double-Sided, Matte/Shadow, Morpher, Multi-Sub-Object, Raytrace, Shellac, and Top/Bottom. Each is briefly described in the following sections.

tip

You can find plug-ins for MAX in many places on the Internet. Common places to look include MAX3D (http://www.max3d.com), Digimation (http://www.digimation.com), or the Discreet Web site (http://www.ktx.com). The Discreet Web site provides links to many more plug-in manufacturers.

- **Standard:** The most common material. Seventy-five percent or more of the materials you create will make use of the Standard material type. Almost all of the parameters found in the standard material are present in other materials as well.

- **Blend:** Simply blends two separate materials (whether they are standard materials or others) by adjusting the strength as a relative percentage. A strength of 50 gives each material equal weight in the blending process.

- **Composite:** Very similar to blend, with several exceptions. A composite material can use more than two materials to combine together. Compositing can combine materials by adding the colors together, subtracting their colors, or multiplying them.

- **Double-Sided:** Used where you are rendering a model with Two-Sided turned on. In this case, both sides of a face are rendered, regardless of the direction of the face normal. This option enables you to apply a material to both sides of the face. Normally, in two-sided rendering, the material on the normal side of the face is repeated on the back side.

- **Matte/Shadow:** Special materials used only under specific circumstances. This material type, when assigned to an object, renders the object invisible in the scene. It does allow the background image or color to show through, and it can receive shadows. As such, it's great for compositing work when you are adding objects on top of a digitized image or animation. Then you can create objects in your scene to mask the animation. A good example might be compositing a plane flying over a lake. If you want the plane to cast a shadow on the lake, you need to use this Matte/Shadow material, applied to an object that is roughly in the position where the lake would be. As the scene is rendered, the object is made transparent to the background image but still receives shadows.

- **Morpher Material:** Designed specifically to work with the Morpher modifier, this option is used to morph from one material to another in the scene, just as you can morph from one object to another.

- **Multi/Sub-Object:** One of the more popular alternative materials, this enables you to assign multiple materials to a single object. Multi/Sub-Object materials are used when you want to keep complex objects as a single object but apply different materials to different portions of the same object.

  In this material, there are submaterials that can be any type of material. The default Multi/Sub-Object material has 10 submaterials. These are assigned a number from 1 to 10 and can each be given a name. If you remember Chapter 6, "Mesh Modeling Tools," and the face-level editing commands, you can select a set of faces and assign them a unique material ID number. This number corresponds to the material number from the Multi/Sub-Object material.

  If you assign a material ID of 3 to a set of faces and then assign a Multi/Sub-Object material to that object, the material in channel #3 of the Multi/Sub-Object material will be assigned to those faces.

- **Raytrace:** The Raytrace material is one of the more complex materials in MAX. It is designed to give you true raytracing capabilities in MAX on an object-by-object basis. Raytracing is used to create effects such as reflection and refraction in the scene. The problem is that it is a time-consuming process. Instead of raytracing the entire scene, you can assign the Raytrace material to objects so that only those objects are traced, thus saving you time. This material also has special features enabling effects such as Black Light or Fluorescent. This material is explored more fully in Chapter 13, "More on Materials."

- **Shellac:** This is a new material for MAX 3 (it was previously available as a shareware plug-in) that enables you to create a shellacked look on an object. It works by combining two materials—a base material and a shellac material. This is a great material for highly polished woods and furniture.

- **Top/Bottom:** Enables you to apply two materials to the same object, basing their placement on a percentage distance from top to bottom. For example, you can set a position value of 50 to set the material division halfway up the object.

  A Top/Bottom material is made up of two materials, the top and bottom materials, which can be swapped. As with other materials that make use of submaterials, you can turn individual materials on and off at will.

As you can see, the various material types in MAX give you enough power and flexibility to spend literally years developing different materials for different purposes. With the addition of plug-in materials, this power is extended even further. Take a look now at how to create a standard material.

Creating a Standard Material

The standard material contains all of the basic material properties you would use to create most of your materials. For example, a teak wood material and a flat white paint material are both created as standard materials. For the most part, you will use standard materials to create most of your materials. The default settings for the Material Editor create standard materials. The process for creating a material is relatively simple, as demonstrated in the following exercise.

Creating Materials

1. Select a material preview window to be active. If all material windows are in use by current materials, you can select the Get Material button to start a new material. This spawns the Material/Map Browser (see Figure 12.9), where you can select the material type or map type to work with. For a standard material, double-click Standard.

2. Just below the Material Preview slots is a drop-down list showing the name of the material (see Figure 12.7). Because you just created the material, it should be named Material #**n**, where **n** is the next available material number. You should rename the material to something more appropriate, such as Yellow Plastic or Blue Glass or whatever material you are about to create.

3. After you name the material, use the Shader and Basic Parameters rollouts to set the shading level, colors, shininess, opacity, and other basic parameters.

4. If necessary, set any extended parameters.

5. When you are happy with the material preview, assign the material to one or more objects in the scene. You can accomplish this in two ways. First, you can click and drag the material preview and drop it on the object. Second, you can select the object and—with the material active—choose the Assign Material to Selection button in the Material Editor. You will know that the material has been assigned in a shaded viewport because the color of the object should change immediately to that of the new material.

6. When material is assigned, the active material preview window shows white triangles in the corners, indicating that the material is now "hot." In other words, if you make any changes to the material at this point, they are immediately reflected in the scene.

   After you have assigned the material or materials, test-render the scene and make any adjustments you see fit in the context of the lighting and cameras from the scene. Now take a closer look at some of the material properties you can control.

Working with Basic Material Parameters

When you create a new standard material, the Shader rollout appears by default. This rollout, shown in Figure 12.13, enables you to change the basic properties of the material. As such, it is the most commonly used rollout.

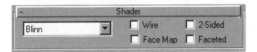

FIGURE 12.13   *The Shader rollout, where you can define the shading algorithm and type of rendering to be used in the material.*

First, you can select the shading level for the material. In this case, you have a choice of seven different levels: Anisotropic, Blinn, Metal, Multilayer, Oren-Nayer Blinn, Phong, and Strauss. Each of these levels was described in Chapter 10, "Understanding Composition Concepts." Selecting the correct shading level has a large impact on the overall quality and believability of the materials. A glossy metal surface is difficult to create without using the Metal or Strauss shading level, for example. By contrast, a flat paint is easier to create with a Blinn or Oren-Nayer Blinn shading level, and plastics are easier with Phong. As you work with the various shading levels, you will gain experience and get a better feel for when to use each shading level.

To the right of the shading level are four check boxes for rendering parameters for the material. For example, 2-Sided forces the material to render on both sides of a face, and Wire forces the material to become a wireframe version, as shown in Figure 12.14. When you have a texture-mapped material, use Face Map to force one copy of the texture maps onto one face. The last is Faceted, which forces the object to be rendered without using any smoothing.

For each material shader you choose, you receive a different Basic Parameters rollout. Most of the controls are the same for each shader type, but how they are implemented varies. For example, a Blinn material shader has Shininess and Shininess Strength spinners to control the highlights on a material. The Anisotropic shader has Specular Level, Glossiness, Anisotropy, and Orientation controls for the same effects. What's different is the fact that the Anisotropic shader can create a noncircular highlight, but a Blinn cannot. Take a look at the basic parameters for a Blinn shader first, as shown in Figure 12.15.

upgrader's note

MAX 2 and earlier versions had a Constant shader. This has been replaced by the Faceted check box, with which you can create constant-like renderings for any shading mode.

Figure 12.14   *A teapot rendered by using the Wireframe shading option. It still uses the material properties, but only the wireframe edges are rendered.*

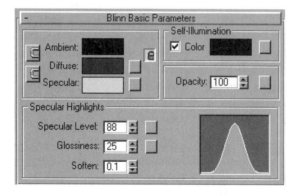

Figure 12.15   *The Blinn Basic Parameters rollout, where you can define such properties as the color, shininess, or opacity of a Blinn shaded standard material.*

The most important part of a Blinn material is, of course, the colors. There are four color swatches you can work with: Ambient (the color of the material in shadow), Diffuse (the general color of the material), Specular (the color of any highlights on the material), and Filter (the color of transparent materials when filtered over a background image). You can adjust colors by double-clicking the color swatch and using the MAX color selector.

Some colors can be "locked" together; if you change one color, the other locked color changes to match. Ambient and Diffuse can be locked, as can Diffuse and Specular, through the two buttons at the far left of the color swatches. You might want to lock two colors together to ensure consistent colors across the surface of the object.

To the right of the color swatches are three smaller, blank buttons. These buttons launch the Material/Map Browser and enable you to replace that color of the material with a bitmap or procedural map. This same bitmap will appear in the Map rollout.

Below the color swatches, you can set the Shininess and Shininess Strength spinners. To the right is a graph of the shininess of the material, enabling you to see a visual representation of how strong the specular highlights are. To the left of this graph is a Soften spinner that enables you to soften specular highlights, if necessary.

Last, you can set the Self-Illumination and Opacity spinners. Self-illumination is used to make the material brighter, as though it has its own light source. This is good for effects similar to neon light. Self-illumination can be controlled in two different ways. The most basic method is to adjust the color swatch. Bright colors result in brighter materials. You can even tint the material to a particular color if you like. Alternatively, you can turn off the check box and adjust the Self-Illumination spinner, which simply makes the material brighter.

The Opacity spinner controls how transparent the material is. When using the Opacity spinner, it is a good idea to set the material preview background to a checkerboard or bitmap so you can better see the transparency of the material.

As mentioned earlier, different shading types use different Basic Parameters rollouts. Figure 12.16 shows you the Anisotropic rollout, which has different controls for the highlights.

The most notable difference between the Anisotropic shader rollout and the Blinn rollout is the highlight graph. Now, you have a 3D graph of the highlight. This is necessary for visualizing the anisotropic highlight. By adjusting the Anisotropy spinner, you can make the highlight narrower or wider. With the Orientation spinner, you can rotate the specular highlight. Thus, you have a much higher degree of control over the highlight. Remember that a noncircular highlight is much more realistic for materials such as metals.

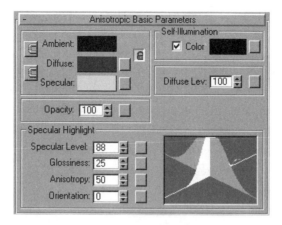

FIGURE 12.16   *The Anisotropic Basic Parameters rollout, where you can set up the color, opacity, and highlights for an anisotropically shaded standard material.*

Having said all that, it is time to see how to create some basic materials. The following exercise shows you how to create the four materials you used in the previous exercises in this chapter: a Red Material, Blue Glass, Green Metal, and a Beige Floor. One of the materials will make use of a map—a good introduction to using maps.

Creating a Red Material

1. Open the Material Editor in a new MAX session.

2. Click the first material slot to make it active. In the Name drop-down list, set the name to Red Material instead of Material #1.

3. For this material, select Oren-Nayer Blinn from the Type drop-down list in the Shader rollout. This creates a nice flat material.

4. Click the Diffuse color swatch to access the color selector and set the RGB colors to 255,5,5. (If you wish, you can use the color swatches instead of typing in a value; simply select a nice, deep red color.)

    Now that you have a basic, flat material, you can create a glass material in a similar manner.

5. Click the next material preview slot and name the material Blue Glass.

6. Set the Shader type to Anisotropic.

7. Set the Diffuse color to 47,47,148, using the color selector or RGB colors. Set the Ambient color to 24,24,74 for a darker version of the same color.

8. Set the Specular Level to 83, Glossiness to 47, and Anisotropy to 0. This disables the anisotropic effect but makes the glass nice and shiny.

9. Set the Opacity to 50 to make the glass transparent. Click on the Background button on the Preview Windows toolbar to enable the display of a checkered background. This makes viewing the opacity of the material much easier.

10. Click the next open material preview slot. Name the material Green Metal.

11. Set the Shading type to Strauss.

12. Set the Color swatch to 49,111,49 for a nice green.

13. Set the Glossiness spinner to 83 and Metalness to 57.

14. In this material, you need to apply a map to create a reflective surface. Expand the Maps rollout.

15. Click on the None button next to Reflection. This launches the Material/Map browser. Select the Raytrace map (the raytrace entry with the green parallelogram next to it) and choose OK.

16. A new rollout appears. Set the Trace Mode to Reflection. Click on the Go to Parent button to return to the Maps rollout.

17. Set the Strength spinner next to Reflection to 10. This makes the reflection effect very subtle.

18. Click the next active material slot and name the material Beige Floor.

19. Set the Shading level to Oren-Nayer Blinn.

20. Set the Diffuse color to 211,199,181 for a nice beige color.

21. Click on the Lock Ambient/Diffuse button to lock the colors together. Choose Yes to the dialog box that pops up.

22. Set the Specular Level to 0. This creates a flat material like a carpet.

As you can see from the previous exercise, creating basic materials is not that difficult. The most important part is choosing the correct shading method and then setting up the colors. As you gain experience, you will learn how to choose these correctly to create beautiful renderings.

Conclusion

Materials are very important to the quality of renderings and have many, many options. This chapter introduced you to the basics of creating and using materials. In particular, you learned the following:

- How to use the Material Editor
- How to create and assign materials
- How to save materials to a library

Now that you have been properly introduced to materials, it's time to learn how to make materials by using methods not covered in this chapter, including how to use bitmaps to create photorealistic materials. The next chapter takes you farther into the realm of materials and the Material Editor.

More on Materials

In the last chapter, you took a look at how to work with materials, assign them, and save them. Now, this chapter explores materials more fully. The following is discussed in this chapter:

- Working with Maps in the Material Editor
- Understanding Mapping Controls
- Using Procedural Maps
- Using Raytraced Materials
- Building More Complex Materials
- Working with Displacement Mapping
- Tips on Building Convincing Materials

Working with Maps in the Material Editor

The Material Editor can handle two types of maps: Bitmaps and Procedural Maps. A *bitmap* is a scanned-in or computer-generated image that is encoded as a series of pixels. When these pixels are small enough and close enough together, they form an image. Bitmaps are stored in a variety of file formats, such as TIFF, Targa, GIF, JPEG, PNG, RLA, and AVI (which is an animated bitmap format). A *procedural map* (covered in more detail later in this chapter) uses mathematical formulas to create the colors. Noise is an example of a procedural map.

Each pixel in a bitmap has a color value assigned to it. Depending on the size of the color value supported, the number of colors in an image will vary. A 24-bit image, for example, can have any of a possible 16.7 million colors assigned to each individual pixel. An 8-bit image has a possible palette of only 256 colors. Obviously, a 24-bit image looks much better than an 8-bit image, but results in a much larger file. Some file formats supported by MAX (such as PNG and RLA) support up to 48-bit color images, which provide the greatest color fidelity.

When it comes to materials, you can use bitmaps to simulate real-world materials. You might photograph a piece of wood, scan the photograph into a bitmap format, use the bitmap in a material, and apply the material to an object. Then, when you render the object, it will look as though it was made of the same wood material. Obviously, it is not quite as easy as that, but using bitmaps greatly increases the realism of the material.

tip

When working with materials, you might sometimes complete many test renderings to see how the materials look. In such cases, you can use 8-bit materials for test renderings and then substitute 24-bit color images for the final renderings. This will save some memory and increase the rendering speed somewhat for the tests.

When you do use a bitmap in a material, it has a profound impact on the memory MAX will need to render the image. Each bitmap used in a material must be loaded into memory (whether real or virtual memory) to render. A 2MB bitmap will require 2MB of memory, so it is always a good idea to use smaller bitmaps and as few as possible.

You can use bitmaps in materials to replace one of the various parts, such as the diffuse color, or to add effects to the material that cannot otherwise be created. An example of such an effect might be a *bump map*, which adds small shadows to the material to make it look like a true 3D surface. Figure 13.1 shows an object using a Diffuse mapped material and an object using a bump map.

As you can see from Figure 13.1, using a bitmap in a material can create both subtle and large-scale changes in a material. In Figure 13.1, a large-scale change is achieved by applying the map to the Diffuse channel, directly affecting the look of the material.

Bitmaps can be applied to a wide range of material properties. In some cases, all of the colors of the bitmap will be used; in other cases, only the black and white or saturation values will be used. Each material property to which you can apply a map is listed here and briefly described:

- **Ambient.** Even though it is rarely done, you can apply a bitmap to the ambient color of a material. The bitmap will appear when the object is in shadow. In general, this color channel is locked with the Diffuse color channel, so a bitmap applied to the Diffuse channel is automatically applied here.

- **Diffuse.** As mentioned earlier, the diffuse color is the general color of the material. Using a bitmap in place of the diffuse color results in a material that looks like the bitmap.

Diffuse mapped

Diffuse and Reflection mapped

Bump mapped

FIGURE 13.1 *Two teapots, one using a bitmap in the Diffuse Color slot and the other using a bitmap in the Bump Map slot. Both teapots rest on a wood table using both Diffuse and Reflection mapping.*

- **Specular.** The specular highlight can also be replaced by a bitmap, which can give the impression of a slightly reflective surface, for example.

- **Shininess.** You can control the shininess of a material through the use of a bitmap. Here, the grayscale colors of the bitmap are used to control where the shininess or specular highlights appear.

- **Shin. Strength.** Just as Shininess and Shininess Strength are related in shading, so are the bitmap versions. Here, the strength of the shininess is controlled by the grayscale colors of the bitmap.

- **Self-Illumination.** Using a bitmap in place of Self-Illumination provides you with control over where the object appears self-illuminated. Black colors of the bitmap are not self-illuminated, but white are, and the colors in between are interpolated appropriately.

- **Opacity.** You can also use a bitmap to control which parts of an object are solid and which are transparent. Black areas are transparent, white areas are solid, and grayscales have differing levels of translucency.

tip

Use the Asset Manager to keep track of all of the bitmaps you might use in MAX. It is a powerful and quick tool for viewing and selecting bitmaps from hundreds of choices. The Asset Manager is covered in Chapter 2, "Touring the 3D Studio MAX 3 Interface."

- **Filter Color.** In this channel, which is used in conjunction with Opacity, you can control the filtering of background colors with a map on transparent materials.

- **Bump.** The second most heavily used map channel is the bump map. Here, the bitmap colors are interpreted to give shade and shadow to the surface of an object, providing the illusion of a 3D surface without the need to create one.

- **Reflection.** Here, a bitmap can be used to simulate the reflection of the surrounding environment.

- **Refraction.** Last, you can apply a bitmap to the Refraction channel. Here, the bitmap is refracted according to the shape of the geometry.

Each of the areas where you can apply a bitmap is shown in Figure 13.2.

In all cases, when you apply a bitmap to use in a specific portion of a material, you can control the strength of the bitmap and whether the bitmap is on or off. You accomplish this in the Maps rollout shown in Figure 13.3. The actual number of map slots will vary, depending on the Shader you choose for the material.

Creating a Mapped Material

To create a mapped material, you can either access the Maps rollout in the Material Editor or simply click on the blank button to the right of many of the material properties, such as diffuse color or transparency. Either action brings up the Material/Map Browser, where you can select the type of map you want to apply to that portion of the material. Map types that can be applied to a material are shown with a green symbol to the left of the Map name; most of the time, you will select Bitmap. The other maps are called procedural maps and are discussed later in this chapter.

note

The Bump Map strength controls are slightly different from those of other map types, which range from 0 to 100 in strength. Bump maps range from 0 to 1,000 in strength, providing you with a higher degree of control.

upgrader's note

Due to the new shader algorithms in MAX 3, you can apply maps to areas beyond those listed here. For example, the Anisotropic shader has a map slot for the Anisotropy value. Maps can also be used in other parts of MAX, such as applying a map to the shadow of a light to create caustic effects.

note

Many times, you will want to create your own maps for use in MAX. Three of the best tools for doing this are Adobe Photoshop, Discreet Paint, and Fractal Design Painter, all of which provide many features you can make use of to create your own maps. MAX accepts Targa, GIF, JPG, PNG, TIF, and other formats from these programs. Paint has the added advantage of working directly with MAX through the Paint map. This provides two-way communication between MAX and Paint, enabling you to use Paint's powerful vector capabilities inside of MAX.

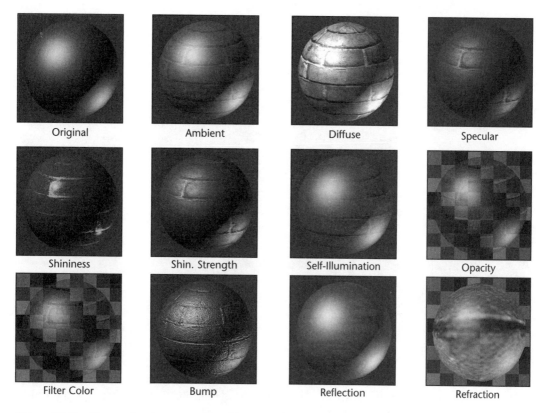

Original	Ambient	Diffuse	Specular
Shininess	Shin. Strength	Self-Illumination	Opacity
Filter Color	Bump	Reflection	Refraction

FIGURE 13.2 *The results when you apply a bitmap to the Ambient, Diffuse, Specular, Shininess, Shin. Strength, Self-Illumination, Opacity, Filter Color, Bump, Reflection, and Refraction channels of a material.*

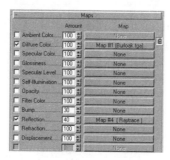

FIGURE 13.3 *The Maps rollout of the Material Editor, where you can define which Map channels are active and how strong they are.*

When you select the Bitmap entry and choose OK, MAX immediately asks you to select a file for use in the material. After you have selected the file, the rollouts of the Material Editor change so you can control the bitmap. Figure 13.4 shows you these rollouts.

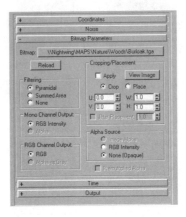

FIGURE 13.4   *The Bitmap rollouts for a material. Through these rollouts, you can precisely control the use of the bitmap in the material.*

When you access the Bitmap rollouts of a material, you are working at a child level of the material—in other words, the bitmap is dependent on the rest of the material. To go to the standard material controls, choose the Go to Parent button in the Material Editor. To return to the bitmap level, simply click the appropriate bitmap button in the Maps rollout.

The two main rollouts to the Bitmap Controls are the Coordinates rollout and the Bitmap Parameters rollout. The Coordinates rollout is covered in the "Working with Mapping Coordinates" section later in this chapter.

Because you were prompted immediately to select a bitmap file for use in the material, the file and its location appear on the Bitmap button. Clicking this button provides you with a file selector, where you can select any supported file type to substitute for the already selected file.

After you have assigned the appropriate bitmap, you can set the bitmap controls, if necessary. There are five sets of controls for each bitmap you load into a material: Filtering, Mono Channel Output, RGB Channel Output, Alpha Source, and Cropping/ Placement.

tip

For you to use a bitmap in MAX, the bitmap file must reside in a directory that MAX is aware of, known as a Map directory. You can select one or more Map directories by choosing Customize/ Configure Paths from the pull-down menu.

The filtering controls determine how the map is antialiased when rendered. *Aliasing* is the appearance of artifacts in a scene, such as jagged lines instead of smooth lines. *Antialiasing* is the process of smoothing out these artifacts. MAX provides two methods of antialiasing bitmaps used in a material: Pyramidal or Summed Area filtering. Both achieve good results, with Summed Area being slightly better but requiring much more memory. In most cases, you should use Pyramidal, unless you are getting aliasing artifacts in your maps or have maps that appear to travel across the surface of the object, in which case Summed Area is better. But, only use Summed area when absolutely necessary.

> **note**
>
> The alpha channel of a bitmap image is an extra 8 bits of color (making the image 32-bit instead of 24-bit) that represents the transparency of the image. The alpha channel is encoded as a 256-level grayscale image, providing 256 levels of transparency. In general, only images that are rendered out of MAX or some other 3D program have alpha channels. Alpha channels are most heavily used in the Video Post or Render Effects for compositing purposes. Video Post and Render Effects are covered in Chapter 18, "Exploring Post Processing Techniques."

There are also two sets of channel outputs. Depending on the material property to which you applied the bitmap, one of these channels will be used. The RGB channel is used for properties such as diffuse color or reflection, and the Mono channel for properties such as bump maps or opacity. Under the Mono channel, you can select whether the mono colors are chosen from the intensity values of the RGB colors or from the alpha channel of the image, if it has one. The RGB output enables you to select the RGB colors or use the alpha channel as a grayscale map, if the bitmap has an alpha channel.

When you are selecting the Alpha option for either the RGB or Mono output channels, you can select the source of the alpha channel under Alpha Source. The three options are Image Alpha, RGB Intensity (which calculates the transparency from the intensity of the colors) or None, where no alpha channel is present.

The last set of controls is very powerful for working with bitmaps. These are the Cropping/Placement controls, which enable you to precisely place a copy of the bitmap, like a decal, on the surface of an object, or to crop the image inside of MAX instead of cropping the bitmap in an image editor such as Photoshop.

The easiest way to make use of the Cropping/Placement controls is to use the View Image button. You will get an interactive editor (shown in Figure 13.5) where you can interactively crop, scale, or position the bitmap (depending on whether Cropping or Placement is active).

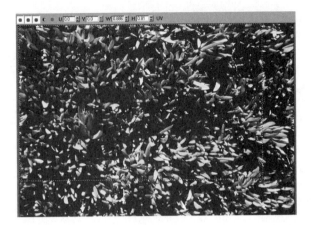

FIGURE 13.5   *The Specify Cropping/Placement dialog box, where you can interactively set the cropping and placement of bitmap images. In this figure, the Placement option is active.*

In the interactive Cropping/Placement editor, a dashed outline appears, representing the cropping or placement boundaries. By adjusting the handles of this outline, you can interactively adjust the bitmap. Alternatively, you can use the number spinners at the top of the dialog box.

After you have applied the bitmap to the material, you can select Go to Parent to return to the main material controls and further adjust the strength of the map in the Maps rollout.

The following exercises show you how to create three different mapped materials for a bowling alley scene. These materials will then be applied in an exercise later in this chapter.

Creating a Wood Floor Material

1. Load the file **MF13-01.MAX** from the accompanying CD. This is the Bowling Alley scene from the end of the previous chapter. You may also load the file you created at the end of the last chapter.

2. Open the Material Editor. Material Slot #4 is unused, so click it.

3. Name the material Alley Floor.

4. Set the Shading Level to Anisotropic.

5. Expand the Maps Rollout and click the None button next to Diffuse Color.

6. In the Material/Map Browser, double-click Bitmap. This opens the Bitmap rollouts in the Material Editor.

7. Select the file cedfence.jpg. (This file should be either in your MAX Maps directory or on the 3D Studio MAX 3.0 CD. If on the CD, copy into the Maps directory first.)

8. Set the U Tiling spinner to 2.0.

9. Choose Go to Parent

10. Set the Specular Level to 50.

11. Put the material in the Material Library.

Creating a Bowling Pin Material

1. Select an open Material Slot. If you need to, switch your Material Previews to 5×3 for more slots.

2. Name the material Bowling Pin.

3. Set the Shading Level to Anisotropic.

4. Expand the Maps rollout and select the None button next to Diffuse Color.

5. Select Bitmap again from the Material/Map Browser and choose OK.

6. Select the file bowling.tga, which is on the accompanying CD.

7. Choose Go to Parent.

8. Set the Specular Level to 75 to make the pin appear polished.

9. Put the material in the Material Library.

Creating a Bowling Ball Material

1. Select another open Material Slot.

2. Name the material Bowling Ball.

3. Set the Shading Level to Blinn.

4. Apply the file marbteal.tga to the Diffuse channel as in the other materials. (This file should have been installed with MAX. If not, it should be available on the MAX 3 CD.)

5. Choose Go to Parent.

6. Set the Specular Level to 50.

7. Put the material in the Material Library.

8. Save the scene as **MF13-01a.MAX**.

As you can see from the last exercise, creating a mapped material is not all that difficult—you simply apply bitmaps to selected areas of the material to generate specific effects.

After you have created the material, you can assign it to objects in the scene, just like any other material. Then, you have to apply mapping coordinates to the objects (if they do not already have them), so MAX will know where and how to place the maps on the objects.

Understanding Mapping Controls

All mapped materials make use of mapping coordinates to correctly place the bitmap on the object. These mapping coordinates make use of a coordinate system called UVW. This is the same as XYZ but corresponds to the bitmap dimensions. UVW is used to help reduce the confusion surrounding which coordinates you are using. If you were to look at a flat bitmap, for example, the X axis is the U direction and the Y axis is the V direction. The W direction is used only with procedural materials.

There are two different ways to create mapping coordinates for an object. The first method is to turn on Generate Mapping Coordinates when you are creating the object. These coordinates are then generated procedurally, based on the type of geometry you are creating. The second, and more flexible, method is to apply the UVW Map modifier to the object. With the UVW Map modifier, you can apply the mapping coordinates, scale them, rotate them, and even select from different types of mapping coordinates, none of which is possible with the Generate Mapping Coordinates options. If you have Generate Mapping Coordinates on and then apply a UVW Map modifier, the modifier takes precedence.

When you apply the UVW Map modifier to an object, you get the rollout shown in Figure 13.6.

When you apply the modifier, mapping coordinates are automatically generated for the object, and a gizmo (sometimes called the Mapping icon) appears, representing the mapping coordinates. Figure 13.7 shows a Plane object with this gizmo present.

The Mapping icon is representative of the scale, orientation, and position of one copy of the bitmap used in the material. By turning on Sub-Object Selection in the UVW Map rollout, you can Move, Scale, and Rotate the Mapping icon to position and control the location of the bitmap on the object.

tip

If you use the UVW Map modifier, it should be the last modifier—or one of the last—that you apply in the stack for the object. If you apply a UVW Map modifier and then use Edit Mesh, for example, to attach more geometry, the attached geometry will not have mapping coordinates because it was attached after the UVW Map modifier in the stack.

If the Mapping icon is smaller than the object, the bitmap will be tiled or copied across the surface. This presents one of the problems with using a mapped material. If the bitmap is a picture of an organic substance such as wood or grass, placing copies of the bitmap next to each other will show a seam. Figure 13.8 shows an example of a box that uses a grass material and shows a tiling error.

You can solve the problem presented in Figure 13.8 by using several different material techniques, such as blended or composite materials and secondary mapping coordinates. The easiest method, however, is to simply use a *tileable bitmap*—one that when tiled across the surface of an object will not show seams. You can either purchase these as material sets from various vendors or use a program such as Photoshop to edit your material until it is tileable.

The best method for solving tiling problems is not to tile the bitmap at all. Instead, create a high-resolution version that has enough detail for your scene, and place it on the object so that it tiles only once. The disadvantage to this method is that a higher-resolution bitmap requires more memory and slightly more time to render.

Mapping Coordinate Types

MAX provides six types of mapping coordinates to match the various types of geometry you might encounter. These mapping types include Planar, Cylindrical, Spherical, Shrink Wrap, Box, Face, and—new to MAX 3—XYZ to UVW. Figure 13.9 shows an example of each type of mapping coordinate.

FIGURE 13.6

The UVW Map Modifier rollout, where you can define exactly how the mapping coordinates are applied to the selected object.

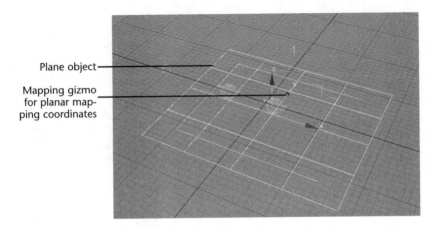

Plane object

Mapping gizmo
for planar map-
ping coordinates

FIGURE 13.7   *The Mapping gizmo, which you can transform to accurately scale and place
the mapping coordinates.*

- **Planar.** Places the bitmap on the surface of an object in a 2D fashion. This works well if the object is flat or relatively flat. The downside is that Planar mapping does not work in all conditions. If you apply Planar mapping to a box, for example, the mapping will look good on one side of the box but will appear stretched along the sides of the box perpendicular to the Mapping icon. You can get around this by rotating the Mapping icon, but then you will have a material that stretches a little across the surface of the object. In general, Planar is great if one surface of the object is showing.

- **Spherical.** Creates a sphere around the object and places the mapping coordinates along that sphere. Use Spherical mapping coordinates with objects such as bowling balls, golf balls, or rocks.

- **Cylindrical.** Use these coordinates on objects that have a cylindrical shape, such as a can or a bowling pin. The bitmap is wrapped around the vertical axis of the mapping coordinates and then, on the ends, projected inward to the center. As an option, you may have the ends capped, with a copy of the bitmap appearing on each end of the cylinder as well.

tip

When transforming the Mapping icon, it is helpful to see the material on the object. If you turn on Smooth + Highlight Shading in the viewport and select the Show Map in Viewport button in the Material Editor, you will see a representation of the bitmap in the viewport that you can interactively adjust. The Show Map in Viewport button is available only when you are adjusting the Bitmap parameters in the Bitmaps rollout and only if the map you are using can be shown in the viewport. Many Procedural maps cannot be displayed in the interactive viewports.

FIGURE 13.8   *A Box object with a grass material applied to it. Notice how you can see the seams between the copies of the grass bitmap.*

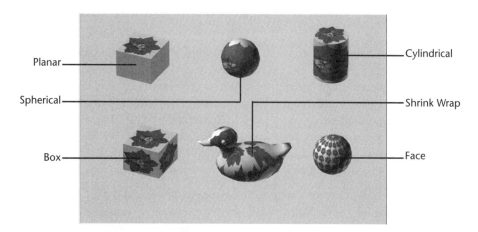

FIGURE 13.9   *The mapping coordinate types as applied to different types of geometry. Correctly selecting and placing mapping coordinates adds to the realism of the material on the object.*

- **Box.** Just like Planar mapping except provides mapping on six sides so you do not have the problem of stretched mapping coordinates. Box mapping is great for boxes, walls, or other objects that have the same material on all sides.

- **Shrink Wrap.** A special mapping coordinate set designed to work with highly organic shapes where cylindrical or spherical mapping isn't good enough. Imagine a sphere made of cellophane surrounding a sculpture. If you sucked all the air out of the interior of the cellophane sphere, the sphere would shrink-wrap itself to the sculpture. This is how Shrink Wrap mapping works. This type of mapping is most commonly used on human or animal figures or other such complex mapping tasks.

- **Face.** Applies one copy of the bitmap to the center of each face in the object. This can be great for creating complex tiled patterns if the faces on the object are evenly spaced.

- **XYZ to UVW.** Converts XYZ coordinates. This enables you to apply mapping coordinates with all the power of the UVW Map modifier but use them with procedural maps. Previously, you did not have this capability.

Applying the UVW Map Modifier

When you apply the UVW Map modifier to an object, Planar mapping coordinates are applied by default. If you select one of the other mapping coordinate types, the Mapping icon changes to match.

After you have applied and selected a mapping coordinate type, there are several controls you can use. First, and most notable, is the channel number. MAX 3 supports up to 100 different mapping channels. When you want to apply a second or third set of mapping coordinates, you must apply a second or third UVW Map modifier and set it to the appropriate mapping channel. Then, in the Material Editor, you can set individual bitmaps to use a particular mapping channel number in the Coordinate rollouts. For example, you could have a material with a diffuse map on one set of mapping coordinates, bump mapping on another, reflection mapping on a third, and so on.

Next, you can choose the type of alignment for the Mapping icon. A Cylindrical Mapping icon is generally created along the Z axis, for example, but can be set to X or Y, as well. Along with the axis alignment, several commands—Fit, Center, Bitmap Fit, Normal Align, View Align, and Region Fit—are available in the UVW Map Modifier rollout for quickly positioning and manipulating the Mapping icons.

The first command is Fit, which makes the Mapping icon fit the size of the selected geometry. The Center button centers the Mapping icon around the geometric center of the selected geometry. Bitmap Fit is one of the more commonly used Mapping icon controls. Each bitmap has its own aspect ratio (ratio of width to height); Bitmap Fit sets the Mapping icon to match the aspect ratio of the bitmap. This prevents unnecessary scaling of the bitmap when rendered. Along the same lines is the Region Fit command, which enables you to fit the Mapping icon to a region you select with the mouse.

The two alignment commands—View Align and Normal Align—align the Mapping icon either to the current viewport or to the Normals of the selected object. Last, you can reset the Mapping icon to its original state or acquire a Mapping icon from another object that already has mapping coordinates. The Acquire command is particularly useful because it enables you to match material scaling between objects.

All of these Mapping icon controls can be adjusted interactively and represent mapping at an object level. You can also control, to an extent, mapping at a material level.

Working with Mapping Coordinates at a Material Level

When you select a bitmap for use in a material, several rollouts appear, including the Bitmap Parameters and Coordinates rollouts. The Coordinates rollout enables you to control the mapping at a material level and apply the mapping changes to all objects with the material assigned to them.

In the Coordinates rollout (see Figure 13.10), you can control the type of coordinates the map will use. You can choose either Texture or Environmental. Texture coordinates rely on coordinates applied to the geometry to which the material is assigned. Use the Environmental coordinates when the bitmap is applied as a background or environment for your scene.

FIGURE 13.10   *The Coordinates rollout of the Bitmap controls, where you can adjust how a map is placed in the scene.*

To the right of the Coordinate Type radio buttons is a drop-down list from which you can choose the type of texture or environmental coordinates you will use. If you select Texture coordinates, for example, you can choose to use Explicit Map channel or Planar XYZ coordinates.

The next set of parameters in the Coordinates rollout controls the position of the bitmap within the Mapping icon. Use the Mapping icon to apply, scale, and rotate the mapping coordinates onto an object. In general, by default, one copy of the bitmap appears within the Mapping icon.

You can set the offset and tiling, mirror the bitmap, set the bitmap to tile if necessary, and rotate and blur the bitmap. All of these controls, except for map blurring, can be controlled either at the material level or at the object level through the UVW Map modifier.

In the following exercise, take some of the materials created in the last exercise and apply them to objects in the scene. Then, apply mapping coordinates to make the materials appear correctly on the objects.

Applying Mapping to a Bowling Pin

1. Load the file **MF13-01a.MAX** that you created in the last exercise. You can also load this file from the accompanying CD.

2. Use Select by Name to select all the Bowling Pin objects and hide all the other objects in the scene.

3. Open the Material Editor. The Bowling Pin material you created in the last exercise should be present. Select and highlight it.

4. Expand the Maps rollout and click the Bowling Pin.tga button next to Diffuse.

5. When the Bitmap rollouts appear, choose Show Map in Viewport.

6. Choose Apply Material to Selection to apply the Bowling Pin material.

7. Minimize the Material Editor.

8. Set the upper-right viewport to a Right view. Choose Zoom Extents and then set the shading level to Smooth + Highlights. The pins should appear with the maps showing, but the mapping coordinates generated during the lathing of the pins are incorrect.

9. With all the pins still selected, go to the Modify command panel and select UVW Map.

10. Set the Mapping type to Cylindrical and the Alignment to Z. The Bowling Pin material should almost immediately appear on the pins, as shown in Figure 13.11.

    Now that the bowling pins have the material and mapping coordinates applied, do the same to the bowling alley.

11. Hide all of the bowling pins and unhide the Lane 1 through Lane 4 objects and the Bowler Setup object.

12. Open the Material Editor and apply the Alley Floor material to the Lane and Bowler Setup objects. Open the Bitmap Parameters of the Diffuse color and turn on the Show Map in Viewport option. Again, these objects have mapping coordinates resulting from the modeling process.

13. Select all of the objects and apply a UVW Map modifier. Set the mapping type to Planar.

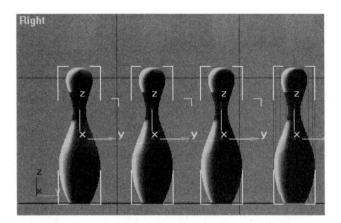

FIGURE 13.11   *The bowling pins after applying the material and mapping coordinates.*

14. Select the Sub-Object button and uniformly scale the Mapping icon down to 20 percent of its original size. You should see the results in the shaded Camera01 viewport, as shown in Figure 13.12.

FIGURE 13.12   *The Bowler Setup and Lane objects after applying the material and mapping coordinates.*

15. Save the file as **MF13-01B.MAX**.

16. On your own, apply the Bowling Ball material and mapping coordinates to the bowling balls that are in the scene.

As you can see, thanks to the interactive renderer, working with mapping coordinates is much easier than it used to be. Don't be afraid to explore and test different mapping coordinates.

Using Procedural Maps

Bitmaps are a powerful method for creating materials, but they are not the only type of maps you can use in a material. The others are procedural maps and are mathematically generated. As such, procedural maps have several distinct advantages over bitmaps.

First, because a procedural map is mathematically generated, it uses much less memory—sometimes at the cost of speed. Second, procedural materials do not require mapping coordinates. You can use mapping coordinates if you want, but most of the time, procedural materials use the World Space XYZ coordinates. Say, for example, that you subtracted a sphere out of a box with a Boolean operation. The resulting void is difficult to correctly map with UVW coordinates, but procedural maps make the object look as though it was cut out of a solid.

You can use procedural maps anywhere you can apply a map to a material. You can also mix and match procedural maps with bitmaps in your scene. The application procedure for a procedural material is the same as for a bitmap, except that instead of selecting the Bitmap option in the Material/Map Browser, you can select any of the procedural materials with a green trapezoid next to them.

Each procedural material has a unique set of controls to define how the material works. A procedural wood has two color controls and a procedural gradient has three.

The following exercise shows how to create a procedural stucco for the bowling alley scene. You apply this stucco as a bump map to the wall material.

tip

If you are running MAX with the Software Z Buffer, you might notice that the material in the interactive viewport appears to be bent. This is due to a speed optimization in the SZB driver. If you right-click the viewport name and choose Texture Correction, the material will appear correct but will take a little longer to redraw. If you are using a hardware accelerator such as a 3dLabs GMX2000, Texture Correction is not available because it is handled in the hardware of the accelerator.

upgrader's note

New to MAX 3 is the XYZ to UVW option in the UVW Map modifier, enabling you to use this modifier to manipulate procedural mapping coordinates.

tip

Max 3 has many procedural maps, some of which are not covered in this book. Refer to the MAX documentation for information on procedural maps not covered here.

Creating a Procedural Stucco

1. Load the file **MF13-01B.MAX** that you created in the previous exercise. You can also load this file from the accompanying CD.

2. Open the Material Editor.

3. Select the Tan Flat Paint material.

4. Expand the Maps rollout and choose the None button next to Bump.

5. Double-click Stucco in the Material/Map Browser to select the procedural map. The Stucco rollouts appear, as shown in Figure 13.13.

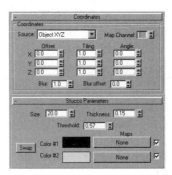

FIGURE 13.13   *The Procedural Stucco rollout, where you can adjust the parameters to create different types of stucco.*

6. Set the Size spinner to 1.0 and leave the rest set to default parameters.

7. Choose Go to Parent.

8. Set the Bump map strength to 150.

9. Unhide all the objects in the scene and render the Camera view. You should now see stucco indentations in the walls, as in Figure 13.14. Save the file.

As you can see from this exercise, using procedural maps is not difficult. Procedural maps do not provide interactive previews, however, so the only way to see what they look like is through the time-consuming process of rendering the scene.

Using Raytraced Materials

The last material issue to look at is a very special material, the raytraced material. Raytracing is a technique for outlining reflections and refractions in scenes. Normally, raytracing is a type of rendering engine, but due to some unique programming, MAX 3 provides raytracing as a material. As such, it is faster than a regular raytracer and can be selectively applied to objects in the scene.

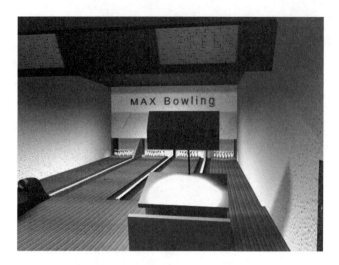

FIGURE 13.14   *The bowling alley scene after applying materials to it. Notice the nice 3D depth in the walls.*

The raytracer comes in two forms in MAX: a raytracing material and a raytracing map. The map version is covered here, and you can explore the raytracing material on your own. The map provides a simple, quick method for getting accurate reflections and refractions and is applied like any other procedural material. You have already used this map several times in exercises earlier in this chapter and in the previous chapter, so you have seen how easy it is to use.

The following exercise shows you how to apply a raytrace map to the reflection of the bowling alley to make the floors look shiny and well oiled.

Using Raytracing to Create Reflections and Refractions

1. Load the file **MF13-01b.MAX** that you worked on in the previous exercise. You can also load this file from the accompanying CD.

2. Open the Material Editor.

3. Choose the Alley Floor material.

4. Expand the Maps rollout and click the None button next to Reflection.

tip

The material version of the ray-tracer provides numerous controls over raytracing parameters, reflection, refraction, material properties, antialiasing, and other advanced topics. Use the material version when you need full control of reflection and refraction parameters in all parts of the material.

5. In the Maps rollout, click the None button next to Reflection. Choose Raytrace and click OK.

6. In the Raytrace rollout, set the Trace Mode to Reflection.

7. Click the Global Parameters button. Turn on Manual Acceleration and choose Close.

8. Choose Go to Parent.

9. Set the Reflection strength to 20.

10. Render the Camera01 viewport to see the results shown in Figure 13.15.

FIGURE 13.15   *The bowling alley after applying a raytrace map to the Lane material. Notice the nice reflections.*

11. Save the file as **MF13-01c.MAX**.

This would be a good time to stop and explore applying materials to the bowling alley scene. Many objects still do not have materials and can be used to explore many of the different material features of MAX. The MAX Material Editor is an extremely powerful tool—don't feel intimidated by it. Even experienced users are always learning new ways of creating and using materials in scenes.

By this point, it should be apparent that the use of maps in materials is easy and helps to make materials more realistic than just using colors.

Tips on Building Convincing Materials

The creation of convincingly realistic materials is one of the keystones of a good rendering or animation. Here are a few tips you can use to help you create better materials:

- If you use a map in the Diffuse Map slot, copy the map to the Specular slot as well. This breaks up the highlight so it looks natural on the material you are creating. The same applies if you use a bump map.

- If the ambient light in your scene is above 0,0,0, make sure the ambient color of your material is darker than the diffuse color. A quick way to do this is to copy the diffuse color into the ambient and then adjust the Blackness slider of the ambient color.

- Along the same lines, if you are using a bitmap for the diffuse color when ambient is above 0,0,0, unlock the Diffuse and Ambient material slots. Then, copy the Diffuse bitmap into the Ambient slot and apply an RGB tint to it to darken the bitmap. This increases the contrast and makes the rendering look more realistic.

- When applying a UVW Map modifier to an object where you are going to use a bitmap, always apply the Bitmap Fit option to the gizmo to make sure you don't stretch the bitmap inside of the material or object.

- When creating glass materials, always turn on two-sided in the Shader rollout. If you can afford the rendering time, apply a Raytrace map to a Reflection or Refraction map, because glass usually has both.

- If you are going to use Reflections in your scene with either the Raytrace map or the Reflection map, keep the strength setting relatively low unless it is a highly reflective object such as a mirror. Usually, values under 30 are good enough.

- When using bump maps in a material, you can sometimes have the problem that the map appears to "dance" in an animation. There are two things you can do: Change the filtering type to Summed Area and apply more blur to the bump map itself or apply SuperSampling, which is discussed in Chapter 14, "Rendering."

- If you have reflections in a material, you might want to have those reflections dimmed to simulate a darker or less perfect surface. To do this, open the Extended Parameters rollout in the material and enable Reflection Dimming.

Conclusion

In this chapter, you learned how to deal with more complex materials, especially those that use maps in them. These types of materials are commonly used to create a wide variety of effects, and knowing how to use them is important to creating a good rendering. This chapter covered the following topics:

- What a bitmap is and how to work with one
- Applying a bitmap to a material
- Creating and adjusting mapping coordinates
- Using procedural maps in materials
- Using Raytracing to create easy reflective effects

Overall, this chapter explored the power of the MAX materials system, including the use of bitmaps in materials, mapping coordinates, procedural methods, and raytracing. Even though just a small portion of MAX's power was uncovered here, you were able to create several materials and add a lot of realism to the bowling alley scene.

Now, it is time to look at how to render the scene and generate still images. That is the focus of the next chapter.

CHAPTER 14

Rendering

Up to this point, the focus of the book has been the interface, modeling, lighting, and materials. Now it is time to look at how to actually render a scene inside of MAX. This relatively simply process has many options you can use to change the look of the resulting image. This chapter focuses on rendering both still frames and animations and covers the following topics:

- Rendering a Scene
- Working with the Virtual Frame Buffer
- Rendering Controls
- MAX Rendering Engine Options
- Dealing with Anti-Aliasing
- Working with the Virtual Frame Buffer
- Render Output
- Rendering for Animations
- Tips on Rendering
- Working with Environments

Rendering a Scene

In MAX, you can render any active viewport except a Track View, Schematic view, or MAXScript Listener viewport. You can also render any section of a viewport. You can control what you are rendering by using the three Render buttons and drop-down list on the Main Toolbar (see Figure 14.1).

With these buttons, you can choose how and which view to render. Render Scene brings up the Render Scene dialog box, where you specify which frames to render, the rendering parameters, and the output filename. Quick Render renders the active viewport at the current frame, Render Type enables you to specify which part of the viewport to render, and Render Last re-renders the last view you rendered with the same settings.

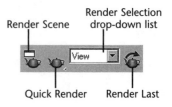

FIGURE 14.1
The Rendering controls located on the Main Toolbar tab of the shelf. You can use these to render the active viewport.

MAX enables you to define two sets of rendering parameters: the production settings and the draft settings. These settings are defined in the Render Scene dialog box. When you are creating or animating your scene, you might want to quickly render low-quality images just to check object placement and motion. For these renderings, you'll want to turn off as many of the time-consuming rendering options as possible—for example, shadows, reflections, map filtering, and motion blur—in the draft settings. In the production settings, you want to specify your final production rendering settings. If you have two sets of rendering parameters, you are less likely to forget to turn on rendering options when you move from draft renderings to production renderings. If you click and hold the Quick Render button, a flyout enables you to choose whether to perform your quick rendering using the draft settings or the production settings.

In the Render Type drop-down list are six options (View, Selected, Crop, Region, Blowup, and Box Selected) that enable you to choose which part of the viewport to render. When you start a rendering by using Region, Crop, or Blowup, a window is displayed in the active viewport as a black dashed line. After resizing or moving this window, you execute the rendering by choosing OK in the lower-right corner of the viewport. The Box Selected option works only if you select one or more objects before executing the Render command in the Render dialog box. Then, these objects are rendered, using their bounding boxes as the rendering area.

To render a scene, first activate the viewport you want to render and choose the Render Scene button from the Main Toolbar to display the Render Scene dialog box shown in Figure 12.2.

The Render Scene dialog box is a *modeless* dialog box. This means if you click the Render button, the dialog box stays open, enabling you to quickly and easily re-render frames in your animation. Three buttons at the bottom of the dialog box facilitate this: The Render button actually renders the scene, Close + Render closes the Render Scene dialog box and renders the current viewport, and Cancel removes any changes you made to the Render Scene parameters and closes the dialog box.

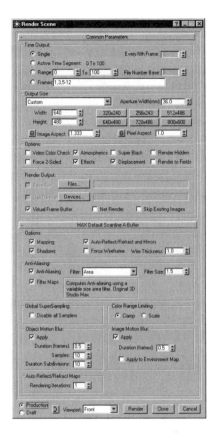

FIGURE 14.2   *The Render Scene dialog box, where you can set up all of the parameters for rendering and execute the actual rendering process.*

Rendering Controls

The Render Scene dialog box parameters shown in Figure 14.2 are described here, section by section. The Render Scene dialog box is divided into two rollouts: Common Parameters, which contains the rendering parameters that are independent of the rendering engine, and a rollout that contains the rendering parameters specific to the rendering engine. The engine shipped with MAX is the Scanline A-Buffer, and the rollout's name is MAX Default Scanline A-Buffer.

At the bottom of the Render Scene dialog box are buttons or options to switch between the Production and Draft rendering settings, transfer settings between the Production and Draft rendering settings, select the viewport to render, and start the rendering process.

upgrader's note

In MAX 2 and earlier, the Render Scene dialog box had a Close button that would close the dialog box and save any changes you made. To close and save in MAX 3, click the X in the upper-right corner of the dialog box.

Two complete sets of common and rendering-engine-specific settings are stored by MAX. One set is called the Production settings, the other the Draft settings. Changing the settings in one set has no impact on the other. To switch between the sets, simply select the appropriate option. If you click the Transfer Settings button, you will be warned that a copy of all the settings will be transferred to the current set. If you click OK, all of the current settings will be replaced.

Image Size

The Time Output area parameters specify which frames are to be rendered. To render just the current frame of the animation, use the Single option. To render the currently active time segment, choose Active Time Segment. To specify a contiguous range of frames, use the Range option and specify the first and last frames of the range. To render a set of individual frames or a set of ranges, use the Frames option.

When you render ranges by using the Active Time Segment or Range options, you can use the Every Nth Frame spinner to determine whether to render every frame, every other frame, and so on. Often, you can do this simply to test an animation.

When you render to a file using any Time Output option other than Single, the frame number is appended to the filename. For example, if you specify an output filename of file.tga and render a range of frames from 0 to 10, the output filenames will be file0000.tga to file0010.tga. The File Number Base lets you specify the base file number from which the filename will increment. For example, if you set the Range of frames to 0–30, Every Nth Frame to 10, and the File Number Base to 100, the output filenames would be file0100.tga, file0110.tga, file0120.tga, and file0130.tga.

Under Customize, Preferences, Rendering, there is an option called Nth Serial Numbering. If this option is on, filenames are incremented by one in rendering sequences, no matter what value you've set for Every Nth Frame. In the previous example, therefore, the output filenames would be file0100.tga to file0103.tga.

Output Size

Options in the Output Size section of the dialog box enable you to set the height and width of the final image in pixels, which are single dots in the image. The higher the resolution, the crisper the image, the longer the rendering time, and the larger the output file.

In the Output Type pop-up list, you can choose either Custom or one of a number of standard film or video formats. With all output types, you can change the width or height of the image by adjusting those fields or by clicking of the preset rendering resolutions. You can also define your own preset by right-clicking of the buttons, which displays the Configure Preset dialog box shown in Figure 14.3. After you set the width and height, the button displays the new values.

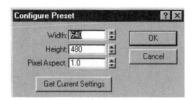

FIGURE 14.3   *The Configure Preset dialog box, where you can set the Preset Buttons to rendering resolutions and aspect ratios you commonly use in your work.*

In Custom mode, you can set the Aperture Width of the camera, the Image Aspect ratio, and the Pixel Aspect ratio. When you choose any of the standard formats, all of these values are locked to the values associated with the standard.

Aperture Width specifies the aperture width of the camera, which alters the relationship between the Lens spinner and the FOV spinner. It has no effect on the view of the scene through the camera. Unless you are trying to match a specific type of camera, this value should not be changed.

The Pixel Aspect ratio refers to the "squareness" of a pixel on the output device. The ratio is formed by dividing the height of the pixel by its width. For computer screens and film, the Pixel Aspect is one—the pixels are square. For other output devices, such as video, the pixels are not square and the Pixel Aspect should be set appropriately.

The Image Aspect ratio refers to the squareness of the entire image on the output device. For a Pixel Aspect ratio of 1.0, the Image Aspect ratio is the image width divided by the image height.

Both the Image Aspect and Pixel Aspect ratios can be locked to their current values by clicking their respective lock icons. If one or both of these are locked, changing the height, width, or aspect ratio fields causes the other fields to adjust to maintain the locked values.

Rendering Options

In the Options section of the Common Parameters dialog box is a set of rendering options that are either enabled or disabled. Depending on your preference, you can set these options to be either be enabled or disabled by default.

If the Video Color Check option is on, MAX checks the colors of the output image versus accepted color standards for NTSC and PAL video outputs. Depending on the preferences set under File, Preferences, Rendering (Video Color Check area), MAX will either correct any colors that are unacceptable or change them to black to warn you.

Choosing Atmospherics enables or disables the rendering of atmospheric effects, such as fog. Because these are sometimes processor intensive, having the ability to turn them off with a single check box at rendering time is helpful.

The Super Black option limits how dark an object can be and is primarily used for compositing purposes. If Super Black is on, no object will be rendered darker than the Super Black Threshold value set under File, Preferences, Rendering. Areas of the image not covered by an object are unaffected by the Super Black option.

If the Render Hidden option is on, hidden objects will be rendered. As you are working, you often will hide objects to make a scene easier to work on. By enabling Render Hidden, you can render these objects without having to unhide them.

The Force 2-Sided option forces the renderer to always render both sides of a face. You'll use this often when you import geometry from other programs, because most other modeling programs, such as AutoCAD, do not track face normals. Objects imported from these programs usually have their face normals pointing in different directions. Using the Force 2-Sided option is effective but increases the rendering time for each frame of an animation.

The Effects and Displacement options enable the use of Render Effects and Displacement Mapping together. *Render Effects* are post-rendering processes such as adding lens flares and glows. *Displacement* is the process of generating new geometry based on a bitmap—often a very slow process if the bitmap or geometry is complex.

Turning the Render Atmospheric Effects option off disables the atmospheric effects and speeds up test renderings. Fog and other such atmospheric effects are computationally intensive and not typically needed if you are just checking your animation.

The Render to Fields option applies only to animation and video output and is discussed in more detail later in this chapter.

Render Output

The Render Output area of the dialog box enables you to determine where the final rendered image goes. Output files can be sent either to a file or to a device. If the Virtual Frame Buffer option is selected, MAX also displays the image in a window called the Virtual Frame Buffer (VFB). Figure 14.4 shows the VFB with a rendering. The Net Render option enables you to use a network of machines to render your animation.

FIGURE 14.4   *The Virtual Frame Buffer, where you can see rendered images as they are generated. Progress of the rendering is indicated by a white line in the VFB.*

MAX can save to a variety of file types. You can set the file type by choosing the Files button in the Render Scene dialog box and then choosing a file type from the List files of the type drop-down list. The file types most commonly used are AVI, which is used for playing back animations on a computer; JPEG, which uses a lossy algorithm to greatly compress images; and Targa, which is used for high-quality images and for images that will be used for video.

You can set up parameters for most file types. Simply choose the file type from the drop-down list and select the Setup button in the Render Output File dialog box. Figure 14.5 shows the setup dialog box for a Targa image file. The image file setup varies from file type to file type.

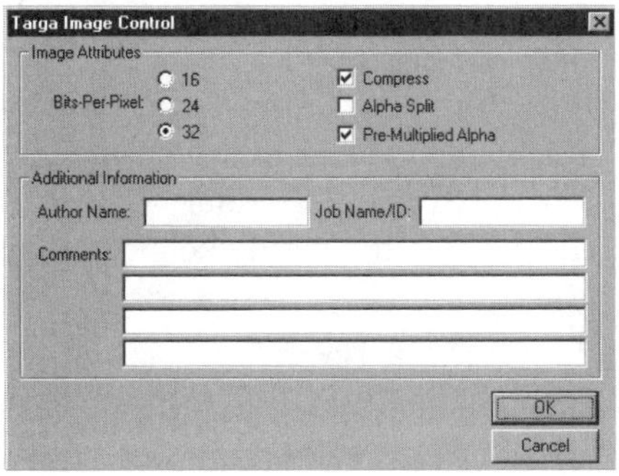

FIGURE 14.5   *The Targa Image Control dialog box, where you can define the parameters for saving different types of Targa files.*

Before you save an image to a specific file type, you can also correct the file's gamma. *Gamma* measures the contrast that affects the midtones of an image, and gamma correction affects the overall brightness of the image. For some output devices (such as video), gamma correction might be necessary for the image to look right. To correct the gamma, you choose the Gamma button and then change the settings in the Output Gamma Settings dialog box.

note

Enable Gamma Correction must be turned on under Customize, Preferences, Gamma before the Gamma button can be selected in the Render Output File dialog box. The system default gamma values are also set up under File, Preferences, Gamma.

Gamma corrections are generally somewhere between 1.0 and 2.5. The higher the value is, the brighter the image will be. You will have to experiment with your output equipment to see whether you need gamma correction at all.

The following exercise steps you through the most common rendering options available in the Render Output dialog box.

Exploring the Common Rendering Options

1. Load file **MF14-01.MAX** from the accompanying CD. The scene consists of a teapot sitting on a table in a room.

2. Click Render Scene and then click Render to render the scene. The Rendering dialog box is displayed, showing the phase and progress.

3. The steam from the teapot and the fog in the room are created by using atmospheric effects. Click Render Scene, turn off Atmospherics, and click Render. The scene will now render without the steam or fog.

4. Click Render Scene, turn on Render Hidden, and click Render to render the scene. A hidden object, a banana sitting on the table, is rendered.

5. Turn Atmospherics back on and, in the Output Size area, click the 640¥480 button. Click Files and specify an output filename of **test.jpg**. After specifying the filename, click Setup. In the JPEG Image Control dialog box, set Quality to 65 and click OK. Then, click OK to exit the Render Output File dialog box and click Render to render the scene. The scene is rendered at the higher resolution and the image is saved to file **test.jpg**.

The parameters in the Common Parameters rollout are used by MAX to determine what is to be rendered. These parameters are used, no matter what rendering engine is used. Parameters specific to the rendering engine have their own rollout.

The next section describes the parameters associated with MAX's default rendering engine.

MAX Rendering Engine Options

The options in the Options area of the Render Scene dialog box turn on or off various aspects of the renderer. These options are frequently turned off for draft renderings when you want to quickly render the scene to check object placement and motion. In this area, you can turn on and off texture mapping, shadow generation, and computation of automatic reflection and refraction maps. If the Force Wireframe option is on, all geometry will be rendered as wireframes, regardless of the material settings. The Wire Thickness value defines the thickness of the wires in pixels.

The following exercise takes you through the Options area.

Exploring the Rendering Engine Options

1. Reload file **MF14-01.MAX** from the accompanying CD.
2. Click Render Scene, turn off Mapping and Shadows, and render the scene. The scene is rendered without texture mapping or shadows.
3. Click Render Scene, turn on Force Wireframe, and render the scene with all objects rendered as wireframes.

As you can see from this exercise, it is very easy to turn off various options to increase the rendering speed. Most of the time, you'll want to turn these off for test renderings and on for final renderings. Now take a look at one of the most important aspects of rendering: Anti-Aliasing.

Dealing with Anti-Aliasing

The options in the Anti-Aliasing area control how texture maps and edges of objects are rendered. *Anti-aliasing* is the process of smoothing edges in an image to prevent jagged or broken-up edges. When Anti-Aliasing is disabled, the image renders faster, but the image quality suffers. Figure 14.6 shows the same scene with and without anti-aliasing. Note the breaking up of the thin helix and the jagged edges on the cylinder on the left in Figure 14.6, and how much smoother these areas look on the right.

Figure 14.6   *The teapot scene from earlier in the chapter, with Anti-Aliasing enabled (left) and disabled (right).*

MAX 3 supports the use of Anti-Aliasing filters. What this means is that you now have the capability to select the anti-aliasing algorithm you feel best suits the needs of the scene on which you are working. MAX has 11 different filters. Each is listed below and briefly described:

■ **Area.** This is the filter that was used in MAX 2.5 and earlier. It uses a variable-size filter to create the anti-aliasing. This filter has a size spinner that is roughly equivalent to the old Pixel Size spinner and basically adds a little blur to the image to smooth it.

■ **Blackman.** This filter is great for creating images that are very sharp.

■ **Blend.** This filter is a blend between an Area filter and a Coarse Sharpen filter. This filter has a Filter Size and a Blend control. Larger sizes and blends result in blurrier, less sharp images. This filter is good for creating a scene that is fairly sharp, but not extremely sharp.

■ **Catmull-Rom.** This is another sharp filter, but also adds edge enhancement. The edges of objects are fairly pronounced when you use this filter.

■ **Cook Variable.** This is a general purpose filter that is capable of producing sharp to blurry images. It has a filter size option. Values over 2.5 create more blur in the image.

■ **Cubic.** This is a set blurring filter that results in a somewhat soft, blurred image.

■ **Mitchell-Netravali.** This filter is the tweaker's dream. It has two variables: Blur and Ringing. By adjusting these, you can create a wide assortment of anti-aliasing effects from sharp and crisp to fairly blurry. It is slower than most of the others, but well worth it.

note

The differences between the filters are too subtle to show in figures in this book. The best way to explore different filters is to re-render the same scene with the same settings except for the Anti-Aliasing filter. In some cases, the difference is clear; in others, it isn't. Experience will tell you which ones you like the best.

- **Quadratic.** Another blurring filter that uses a different method.
- **Sharp Quadratic.** A version of quadratic that adds a sharpening effect.
- **Soften.** This is an adjustable Gaussian filter that creates a mild blurring effect. Its filter size variable affects the amount of blurring.
- **Video.** This blurring filter is designed to work with NTSC or PAL video output.

As a guideline, select filters that create sharper images for stills or prints. When going out to video, select one of the filters that blurs the image a little—this will make the output on TV look better. For film or other output options, select the filter that best suits the effect you want.

Filter Maps is the second option in the Anti-Aliasing section of the Render Scene rollout. Turning off Filter Maps disables the filtering of all bitmaps. Bitmap filtering is a memory-intensive task that slows down rendering times. Generally, unless you are doing test renderings, you should always leave Filter Maps on because it will produce the best-looking materials that use bitmaps.

The third and last option for handling anti-aliasing in your scene occurs at the material level and is called SuperSampling. This technique involves anti-aliasing any maps used in a material, above and beyond the filtering process. Turning on SuperSampling increases rendering times but is usually worth it in the end. The SuperSampling controls are located in each material under the SuperSampling rollout, which is shown in Figure 14.7.

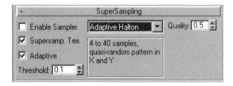

FIGURE 14.7   *The SuperSampling rollout in the Material Editor, where you can enable or disable SuperSampling and select the type of sampling filter you would like to use.*

Like the anti-aliasing filters in the Render Scene dialog box, you can also select SuperSampling filters to sample the materials in different ways (you can choose from four different filters). SuperSampling can be enabled or disabled on a material-by-material basis, or you can apply it globally for the entire scene by turning on the Disable All Samplers option in the Render Scene dialog box.

The following exercise explores the Anti-Aliasing options for the rendering engine.

Exploring the Rendering Engine Anti-Aliasing Options

1. Reload file **MF14-01.MAX** from the accompanying CD.

2. Click Render Scene and then click Render to render the scene. Click the Clone Virtual Frame Buffer button to create a copy of the VFB.

3. In the Render Scene dialog box, set the Anti-Aliasing filter to Mitchell-Netravali. Render the scene and compare the rendering in the VFB to the previous rendering. You should be able to see subtle differences in the scene.

4. Set the Anti-Aliasing filter to Blend. Set the filter size to 4 and re-render. The differences between this rendering and the last should be more pronounced.

   Anti-aliasing is extremely important to high-quality imagery. By combining the methods mentioned in the previous section, you will be able to produce very crisp, clear imagery. The only problem is that with the number of anti-aliasing options, it will take you a while to decide which combinations work best for you. Don't be afraid to experiment.

Raytraced Shadows

The final rendering option to look at is the Max Quadtree Depth parameter, which controls the time versus memory requirements for raytraced shadows. In MAX 2, the Quadtree controls were in the Render Scene dialog box; in MAX 3, they are located in the Raytraced Shadow Params rollout of the individual lights. Higher values make the process of creating raytraced shadows faster but take more RAM than lower values. The lower the value is, the slower the raytraced shadows are to create, but the less RAM you use. Recommended values are between four and eight. Below four, the quadtree gets too small and performance suffers; above eight, too much RAM is used and the rendering speed does not increase proportionally.

Table 14.1 shows the rendering time and memory requirements for different Max Quadtree Depth settings in a simple scene. The default setting is seven.

Table 14.1   Max Quadtree Depth Settings

Max Quadtree Depth	Rendering Time	MAX Memory Requirements
4	16:01 minutes	42.0 megs
5	6:06 minutes	43.0 megs
6	2:36 minutes	43.2 megs
7	1:31 minutes	43.3 megs
8	1:09 minutes	44.4 megs
9	1:04 minutes	46.2 megs
10	1:04 minutes	50.5 megs

As you can see from the table, adjusting the Quadtree limit can be useful and can also be a waste of resources. It really depends on the complexity of the scene with which you are working. Now take a closer look at the virtual frame buffer.

Working with the Virtual Frame Buffer

When you render an image, you will typically output to the Virtual Frame Buffer (VFB), as well as to an output file or device. The VFB remains open after the rendering operation is complete, showing the results of the last frame rendered. You also use the VFB when viewing bitmap files in the Material Editor or via File, View File.

Virtual Frame Buffer Tools

Located across the top of the VFB is a set of command buttons, a drop-down list, and a color swatch, as shown in Figure 14.8.

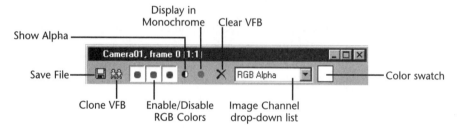

FIGURE 14.8   *The Virtual Frame Buffer's toolbar. You can use the VFB to view and compare images.*

Three buttons—Enable Red Channel, Enable Green Channel, and Enable Blue Channel—turn on and off the display of the red, green, and blue components of the image, respectively. If the button is pushed in, that color component is included in the image display. The Display Alpha Channel button causes the alpha (transparency) channel of the image to be displayed rather than the RGB channel data.

The Monochrome button displays the image in monochrome. The monochrome (or grayscale) value shown for each pixel is the average of the enabled color channel values. Enabling all three color channels provides the same values used by monochrome material map channels, such as for bump or opacity maps.

The Clear button clears all values in the image. The Save Bitmap button enables you to save the image shown in the VFB to a file. The Clone Virtual Frame Buffer button creates a new VFB containing the image shown in the original VFB. Cloning a VFB when you are adjusting materials or lighting enables you to see before and after images—render the scene, clone the VFB, modify the materials or lighting, and re-render.

The Image Channel drop-down list enables you to display additional image channels if they're present in the image. Typically, only the RGBA (Red, Green, Blue, Alpha) channels are present in an image, but if you are outputting to an .rla file, or if the image was rendered in Video Post, additional channels might be present.

In the Virtual Frame Buffer image, you can read the color/alpha value and coordinate location of any pixel. To do this, right-click and hold over the image. While the right mouse button is held down, a dialog box displays the following information about the pixel under the mouse pointer (see Figure 14.9):

- **Image.** Displays general information about the image (Width, Height, Aspect, Gamma, and Image Type).

- **Pixel (X, Y).** For the pixel under the mouse pointer, Pixel displays the RGBA color values and the percentage of each color. Also shown is the monochrome value of the pixel.

- **Optional Pixel Data.** If the image contains additional information, (such as that saved in an .rla file), this area displays that information.

In addition, a color swatch in the title bar stores the color value of the last pixel you clicked. You can drag and drop this color swatch to any other color swatch in MAX, or you can click the color swatch to display the Color Selector dialog box for further detail.

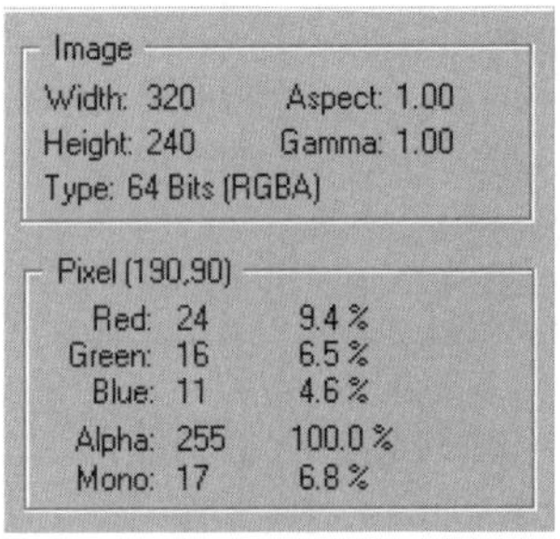

FIGURE 14.9   *The VFB when you right-click the image. Notice the amount of information displayed in the pop-up dialog box.*

Zooming and Panning the Virtual Frame Buffer

You can zoom in and out and pan the image in the VFB. You can even do this while a scene is rendering. To zoom in by two, press Ctrl and left-click. To zoom out by two, right-click. To pan the image, press Shift and left-click and drag or use the VFB scrollbars.

You should now have a good understanding of the rendering process and the effects of the rendering options on the rendered image. Because a full production rendering can take a significant amount of time, it is important to understand the effect of the various options on the rendering speed and image quality. Understanding these trade-offs is actually more important for rendering still images than for rendering animations. Any rendering defects are usually quite noticeable in a high-resolution still image. Animations are typically rendered at a lower resolution and object motion tends to draw the viewer's attention, making rendering defects less noticeable.

If you have a three-button mouse or a Microsoft Intellimouse, you can use its third-button or wheel to zoom and pan. Roll the wheel to zoom in or out. To pan, press the wheel and drag, or drag by using the middle button on a three-button mouse. You must have the Pan/Zoom option chosen in the Customize, Preferences, Viewports dialog box to use the third button for panning and zooming.

Rendering for Animations

To render an animation, you start by activating the view you want to render. Then choose the Render Scene button on the main toolbar, just as you would for a still frame. (Alternatively, you can select the view in the Render Scene dialog box.) In the Render Scene dialog box, several settings apply to rendering animations. These include the Time Range, Video Color Checking, Motion Blur, Field Rendering, and Net Rendering.

Animation is nothing more than the display of a sequence of images at a rate fast enough to give the illusion of motion. To achieve this effect, you have to render many still frames. In the Time Output area of the Render Scene dialog box, you define which frames you are going to render. You can render the active time segment, a specific range, or specific sets of frames.

Animations typically are rendered with the intent of outputting the animation to videotape. Unfortunately, videotape is not a great medium, because neither the NTSC standard or the PAL video standard support as wide a color range as MAX does. If you are rendering the animation with the intention of taking it to videotape, you should turn on the Video Color Check check box in the Options area of the Render Scene dialog box. This enables you to check the colors of each output image relative to acceptable color ranges for the videotape type (NTSC or PAL) to which you are recording. You can define how Video Color Check is performed by choosing Customize, Preferences and clicking the Rendering tab in the Preference Settings dialog box (see Figure 14.10).

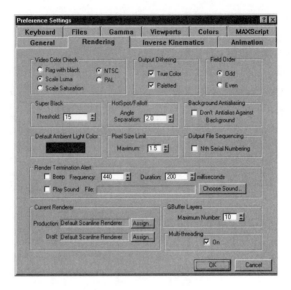

FIGURE 14.10   *The Rendering tab of the Preferences dialog box. This is where you can define some of the defaults for rendering.*

In the Video Color Check area in the upper-left corner of the Rendering tab, you can determine how MAX handles the color checking. First—and most important—you should choose the video standard to which you are outputting. In the United States and Japan, it is NTSC; in other places, it might be NTSC or PAL, but more than likely PAL. Then you can determine how MAX should handle colors in your images that are not compatible with the standards.

The options found in the Video Color Check area are described in the following list, with their effects:

- **Flag with Black.** Each pixel that is out of the acceptable color range is colored black. You can adjust the materials or lighting so the material does not exceed acceptable color limits.

- **Scale Luma.** Each pixel's luminance is scaled up or down until the color is within the acceptable range. If the pixel's color is already within the range, it is not scaled.

- **Scale Saturation.** Each pixel's color saturation is scaled up or down until the color is within the acceptable range. If the pixel's color is already within the range, it is not scaled.

Very bright green colors fail video color checking. Even if a color passes video color checking, that does not mean the color will look good when viewed on a video monitor. All very bright colors tend to bleed when displayed on a video monitor, with bright red being the worst. When you design your colors in Material Editor, keep the saturation value of your colors at less than 200.

Motion Blur

If you look at a still frame from a movie or from a video, you will notice that the edges of moving objects are rather blurred along the direction of motion. This happens because the object is in one position when the shutter opens and in another when the shutter closes. The captured image is actually of the object in all its positions between the opening and closing of the shutter. You can use motion blur in MAX to approximate this effect. In a playback of animated sequences, motion blur provides a smoothness of motion that is not present if motion blur is not applied. Figure 14.11 shows a scene rendered without motion blur, and Figure 14.12 shows the same scene rendered with motion blur.

FIGURE 14.11   *A scene rendered without motion blur.*

MAX supports three types of motion blur: Object, Scene, and Image. MAX performs Object motion blur by rendering multiple copies of selected objects within a single rendering. Scene motion blur is performed by rendering the scene multiple times and then compositing the resulting images. Image motion blur is performed by rendering the objects once and calculating a linear motion vector for each pixel, which is then blurred along its motion vector. Object and Image motion blur are performed either by using Render Scene or in Video Post. Scene motion blur can be performed only in Video Post.

To perform Image or Object motion blur on an object, you first need to turn on Motion Blur for the object. To do this, right-click the object and choose Properties from the pop-up menu to display the Object Properties dialog box shown in Figure 14.13. In the Motion Blur area of this dialog box, you can specify whether to perform no motion blur, Object motion blur, or Image motion blur on the object. The Multiplier field for Image motion blur is described later in this section.

FIGURE 14.12   *The same scene rendered with motion blur.*

FIGURE 14.13   *The Object Properties dialog box, where you can enable or disable motion blur for individual objects.*

After you have turned on motion blur for one or more objects, you need to set the motion blur parameters in the Render Scene dialog box. In the MAX Default Scanline A-Buffer rollout, there are parameters for both Object and Image motion blur (see Figure 14.14). For each type of motion blur, you need to click Apply so that type of motion blur will be calculated. Both motion blur areas also contain a Duration (Frames) field that specifies how much time to include in the motion blur around the frame being rendered—think of this parameter as determining how long a camera's shutter would be open. This exposure time is centered around the frame;

for example, if you are rendering frame 10 and set a Duration value of 1, the exposure period will be from frame 9.5 to 10.5. For a Duration value of 0.5, the exposure period will be 9.75 to 10.25. Typical Duration values are in the range of 0.3 to 0.5.

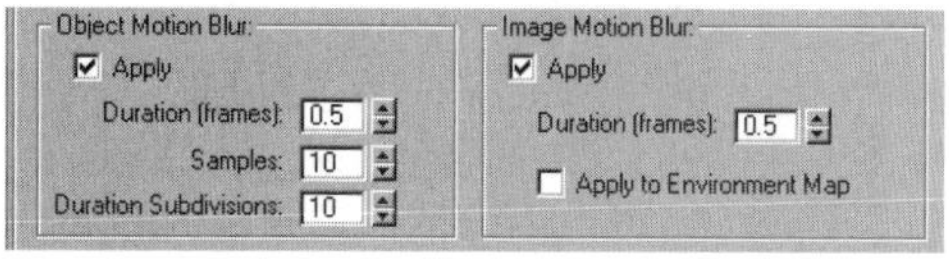

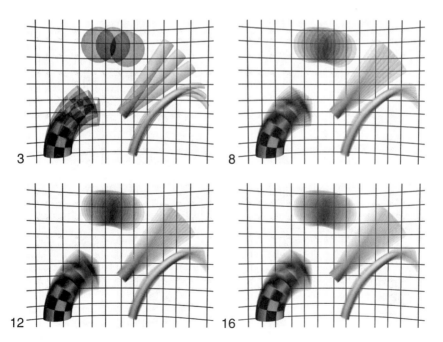

FIGURE 14.14   *The Motion Blur controls in the Render Scene dialog box. Here, you can define exactly how the motion blur is created.*

When you're using Object motion blur, two additional settings are available: Duration Subdivisions and Samples. The Duration Subdivisions parameter sets the number of copies of the object to render per frame. If this parameter is set to three, one copy of the object will be rendered at the beginning of the exposure period, one at the middle, and one at the end. Figure 14.15 shows a scene rendered with Duration Subdivisions values of 3, 8, 12, and 16. Notice that as the Duration Subdivisions value increases, the number of copies increases, and the resulting motion blur looks smoother.

FIGURE 14.15   *Renderings of a scene, using Object motion blur with Duration Subdivisions values of 3, 8, 12, and 16.*

The Samples parameter controls how many times these copies are sampled in the final rendered image. It is best to think of Samples in terms of the percentage 100 (Samples/Duration Subdivisions). At 100%, all pixels from each copy of the object are included in the rendered image. At 50%, half of the pixels from each copy are included, or 2 lower than the Duration Subdivisions value. Figure 14.16 shows a scene rendered with a Duration Subdivisions value of 12 and Samples values of 6, 8, 10, and 12. Notice that as the Samples value increases, each copy of the objects becomes more solid. resulting in dithering of the image. Typical Duration Subdivisions values are in the range of 10 to 16, with Samples set at one.

Image motion blur has two additional settings: Multiplier in the Object Properties dialog box and Apply to Environment Map in the Render Scene dialog box. By using the Multiplier parameter, you can increase or decrease the amount of Image motion blur on an object-by-object basis. For example, with the Multiplier value set to two, the object's "streak" is twice as long as when the Multiplier value remains at one. The total length of an object's streak is a function of the Multiplier value and the Duration value. If the Apply to Environment Map option is turned on, environmental background images will also be blurred, based on the amount of camera motion. Figure 14.16 shows the same scene as in Figure 14.15, rendered with Image motion blur.

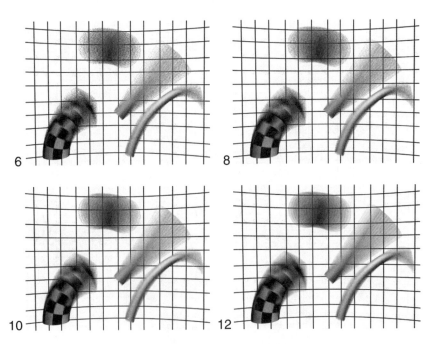

Figure 14.16 *Renderings of a scene, using Object motion blur with Samples values of 6, 8, 10, and 12.*

As explained previously, Image motion blur is performed by calculating a linear motion vector for each pixel and then blurring the pixel along its motion vector. The motion vectors are based on the difference in a pixel's position at a time slightly before the rendering time and its position at the rendering time. As a result, Image motion blur will not be accurate if the point on the object corresponding to a pixel is not moving in a straight line. Also, Image motion blur will not be accurate if the point on the object is not coming into the frame as it moves. This is most evident at frame 0, where typically there is no motion coming into the frame. Figure 14.17 shows an Object motion blur rendering in which the object is moving with a curvilinear trajectory. Figure 14.18 shows the same object rendered by using Image motion blur. Although Image motion blur is typically faster to perform than Scene or Object motion blur and usually looks better, the limitations of Image motion blur sometimes prevent its use.

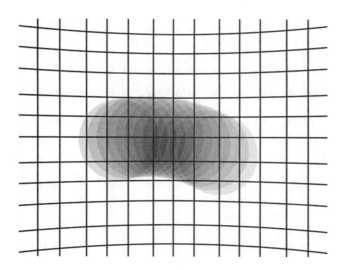

Figure 14.17   *Rendering by using Object motion blur of an object moving with a curvilinear trajectory.*

Animated object transforms, object deformations, and camera transforms are reflected when performing Object or Image motion blur. Animated environmental effects (including background images), camera parameters (such as FOV), and object materials are not reflected in the execution of Object or Image motion blur. Also, changes in the environmental background image due to camera transforms are not reflected with Object motion blur but can be with Image motion blur.

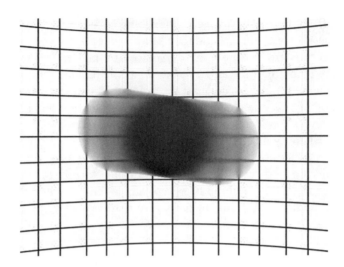

FIGURE 14.18   *Rendering by using Image motion blur of an object moving with a curvilinear trajectory.*

You should note that motion blur can slow down the rendering process substantially and should be used only when necessary. Memory requirements depend on the number of faces in objects selected for Object motion blur and on the size of the output image for Image motion blur. For Object motion blur, additional memory is required for each copy of the object created. For Image motion blur, an additional 14 bytes per pixel are required. (For a 640×480 image, this means an additional 4.3MB of memory.)

You can perform Scene motion blur only from Video Post. When you add a scene event to the Video Post queue, the dialog box shown in Figure 14.19 is displayed. To turn on Scene motion blur, set its check box in the Scene Options area. When you execute a Video Post queue when a scene event has Scene motion blur turned on, you will see that the scene is rendered multiple times per frame and then the separate images are composited. The Duration field specifies how much time to include in the motion blur around the frame being rendered. The Duration Subdivisions field sets the number of times to render the scene per frame. The Dither % field specifies the amount of dithering to use when compositing the individual scene images from each subdivision rendering into the final image for the frame. Scene motion blur can be used in conjunction with Object and Image motion blur if needed.

In the following exercise, you render a bowling alley simulation. The scene will be rendered with no motion blur, Object motion blur, and Image motion blur to show you the differences in image quality and rendering time in a real-world example.

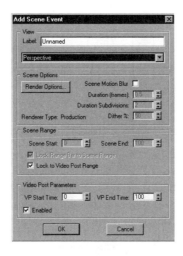

FIGURE 14.19   *The Add Scene Event dialog box in Video Post, where you can enable or disable Scene motion blur.*

Rendering an Animation

1. Load file **MF14-02.MAX** from the accompanying CD. This scene contains the results of the dynamic simulation in the bowling alley.

2. Select the Camera03 viewport and click Render Scene. Select Range and set the range to frames 15–50 in the Time Output area. In Output size, select 320×240.

3. Choose Files and type an output filename of **MF14-02.AVI**.

4. Choose Setup, Cinepak Codec. Set the Compression Quality to 70. If Key Frame is turned off, turn it on and set it to 15 frames. Click OK to close the Video Compression dialog box and click Save to close the Render Output File dialog box.

5. Now, click Render to render the animation. When the rendering is complete, choose File, View File to view **MF14-02.AVI**.

6. In the Front viewport, select all the pins and the bowling ball. Right-click the selected objects and choose Properties from the pop-up menu. In the Object Properties dialog box, turn on Object in the Motion Blur area.

7. Select the Camera03 viewport and render the animation to file **MF14-02B.AVI**. When the rendering is complete, view **MF14-02B.AVI**.

8. Right-click one of the selected objects and choose Properties from the pop-up menu. In the Object Properties dialog box, turn on Image in the Motion Blur area.

9. Select the Camera03 viewport and render the animation to file **MF14-02C.AVI**. When the rendering is complete, view **MF14-02C.AVI**.

When viewing the AVI files from the previous example, you can see that the use of motion blur makes the animation look much more realistic, but at a cost of increased rendering times. Rendering time was approximately three times longer when you used Object motion blur, but only about 10% longer when you used Image motion blur. In the previous example, the limitations of Image motion blur are not obvious while playing back the animation, so Image motion blur should be used in this case.

Field Rendering

The most important aspect of rendering an animation for video output is probably field rendering. Video output displays information in an interlaced manner. This means the video output first displays every other scanline of information and then repeats by displaying the scanlines it missed the first time. Most computer monitors are noninterlaced, so all scanlines are refreshed in order.

To get the smoothest motion in your animations when they are played back on a TV screen, you should always use field rendering. This causes MAX to render every other scanline of the frame and then to come back and render the scanlines it missed. When MAX renders the second set of scanlines, however, it moves forward in time in the animation by half a frame. Field-rendered images don't look as good as still frames because of this, but the motion on a videotape is excellent. Rendering to fields increases the overall processing time for the animation, of course.

When you render to fields, you must determine which field of the frame is rendered first. You can render either odd or even fields first. You set this value in the Preference Settings dialog box on the Rendering tab, as shown in Figure 14.20. Before you decide which field order to use, you should match the order to the output device you are using. A DPS Perception Video Recorder (PVR), for example, can accept either order of field rendering; you just need to match the setting in MAX to the settings on the PVR. You should check the documentation on your output hardware or software to see which field order to use.

When you do field rendering, the playback of the animation changes slightly. Instead of referring to the playback speed as 30 frames per second, you say it plays back at 60 fields per second. Remember, each frame has two fields. When the documentation of a specific output device specifies 60 fields per second, this refers to the field-rendering playback speed.

In the next section, special effects that can be rendered in the scene are described. These special effects, called environmental effects, are not based on scene geometry. Rather, they form the background against which the scene geometry is rendered or are effects that are applied to part of the scene or the entire scene volume.

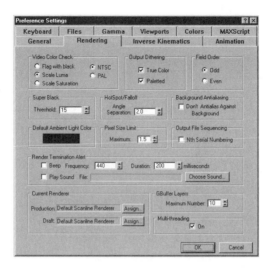

Figure 14.20   *The Rendering tab of the Preferences dialog box, where you can set the field order for field-rendered images.*

Working with Environments

For many scenes, you need to simulate real-world environments so you can create the realism and sense of space critical to a rendering. For example, a nighttime scene in the early spring or late fall, such as around Halloween, would greatly benefit from the use of fog to create a sense of ambiance and mood. These environments can be earthly or alien, day or night, but in all cases, careful use of environmental effects greatly enhances the realism and overall impact of the image or animation.

This section focuses on how to create environmental effects. In particular, you learn how to work with volumetric fog, fog, combustion, and environment background.

Environmental effects in MAX are accessed by choosing Environment from the Rendering pull-down menu. This displays the Environment dialog box shown in Figure 14.21. The dialog box is divided into three areas: Background, Global Lighting, and Atmosphere. The Environment Background controls in the Background section of the dialog box are covered later in this chapter.

The Global Lighting section contains the Ambient color swatch, along with two controls that globally affect all lights in the scene except the ambient light. The Tint color swatch tints all lights in the scene by that color; click the color swatch to display the color selector. The Level value acts as a multiplier to all lights in the scene except ambient light. Thus, a level of one (default) preserves the normal light settings, higher numbers raise the lighting, and lower numbers reduce the lighting.

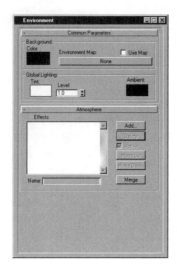

FIGURE 14.21   *The Environment dialog box, where you can add and edit environmental effects for your scene.*

The Atmosphere section enables you to create and add four types of atmospheric events to your rendering: Combustion, Fog, Volumetric Fog, and Volumetric Lights. Choosing the Add button in the Atmosphere section displays the Add Atmospheric Effect dialog box, in which you can add one of these four atmospheric effects. Volumetric Lights were previously described in Chapter 11, "Working with Lights and Cameras."

Volumetric Fog

Volumetric fog is similar to a volumetric light except that the fog can permeate the entire scene or be confined within an atmospheric gizmo. Many of the parameters for volumetric fog are the same as for volumetric lights. Volumetric fog is used instead of regular fog to give it some irregularity and make it look more realistic. When you choose this option from the list in the Add Atmospheric Effect dialog box, MAX displays the Volume Fog Parameters rollout shown in Figure 14.22.

An atmospheric gizmo specifies the volume in the scene to which an atmospheric effect is limited. You create atmospheric gizmos by using the Helpers category of the Create panel and choosing Atmospheric Apparatus from the pop-up menu list. You can create gizmos in three shapes: box, cylinder, and sphere (which can be a sphere or a hemisphere). As with their matching geometry types, you create gizmos by dragging the mouse to create the initial dimensions.

After you create an atmospheric gizmo, it can be moved, rotated, or scaled. By performing nonuniform scaling on the gizmo, you can directionally stretch or compress the fog. If you scale an atmospheric gizmo in its vertical direction, for example, you can create effects, such as steam rising off of water.

FIGURE 14.22   *The Volumetric Fog Parameters rollout, where you can define how the volumetric fog will appear in the scene.*

The atmospheric gizmos to which you apply a Volume Fog are specified in the Gizmos area of the Volume Fog Parameters rollout. If no atmospheric gizmo is specified, the Volume Fog is applied to the entire scene. When you apply Volume Fog to a gizmo, the fog fills the entirety of the gizmo. By increasing the Soften Gizmo Edges value, you can soften the fog at the edges of the gizmo so that the shape of the gizmo is not noticeable. Normally, you want the fog to apply to both the background and the objects in the scene. If you are compositing the rendered image with other images, you might want only the objects to be fogged. In this case, you should turn off Fog Background, which will prevent fogging of areas where no objects are located.

MAX renders a Volume Fog by stepping through the fog and calculating the fog intensity at each step. The number of steps evaluated is specified by the MAX Steps value. In most cases, a much lower MAX Steps setting can be used for Volume Fogs that are applied to atmospheric gizmos. Because the rendering time gets longer as the MAX Steps value gets higher, it is best to perform test renderings starting with a low value and increasing it until the aliasing that occurs at low values disappears.

For Volume Fogs applied to a gizmo, the step size is based on the size of the atmospheric gizmo. Because Volume Fogs that are not applied to an atmospheric gizmo extend to infinity, you need to specify the Step Size for MAX to use. Again, some experimentation is needed to determine the proper Step Size value to use, but an initial value can be estimated by taking the distance from the camera to the farthest object and then dividing that distance by the MAX Steps value.

The following exercise shows how to create and use volumetric fog.

Creating and Using Volumetric Fog

1. Load the file **MF14-03.MAX** from the accompanying CD. Render the Camera viewport to see what it looks like at the moment (see Figure 14.23).

FIGURE 14.23   *The temple scene before adding volumetric fog.*

2. Choose Rendering, Environment and select the Add button.

3. Choose Volume Fog from the Add Atmospheric Effects dialog box. Set Density to 5, Size to 10, and Uniformity to 0.1 and turn on Exponential and Turbulence.

4. Render the Camera viewport. Figure 14.24 shows the rendered scene.

5. In the Helpers branch of the Create command panel, choose Atmospheric Apparatus from the drop-down list.

6. In the Top viewport, create a CylGizmo centered on the camera. Give it a radius of about 1000 and a height of 15.

7. In the Environment dialog box, click Pick Gizmo and click the CylGizmo.

8. Render the Camera viewport to see what it looks like at the moment (see Figure 14.25).

   Volume Fog creates a three-dimensional fog in the scene. You can use Volume Fog to create fog that moves through the scene over time, as well as fog or clouds that you can walk or fly through. By assigning Volume Fog to atmospheric gizmos, you limit the volume of the scene to which the Volume Fog is applied.

FIGURE 14.24   *The scene, with Volumetric Fog applied to the entire scene.*

FIGURE 14.25   *The scene with Volumetric Fog applied to an atmospheric gizmo.*

Fog

The Fog atmospheric effect is a standard generic fog. When compared to a Volumetric Fog, a standard fog does not have very much in the way of noise controls to add nonuniformity and realism to the fog. Standard fog is based on the Near and Far range settings for the current camera view—in other words, Fog is view dependent.

When you choose Fog from the Add Atmospheric Effect dialog box, you see the rollout shown in Figure 14.26.

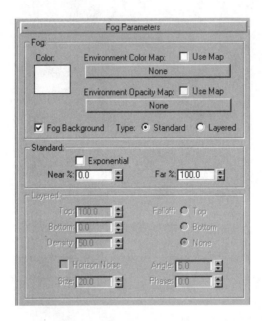

FIGURE 14.26   *The Fog rollout in the Environment Dialog Box. Here, you can define how regular fog appears in your scene.*

The Fog Parameters rollout is divided into three areas: Fog, Standard, and Layered. The Fog area controls the way the fog appears in the scene, regardless of fog type.

Choosing the Standard fog type activates the Standard area of the dialog box, which has only three controls. Near % sets the percentage of fog at the near camera range, Far % sets the percentage of fog at the far camera range, and the Exponential control works the same as with Volumetric lights.

Choosing the Layered fog type activates the Layered area of the dialog box. With a layered fog, you can vary the density of the fog from top to bottom.

The following exercise shows how to create a Fog atmospheric effect.

Creating and Using Fog

1. Load the file **MF14-03.MAX** from the accompanying CD. (Reload this file from scratch if you worked on the previous exercise.)
2. Select the camera and, in the Modify command panel, choose Show in the Environment Ranges area.
3. Set the Near range to 70 and the Far range to 500. The fog will start at the Near range and grow progressively more dense as it approaches the Far range.
4. Choose Rendering, Environment, and select the Add button.
5. Choose Fog from the Add Atmospheric Effects dialog box. In the Standard section, set Near % to 20, and Far % to 75.
6. Render the Camera viewport. Figure 14.27 shows the rendered scene.

FIGURE 14.27   *The scene rendered with Standard Fog.*

7. Change the fog type to Layered, set Top to 20, Density to 15, and Falloff to Top.
8. Render the Camera viewport. Figure 14.28 shows the rendered scene.

FIGURE 14.28   *The scene rendered with Layered Fog.*

For further practice on your own, experiment with the Horizon Noise angle to see how increasing the angle "pushes down" the solid fog in the rendered image. Also try using either an environment or opacity map to see how it affects the fog.

In most cases, it is better to use Volume Fog, rather than Fog, when applied to a Box atmospheric gizmo. Volume Fog provides better control over the fog generation, and you can adjust its parameters to achieve a more realistic fog effect.

Combustion

Combustion is used to produce animated fire, smoke, and explosion effects. Because no geometry is required to produce these effects, they're virtually RAM-free and render much more quickly than would a particle system. When you choose Combustion from the Add Atmospheric Effects dialog box, you see the rollout shown in Figure 14.29.

Combustion is similar to Volume Fog in that it is applied to an atmospheric gizmo. The combustion effect is constrained to the atmospheric gizmo, which can be moved, rotated, or scaled. By performing nonuniform scaling on the gizmo, you can directionally stretch or compress the combustion effect. For example, if you scale an atmospheric gizmo up in one direction, you can create a jet's exhaust.

Combustion can be used to create either fires or explosions. How the various Combustion parameters affect the Combustion effect depends on which of these you are creating. To create fires, you turn off the Explosion option in the Explosion area. To create explosions, you turn on this option.

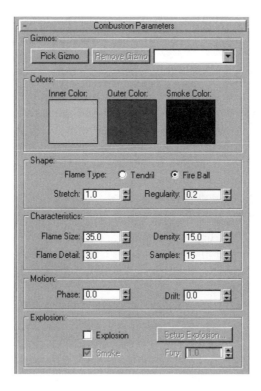

FIGURE 14.29   *The Combustion rollout, where you can set up combustion type effects for your scene.*

When Explosion is off, the color of the flame varies between the Inner and Outer colors defined in the Colors area. The flames rise based on the rate of change of the Drift value, and they churn based on the rate of change of the Phase value. Typical fires, such as campfires and candles, have fairly high rates of change for the Drift value and low rates of change for the Phase value. For pool fires (such as an oil spill), the rate of change on the Phase value would be high to give a turbulent fire.

If Explosion is turned on, the Phase value controls the timing of the explosion. An explosion goes through three phases: Expansion (Phase=0 to 100), Burnoff (Phase=100 to 200), and Dissipation (Phase=200 to 300). The maximum intensity of the explosion occurs as a Phase value of 100. When Smoke is turned on, the flame colors will turn to the smoke color as the phase parameter goes from 100 to 200. The flames rise based on the rate of change of the Drift value, and they churn based on the Fury value.

There are two Flame Types from which you can choose in the Shape area: Tendril, in which the flames are pointy at the ends and have veins along their centers, and Fire Ball, in which the flames are more puffy and round, as if they are balls of fire. Tendrils are most often used for fire effects, whereas Fire Ball is typically used for explosions.

The length of individual flames in the gizmo is controlled by the Stretch parameter, and the Regularity parameter affects the overall shape of the fire. By decreasing the Regularity value, you can pull the flames in from the edges of the gizmo so that the shape of the gizmo is not noticeable. The Stretch value is usually based on the intensity of the fire—weak fires have a low Stretch value, but a blazing bonfire has a high Stretch value. Open fires typically have low Regularity values; a constrained fire, such as in a fireplace, would have higher Regularity values.

In the Characteristics area, you can adjust the characteristics of the flames. Flame Size specifies the size of the individual flames or tendrils. This does not influence the overall size of the effect but instead acts on the characteristic appearance of the fire. Flame Detail specifies the amount of detail within the individual flames. If this parameter is low, the flames will be smooth with little detail; larger values provide more detail. Density specifies the density or overall strength of the effect, and Samples specifies the rate at which the volume is sampled. Higher values give more precision and generally produce better results but at the expense of slower rendering times.

The Setup Explosion button is an aid for quickly setting up explosions. Clicking this button displays the Setup Explosion Phase Curve dialog box in which two spinner controls specify a start and end time for the explosion. After you click OK, the existing phase curve is discarded and a new phase curve is created that represents an explosion over the specified interval. Only the Phase values are set by using Setup Explosion, and the remaining parameters need to be adjusted to give the desired effect.

The following exercise uses Combustion to add jet exhausts to an airplane.

Using Combustion

1. Load the file **MF14-04.MAX** from the accompanying CD. The scene shows an airplane flying over a lake, and you want to use Combustion to add the jet exhausts. Two SphereGizmos have already been created in the scene and are nonuniformly scaled to achieve the proper shape.

2. Choose Rendering, Environment and select the Add button.

3. Choose Combustion from the Add Atmospheric Effects dialog box.

4. In the Gizmos area, click Pick Gizmo and select one of the SphereGizmos in the Top viewport. Repeat and select the other SphereGizmo.

5. In the Shape area, set Stretch to 0.01 and Regularity to 0.5. In the Characteristics area, set Flame Size to 4, Flame Details to 3, and Density to 200.

6. Render the Camera viewport. Figure 14.30 shows the rendered scene.

Figure 14.30   *The scene after adding a combustion effect to the plane. This scene also shows a good use of the Matte/Shadow material.*

The parameter values to be used in Combustion vary greatly, depending on the type of fire or explosion you are modeling. Typically you use an atmospheric gizmo approximating the overall shape of the fire or explosion, specify the shape of the flames as Tendrils or a Fire Ball, and specify whether a fire or explosion is being modeled. If an explosion is being modeled, the you then set the Phase values to establish the timing of the explosion. Next, you adjust the colors and density to set the overall color and brightness. Finally, you adjust the remaining parameters to give the flames the desired look. A lot of experimentation might be required to get the exact effect you desire.

Environment Maps

Environment maps are used in two places in MAX: the Background environment map and the Fog Color and Opacity maps. Environment mapping enables you to map a bitmap to the environment rather than to a particular object. If you want to render your scene on top of a city background, for example, you could use a Background environment map with screen environment mapping. Also, if you want to create an animation of a scene with a sky background, you could use a Background environment map with Spherical or Cylindrical environment mapping.

The mechanics of applying and using environment maps for Fog are the same as for the background. In this section, only the Background environment map is discussed, but the information also applies to the Fog environment maps.

You can use four types of environmental mapping: Screen, Spherical, Cylindrical, and Shrink Wrap. Spherical mapping, for example, creates an infinitely large sphere around your scene and maps the background to the inside of the sphere. The background controls are located in the Background area of the Environment dialog box.

The Background controls are rather simple to use. By clicking the color swatch, you can use the standard color picker to define a color for the background. For all areas of the rendered image where no object appears, the background color will be displayed. To the right of the color swatch is the Environment Map button. To assign a map to the background, click the Environment Map button to display the standard Material/Map Browser dialog box.

Because the environment map is a map, you can use any of the standard map types, such as Gradient, Bitmap, Mask, and so on. When you choose a map type, its name is displayed on the Environment Map button. To adjust the parameters associated with the map, or to assign a bitmap if the Bitmap map type is chosen, you must assign the map to a slot in the Material Editor. You can do this by opening the Material Editor and dragging from the Environment Map button to a Material Editor slot. This will display the Instance (Copy) Map dialog box, in which you should specify to instance the map so that any changes made to the map in Material Editor will be automatically reflected in the environment map. Alternatively, you can define a map in Material Editor and drag that map to the Environment Map button. At this point, you adjust the map parameters in Material Editor in the same fashion as you would adjust any other map.

If the assigned map is a 2D map (such as Bitmap, Checker, or Gradient), you will see, at the top of the Coordinates section of the rollout, options on whether to use Texture or Environment coordinates and which type or subset of mapping coordinates to use. For environment maps, you must choose Environment coordinates. In the Mapping drop-down list, you can choose the type of environment coordinates you are going to use. Descriptions of the four choices follow:

- **Spherical.** Enables you to map the environment to the inside of an infinitely large sphere. The map is applied around the sphere, and then its upper and lower edges are pulled in to the poles of the sphere. Watch out for two things. First, be sure to use a high-resolution bitmap; otherwise, the background will look stretched and fuzzy. Second, there will always be a seam where the map starts and ends on the sphere; try to keep that seam behind the camera and out of view when rendering.

- **Cylindrical.** Enables you to map the environment to the inside of an infinitely large cylinder instead of a sphere. The same warnings that apply to spherical mapping apply here.

- **Shrink Wrap.** Enables you to map the environment to the inside of an infinitely large sphere. The map is draped around the sphere, with all four edges pulled in to one pole of the sphere.

- **Screen.** Enables you to map the environment directly to the view. As the view changes, the screen mapping travels along with the view. This is great for still images and can be used when you want to match your scene to a real background.

After you have chosen the environment mapping type, the environment is set; this is the way it will render until you disable the environment mapping in the Environment dialog box. You can disable the environment map by turning off Use Map in the Background area of the Environment dialog box.

The following exercise shows you how to create an environment map.

Creating and Using an Environment Map

1. Load the file **MF14-05.MAX** from the accompanying CD.

2. Choose Rendering, Environment from the pull-down menus.

3. Click the Environment Map button in the Background area. Double-click Bitmap in the Material/Map Browser to assign it as the map type. Select **Cloud2v.jpg** as the map to use.

4. Open the Material Editor and drag from the Environment Map button to the Material Editor slot #6. In the Instance (Copy) Map dialog box, specify to instance the map.

5. In the Coordinates rollout, make sure Environ is selected and set Mapping to Screen. Set the W Angle to 90.

6. Render the Camera view. Figure 14.31 shows the rendered scene.

FIGURE 14.31   *The scene after applying a bitmap to use as the background.*

7. In the Material Editor, change the map type from Bitmap to Cellular, discarding the old map.

8. In the Cell Characteristics area, change Size to 2 and Spread to 0.02.

9. Render the Camera view. Figure 14.32 shows the rendered scene.

FIGURE 14.32 *The scene after using a Cellular map as the background to simulate a star field.*

Environment maps are useful for assigning fixed or animated backgrounds to your scene. This can reduce the amount of modeling required to duplicate the background or allow the use of "real-world" images in the background. If the background objects in a scene aren't affected by the foreground objects, the background objects can be rendered to an image, which can be used as the background. This can also significantly reduce rendering time.

Perspective Matching

Perspective matching makes use of a screen-environment mapped background and the camera's horizon line to match the perspective of your scene to the background. This is done when you want to render your scene into a photograph or other such background. Architects often use this feature to render buildings into the site context. For best results, and to decrease rendering time, always try to use background bitmaps that are the same size and resolution as your final output.

After you have set up the environment map, use a shaded view of your Camera viewport to perform the perspective match. In this shaded view, you can turn on the background and use the camera controls to change the Camera view to match the perspective of the background. To turn on a background image, choose Views, Viewport Background, which displays the dialog box shown in Figure 14.33.

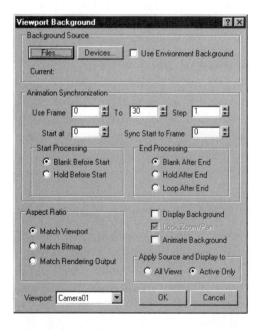

FIGURE 14.33   *The Viewport Background dialog box, where you can load images into the viewports as backgrounds.*

In the Background Source section, choose Use Environment Background to use the same bitmap you are using as the screen environment map. Alternatively, if you want to be able to zoom in and pan on a bitmap background in orthographic viewports, click Files and select the bitmap file being used as a background. In the Aspect Ratio area, turn on Match Bitmap and turn on Lock Zoom/Pan.

tip

You can zoom in and pan on a bitmap in Perspective and Camera viewports, but you need to use virtual viewports to do so. See the MAX documentation for information on virtual viewports.

To turn on the background display in the viewport, turn on Display Background at the bottom right of the Viewport Background dialog box. When you choose OK, the image is displayed as the background of the current viewport.

The following exercise shows how to create and use perspective matching.

Creating and Using Perspective Matching

1. Load the file **MF14-06.MAX** from the accompanying CD.
2. Choose Rendering, Environment. Assign bitmap lake_mt.jpg as the background environment map and set the environmental mapping type to Screen.
3. Close the Environment and Material Editor dialog boxes.
4. Click the Camera viewport name to activate it, if it is not already active.
5. Choose Views, Viewport Background, and turn on Use Environment Background and Display Background.
6. Select the camera and, in the Modify command panel, turn on Show Horizon for the camera. A line appears in the Camera viewport, as shown in Figure 14.34.

FIGURE 14.34 *The camera viewport, showing the background image and the horizon line.*

7. Activate the Camera viewport if it is not active.

8. Choose Orbit Camera from the Viewport control buttons.

9. Click and drag around in the viewport until the horizon line matches the shoreline in the background image; then release the mouse button.

10. Render the Camera viewport. Figure 14.35 shows the final rendering.

FIGURE 14.35   *The scene after perspective matching.*

Perspective matching enables you to set up the camera so that the ground plane associated with the objects in your scene matches that of the background image. Special effects can show objects in the scene interacting with the background image. You accomplish this with "shadow catchers," created by assigning Matte/Shadow materials to objects in the scene and using the Camera Mapping modifier to apply to objects a mapping that matches the background image mapping.

Conclusion

Rendering and output are important issues that will grow familiar as you work with MAX. Environmental effects are important to creating ambiance and mood in certain scenes. Backgrounds are necessary to provide an extra hint of realism to most renderings or animations. Making use of these tools will greatly enhance not only your skills, but your overall output quality. This chapter taught you the following:

- Common rendering parameters
- Multithreaded rendering
- Working with the Virtual Frame Buffer

- Creating and rendering a scene
- Working with environmental effects

This concludes the fundamentals on composition and rendering. Although you have learned the basics here, you'll learn much more with experience. Practice these tools—the most important tools for producing a rich, powerful rendering.

PART IV

Animation Fundamentals

CHAPTER 15

Understanding Animation Concepts

Up to this point, you have explored numerous features of MAX: the user interface, modeling, editing, composition, materials, rendering, and environments. But these are only part of what MAX brings to you. One of the most powerful features of MAX is its capability to animate almost any geometry, light, camera, or modifier.

This chapter examines the basics of computer animation in MAX. In this chapter, you will learn about the following topics and how they apply to animating with MAX:

- What Can Be Animated in MAX
- Animation Fundamentals
- Understanding Time in Computer Animation
- Advanced Animation Topics

The rest of the chapter discusses the basic and advanced concepts of animation in relation to 3D Studio MAX. You will read about practical application of these concepts in the next several chapters.

What Can Be Animated in MAX

You can animate all object, sub-object, and gizmo transforms in MAX, as well as most object, modifier, material, and atmospheric effect parameters. In Video Post, you can animate many of the parameters of the Video Post filters. The same applies for render effects and even some of the rendering engine parameters. Parameters that you cannot typically animate are time-related parameters (such as the detonation time in the Bomb space warp and the start and life parameters in the particle systems) and space-warp and particle-system icon sizes. On/off or multiple-choice options in the command panels are sometimes animatable and sometimes not.

The easiest way to discover which parameters you can animate is to create the object, apply the modifier, or create the material, and then display all of the tracks for the object, modifier, or material in Track View. Track View, which will be described in Chapter 16, "Exploring Basic Animation Methods," shows all available animatable parameters by name.

Another way to discover whether a parameter that has a spinner is animatable is to turn on the Animate button and adjust the spinner. If a red bracket appears around the spinner, the parameter is animatable. The red bracket also indicates the presence of an animated key.

Animation Fundamentals

This section introduces concepts associated with basic animation. As you become familiar with the more fundamental animation concepts and methods, you will find it easier to perform your job as an animator. A good understanding of the fundamentals of animation will also make understanding and working with advanced animation topics—character animation, for example—much easier. The concepts covered include understanding controllers and understanding time in computer animation.

Understanding Controllers

Whenever you create animation in MAX, an animation controller is assigned to each animated parameter for the objects. These controllers store the data associated with the animation and define how the animation data is interpreted into the animation. There are four basic types of controllers:

- Key-based controllers
- Procedural controllers
- Compound controllers
- System controllers

The following sections describe the basic differences of these four controller types. The various controllers themselves will be described in Chapter 16, "Exploring Basic Animation Methods," and in Chapter 17, "Exploring Other Animation Methods."

Key-Based Controllers

The most common method used for creating animation is keyframing. *Keyframing* is a process whereby objects are positioned at critical frames and someone or—in the case of MAX—an animation controller creates the animation between the critical frames. A *keyframe* is any frame of an animation in which a specific event is supposed to occur. The frames between keyframes are called *in-betweens*, or *tweens*.

Keyframing in MAX works by setting the current frame of the animation to the desired time (by adjusting the Time slider at the bottom of the interface), turning on the Animate button (which tells MAX that the following changes are to be animated over time), and creating the Keyframe event. In MAX, the Keyframe event can be not only a change in the transform (Position, Rotation, or Scale) of an object, but also a change in any of its animatable parameters. The new value for the transform or parameter is stored in a key by the animation controller assigned to the object's transform or parameter.

Say, for example, that you want to create an animation of a cylinder bending 90 degrees over 30 frames. You would first create a cylinder and apply a Bend modifier. You would then move to frame 30, turn on the Animate button, and change the Bend modifier's Angle parameter to 90. At that point, MAX would assign a controller to the Angle parameter of the Bend modifier, create a key at frame 0 to store the initial Angle value, and then create another key at frame 30 to store the new Angle value. If you play back or render the animation, the cylinder would smoothly bend 90 degrees over the 30 frames.

You can tell if an object has a Position, Rotation, or Scale key at a specific frame because a white bounding box appears around the object. For other parameters, a red bracket appears around the parameter's spinner if a key for it exists at that frame.

MAX ships with a variety of key-based controllers, including the Bézier, Linear, and Smooth controllers. Each of these controllers stores the animation data in keys. The difference between the controllers is how the output values between keys (the tween values) are calculated.

Procedural Controllers

Procedural, or parametric, controllers do not store keys; rather, their output is based on initial data values supplied by the user and on the equation the controller implements. Procedural controllers enable you to create motions or effects that would be difficult or tedious to create by using key-based controllers, such as attaching an object to the animated surface of another object, having an object travel along an existing spline, or having a light blink on and off in a complex periodic fashion. Examples of procedural controllers are the Surface, Path, and Waveform controllers.

Compound Controllers

Compound controllers combine the output of a set of controllers, yielding results in a format that MAX expects. An example of a compound controller is the Position/Rotation/Scale (PRS) controller. The PRS controller takes data from individual Position, Rotation, and Scale controllers and outputs to MAX the transform matrix for the object. Other compound controllers include the Look At, List, and Euler XYZ controllers.

System Controllers

Although the previous controllers all control a parameter or transformation of a single object, system controllers control multiple aspects of multiple

note

If you want to see all of the controllers that are available in MAX, simply open a copy of Track View by choosing Track View, New Track View. Then, click on the Filters button on the left side of the Track View toolbar. This launches a filtering dialog box where you can control what is displayed in Track View. In the middle of the dialog box is a Hide by Controller list, which shows you all of the available controllers.

objects. Typically, although the parameters associated with the system can be animated, the parameters or transforms of individual objects cannot be animated. In cases where the individual object transforms can be animated, the system controller maintains control over these transforms and can limit the transforms to meet the requirements of the system. Examples of system controllers are the new Bone IK controller, the Sunlight controller, and the Biped portion of Character Studio.

As previously described, keys store the data values for a parameter at a particular time. In MAX, as with most animation packages, time is not continuous but rather is defined in small discrete chunks.

Of course, using different types of controllers to create different types of animation isn't very helpful without a good understanding of how time is interpreted by MAX.

Understanding Time in Computer Animation

Time is one of the most important elements to understand when learning about computer animation. Computer animation is achieved by displaying a series of individual frames at a speed fast enough to create the illusion of motion. This is the same principle used in simple hand-drawn animation, film, and television.

In general terms, animation playback is not considered smooth unless you can achieve a speed of at least 20 frames per second (FPS), but the actual speed for which you will design your animation depends on what medium you use to record the animation. The film industry, for example, has standardized on 24 FPS, whereas 30 FPS is the standard for video in the United States.

MAX supports three standard frame rates—two for video and one for film—and a user-defined custom frame rate. The three standard frame rates are

- **NTSC:** Stands for the National Television Standards Committee and is the standard for television broadcast in the United States and Japan. The frame rate for NTSC is 29.97 frames per second.

- **PAL:** Stands for Phase Alternate Line and is the standard for television broadcast in most European countries. The frame rate for PAL is 25 frames per second.

- **Film:** The frame rate for film is 24 frames per second.

note

Although the true NTSC frame rate is 29.97 frames per second, MAX uses a frame rate of 30 FPS when the NTSC frame rate option is selected. The difference between MAX's and the actual NTSC frame rate is one frame in 33.33 seconds, or about one second in 1,000 seconds. Although this should not normally affect you, you need to be aware of this if you are lip synching or need the animation to have a specific duration.

MAX enables you to set the overall playback speed of the animation to any of these standards or, by using the Custom frame rate, to any frame rate you want. After you have set this information, you can display and work with time in MAX as frames, minutes, and seconds, or as fractions of seconds (called *ticks*). These settings are available in the Time Configuration dialog box, which you can access by right-clicking on the playback arrow. Figure 15.1 shows you this dialog box.

FIGURE 15.1   *The Time Configuration dialog box, where you can define how time is interpreted by MAX as well as how time is read back and the overall length of the animation.*

Advanced Animation Topics

This section introduces concepts associated with more advanced animation methods and techniques. As you become familiar with the more basic animation methods, you will start to run into situations when these techniques make it easier to perform your job as an animator. The techniques covered are the following:

- Trajectories
- Ghosting
- Pivot points
- Links and chains
- Skeletal deformation
- Morphing
- Space warps
- Character animation
- Motion blur
- Soft and hard body dynamics

Trajectories

When you create animations in MAX in which the position of the objects changes, the object motions can be thought of as *trajectories*, or motion paths. A trajectory is usually a line, such as a Bézier spline, that passes through each keyframed position. As described earlier, the trajectory between the keyframes is a function of the controller being used. The controller affects the curvature of the trajectory and how fast the object moves between the keyframes. By viewing an object's trajectory, you can see how the object will be moving and detect any unexpected motion resulting from how the controllers interpolate the motion between keyframes. MAX provides the capability to display object trajectories from the Motion and Display command panels. Figure 15.2 shows the trajectory for a sphere whose position is animated over time.

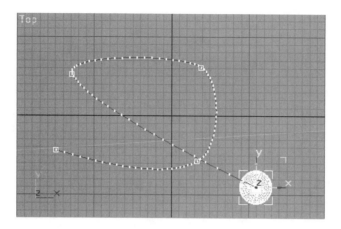

FIGURE 15.2   *A sphere, displaying its motion path. You can edit the motion path indirectly by adjusting the animation controller, or directly by editing the position of the keys.*

Ghosting

Ghosting is a method of displaying wireframe or shaded "ghost" copies of an animated object at a number of frames before and after the current frame. Although showing an object's trajectory shows how the object is moving over time, ghosting gives you "snap-shots" of what the object looks like over time. These snapshots show the effect on the object of any rotation and scaling or of any modifiers or space warps.

Ghosting is particularly useful in character animation, where it gives you a sense of the timing of the character's motion. MAX provides the capability to display object ghosts from the View menu, with ghosting options being set in Customize, Preferences, Viewports. Figure 15.3 shows two frames of ghosting before and after the current frame for an animated sphere.

Pivot Points

Every object you create in MAX has an associated pivot point. Think of the pivot point as the anchor point of the object. As you move, rotate, or scale an object, these transforms are applied to the pivot point and then the transform is passed on to the object geometry. The practical effect of this is that if you are rotating or scaling an object, the object geometry is rotated or scaled relative to the pivot point. Figure 15.3 shows two boxes (and ghosts of the boxes) that have identical rotation and scaling but different locations for their pivot points. The location of the pivot point for the top box is located at its center (as indicated by the axes tripod), and the pivot point for the bottom box is located at its left edge.

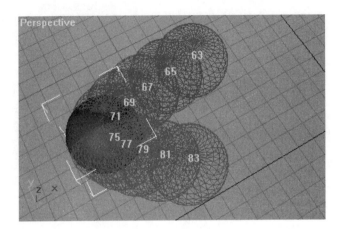

FIGURE 15.3   *The same animated sphere, showing ghosting in the viewports. Note the frame numbers are displayed for each ghost. The ghosting parameters are controlled via the Viewports Preferences.*

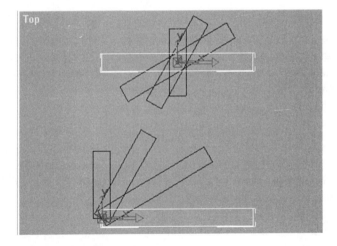

FIGURE 15.4   *The location of an object's pivot point affects how the rotation and scale transforms are applied to the object geometry.*

As can be seen from the ghosts, the rotation and scaling on the two objects are applied relative to pivot points. The effect is useful when animating both mechanical objects and characters. In both cases, you should locate the pivot points at the joint location. You can even move the pivot point away from the object, making it appear that the object is rotating around another object. You can adjust the pivot point location and orientation in the Hierarchy command panel (see the "Working with Hierarchies" section in Chapter 16).

Links and Chains

Clearly, adjusting the pivot point of an object is of great benefit when you are animating a single object. But there are other times, especially in character or mechanical modeling, when you want to animate an object by transforming it and have other objects repeat the same transform. If, for example, you rotate the upper arm of a character, you want the lower arm, hand, and fingers to move along with the upper arm, as they would in real life. Although you can manually keyframe their motion, this would quickly become tedious and frustrating.

The solution here is to link one object to another and form a hierarchical chain. The linked object becomes the child and the object linked to becomes the parent. You can build entire chains of linkages this way, with the restriction that a child can have only a single parent. You perform object linking by using the Link tool, described in the "Working with Hierarchies" section in Chapter 16.

When you transform a portion of a linked chain, the transform can be propagated in two directions: up the chain or down the chain. If the transform is being propagated down the chain, forward kinematics is being applied. If the transform is being propagated up the chain, inverse kinematics is being applied. Figure 15.5 shows two arms and their ghosts. The top arm was animated by rotating the upper arm and uses forward kinematics. The bottom arm was animated by repositioning the hand and uses inverse kinematics.

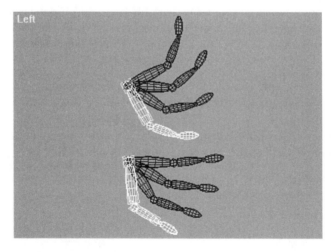

FIGURE 15.5   *Forward kinematics propagates motion down a linked chain, whereas inverse kinematics propagates motion up a linked chain.*

Forward Kinematics

With forward kinematics, when you transform a parent object, any children objects are transformed along with the parent. The effect is as if a rigid bar has attached the child's pivot point to the parent's pivot point. If you move the parent, the child also moves so that its position relative to the parent remains constant. If you rotate the parent, the child both moves and rotates such that the position and orientation of the child relative to the parent remains constant. This can be seen in the top arm in Figure 15.5, where, as the upper arm was rotated, the lower arm and its children moved and rotated to remain fixed, relative to the upper arm.

Although the children are being rotated and moved as the parent is transformed, transform keys are not being generated for the children. By linking the objects, you have told MAX to perform these transforms automatically.

Forward kinematics affects only the children of an object. If you select and move an object in the middle or at the end of a chain, that object will move away from its parent object.

Inverse Kinematics

With inverse kinematics (IK), you transform a child object and MAX calculates the position of the parent objects. Other than the fact that the motion is being propagated up the chain rather than down the chain, the other main difference between forward and inverse kinematics is that only one result is possible from forward kinematics, whereas multiple results are possible from inverse kinematics. The final position of the parents is called the IK solution. This solution is based on the motion of the object transformed and the joint constraints applied to the object and its parents.

In the bottom arm shown in Figure 15.5, joint constraints were applied to each object to ensure that the objects would not move away from one another and to ensure that the joints only rotated about the appropriate axes. After activating IK, the hand was then moved. While the hand was being moved, MAX calculated the IK solution in real time, showing the position of each of the objects in the arm.

If you select and move the lower arm, both forward and inverse kinematics will be applied; forward kinematics will be applied to the hand and inverse kinematics to the upper arm.

Further details on inverse kinematics are provided in the "Basics of IK" section in Chapter 16.

Skeletal Deformation

In Figure 15.5, the upper arm, lower arm, and hand are all separate objects. If the arm were a single object, there obviously wouldn't be any way to set up a linkage to achieve the desired motion of the arm.

If you want to deform an object, such as an arm, that is modeled as a single mesh, a method called *skeletal deformation* is commonly used. A skeleton is constructed beneath the object and is animated. The mesh is then attached to the skeleton by using a skeleton deformation modifier or space warp. This modifier or space warp takes the movement of the skeleton and deforms the mesh of the object to match.

MAX 3 ships with a skeletal deformation tool called Skin. This tool is implemented as a Modifier and can be applied to any mesh object. The two available plug-ins that provide more skeletal deformation are the Physique portion of Character Studio and Bones Pro for MAX.

Morphing

Morphing is a method you can use to create an animated mesh by transforming one object into another over time. To morph, you establish two or more target objects and set keyframes that specify the percentage influence of each target object at that time. The resulting morph object is based on the relative position of the target's vertices from the target's pivot points and the percentage influence of the target objects. When you're using morphing, each object must contain the same number of vertices, and the vertices in each target must be created in the same order. In practical applications, one initial morph target is usually created, and then the remaining targets are created by cloning the initial target and editing the clones at the sub-object level.

MAX 3 also supports another form of morphing through the Morpher object modifier. With this modifier, you can use morphing as an animation tool and as a modeling tool. The Morpher also adds more control over the ability to morph materials through the use of a Morpher material that is now available as well.

Morphing is a handy tool for detailed and fluid animation of objects. A common application is for facial animation, where targets are made to represent different facial expressions by using sub-object editing for skeletal deformation. The animator then can combine the different targets with varying influence levels to achieve fluid movement and unique facial expressions. An example frame from a facial animation using morph targets is shown in Figure 15.6.

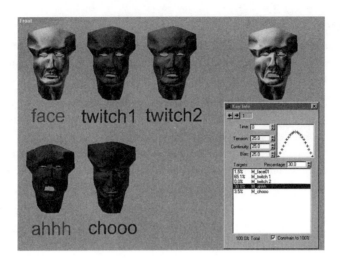

Figure 15.6   *Morphing enables you to combine several target objects to form a new, unique object.*

Morphing is described in more detail in the "Animating Using Morphing" section in Chapter 16.

Space Warps

Space warps are a means of defining an area in 3D space that has an automatic effect on selected objects passing through its influence. Only objects bound to the space warp are affected by the space warp. The difference between a modifier and a space warp is that a modifier always has the same effect on an object, no matter a where the object is located, whereas the effect a space warp has on an object is dependent on the location and orientation of the object relative to the space warp. Depending on the type of deformation selected, the object might respond to gravity effects, become wavelike, disintegrate, or change its path. In Figure 15.7, the text is deformed along a spline and a wave is applied to a box.

Space warps make it easier to cause certain effects to occur on cue (such as having an object shatter as it strikes a floor) or to apply external forces to particle systems. Further details on using space warps is provided in the "Using Space Warps" section in Chapter 16.

FIGURE 15.7   *Space warps deform objects based on the location and orientation of an object relative to the space warp.*

Character Animation

The goal of character animation is to provide a sense of life and personality to a character. The character can be not only a human or animal model, but any object. As Buzz Lightyear would say, "Character animation is moving with style." In television commercials and in films, we have seen dancing cars, gas pumps, and cereal boxes. What makes the objects appear alive is not how they look, but how they move.

In fact, performing character animation for an "inanimate" object is easier than for a human or animal. Because the viewer does not have any preconceived notions of how the inanimate object would move if it were indeed alive, you have the freedom to have the object move as you want. After a lifetime of observing the movement of humans and animals, viewers will quickly detect nonlifelike movement associated with these types of models.

Generally, you can base how a character would move on how you would perform the same motion. The use of full-length and hand-held mirrors allow you to see how you would perform the motion both overall and in detail. By using a camcorder and a stopwatch to record yourself performing the motion, you can identify "keyframes" and the timing between those keyframes.

Motion Blur

If you take a picture of a fast-moving object, you will notice that the edges of the object are not sharp and that the position of the object appears to be spread out.

This is a result of the object's being in one position when the shutter opens and in another when the shutter closes. The image captured on film is actually of the object in all of its positions between the opening and closing of the shutter.

The use of motion blur in MAX approximates this effect. In still images rendered with motion blur, fast-moving objects are blurred more than slower-moving objects, giving an impression of their relative speeds. In playback of animated sequences, motion blur provides a smoothness of motion that would not be present if motion blur were not applied. Figure 15.8 shows a rendering of two bowling pins that each have the same motion. One pin was rendered with motion blur and the other without.

FIGURE 15.8   *A rendering of two bowling pins that each have the same motion. The right pin was rendered with a motion blur, the left without.*

Three different types of motion blur are available in MAX and are described in the "Motion Blur" section in Chapter 14, "Rendering."

Soft and Hard Body Dynamics

The term *dynamics*, as used in MAX, refers to a system of controls used to produce animation that simulates real-world physics. Using dynamics allows the animator to create virtual environments where realistic object movements can be achieved, based on the object's physical properties and the forces acting on the object.

You can, for example, create a scene representing a bowling alley and set up the scene for dynamics by selecting the objects to be included in the dynamics simulation, defining the object properties, defining which object collisions to detect, and applying an initial motion on the bowling ball. The dynamics system then uses this information to calculate and generate keys for the positioning and rotation of each object in the dynamic simulation over a range of frames.

The two types of dynamics are hard-body (sometimes called rigid-body) and soft-body. In hard-body dynamics, when objects change their velocity or collide with another object, the objects are not deformed. For example, if a sphere hits another object, the sphere remains spherical. Hard-body dynamics are implemented in MAX 3 through the Dynamics utility, which is described in the "Working with Dynamics" section in Chapter 16.

In soft-body dynamics, when objects change their velocity or collide with another object, the objects can deform based on their physical properties. Now, if a sphere hits another object, the sphere becomes squashed. Soft-body dynamics can also be used to simulate flexible objects such as hoses, antennae, or even hair. MAX 3 implements soft-body dynamics through the use of the Lag modifier, which is covered in Chapter 16.

Conclusion

This chapter described the fundamentals of computer animation on which the following chapters will build. From this chapter, you should have a basic understanding of the following terminology and techniques:

- Basic animation controllers
- Animation frame rates
- Ghosting and trajectories as animation aids
- Forward and inverse kinematics
- Object deformation, using skeletal deformation, morphing, and space warps
- Character animation
- Motion blur
- Hard- and soft-body dynamics

Although this was only an overview, you should now have an understanding of the basic animation concepts and how they are applied in MAX. In the following chapters, you will delve into the methods and techniques of animation in MAX.

CHAPTER 16

Exploring Basic Animation Methods

In Chapter 15, "Understanding Animation Concepts," you were introduced to the basic types of animation controllers and learned how to set and control time in MAX. This chapter builds on those concepts to create and adjust animations. The following topics are covered:

- Configuring Time in MAX
- Creating a Keyframed Animation
- Introduction to Track View
- Viewing and Working with Function Curves in Track View
- Working with Controllers
- Procedural and Compound Controllers and Their Uses
- Using Advanced Track View Controls
- Pulling It All Together

Configuring Time in MAX

All animation time in MAX is configured through the Time Configuration dialog box (see Figure 16.1). This dialog box is accessed by either clicking the Time Configuration button or right-clicking any animation playback button. The frame rate, time display, playback options, key step options, and the start and end of the active time segment are configured and controlled through this dialog box, where you also can rescale the amount of time in the active time segment. A new element of this dialog box in MAX 3 is the capability to play back the animation in the viewports backward or to ping-pong the animation. To make use of these two new features, the Real Time option must be turned off.

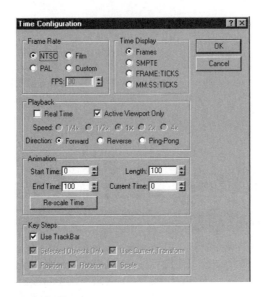

FIGURE 16.1   *The MAX Time Configuration dialog box, where you can define how time is interpreted within MAX.*

Setting the Frame Rate

MAX provides three predefined frame rates and enables you to define your own custom frame rate. The predefined rates cover the standard frame rates used for video and for film. If the Custom frame rate is selected, you can adjust the FPS spinner to set the frame rate.

Internal to MAX, all time-related data is stored in a unit of measure called *ticks*. Each second is divided into 4,800 ticks, but the number of ticks per frame varies, based on the frame rate. This feature ensures that, even as you change the frame rate, the length of the animation in seconds remains constant. You can create an animation of a given duration for television and then output for film with the same duration by simply changing the Frame Rate to Film. If you had a 30-second animation developed for video at 30 FPS, for example, the total number of frames would be 900. If you then changed the frame rate to Film (at 24 FPS), the length of the animation would still be 30 seconds, but the new frame count would be 720.

Setting the Time Display

The Time Display options control how time is displayed on the Time slider and in any dialog box where you change a time-related parameter for the animation. Each of these options is described in the following list:

- **Frames.** Displays time as frames.
- **SMPTE.** Stands for Society of Motion Picture and Television Engineers. This option displays time as Minutes:Seconds:Frame.
- **Frame:Ticks.** Displays time as frames, followed by the tick offset from the frame. For a frame rate of 30, each frame contains 160 ticks. Thus, you would display the time and control the animation at a resolution of 1/160 of a frame.
- **MM:SS:Ticks.** Displays time as minutes and seconds, followed by the tick offset from the second.

Changing the Playback Options

Three Playback options are available in the Time Configuration dialog box: Real Time, Active Viewport Only, and Direction. If the Real Time option is chosen, MAX tries to play back the animation in the viewport at a user-specified multiple of the given frame rate. MAX skips frames of the animation if it is unable to maintain this frame rate. To see all frames in the viewport playback, turn off this option. The Direction option enables the viewport playback to go forward, backward, or ping-pong. This option is only available when Real Time is off.

If the Active Viewport Only option is chosen, viewport playback will occur only in the active viewport. If this option is off, playback will occur in all viewports.

Changing and Rescaling Animation Time

The Start Time and End Time fields enable you to change the length of the active time segment. The active time segment is the time range you can move within by using the Time slider and the animation playback buttons. When you change the Start Time, End Time, or Length in the Time Configuration dialog box, only the definitions of the begin and end points of the active time segment are changed. The time associated with any keys in the animation does not change.

The Rescale Time button brings up the Rescale Time dialog box, where you can rescale the current time segment. MAX rescales the time segment by stretching or shrinking the time between animation keys within that segment. Any animation keys that occur either before or after the current time segment are moved earlier or later in time, depending on whether you adjust the Start Time or the End Time. Any time-related parameters are also affected. For example, parameters in the particle systems include the start time and life of the particles. The time value for these parameters will be scaled appropriately.

Changing the Key Steps Options

The Key Steps options are used in conjunction with the Key Mode Toggle button and the Previous Key and Next Key buttons discussed in the next section. When the Selected Objects Only option is chosen, MAX jumps to the previous or next frame containing a transform (Position, Rotation, Scale) key for the selected object only. If this option is off, MAX jumps to the previous or next frame containing a transform key for any object in the scene. Which transform keys are searched for depends on the setting of the Use Current Transform option.

If the Use Current Transform option is chosen, MAX jumps only to frames containing a transform key of the same type as the transform currently selected in the toolbar. If the Use Current Transform option is off, the Position, Rotation, and Scale options at the bottom of the dialog box are enabled and you can specify the types of transform keys to which MAX will jump.

In the following example, you use the time configuration tools to change the length of an animation.

Changing the Length of an Animation

1. Load the file **MF16-01.MAX** from the accompanying CD.

2. Access the Time Configuration dialog box by either clicking the Time Configuration button or right-clicking any animation playback button.

3. The current time display is SMPTE, the Frame Rate is NTSC, and the length of the animation is four seconds. Switch between frame rates and notice that the length of the animation remains at four seconds.

4. Change the Time Display to Frames and again switch between frame rates. Notice that the length of the animation now changes as you switch between frame rates.

5. Change the Time Display back to SMPTE and click Rescale Time. In the Rescale Time dialog box, change Length to two seconds and click OK. The total length of the animation is now two seconds. If you play back the animation now, the animated changes in the scene will happen twice as fast.

6. Change the End Time to four seconds. If you play back the animation now, the animated changes in the scene will occur over the first two seconds and then stay constant over the remaining two seconds.

Using the Time Controls

The Time controls are used for creating animation and moving between frames in an animation. The Time slider, Animate button, and animation playback buttons are located in the lower portion of the main MAX window, as shown in Figure 16.2.

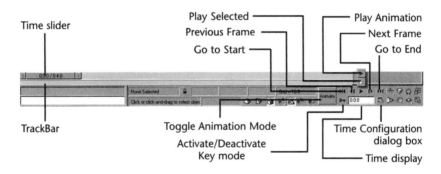

FIGURE 16.2 *The MAX Time Controls, where you can control the interactive playback of animations in the MAX viewports.*

The Time slider displays the current frame or time of the animation, as well as the overall number of frames or amount of time in the active time segment. By positioning this slider with the mouse, you define the current frame or time. The small arrow keys on either side of the Time slider duplicate the function of the Previous Frame/Previous Key and Next Frame/Next Key buttons.

The Animate button toggles MAX in and out of Animation mode. When MAX is in Animation mode, changes to any animatable parameter or object transform cause an animation key to be generated. You know MAX is in Animation mode when the current viewport is outlined in red and the Animate button turns red.

To the right of the Animate button is a series of buttons with which you can move through time and control the interactive playback of animations in MAX. By using these buttons, you can move the start or end of the active time segment, play back the animation, or manually set the current frame. As described previously, the Key Mode Toggle enables you to move between frames containing transform keys for the selected objects.

As you move through time, the MAX viewports update to reflect the animated changes to the scene objects. Typically, you will view your objects by using the Wireframe rendering level of the interactive renderer. By using the Smooth or Facets rendering level, you can more easily visualize the completed animation. Unfortunately, most scenes will not play back smoothly in the interactive renderer, but you can use the speed of the renderer to generate preview animations.

tip

For an even more blatant indication that the system is in Animation mode, add the following two lines to your 3dsmax.ini file:

```
[RedSliderWhenAnimating]
Enabled=1
```

When Enabled is set to 1, the Time slider background turns red whenever Animation mode is on. When Enabled is missing or is set to 0, the background color of the Time slider does not change.

Previewing Animations

A preview animation uses the interactive renderer to create a simple version of the animation. Animators use these mostly to check the motion of objects in the scene. Because a preview animation is generated with the interactive renderer, you can apply lighting, opacity, and materials. None of these are as accurate as the scanline renderer, however, and should only be used to help test the motion. For the final testing of the lighting, opacity, and materials, render individual frames of the animation by using the scanline renderer.

Generating a preview animation is a simple task. Under the Rendering menu, you can choose to make, view, and rename previews. The Make Preview command displays its dialog box, shown in Figure 16.3, in which you set the preview settings.

The Make Preview dialog box is divided into six sections:

- **Preview Range.** Enables you to define the time segment to render. You can choose the active time segment or a custom range.
- **Frame Rate.** Enables you to set the target frame rate for the animation file. Every Nth Frame enables you to create a preview of a regular sampling of the animation.

- **Image Size.** Enables you to set the resolution of the preview images as a percentage of the image resolution set in the Render Scene dialog box.
- **Display in Preview.** Enables you to pick the type of objects to be shown in the preview animation.
- **Rendering Level.** Enables you to select the rendering level used by the interactive renderer while generating the preview animation.
- **Output.** Enables you to choose the output file type or device. The default file type is AVI.

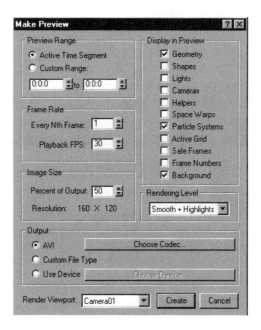

FIGURE 16.3   *The Make Preview dialog box, where you can define and generate preview animations.*

After setting the desired options, generate the preview animation by choosing Create.

The View Preview command loads the media player and the last preview animation that was generated. The Rename Preview command enables you to change the name of the file so you do not overwrite it the next time you generate a preview animation.

Creating a Keyframed Animation

The mechanics of creating a keyframed animation are simple: You move to a frame other than 0 and turn on the Animate button. Then, you adjust an object's position, rotation, or scale, or adjust a parameter in a command panel or dialog box.

The following exercise shows you how to create a simple keyframed animation in which you animate a variety of objects.

Creating a Keyframed Animation

1. Load file **MF16-02.MAX** from the accompanying CD. Figure 16.4 shows what this file looks like before any animation is applied.

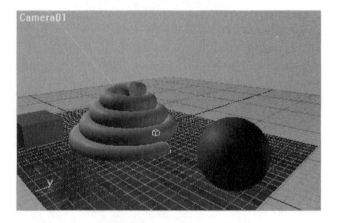

FIGURE 16.4   *The scene before any animation is applied.*

2. Click the Time Configuration button and set the time display to SMPTE. The time will be displayed as MIN:SEC:Frames, a readout that is much easier to understand than raw frame numbers. Set the End Time to 0:4:0 (four seconds) and click OK.

3. At time 0:0:0, turn on the Animate button and select the tubular object in the middle of the viewports.

4. Open the Modify command panel and expand the Deformations rollout. Click Scale to apply a scale deformation to the Loft object. Click the right endpoint of the scale deformation spline and drag it down to a value of five, as shown in Figure 16.5.

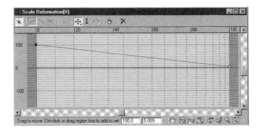

FIGURE 16.5   *The Scale Deformation graph at frame 0.*

5. Set the current frame to 0:4:0 and drag the right endpoint of the scale deformation spline back to its original value of 100. Close the Scale Deformation window.

6. Play back the animation. If MAX skips too many frames during playback, go back to the Time Configuration dialog box and turn off Real Time Playback.

7. Set the current frame to 0:2:0 and select the sphere on the right side of the scene.

8. Apply an XForm modifier to the sphere. Click Select and Squash on the Main Toolbar tab of the shelf. In the Front viewport, scale the sphere down in the X and Y axes to approximately 50%. The scene should appear similar to that seen in Figure 16.6. Turn off the Sub-Object mode button for the XForm modifier.

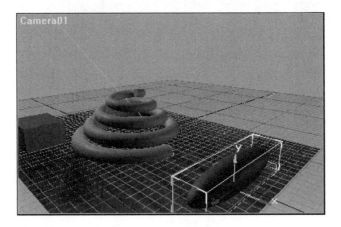

FIGURE 16.6   *The sphere after applying an animated nonuniform scale to it.*

9. Switch to the Camera viewport and set the current frame to 0:4:0. Click Select and Rotate in the MAX toolbar and rotate the sphere 720 degrees around the Z axis.

10. Set the current frame to 0:2.0. Open the Material Editor by clicking the Material Editor button in the MAX toolbar. Select the second material slot (material Cone). In the Basic Parameters rollout, set the Opacity value to 100.

11. Set the current frame to 0:4.0 and set the opacity to 0. Turn off Animate and close the Material Editor dialog box.

12. On the MAX menu bar, click Rendering, Environment. Add a Volume Light to spotlight Spot01. Set the following parameter values:

    Density: 1.0
    Noise On: Checked
    Amount: 0.5
    Uniformity: 0.5
    Size: 5.0
    Wind Strength: 0.5

13. Close the Environment dialog box.

14. Set the current frame to 0:4.0 and turn on the Animate button.

15. Select spotlight Spot01. Click Select and Move and move Spot01 to the right side of the scene in the Top viewport, as shown in Figure 16.7.

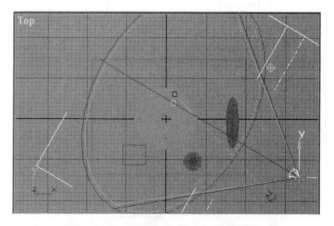

FIGURE 16.7   *The correct position of the spotlight after animating it.*

16. Set the current frame to 0:1.0 and select the camera. Move the camera to the upper-right corner of the Top viewport.

17. Set the current frame to 0:2.0 and move the camera to the upper-left corner of the Top viewport.

18. Set the current frame to 0:3.0 and move the camera to the lower-left corner of the Top viewport.

19. Set the current frame to 0:4.0 and move the camera back to its original position at the lower-right corner of the Top viewport.

20. Save the file as **MF16-02a.MAX**. This file—saved up to this point—is also provided on the CD for reference purposes. It will be used in later exercises to illustrate other points, so keep it handy.

21. Turn off Animate, activate the Camera viewport, and play back the animation. Although the animation should play back relatively quickly, it won't play back in real time.

22. On the menu bar, select Rendering, Make Preview. Click Create in the Make Preview dialog box to create an animation preview. After MAX finishes creating the preview, Media Player starts automatically to show the preview.

Click the Play button to play the animation. You should see the camera view rotating around the model, the lighting constantly changing, the sphere spinning and shrinking, and the wound-up tube getting larger at the top.

This exercise illustrates some points about keyframe animation and how easy it is to use. For now, you will not render the file; that will come later. However, if you want to see the final rendering, load **MF16-02a.avi** from the accompanying CD by choosing File, View File.

Understanding Trajectories

Clearly, being able to control motion in a scene is terrific, but so is being able to see the motion path in the scene. To see the motion path, select the object that is in motion and then choose the Trajectories button in the Motion command panel. MAX displays the motion path for the selected object, as shown in Figure 16.8.

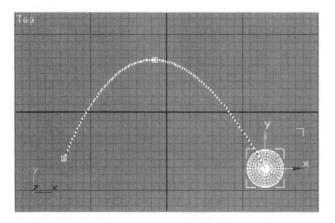

FIGURE 16.8   *The Motion Path for an object.*

The motion path is displayed as a blue line; the white boxes on the line represent the position keys for the object. Depending on which position controller you use, this path can be a straight line, a Bézier line, or a TCB line. In this figure, it is a Bézier line.

To interactively change the position of keys, choose the Sub-Object button at the top of the Trajectories rollout and then use a transform (such as Select and Move) to reposition any key. As you do this, you can watch the changes that occur in the motion path.

In the following exercise, you use the Trajectory display to show and adjust the motion of an object.

> **note**
>
> You have two ways to display an object's trajectory while in other command panels or when the object is not selected:
>
> - By turning on Trajectory in the Display Properties rollout of the Display command panel while the object is selected.
>
> - By right-clicking the object, selecting properties from the pop-up menu, and turning on Trajectory in the Display Properties area of the Object Parameters dialog box.

Editing an Animation by Using Trajectory

1. Continue using the scene that resulted from the previous exercise, or load **MF16-02a.MAX** from the accompanying CD.

2. Select the camera in the Top viewport.

3. Click the Motion command panel tab and click Trajectories. The trajectory of the camera is shown in the viewports. Click Zoom Extents to zoom the Top viewport back to show the entire trajectory.

4. Move to frame 0:2.15 and turn on Animate. Move the camera in the Top viewport. As you move the camera, the trajectory display is updated to show the new trajectory.

5. In the command panel, click the Sub-Object button to enter Sub-Object Keys mode.

6. In the Top viewport, select any of the keys along the trajectory and move it. As you move the key, the trajectory display is updated to show the new trajectory. Moving a key is the same as setting the current frame to the frame associated with the key and moving the object.

Setting keys and displaying trajectories in the MAX viewports are fundamental controls of animation. Although the values for keyframed parameters can be adjusted in the viewports or in the command panels, you first need to move to the frames associated with those keys. There is no way to move between frames containing keys for a parameter other than transform keys. Track View provides a direct way of viewing, adding, and modifying keys for all parameters.

Introduction to Track View

Adding keyframes to an animation in MAX is a relatively simple task, but editing, modifying, and deleting one or more keys can be difficult unless you use Track View—a powerful dialog box that enables you to edit all keys in your scene along a timeline. Through this dialog box you can control the speed, motion, and spacing of keys, as well as create, delete, move, and copy keys.

Opening Track View

You can access the Track View dialog box at any time by choosing the Open Track View button on the main toolbar (see Figure 16.9). The Track View dialog box is divided into two windows and two rows of buttons: the Hierarchy Tree and Track windows and the Control and View buttons.

Hierarchy Tree window

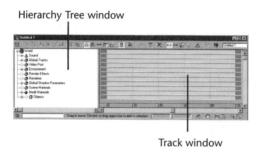

Track window

FIGURE 16.9   *The Track View dialog box, where you can view and edit animation keys in a variety of ways.*

The Hierarchy Tree and Edit Windows

The Hierarchy Tree window, on the left of the Track View dialog box, is an expandable tree list of all elements in the scene, including materials, sounds, objects, and environmental effects. You can expand any of the tree's branches by clicking the plus (+) button next to the branch name. Figure 16.10 shows an expanded tree.

As you can see from Figure 16.10, even something as simple as a box can have 10 or more animatable parameters associated with it. When you create a key, you create it for a specific parameter of an object—such as its position or rotation—and at a specific time.

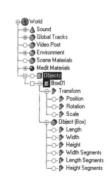

FIGURE 16.10

The Track View hierarchy tree, where objects are displayed according to their relationships to other objects in the scene.

If an object parameter has a key, that key will appear in the Edit window in the parameter's track at the frame where the key is located. Frames are numbered across the top of the Edit window, in a timeline. If a parameter is not animated, the static data value for that parameter is shown in the track. Figure 16.11 shows a Track View with some keys assigned.

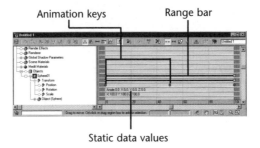

Animation keys   Range bar

Static data values

FIGURE 16.11   *An object in Track View with a set of animation keys assigned to it.*

Take the Sphere01 object shown in the Hierarchy Tree window, for example. If you expand its tree as shown in Figure 16.11, you can access the transforms or the object parameters themselves. In this example, the box was moved to a new location at frames 0, 50, and 100. The keys for the position of the sphere show up under the Position Transform track. Because the rotation and scale of the box were not animated, the static data values for these parameters are shown in their respective tracks.

In the Edit window, the start and end times of the animated transforms are represented by the white boxes at each end of the range (the heavy black line) in the Transform track. The range represents the total length of time this object is being animated by some sort of transform. The specific transforms are located below the Transform entry in the tree.

In the Position track in Figure 16.11, the gray spheres at frames 0, 50, and 100 represent the keys created in the animation. From Track View, you can delete the individual keys, move them, copy them, and so on. If you clicke of the gray spheres, it turns white to indicate that it has been selected. After it has been selected, you can easily transform the key.

upgrader's note

The TrackBar is a new feature in MAX 3. Figure 16.11 shows a set of keys in the Position track. These same keys appear in the TrackBar when the Sphere01 object is selected, giving you quick access to the keys without a need to go through Track View.

Track View works with different modes to achieve different levels of functionality. When Track View is set to a specific mode, you can edit the tracks in only certain ways, depending on the mode. In Edit Key mode, for example, you can edit individual keys; in Edit Ranges mode, you can edit a range of keys but not an individual key. Each mode is activated by selecting the appropriate mode button from the Track View toolbar (see Figure 16.12). The modes are listed here and explained briefly:

- **Edit Keys.** Edit the time or value of individual keys or selected sets of keys.
- **Edit Time.** Add, delete, copy, stretch, or shrink time. Underlying keys are affected based on the changes made to time.
- **Edit Ranges.** Slide or move time ranges and their underlying keys quickly. Individual keys are not displayed.
- **Position Ranges.** Edit ranges independent of their underlying keys. Used primarily with Out-of-Range Types.
- **Function Curves.** Display curves to show how animation values change over time.

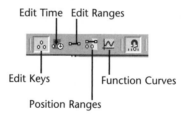

FIGURE 16.12   *The Track View toolbar, where you can access the various commands available.*

Making Basic Adjustments to Keys

In Edit Keys mode of Track View, you can make many adjustments to both the time and values associated with keys. Figure 16.13 shows the Edit Keys mode Track View toolbar buttons. To add a key to a track, click Add Keys and click in the track to add a key at that location in time. The data value assigned to the key is the interpolated value at that time if the track is animated or the track's static data value if the track is not animated.

To delete one or more keys, select the key(s)—either by clicking them (hold down Ctrl while clicking to add keys to the selection set) or by dragging a selection box around them—and then click Delete Keys. If an object name label (signified by the yellow cube in the Hierarchy Tree window) is selected when you click Delete Keys, MAX asks whether you want to delete all keys for that object. If you respond yes, all of the object's keys will be deleted. If you answer no, no keys (including any selected keys) will be deleted.

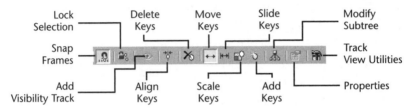

FIGURE 16.13   *The Edit Keys mode Track View toolbar buttons.*

To move one or more keys, simply select the key(s), click Move Keys, and drag the keys left or right. Moving keys does not affect the data values associated with the keys—only the time at which the keys are located. To clone one or more keys, select the key(s), click Move Keys, and drag them left or right while holding down the Shift key. For each of the selected keys, a new key (containing the same data value as the original key) will be created when you release the mouse button. The position of the new keys in time will offset from the original keys by the amount that you dragged the mouse. Figure 16.14 shows you an object with a key at frame 20 that was moved to frame 30 and then cloned to frame 50.

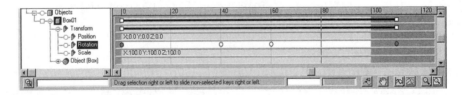

FIGURE 16.14   *The Track View, showing the effect of moving and cloning keys.*

Moving a set of keys does not affect nonselected keys. At times, you will want to slide the preceding or subsequent keys by the same amount that you move the selected keys. To slide a set of keys, perform the same actions as for moving the keys, except click Slide Keys rather than Move Keys. As you move the selected keys to the left, any preceding keys are also moved to the left. As you move the selected keys to the right, any subsequent keys are moved to the right. Again, the data values associated with the keys are not changed—only the time at which the keys are located. Figure 16.15 shows the same object as Figure 16.14, but the keys at frames 30 and 50 were shifted right 10 frames. Note that the key at frame 100 is now at frame 110.

FIGURE 16.15 *The Track View, showing the effect of sliding keys.*

In some cases, you will want to modify not only the keys on selected objects or tracks but also keys on their descendants. You might have a completed animation in which keys are present on multiple objects at frame 100, for example, but you need to move all of these keys to frame 120. The easiest way to do this is to click Modify Subtree to turn it on, select the key at frame 100 in the Objects track, and move that key. This will move all the keys under objects that occur at frame 100. If you also have animated material, Video Post, or environmental effects, you would select the corresponding key in the World track and move it. Figure 16.16 shows two Track Views of the same scene. In the top Track View, Modify Subtree is off and range bars are shown in each parent track. In the bottom Track View, Modify Subtree is on and keys are present in each parent track. These keys signify that at least one key is present in a descendent at that frame, and when you perform an action on the parent key, all descendent keys will be affected similarly.

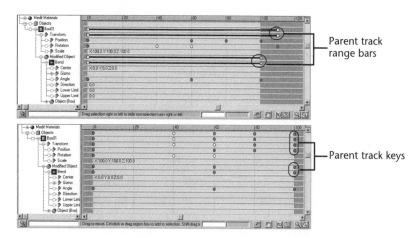

FIGURE 16.16 *Two Track View displays, showing the effect of having Modify Subtree off and Modify Subtree on.*

Most key-based controllers enable you to change the data values and interpolation parameters for each key. To change these values for a key, right-click the key. If the controller allows these values to be modified in Track View, the Key Info dialog box is displayed. Figure 16.17 shows the Key Info dialog box for a Bézier key. The fields in this dialog box vary for each controller type and are described in the section "Using Key-Based Controllers."

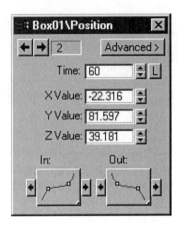

FIGURE 16.17   *The Key Info dialog box for a Bézier position key.*

In the following exercise, you use the various Edit Key tools to modify the keys for an animation.

Editing Keys in Track View

1. Reload **MF16-02a.MAX** from the accompanying CD.

2. Open Track View by clicking Open Track View. The state of active track views is saved with the .MAX file. This file was saved with one active track view called Animated Only, which was configured to show only the animated tracks and their parent tracks. Right-click the track name "Objects" in the Hierarchy Tree window and select Expand All from the pop-up menu to display the animated tracks.

3. Select the keys at time 0:4:0 for the Def.Scale(X) and Def.Scale(Y) points on object Loft01. With the Move Keys button active, drag these keys to 0:2:0.

4. Select the Def.Scale keys at time 0:0:0 and drag these keys to time 0:4:0 while holding down the Shift key. This clones the keys at time 0:0:0 and places the clones at 0:4:0. If you play back the animation, the wound-up tube gets larger at the top up to 0:2:0 and then shrinks back down.

5. The Def.Scale keys at frame 0:4:0 are still selected. Click Delete Keys or press the Delete key on your keyboard to delete the Def.Scale keys.

6. Click Modify Subtree to turn on Subtree mode. Click and drag down the time ruler to show the keys in the World track. Click the World track key at time 0:2:0 to select all the keys in the scene at time 0:2:0. Hold down the Ctrl key and left-click the key on the Camera01 track to deselect the camera keys. Drag the remaining selected keys to time 0:3:0. Turn Modify Subtree back off.

7. Select the Position key for Camera01 at time 0:1:0. Click Slide Keys and move the selected key to time 0:2:0. As you move the key, notice that the keys to the right also move to the right. The time between keys remains constant.

8. Select the Position keys for Camera01 from time 0:2:0 to 0:4:0. Click Scale Keys and move the keys so that the leftmost key moves to time 0:12:0. As you move the keys, notice that the time between selected keys is reduced. The keys at frame 0:0:0 and 0:5:0 are not affected.

9. Select the key at time 0:0:0 for the Scale track of Sphere01's XForm gizmo and then right-click the key. The Key Info dialog box is displayed, showing the values associated with the key. Set Z Value to 100 and close the dialog box. When you look at the sphere in the viewports, notice that the sphere is scaled up to 200 percent along the vertical.

10. Click Add Keys and then click the Scale track of Sphere01's XForm gizmo at time 0:2:0. A key is created at this time. Right-click the key to display its values. The values stored in the key are the interpolated scale values at that timepoint. Change the X, Y, and Z values to 0 and close the dialog box. If you play back the animation in the viewports, the sphere scales down to nothing over the first two seconds and then expands again over the next second.

In this section, you learned how to use the Edit Keys mode of Track View to adjust the position of keys in time, create and delete keys, and change the values associated with keys by using the Key Info dialog box. Although the Edit Keys mode makes it easy to edit keys, it doesn't help you understand how the animation values change over time. For this, you use the Function Curves mode of Track View.

Working with Function Curves

The Function Curves mode of Track View displays curves showing how animation values change over time for selected tracks. These curves make it easier for you to see how the object is acting in the animation. For example, a Position function curve might have sloped lines. The steeper the lines, the faster the object is moving. Figure 16.18 shows you a Position function curve.

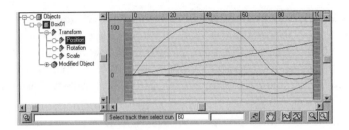

FIGURE 16.18   *The function curve for an object's Position track shows the X, Y, and Z position values of the object over time.*

To display the function curve for a track, select the track's name in the Hierarchy Display window and click Function Curves. The Edit window is replaced with the Function Curve display. The horizontal axis of this display is time and the vertical axis is the output value(s) of the selected controller. Figure 16.19 shows the Track View toolbar buttons in Function Curves mode.

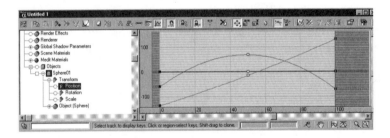

FIGURE 16.19   *The Track View toolbar buttons in Function Curves mode.*

You will see one or three curves, depending on the type of track being displayed. For tracks whose controllers output one value (length, width, radius), a single curve is displayed. For tracks whose controllers output three values (scale, position, color), three curves are displayed. The red curve represents the X or red value, green the Y or green value, and blue the Z or blue value.

The only tracks that do not display a function curve are the Object and Modifier gizmo rotation tracks. These tracks do not display a function curve because all rotation controllers are based on *quaternion controllers*, which have four data values associated with each key. A function curve display from one of these controllers would appear to be gibberish. One rotation controller, the Euler XYZ, enables you to bypass this restriction. The Euler XYZ controller takes as input three separate controllers and outputs the quaternion representation of these three values. Although you cannot display the function curve for the Euler XYZ controller itself, you can display the function curves for its three input controllers.

Track View enables you to display the function curves for more than one track by clicking the track names while holding down the Ctrl key. When you click a curve, that curve becomes active. You can tell which track an active curve is associated with because the green triangle next to the track name becomes highlighted. You can also set the track's curve as active by clicking this green triangle.

When a curve is active, its vertices are displayed as solid black boxes. These vertices correspond to the keys for that track. When you click the vertices or drag a selection region around them, the vertices become selected and the inside of the box turns white. The data values or time for these vertices can then be edited. When you click Show Selected Key Stats, the time and data value for each selected key is displayed. Any change to the time or value of a vertex automatically updates the values for its associated key.

Vertices can be added, deleted, moved, and scaled in a manner similar to performing the same functions in Edit Keys. The only difference with moving vertices is that you can move a vertex vertically, which changes the selected vertex's data values. An additional function is Scale Values, which enables you to scale the selected vertex's data values. As you perform these functions, the function curve is updated in real time to reflect the changes you made.

In the following exercise, you use the various Function Curve tools to modify the keys for an animation.

Working with Function Curves in Track View

1. Reload file **MF16-02a.MAX** from the accompanying CD.
2. Open Track View by clicking Open Track View. Right-click the track name Objects in the Hierarchy Tree window and select Expand All from the pop-up menu to display the animated tracks. Click Function Curves to enter Function Curves mode.
3. Click Position under Spot01's transform to display the Position function curves. Then, click one of the curves to select the curves.
4. Click Add Keys and click one of the curves at time 0:2:0. A new position key is created at this timepoint.
5. Click Move Keys and then click one of the curves to deselect the key you just created.
6. The red curve shows the X coordinates of the spotlight. Click the vertex at time 0:2:0 on this curve and drag it down to about 110 degrees (watch the key value field at the bottom of Track View). The shape of the curve changes to show the object moving slowly in the X direction at the beginning of the animation and then moving faster in the X direction as the animation progresses.
7. Move the vertex selected in step 6 to the left and right. As you move this vertex, the other vertices at this timepoint also move. All three values are stored in the same key, and changing the time value of one value changes the time value of all values.

When you are editing parameter values or changing controller interpolation parameters, you will usually want to do the editing in Function Curves mode. Because the actual parameter values used on all frames are shown by the curve, you can see the effect of changes in the controller's interpolation parameters between keyframes.

Working with Controllers

Whenever you create animation in MAX, some sort of controller is assigned to the animated parameters of the objects. There are two classes of animation controllers: key-based and procedural. *Key-based* controllers store the animation data in keys and output values to the parameters based on the key's values and the controller's interpolation method. The various types of key-based controllers interpolate between keys in different ways. *Procedural* controllers do not store keys; rather, their output is based on initial data values supplied by the user and the equation implemented by the controller.

Assigning Controllers

You can assign or replace controllers for all parameters through the Track View dialog box. You can also replace controllers assigned to object transforms (Position/Rotation/Scale) through the Motion command panel.

The controller assigned to a track can be changed in Track View by selecting the track's name in the Hierarchy Display window and then clicking Assign Controller. An Assign Controller dialog box is displayed, showing which controllers can be assigned to that track. Figure 16.20 shows the Assign Position Controller dialog box for an object's Position track.

As you can see from the list of controllers shown in Figure 16.20, 15 different animation controllers can be assigned to the Position track of an object. If you switch between a procedural and a key-based controller or between procedural controllers, any previously defined animation for that track will be lost. If you switch between key-based controllers, any previously defined animation for that track will be transferred to the new controller.

When you select a controller from the Assign Controller dialog box, you have the option to make it the default controller. If you do, the new default controller will be used for all new controller assignments for parameters using that data type. You should be very careful about changing the default, because the effects might be more widespread than you realize. For example, position controllers are used not only for the object's position, but also for the gizmo and center point of object modifiers. Making the Path controller the default position controller is a sure path to confusion because all objects will be created at the world center and will be unmovable.

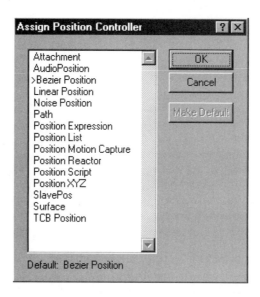

FIGURE 16.20   *The Assign Position Controller dialog box for Position tracks. Here, you can assign controllers to handle position-based animation in different ways.*

The controllers assigned to an object's Transform tracks can also be changed in the Motion command panel. When you click the Motion command panel tab with an object selected, a series of rollouts similar to those shown in Figure 16.21 is displayed. At the top of the Motion command panel, look for the Assign Controller rollout, which shows which controllers are assigned to the object transforms. You can change a controller by highlighting the Transform track and clicking the Assign Controller button. A Replace Controller dialog box is displayed.

The rollouts displayed below the Assign Controller rollout vary according to which transform controller is being used, which track is selected at the bottom of the transform controller's rollout, and which controller is being used for the selected track. In Figure 16.21, the transform controller is the Position/Rotation/Scale (PRS) controller, so the second rollout is the PRS Parameters rollout. The Position track is selected at the bottom of this rollout. The position controller is the Bézier controller, which uses the third and fourth rollouts: Key Info (Basic) and Key Info (Advanced). Although different controllers cause different rollouts to be displayed, the general rollout structure is the same.

The rollouts associated with key-based controllers enable you to change the data values and interpolation parameters for each key in a manner similar to the Key Info dialog boxes in Track View. If a key is present for the selected controller on the current frame, the controller's rollouts will display these values. The various fields in these rollouts are described in the following sections for each controller type.

Key-Based Controllers

All key-based controllers store their animation data in keys. The difference between the controllers is how the output values between keys are calculated. When plotted over time, the output values of a controller form the controller's function curve.

Bézier Controllers

The most used controller is the Bézier controller, which interpolates between keys based on a Bézier spline that passes through the keys' values. When you select a Transform track in the Motion command panel that has a Bézier controller assigned to it, you see the Basic and Advanced Key Info rollouts shown in Figure 16.22.

At the top of the rollout is the time or frame number of the current key. You can change the time of the key by adjusting this number. Use the two black arrow buttons in the rollout's top-left corner to move to the next or previous key. Alternatively, you can click the L button next to the spinner to lock the key to the specified time so you cannot move it by accident. Below the frame number are X, Y, and Z spinner fields that show the key's data values.

FIGURE 16.21

The Motion command panel rollouts for a PRS controller and the expanded Assign Controller rollout.

Below the value spinner fields are two large buttons that control the shape of the function curve as it enters (In) and leaves (Out) the key. These buttons enable you to define how the tangent of the Bézier line is defined on the in or out side of the key. When you click and hold the large buttons, you will see the tangent types shown in Figure 16.23.

Each of the six Bézier tangent controls causes the tangent curve of frames before or after the key to react differently. The default is the first tangent curve type, which produces a nice smooth line through the key. The effect of the others is similar to the graphic representation on the button. For example, the third button from the top of the list (the Step tangent type) causes the output of the controller to remain at a constant value until the next key is reached. At that time, a step change to the new key's value occurs.

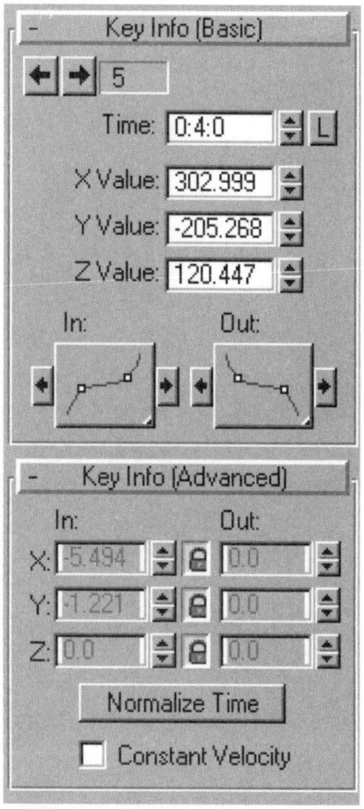

The last Bézier tangent type is the Custom tangent type. When you choose this button, the Key Info Advanced rollout becomes available. The In and Out controls enable you to control the rotation of the tangent handles of the function curve so you have precise control over the tangent points. Adjusting the tangent points is better done in the Function Curves mode of Track View because you can manipulate the tangent points directly and see the results of your changes on the curve immediately (see Figure 16.24).

The Normalize Time control repositions the selected keys in time so that the average rate of change is equal between the preceding and following keys for all selected keys. The Constant Velocity option adjusts the calculation of the interpolated values between keys to keep the absolute velocity of an object the same between the selected keys and their following keys.

FIGURE 16.22
A Bézier controller's basic and advanced Key Info rollouts in the Motion command panel.

In the following exercise, you use the Bézier tangent controls to adjust the movement of an object.

Using the Bézier Controller

1. Load **MF16-03.MAX** from the accompanying CD. In this scene, a rotating paddle hits a ball.

2. Advance to frame 18, where the paddle is just about to hit the ball. You want the ball to remain stationary until the paddle hits the ball, so create a position key for the ball at this frame.

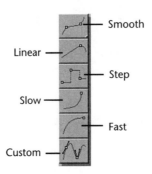

FIGURE 16.23   *The Bézier Controller's tangent types.*

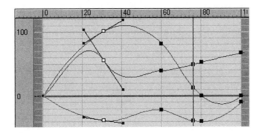

FIGURE 16.24   *The tangent points for a Bézier controller with a Custom tangent type can be directly manipulated in the Function Curves mode of Track View.*

3. Select the ball and right-click the Time slider. In the Create Key dialog box, turn off Rotation and Scale and click OK. This creates a position key for the ball, using its current position.

4. Advance to frame 100 and turn on Animate. Click Select and Move and Restrict to X. In the Front viewport, move the ball right to the edge of the base and play back the animation. Between frames 0 and 18, the ball is moving slightly to the left and then back to the right. This motion is due to the interpolation parameters for the controller.

5. Click Open Track View and expand the hierarchy tree to display the Position track for the ball. Select the Position track name and click Function Curves. Click one of the curves to show the keys for the track (see Figure 16.25). As can be seen from the function curves for the X axis (the red curve), the X value is not remaining constant between frames 0 and 18.

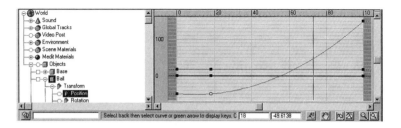

FIGURE 16.25   *The ball's Position function curve before changing the tangent types.*

6. Right-click the X-axis vertex at frame 0. In the Key Info dialog box, set the Out tangent type to Step and play back the animation. The ball now remains in position between frames 0 and 18, but the ball starts off moving slowly at frame 18 and speeds up as it approaches frame 100. You need to have the ball moving fast at frame 18 and slow to a stop at frame 100.

7. In the Key Info dialog box, click the right arrow to move to key 2, which is the key at frame 18. Set the Out tangent type to Fast (third from the bottom of the flyout). Click the right arrow to move to key 3 (frame 100). Set the In tangent type to Slow (second from the bottom of the flyout). Figure 16.26 shows the Position function curve at this point.

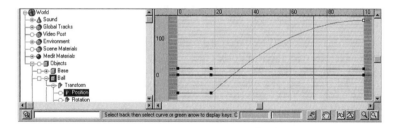

FIGURE 16.26   *The ball's position curves after changing the tangent types.*

8. Close the Key Info dialog box and Track View. Play back the animation. The ball's motion now looks okay, but you still need to do some work on the initial rotation of the paddle. Save this file as **MF16-03a.MAX**. You will use this file in the next example to adjust the paddle rotation.

In the previous example, you adjusted the tangent types to control the interpolation of the ball's position between keyframes. You can fine-tune the interpolation by using the Custom tangent type and adjusting the tangent vectors at the keys to achieve the exact motion you want.

TCB Controllers

Tension/Continuity/Bias (TCB) controllers inter-polate between keys based on five interpolation parameters assigned to each key: Tension, Continuity, Bias, Ease To, and Ease From. The shape of the controller's function curve is based on each key's data and interpolation parameter values. When you select a track with a TCB controller in the Motion command panel, MAX displays a Key Info rollout similar to the one shown in Figure 16.27. To access the same controls in Track View, right-click one of the controller's keys.

The Key Info rollout has the same keyframe number and lock controls and the same X, Y, and Z spinners as the TCB controller rollout. Below the frame number are X, Y, and Z spinner fields that show the key's data values. The TCB controller is assigned to an object's Position track, so these data values show the X, Y, and Z position values at the current frame. Adjusting any of these data values adjusts the position of the object.

Below the key's value fields is the TCB graph, which shows the effect of the key's interpolation parameters. The red tick at the top of the curve represents the current key and the ticks on either side represent an even division of time on either side of the key. Although handy, the TCB graph doesn't provide a good representation of the effect of changing the interpolation parameters on the function curve. It is better to adjust the interpolation parameters in the Function Curves mode of Track View.

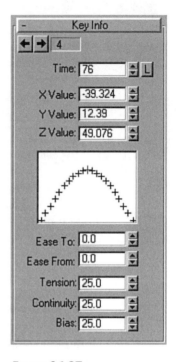

FIGURE 16.27
A TCB Position controller's Key Info rollout in the Motion command panel.

The Tension value controls the amount of curvature of the function curve through the key. High Tension values result in no curvature (a straight line); low Tension values result in increased curvature.

The Continuity value controls the angle between the In and Out tangents of the function curve. Only a setting of 25 will give you a smooth function curve through the key. High Continuity values cause the function curve to overshoot the key's value on each side of the key; low Continuity values cause the function curve to approach a straight line between the current key and each adjacent key.

The Bias value controls the rotation of the In and Out tangents of the function curve. High Bias values cause the function curve to overshoot the key's value as it leaves the key, and low Bias values cause an overshoot as it enters the key. High Ease To and Ease From values slow the rate of change of the function curve as it enters and leaves the key, respectively.

In the following exercise, you use the TCB interpolation parameters to adjust the rotation of the paddle from the last example.

Using the TCB Controller

1. If you did not complete the last example, load **MF16-03a.MAX** from the accompanying CD.

2. Play the animation and watch the rotation of the paddle over the first 20 frames. The paddle rotates at a constant speed, but you would expect it to start off rotating slowly and speed up as it approaches the bottom of the swing.

3. To see the rotation of the paddle, choose Customize, Preferences, Viewports. Set Ghosting Frames to 10, set Display Nth Frame to 2, and turn on Ghost Before and After. Click OK to close the Preference Setting dialog box. Click the Views menu item and turn on Show Ghosting. Select the paddle in the Front viewport to show its ghosts (see Figure 16.28) and click Min/Max Toggle to maximize the Front viewport.

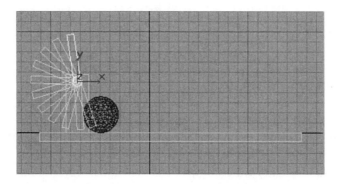

Figure 16.28   *The paddle's ghosts show the position of the paddle in the surrounding frames.*

4. Click the Motion command panel tab. In the PRS Parameters rollout, click Rotation to display the rotation controller parameters.

5. Go to frame 0, where the first rotation key for the paddle occurs. In the Key Info rollout, set Ease From to 50.

6. Go to frame 20, where the third rotation key for the paddle occurs. In the Key Info rollout, decrease Angle so that the paddle is just hitting the ball.

7. Look at the animation at frames 18 to 20. The paddle is hitting the ball at frame 18 and rebounding from the ball at frame 20. At frame 19, the paddle is passing slightly into the ball. In Customize, Preferences, Viewports, set Ghosting Frames to 1 and Display Nth Frame to 1.

8. At frame 19, note the position of the left side of the ball in the Front viewport. Go to frame 18, where the paddle is hitting the ball and the second rotation key for the paddle occurs. Using the paddle's ghost as a guide, adjust Ease From so that the paddle barely touches the ball at frame 19. The Ease From value should be approximately 20. Turn off ghosting and play back the animation.

In the previous example, you adjusted the TCB interpolation parameters to achieve the proper rotation of the paddle. Displaying ghosts while adjusting interpolation parameters enables you to see the effects of these changes quickly.

On/Off Controller

The On/Off controller is used for object and modifier parameters that can be either on or off. In Track View, the On/Off controller displays a solid blue color in frames that are on and no blue in frames that are off. Each key you add to an On/Off controller causes the On/Off state to change at that key. An effect of this is that when you add a key, the On/Off state of all sections following that key is flipped.

The following exercise steps you through the use of the On/Off controller.

Using the On/Off Controller

1. Create a box and click Open Track View.

2. Expand the hierarchy tree to show the track immediately under object Box01. Click the Box01 track name to select it.

3. Click Add Visibility Track on the Track View toolbar. A Visibility track is added to Box01. The default controller is assigned to Visibility tracks in the On/Off controller and the controller state defaults to being on. Whenever the controller is in the on state, the object is visible. Whenever the controller is in the off state, the object is invisible.

4. Click Add Keys and then click in the Visibility track at frame 20. A key is added at frame 20 that sets the controller to the off state for frame 20 and subsequent frames.

5. Click in the Visibility track at frame 80. A key is added at frame 80 that sets the controller to the on state for frame 80 and subsequent frames.

6. Click in the Visibility track at frame 40. A key is added at frame 40 that sets the controller to the on state. Because the controller state entering frame 80 changed from off to on, the key at frame 80 now changes the controller state from on to off for frame 80 and subsequent frames. Figure 16.29 shows the Visibility track for the box, showing it as visible up to frame 20, invisible from frames 21 to 39, and visible after frame 39. Play back the animation to see the results in the MAX viewports.

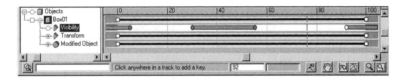

Figure 16.29   *A Track View display of an On/Off controller assigned to an object's Visibility track.*

Although the On/Off controller is used as the default controller for Visibility tracks only, it can also be used for other parameters that are on or off (for example, the smoothing tracks for most primitives).

In this section, most of the key-based controllers were described. Several additional key-based controllers were not described; however, those controllers are derived from the described controllers. For example, the Linear Position controller is the same as the Bézier Position controller, except with all the tangents set to Linear.

The procedural controllers are described in the next section. Procedural controllers do not store keys; instead, their output is based on initial data values supplied by the user and the subsequent equation implemented by the controller.

Procedural Controllers

Most procedural controllers have an associated Properties dialog box. You can display this dialog box by selecting the track name to which the controller is assigned in the Motion command panel or in Track View and then right-clicking the track name and selecting Properties from the pop-up menu. Alternatively, you can select the track name in Track View and click the Properties button, or simply right-click the track in the Edit window.

The Path Controller

The Path controller enables you to restrict the motion of an object to a spline. The position of the object is based on the spline and a percentage value. At a percentage value of 0, the object is positioned at the first vertex of the spline; at a percentage value of 100, the object is positioned at the end of the spline. As the percentage value increases from 0 to 100, the object moves along the spline. The Path controller can only be assigned to the Position track of an object.

When you assign the Path controller to an object, the rollout displayed in the Motion command panel resembles the one shown in Figure 16.30. The Pick Path button enables you to choose the shape along which the object is to travel. If you select a shape that contains multiple splines, only the first spline is used as the path. In the Path Options section, the % Along Path field specifies where along the spline the object is to be located. When the Path controller is first assigned to an object, two keys are automatically created: The percentage value is set to 0 at the first frame of the current time segment and to 100 for the last frame.

FIGURE 16.30

A Path controller's Path Parameters rollout in the Motion command panel.

When the Follow option is off, the object moves along the path without changing its orientation. Turning on the Follow option forces the object to reorient itself as it travels along the path so that the object is always pointing in the same direction as the path. The Axis options at the bottom of the Path Parameters rollout specify which of the object's local axes is to point along the path and whether that axis points forward or backward.

The Bank option forces the object to tip laterally as it travels along the curves of the spline. The degree of banking at a given point is a function of the curvature of the spline at that point. When Bank is active, you can set both the amount and the smoothness of the bank.

The Allow Upside Down option is used to avoid flipping an object when it follows a path that is pointing straight up or down. The Path controller normally tries to keep one of the object's local axes (usually the Z axis) pointing in the same direction as the world's Z axis. If you have a plane doing a loop, however, the plane would normally be upside down at the top of the loop. Turning on the Allow Upside Down option allows the plane to turn upside down in this case.

If the Constant Velocity option is off, MAX positions the object on the spline over time, based on the number of spline vertices, not on the length of the spline. If you are using a spline with three vertices (start, middle, and end) at a % Along Path value of 50, the object will always be located at the middle vertex regardless of the distance between vertices. If Constant Velocity is on, however, MAX positions the object on the spline over time based on the actual length of the path. If you have a path 100 units long, the object will be located 50 units along the path when the % Along Path value is 50.

The following example shows how the various Path controller options affect the position and orientation of an object, and what type of spline paths can cause unexpected rotations of the object.

Using the Path Controller

1. Load file MF16-04.MAX from the accompanying CD.

2. Select the airplane and, in the Motion command panel, select the Position track. Click Assign Controller and choose Path in the Assign Position Controller dialog box.

3. Click Pick Path and select object Path01 as the path. The airplane will move to the beginning of the path, but its orientation will not change.

4. Click Play Animation to view the animation. The airplane moves along the path, but its orientation remains fixed and the plane points in the wrong direction.

5. Turn on the Follow option and set Axis to Y. The front of the airplane now points in the direction in which it is moving.

6. In the MAX toolbar, set Reference Coordinate System to Local so you can see the object orientations more clearly. Click Play Animation to view the animation. The front of the airplane continues to point in the direction in which it is moving, but the airplane rolls between frames 51 and 55, is right side up at the top of the loop, and rolls again between frames 67 and 70.

7. Click the Allow Upside Down option to turn it on and play back the animation. The airplane no longer rolls and it is upside down at the top of the loop.

8. You will notice that the airplane moves slowly over the first 20 frames and then speeds up because there is an extra vertex located near the beginning of the spline. Turn on Constant Velocity and play back the animation—the airplane now follows the path at a constant speed.

9. Click Pick Path and select Path02 as the path. Drag the Time slider and notice that the plane rolls upside down at about frame 80 and returns to an upright orientation at about frame 89. This behavior occurs because Path02 is nonplanar (see the previous warning). The only way to correct this behavior is to manually add rotations to the airplane to counteract the roll.

10. Select the cone, assign a Path controller to the cone, and select object Path03 as the path.

11. Turn on the Follow and Bank options and play back the animation. The cone banks excessively over frames 14 to 37 and frames 63 to 88.

12. Turn down the Bank Amount to approximately 0.05 and play back the animation. The cone now banks more reasonably at the ends of the ellipse.

The Path controller is frequently used for controlling the motion of a camera through a scene. To set up a walk-through of an architectural model, you can create a spline representing the path of the camera and then assign the camera to that spline by using the Path controller. By animating the % Along Path, you can have the camera pause as it moves along the path to look around at the scene at that point.

Noise Controllers

Noise controllers are used to generate random values. An example Noise Controller Properties dialog box is shown in Figure 16.31. To access this dialog box, right-click the Noise controller and choose Properties from the pop-up menu. At the top of this dialog box, you can set the three controller parameters:

- **Seed.** Sets the initial value for the random number generator
- **Frequency.** Controls how rapidly the noise values change
- **Strength.** Specifies the range of output values

If the >0 option is unchecked, the output values are centered around 0. If this option is checked, the output values range from 0 to the Strength value.

In the lower portion of the dialog box, Fractal Noise and Roughness specify whether to generate the noise values by using a fractal Brownian motion and, if so, how much high-frequency noise to use. The Ramp In and Ramp Out parameters set the amount of time noise takes to build to or fall from full strength.

In the following exercise, you add a touch of noise to the rotation of an air-speed-measuring device by assigning a List controller to the Rotation track and adding a Noise controller with low strength settings.

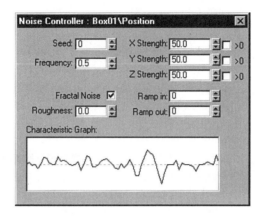

FIGURE 16.31   *A Noise Controller's Properties dialog box.*

Using the Noise Controller

1. Load MF16-05.MAX from the accompanying CD.

2. Select the cylinder that forms the base of the unit.

3. Click the Motion command panel tab and open the Assign Controller rollout.

4. Select the Rotation track and click Assign Controller. Select the Rotation List controller from the Assign Rotation Controller dialog box and click OK.

5. Click the plus sign next to the Rotation controller. This displays the list of Rotation controllers being combined.

6. Select the track labeled Available and assign a Noise Rotation controller to that track by using Assign Controller.

7. Select the Noise Rotation track and right-click the track. Select Properties from the pop-up menu. In the Noise Controller dialog box, set the X and Y strengths to 0, set the Z strength to 20, set Frequency to 0.2, and turn off Fractal Noise. Then, close the Noise Controller dialog box.

8. Turn on Animate and advance to frame 75. In the Top viewport, rotate the cylinder approximately –90 degrees about the Z axis.

9. Activate the Perspective viewport and play back the animation.

As can be seen in this example, adding a small amount of noise to an object's position or rotation can make the object's motion appear more realistic.

Waveform Controllers

Waveform controllers are used to generate regular, periodic waveforms. An example Waveform Controller Properties dialog box is shown in Figure 16.32. At the upper-left of the dialog box is the Waveform List window, which shows the currently defined waveform generators. The buttons to the right of the Waveform List window enable you to add, delete, and reorder the waveform generators. The waveform generators are evaluated in a downward order, with each waveform generator acting on the output of the previous waveform generator.

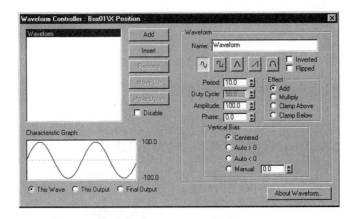

FIGURE 16.32   *A Waveform Controller's Properties dialog box.*

The Characteristic Graph shows one of three displays. If the This Wave option is selected, only the shape of the waveform being generated by the selected waveform generator is displayed, independent of all other waveform generators. If the This Output option is selected, the output from the selected waveform generator— including its effect on the input waveform—is displayed. If the Final Output option is selected, the output from the final waveform generator is shown.

In the Waveform area, you can rename the waveform generator and set the characteristics of the waveform (shape, period, amplitude). In the Effect area, you select how the selected waveform generator acts on the previous waveform generator's output. In the Vertical Bias area, you specify the value around which the waveform is centered.

In the following exercise, you use the Waveform controller to have a set of lights flash on and off along a runway.

Using the Waveform Controller

1. Load file MF16-06.MAX, select the Camera viewport, and play back the animation.

   The scene is based on the Path controller example scene, where the airplane is coming in for a landing. Notice the runway lights that run alongside the runway. You want these lights to be flashing on and off.

2. Open Track View and expand the hierarchy to show Cylinder01. Expand Cylinder01 and then expand the Lights material track under Cylinder01. Expand the Parameters track under Lights (see Figure 16.33).

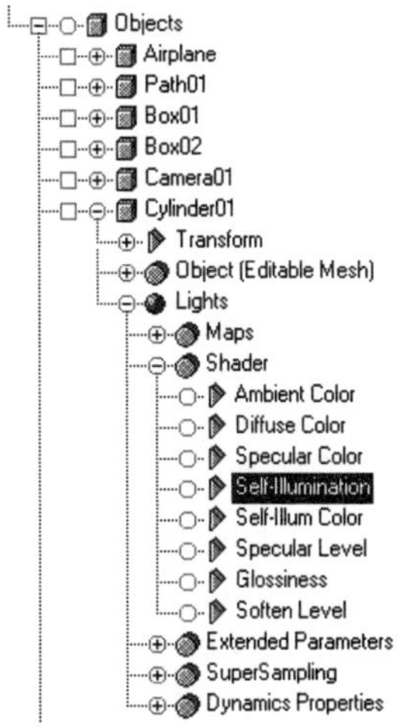

3. Select the Self-Illum. track and click Assign Controller. Choose the Waveform Float controller and click OK.

4. Right-click the Self-Illum. range bar to display the Waveform Controller Properties dialog box.

FIGURE 16.33
The Track View hierarchy tree, expanded to the parameters of the material assigned to the runway lights.

5. Select the Square waveform type and set the Period to 20, the Duty Cycle to 20, the Amplitude to 50, and the Vertical Bias to Auto > 0. Figure 16.34 shows the Waveform Controller dialog box with these settings.

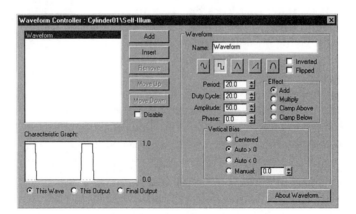

FIGURE 16.34   *The Waveform Controller dialog box.*

6. Close the Waveform Controller dialog box and Track View.

   Play back the animation. The lights now flash on and off as the airplane approaches the runway.

As can be seen in the previous example, generating a periodic waveform is very easy. By combining multiple waveforms in a Waveform controller, you can generate complex periodic motions to duplicate the motion of mechanical systems. By using several waveforms whose periods can all be evenly divided into a longer period, you can generate what appears to be noise but can be looped over this longer period.

The Attachment Controller

The Attachment controller is used to position an object on the surface of another object. The purpose of this controller is to "link" an object to the surface of another object that is being deformed. For example, if you use the Attachment controller to attach a sphere to the top of a cylinder and then you bend the cylinder, the sphere remains attached to the top of the bent cylinder.

When you apply an Attachment controller in the Motion command panel, you get the rollout shown in Figure 16.35. Use this rollout to select the object to attach to by clicking the Pick Object button. To specify the attachment position on the object, click the Set Position button and then click and drag the mouse over the surface of the object being attached to. When you release the mouse button, the controlled object are positioned at that point on the surface, and the face number and barycentric coordinates within that face are displayed in the Position area of the rollout. In the Attach To area of the rollout, if Align to Surface is checked, the local Z axis of the controlled object will be aligned to the surface normal of the surface object.

You can animate the position of the controlled object relative to the surface by moving to another frame, clicking Set Position, and setting a position on the surface. The parameters in the TCB area of the rollout control the interpolation of the controlled object's position between position keys (see the section "TCB Controllers" for information on these parameters);

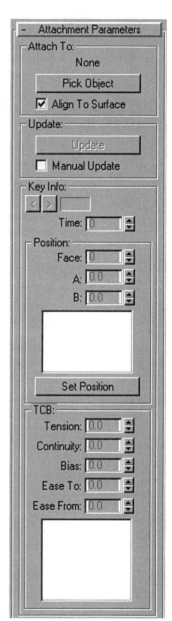

Figure 16.35
An Attachment Controller's Attachment Parameters rollout in the Motion command panel.

however, the results of animating the position of the controlled object might not be what you expected. The controlled object does not follow the surface between the position keys—rather, it moves in a straight line between these points. An example of this is shown in Figure 16.36, where two position keys have been set and the controlled object's motion path is displayed.

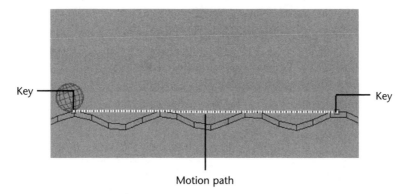

Key

Key

Motion path

FIGURE 16.36   *The effect of animating the attachment point on a deforming object.*

In the following exercise, you use the Attachment controller to attach a set of weights to a bending bar.

Using the Attachment Controller

1. Load file **MF16-07.MAX** from the accompanying CD. This scene shows a set of weights and a weight bar that is animated to move up and down. In this animation, you want the bar to bend as it is being lifted and the weights to respond appropriately.

2. Select object Weights-L and, in the Motion command panel, assign an Attachment controller to the object's Position track.

3. Click Pick Object and click the Bar object.

4. Click Set Position and position Weights-L near the end of Bar. The weights' orientation flips, based on the face of the bar to which they are attached. Make sure when you place the weights that the small weights are facing outward along the bar. Click Set Position to turn it off.

5. Repeat steps 2 through 4 for object Weights-R.

   In the Front viewport, you can see that the center of the weights is not aligned with the center of the bar. This occurs because the pivot points of the weights are located at their center and the pivot points are being attached to the surface of the bar.

6. To center the Weights-R object on the bar, activate the Front viewport, open the Hierarchy command panel, and click Affect Object Only. Click Align on the MAX toolbar and select the rod to align to. In the Align Selection dialog box, choose X Position, Y Position, and Center for both Current Object and Target Object. Click OK.

7. Select Weights-L and repeat step 6.

   If you play back the animation, notice that the weights now follow the bar's motion. It is time to bend the bar.

8. Apply a Bend modifier to the Bar object. Set the Bend Direction to 90 and drag the Bend Angle spinner up and down. The weights follow the bending of the bar. Set the Bend Angle to 0.

9. Advance to frame 8, turn on the Animate button, and set the Bend Angle to 57. Advance to frame 92 and Shift + right-click the Bend Angle spinner up-arrow to set a key at frame 92. Advance to frame 100 and set Bend Angle to 0.

   If you play back the animation, you will see that the bar keeps bending between frames 8 and 92, causing the bar to form almost a full half circle. You need to stop the bending between these two frames.

10. Open Track View, right-click Filters and select Animated Tracks Only from the drop-down menu. Right-click Objects and select Expand All from the drop-down menu.

11. Right-click the second key in Bend's Angle track to display the Key Info dialog box. Click and hold on the Out tangent-type button, and select the Step tangent type (third from the top).

12. Close Track View and play back the animation.

Compound Controllers

A compound controller takes as its input the output data of other controllers. It combines this data with any of its own parameter data and then manipulates the data and outputs the results. When the compound controller is displayed in the Motion command panel or in Track View, you can expand the display to show the controller's input to it by clicking the plus sign to the left of the controller.

> **note**
>
> MAX provides some additional, more advanced procedural controllers. These advanced controllers are used for such special purposes as controlling parameters based on audio files, motion control device data, and user-defined equations. There's even a Reactor controller that enables objects to react to other objects in the scene. These controllers are beyond the scope of a Fundamentals book. For more information on these controllers, refer to your MAX documentation and to New Riders' *Inside 3D Studio MAX 3.0 Volume III, Animation*.

PRS Controller

The Position/Rotation/Scale (PRS) controller is the default controller assigned to the Transform track of objects and modifier gizmos. The PRS controller has three input controllers: Position, Rotation, and Scale. The PRS controller combines the output of these three controllers and outputs the transform matrix required by MAX. No parameters or options are associated with the PRS controller.

The Look At Controller

The Look At controller forces one object to always face another. The Look At controller is used as the default controller for targeted cameras and lights. When a Look At controller is applied to the Transform track of an object, the Position/Rotation/Scale transforms are replaced with Position/Roll Angle/Scale transforms. When you apply a Look At controller in the Motion command panel, you get the Look At Parameters rollout shown in Figure 16.37.

FIGURE 16.37
A Look At controller's Look At Parameters rollout in the Motion command panel.

After assigning a Look At controller, click the Pick Target button and select the object to be looked at. The Axis options specify which of the object's local axes is to point toward the target object and whether the positive or negative direction of that axis points toward the target object.

The Link Control Controller

When you link one object to another by using the Select and Link tool, that object is always a child of the object to which it is linked. Creating and animating hierarchical linkages is described in Chapter 17, "Exploring Other Animation Methods." By using the Link Control controller, you can animate the transfer of hierarchical linkages between objects. You can have one object as the parent of an object over a certain time range and then switch parent objects. When a Link Control controller is applied, the original PRS or Look At controller becomes an input to the Link Control controller, enabling you to animate the object relative to its linked objects. When you apply a Link Control controller in the Motion command panel, you get the Link Parameters rollout shown in Figure 16.38.

The two commands in the Link Parameters rollout are Add Link and Delete Link. Add Link enables you to specify an object for linking. By selecting an object in the Linkage list and clicking Delete Link, you can delete the linkage to that object. A Start Time field lies just below the Linkage list. When an object is selected in the Linkage list, Start Time is the time at which that object will start to act as the parent of the current object. The only exception to this is the first object in the list, which is the parent of the current object until the time when the second object becomes the parent. Thus, there is always a parent to the current object.

In the following exercise, you use the Link Control controller to pass a ball between a set of rotating rods.

FIGURE 16.38
A Link Control controller's Link Parameters rollout in the Motion command panel.

Using the Link Control Controller

1. Load **MF16-08.MAX** from the accompanying CD.

   This scene consists of a ball, three rotating boxes, and a stationary dummy object.

2. Select the ball and, in the Motion command panel, select the Transform track, click Assign Controller, and choose Link Control.

3. At frame 0, click Add Link and then select the dummy object. The object name "Dummy- world" appears in the Linkage list with a Start Time of 0.

4. Advance to frame 5. With Add Link still selected, click Box1.

5. At the following frames, add the following objects as links: frame 20, Box2; frame 30, Box3; frame 50, Box2; frame 60, Box1; frame 85, Dummy-world.

6. Click Add Link to turn off link selection and play back the animation. As the boxes rotate past each other, the ball is passed from the end of one box to the end of the next.

Link Control is very useful in character animation. You will often need the character to interact with objects in a scene—for example, to pick up and carry off an object. By using Link Control on the object, you can link the object to a stationary object until it is picked up and then transfer the linkage to the character.

List Controllers

You use a List controller to create a list of controllers whose outputs are added together. When you assign this controller type in the Motion command panel, you get the Position List rollout shown in Figure 16.39.

Each controller you add to the List controller gets added to the bottom of the list. To add a controller to the list, select the Available track in the Assign Controller rollout and click Assign Controller. The new controller is added to the list immediately above the Available track.

You can cut, delete, and paste controllers into and out of this list. Any one controller in the list is set as the active controller. If the active controller is a key-based controller, you can interactively set keys for the track to which the List controller is assigned, and the keys will be stored in the active controller. If a procedural controller is active, you will not be able to interactively set keys for the track. As an example, suppose you have an object with a List controller assigned to the Position track and Noise and Bézier Position controllers assigned in the List controller. If the Noise controller is the active controller, you will not be able to move the object interactively in the scene. If the Bézier controller is active, you will be able to move the object, and keys will be stored in this controller.

If you want to assign a List controller to a track other than a Transform track, you must perform the assignment in Track View. Although you can assign controllers to the List controller in Track View, you cannot delete controllers from the list, nor can you set which controller is active.

FIGURE 16.39
A List Controller's Position List rollout in the Motion command panel.

tip

List controllers are useful for offsetting the output of procedural controllers. For example, suppose you have a sphere whose radius you want to vary between 50 and 60 by using the Noise controller. In this case, you would apply a Bézier controller to the Radius track and set its value to 55. You would then apply a List controller to the Radius track. The prior Bézier controller would automatically become an input to the List controller. Finally, you would add a Noise controller to the List controller and set its strength to 10.

XYZ Controllers

Many parameters in MAX don't consist of a single value but rather a set of three values. Examples of these are the various color (red, green, blue), position (x, y, z), scale (x, y, z), and rotation (x, y, z) parameters. The XYZ controllers are used to combine the outputs of three separate controllers (each outputting a single value) into a format understood by MAX. This enables you to animate each of these values independent of the others.

Using Advanced Track View Controls

Track View contains a wide variety of tools for adjusting the values and times associated with keys. Many of these tools are beyond the scope of this book. This section covers some of the tools and controls you are most likely to need while creating animations. Refer to the MAX documentation for tools not discussed here.

Filters

In even a simple scene, a full display of all the tracks in Track View can result in hundreds of pages. The capability to filter the display to show only the portions that interest you is critical for efficient Track View use. Clicking Filters displays the Filters dialog box, shown in Figure 16.40. Right-clicking Filters displays the drop-down menu shown in Figure 16.41, with the most frequently used options from the full Filters dialog box.

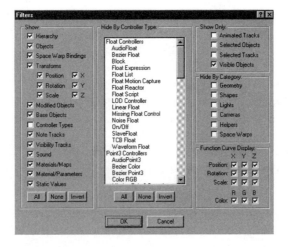

FIGURE 16.40   *By using the Filters dialog box in Track View, you can display only the information you need.*

The Show area of the Filters dialog box contains a list of check boxes specifying how the hierarchical display will be formatted and which components will be displayed. In the Hide By Controller Type area, any controllers selected in the list will not be displayed. The Show Only area filters items based on their animation, selection, and visibility states. The Hide By Category area filters objects based on their type. The Function Curve Display area filters which axes are displayed in Function Curves mode.

Adding Visibility Tracks

The Add Visibility Track button, located on the toolbar of the Track View dialog box, adds a new track to the selected object. This track controls the visibility of the object over time. When the track is added, it is automatically assigned an On/Off controller. When you add keys to the Visibility track, the keys set the visibility of the object to either off or on. When the time passes a key, the visibility of the object is set until it reaches another key or the end of the animation.

The visibility of an object does not need to be either on or off. By assigning another controller to the Visibility track (such as a Bézier controller), you can achieve gradual visibility. The object is invisible at controller values of zero or less and then grows increasingly visible as the controller value approaches 1. The object is fully visible at controller values of 1 or more.

When you assign a Visibility track to a parent object, the visibility of all children objects is similarly affected. If you do not want a child object to inherit the parent's visibility, right-click the child object, choose Properties from the pop-up menu, and turn off Inherit Visibility in the Rendering Control area of the Object Properties dialog box.

FIGURE 16.41
The Filters drop-down menu provides easy access to the most common filters.

note

You can change the object properties for multiple objects by selecting the objects, right-clicking one of the selected objects, and choosing Properties from the pop-up menu. Any changes made in the Object Properties dialog box are applied to all selected objects.

Out-of-Range Types

The Parameter Curve Out-of-Range Types (ORT) button displays the ORT dialog box shown in Figure 16.42, where you can control how the animation of a selected track occurs outside the animated range you have defined. The default ORT is Constant, which uses the value at the beginning of the range for all frames before the range and the value at the end of the range for all frames after the range.

Below each out-of-range type are two buttons. The one on the left represents what happens to the selected track before the animation enters the range in which you defined the animation. The button on the right defines what happens when the animation leaves the range you defined. You can select the left and right buttons in any combination of out-of-range types. For example, you could set the animation to be constant when entering the range and linear after leaving the range.

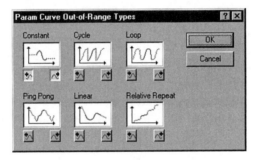

FIGURE 16.42   *The Out-of-Range types control how the animation of a track occurs outside of the animated range of the track.*

Copying and Pasting Time

You will often have a section of an animation defined for one object and want to copy that animation to another object or to the same object but at a different time. You can do this by using the Copy Time and Paste Time functions in Edit Time mode.

To copy a group of keys, enter Edit mode and select the track(s) from which you want to copy the keys. In the Edit window, click at the start of the time range you want to copy and then drag the mouse to the end of the time range. Click Copy Time to copy that block of time (and the enclosed keys in the selected tracks) to the Time Clipboard. To paste from the Time Clipboard, select the track(s) to which you want to paste, click in the Edit window to define the insertion point (or click-and-drag to define a block of time), and then click Paste Time. The Paste Time dialog box is displayed, asking whether you want to Paste Absolute or Paste Relative. If you choose

Paste Absolute, the keys are pasted with their original values. If you choose Paste Relative, MAX subtracts the track value at the insertion point from the pasted keys' values and adjusts the value for any keys after the insertion range by the net change over the range being pasted. During the actual paste operation, the insertion range (if defined) is deleted, forming an insertion point, and then the Time Clipboard range is inserted at the insertion point. Any keys after the insertion point are pushed to the right by the size of the pasted block.

Copying and Pasting in the Hierarchy Tree Window

You can copy and paste controllers, objects, and modifiers in the Hierarchy Tree window. Generally, a copied item can be pasted only on a like item. The exception to this is that a modifier can be pasted on an object. If you are copying a controller, you can paste only to tracks that can accept that type of controller. You can, for example, paste a Position controller to a Position track, but not to a Rotation track.

To copy an item, select the item's name in the Hierarchy Tree window and click Copy. To paste, select one or more compatible items (the targets) and click Paste. The Paste dialog box is displayed, asking whether you want to paste as a Copy or as an Instance and whether to also replace any instances of the targets that might exist.

Pulling It All Together

By using the various commands and modes of Track View and by using the appropriate animation controllers, you can easily build on a simple animation to create a more detailed and lifelike animation. In the following exercise, you use many of the tools in Track View to create an animation.

The Bouncing Ball

1. Load **MF16-09.MAX** from the accompanying CD. This scene consists of a ball sitting at the top of a flight of stairs. In this animation, you want the ball to bounce down the stairs and roll away on the floor.

2. Select the ball, advance to frame 15, and turn on the Animate button.

3. Move the ball so that it rests on the center of the first step down. Go to frame 5 and move the ball vertically so that the bottom of the ball is about one step's height above the top step.

4. Right-click the ball, choose Properties from the pop-up menu, and turn on Trajectory. Click OK.

5. Apply an XForm modifier to the ball. Choose Select and Squash in the MAX tool-bar and choose Restrict to Y. Right-click Select and Squash to display the Scale Transform type-in. Shift + right-click any of the spinners to set a scale key at this frame and close the Transform type-in.

6. Go to frame 0 and squash the ball to about 80 percent along the Y axis.

7. Open Track View, right-click the Filters button, and choose Animated Tracks Only from the pop-up menu. Right-click the Objects track name and choose Expand All from the pop-up menu.

8. Select the key in frame 0 of the Ball/XForm/Gizmo/Scale track and clone the key to frame 15 by dragging the key while holding down the Shift keyboard key. Clone the scale key at frame 5 to frame 14. Select and delete the keys in the gizmo's Position track and collapse and expand the Gizmo tracks.

   At this point, drag the Time slider back and forth, watching the motion and scaling of the ball. The ball is scaling between frames 6 and 14, but it should not be.

9. Right-click the gizmo Scale key at frame 5. Click and hold on the Out Tangent Type button and select the Step tangent type (third from the top).

10. Select the ball's Position track and the gizmo's Scale track. Click Edit Time and, in the Edit window, drag the mouse from frame 0 to 15. Click Copy Time.

11. Click at frame 15 in a track in the Edit window to define the insertion point and click Paste Time. In the Paste Track dialog box, choose Paste Relative and click OK. Figure 16.43 shows the Track View display at this point.

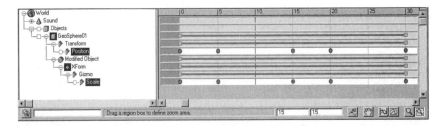

Figure 16.43   *The Track View display after pasting the object's Position track and the gizmo's Scale track.*

Again, drag the Time slider back and forth, watching the motion of the ball. The motion of the ball as it hits the first step is definitely off.

12. Back in Track View, switch to Edit Key mode and right-click the key at frame 15 in the ball's Position track. Set the In tangent type to Fast (fourth from the top). Next to the In Tangent Type button, click the small arrow pointing to the right to set the Out tangent type to Fast. Use the right-arrow button at the top of the

dialog box to advance to key number 5. Set the In and Out tangent types to Fast in the same manner as before.

Drag the Time slider back and forth again—much better. Figure 16.44 shows the ball's trajectory at this point.

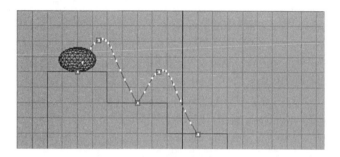

FIGURE 16.44   *The ball's trajectory after adjusting the In and Out tangent types.*

13. Go back to Edit Time mode in Track View and select a time range of 15 to 30. With the Position and Scale tracks selected, click Copy Time. Click at frame 30 to define the insertion point and click Paste Time, Pasting Relative. Paste at frame 30 six more times. From the ball's trajectory in the viewport, you can see the ball bouncing down the stairs.

14. Select the ball if it is not currently selected. Go to the Motion command panel and click Trajectories. Click Sub-Object to enter Keys mode. Move the keys where the ball is hitting the steps or floor to line up the keys with the steps or floor. Move the key at the top of the last bounce so that it is a little bit above the floor.

15. Click again on the Sub-Object button to exit Keys mode. Go to frame 160 and, with Animate on, move the ball to the end of the floor. Figure 16.45 shows the trajectory of the ball at this point.

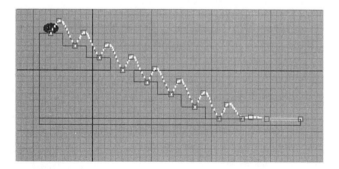

FIGURE 16.45   *Align the keys to the steps and floor by using Sub-Object Keys mode in the Motion/Trajectories command panel.*

16. You really don't want the ball to squash at the last animated frame. In the Edit Key mode of Track View, delete the gizmo's Scale key at frame 135.

17. Click Min/Max Toggle to show all four viewports. Activate the Camera view and play back the animation. The motion of the ball around frame 135 is a bit off. In Track View, right-click the ball's position key at frame 135. Change the In and Out tangent type to Smooth (the first tangent type in the flyout). Click the right arrow next to the Out tangent button to set the In tangent of the next key to Smooth.

Now, play back the animation. Everything looks pretty good, except that the ball is not rotating.

18. Right-click the ball and choose Properties from the pop-up menu. Turn off Trajectory and click OK.

19. Go to the Modify command panel and go down the Modifier stack to the GeoSphere. Add an XForm modifier. You want to rotate the ball before the scaling is performed on the ball, so the rotation XForm must be before the scale XForm in the stack.

20. In the viewports, you can see that the center of the gizmo is located at the base of the ball. In the Sub-Object list, select Center. Turn off Animate, click Align in the MAX toolbar, and select the ball as the object to which to align. Turn on all three Position options, set the Target Object to Center, and click OK. Finally, click the Sub-Object button to turn off Sub-Object mode.

21. In Track View, right-click Filters and turn off Animated Tracks Only. Scroll down the hierarchy tree until you find the XForm modifier directly above Object (GeoSphere), as in Figure 16.46. Select the Xform's Gizmo Rotation track and click Assign Controller. Select Euler XYZ from the Assign Rotation Controller dialog box and click OK. Expand the Rotation track branch.

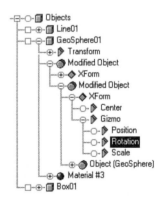

22. Select the Y Rotation track, click Add Keys, and create keys at frames 0 and 80 for the Y Rotation track. Right-click the Rotation key at frame 80 and set its value to 360.

FIGURE 16.46
The Track View hierarchy tree expanded to the Gizmo Position track of the Rotation Xform Modifier.

23. Click Parameter Curve Out-Of-Range Types and then click the arrow pointing to the right under Relative Repeat. Click OK to exit the dialog box and play the animation.

In this exercise, you have seen how the various animation tools in MAX work together to enable you to quickly go from a basic scene without any animation to the completed animated scene.

Conclusion

This chapter described the basic tools used for animating your scene. From this chapter, you should have a basic understanding of the following tools and techniques:

- Basic keyframed animations
- Keys and function curves in Track View
- Key-based and procedural controllers
- Various key-based controller types

Although you can create many animations by using just these basic tools, they might not be adequate for animating scenes with special requirements. The next chapter explores more advanced animation tools and techniques.

CHAPTER 17

Exploring Other Animation Methods

This chapters focuses on advanced animation methods, with particular emphasis on using the following tools and techniques:

- Creating Object Hierarchies
- Adjusting Object Pivot Points
- Using Inverse Kinematics
- Creating Skeletal Deformations
- Using Space Warps
- Animating with Morphs
- Animating with Rigid-Body Dynamics

By the end of the chapter, you will have a good idea of how to create complicated animations and special effects by using these tools and techniques.

Creating Object Hierarchies

Chapter 16, "Exploring Basic Animation Methods," described how to animate single objects by moving, rotating, and scaling. At times, especially in character or mechanical animation, you want to animate an object by transforming it and have other objects repeat the same transformation. For example, if you animate the upper arm of a character, you want the lower arm, wrist, and hand to animate with the upper arm, as they would in real life. You can accomplish this in Track View by copying and pasting keys between tracks, but that process quickly becomes tedious.

The solution is to link one object to another and form a hierarchical chain. The linked object becomes the *child* and the object it is linked to becomes the *parent*. When the parent object is transformed, the child object is also transformed, but if you transform the child, the parent is not transformed. This transfer of transforms from parent to child is called *forward kinematics*.

To link two objects together, you must use a selection tool called Select and Link. This tool and its sister tool, Unlink Selection, are on the Main Toolbar of the Tab Panel, as shown in Figure 17.1.

Select and Link ——————— Unlink Selection

FIGURE 17.1   *The Select and Link/Unlink tools on the Main Toolbar tab of the Tab Panel.*

To link an object as a child to another (parent) object, choose Select and Link. When you place the cursor over a selected object, it changes to the Make Link cursor. Click the object you want to be the child and drag to the object you want to be the parent. A line forms between the two, and the cursor changes to the Accept Link cursor. When you release the mouse button with the Accept Link cursor visible, both objects are highlighted for a moment and then return to normal. Although they look the same as they did before you linked them, the objects no longer act the same. When you move the parent now, the child moves with it.

Using this manner of linking, you can form a hierarchical tree that is very powerful for character animation. For example, you can link the hand of the character to a forearm, the forearm to an upper arm, and the upper arm to a torso object. Then, when you rotate the upper arm, the forearm and hand rotate with it.

The following exercise shows you how to link objects together quickly.

Linking Objects Together

1. Load the file MF17-01.MAX from the accompanying CD. Figure 17.2 shows this file loaded in MAX.

2. Choose Select and Link, and click the ball at the end of the last arm segment.

3. Click and drag up to the first arm segment and let go over that segment. The ball and arm should highlight briefly to indicate they are linked.

4. Link the first arm segment to the first circular joint.

5. Link the first circular joint to the second arm segment.

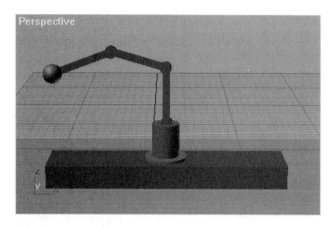

FIGURE 17.2   *The scene, showing a mechanical arm before the parts are linked together.*

6. Moving to the right and downward, continue linking each object to the next object. Link all objects except the ground object.

7. Choose Select Object and then Select by Name. At the bottom of the Select Objects dialog box, turn on Display Subtree. As shown in Figure 16.3, the Object list shows the object names listed from the parent down, with each child indented from its parent. Close Select by Name.

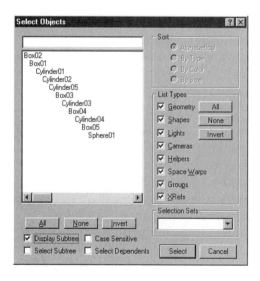

FIGURE 17.3   *The Select Objects dialog box, showing how a linked hierarchy is displayed.*

8. In the Front viewport, starting at the left, select the first circular joint and rotate it 45 degrees. Notice the way the rest of the arm responds.

9. Rotate the second joint –30 degrees. Notice that the part of the arm that is lower in the hierarchy chain moves, but the objects higher in the hierarchy chain do not move.

10. Save the file as MF17-01a.MAX for use in a later exercise.

The transfer of motion from a parent object to its children, as shown in the previous exercise, is the basis of forward kinematics. By applying this type of animation with keyframes, and with some work, you can produce character animation.

Adjusting Object Pivot Points

While animating an object in MAX, you might need to rotate an object around a specific point, such as the center or one end. The point around which the object rotates and scales is called the object's *pivot point*. The point on a parent object around which its child objects are rotated and scaled is also called the *pivot point*. When an object is created in MAX, you generally should place the pivot point at either the center or the base of the object.

You can adjust an object's pivot point by selecting the child object and clicking the Hierarchy command panel tab. On the Hierarchy command panel are three buttons that enable you to work with three different aspects of hierarchical relationships between objects. To adjust an object's pivot point, first select the Pivot button (see Figure 17.4). In the Adjust Pivot rollout, you can adjust the location and orientation of an object's pivot point independent of the object's mesh, or vice versa, and you can apply a rotation or scaling effect on the pivot point that affects the position of any children.

FIGURE 17.4

The Hierarchy command panel, where you can adjust the Pivot, Inverse Kinematics (IK), and Link Info of the selected object.

- When the Affect Pivot Only button is selected, you can move or rotate the object's pivot point, and only the pivot point is adjusted (the object mesh and any child objects are not affected).

- When the Affect Object Only button is selected, you can move, rotate, or scale the object's mesh, and only the mesh is adjusted (the object's pivot point and any child objects are not affected).

- When the Affect Hierarchy Only button is selected, you can rotate or scale the position of any child objects with respect to the object's pivot point, but the object's mesh and pivot point are not affected.

When either the Affect Pivot Only button or the Affect Object Only button is selected, the Alignment area buttons are enabled. These buttons are shortcuts for placing or orienting the pivot point with respect to the object mesh or the world, or the object mesh with respect to the pivot point or the world.

The Reset Pivot button simply resets the object pivot to its original position and resets the orientation from when the object was created.

The commands in the Adjust Transform rollout are used primarily for linked hierarchies. When the Don't Affect Children button in the Move/Rotate/Scale area is selected, the object can be moved, rotated, or scaled, and any child objects will not inherit that particular transform. The Transform button in the Reset area aligns the pivot point orientation to the world orientation and does not affect the object's mesh or child objects. The Scale button sets the base scale value of an object to its current scale value and sets the current scale value to 100%.

The following exercise shows you how to use the Pivot options on the Hierarchy command panel.

Adjusting Pivot Points

1. Load the file **MF17-01.MAX** again. (If you are continuing from the last exercise, please reload the file from the accompanying CD.)

2. Select one of the arms of the object and rotate it a couple of degrees. Notice how it rotates around one end point.

3. Click the Hierarchy command panel tab.

4. Choose Affect Pivot Only. The Pivot icon appears as a tripod, as shown in Figure 17.5.

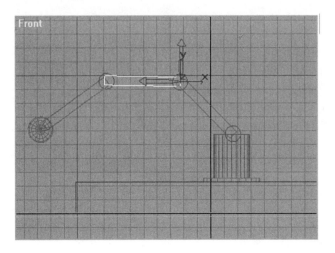

FIGURE 17.5   *The Pivot icon, with which you can adjust the pivot point's location and orientation.*

5. Choose Center to Object. The pivot point is centered on the object. Turn off Affect Pivot Only and rotate the object again. It now rotates around the pivot point.

6. Turn on Affect Pivot Only and drag the pivot point to a new location on the screen.

7. Again, turn off Affect Pivot Only and try to rotate the arm. It rotates around the pivot point.

8. Choose Affect Object Only. Move the arm to a new location. Notice how the arm moves and the pivot point does not. Again, if you try to rotate the object, it rotates around the pivot point.

9. Finally, with Affect Object Only on, choose Align to World in the Alignment area. The object mesh is now aligned to the world coordinate system.

Selecting the location of the pivot point for an object is critical when you are using forward or inverse kinematics. The orientation of the pivot point is also important when using rotational limits in inverse kinematics (described later in this chapter). The rotational limits are specified by using object local axes, which are the object's pivot point axes.

Controlling Child Inheritance

You can control which of the parent's transforms are passed to a child by selecting the child object and clicking the Link Info button on the Hierarchy command panel tab (see Figure 17.6). On the Link Info panel, you can control which transforms can be directly applied to an object (the Locks rollout) and which transforms are inherited from the object's parent (the Inherit rollout).

In the Locks rollout, if you select any axis in the transform area, you cannot directly transform the selected object along that local axis. For example, if you have Move's Z axis checked, you can use Select and Move to move the object along its local X and Y axes but not its local Z axis. If the object is a child object and you move the parent object, the child object moves with the parent, no matter which locks are set.

Inherit, the second rollout, determines which transforms a child object inherits from the parent. For each selected axis in the transform area, the selected object inherits the parent's transform along that world axis. For example, if you have Move's X and Y axes cleared, the object moves up and down as its parent object moves but not side to side with the parent. If you were creating a Ferris wheel, you would want to attach the cars to the wheel as child objects so the cars would rotate as the wheel rotates. You would not want the cars to inherit any of the wheel's rotation, however, so you would clear all the axes for Rotate. Otherwise, the cars would rotate about their local axes along with the Ferris wheel and dump out their passengers.

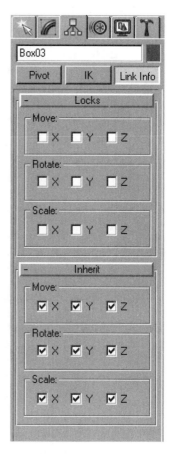

FIGURE 17.6
The Link Info rollouts, where you can control which transforms of a parent object are passed on to the child.

Using Inverse Kinematics

There are two ways to create character or mechanical animation efficiently and effectively. The first is forward kinematics, which you have just seen. In forward kinematics, you animate a hierarchical chain by transforming parent objects and affecting child objects with that transform.

Inverse kinematics (IK) does just the opposite. Instead of transforming the parent, you transform the child, and the parent objects are affected all the way up through the chain. This is only part of IK's power. IK also enables you to place restrictions on how the joints work. In IK, you can use two types of restrictions: Rotating and Sliding. You can restrict the joints in any axis to any amount of rotation or to any distance, and by setting information such as joint precedence, damping (diminishing the strength of), and so on, you can easily make the animation more lifelike.

The downside of IK is that you give up some control of the animation to the IK system by relying on the IK system to calculate certain keyframes and motion. The results are good in some cases, but troublesome in others. Despite its downside, IK is extremely powerful for the creation of character and mechanical animation.

To use IK, you must first perform the linking operation used in forward kinematics. When linking, always start with the last object in the chain and work your way back to the parent object. Because it is inverse kinematics, the child objects affect the parent; therefore, the last object on the link chain should be a child object. After you have linked the objects, you can apply the IK parameters to the joints between the objects.

After the IK parameters have been set, you turn on inverse kinematics by choosing the IK button on the Main Toolbar (see Figure 17.7). Then, whenever you manipulate an object that is part of an IK chain, the IK constraints are used. When the IK button is active, it turns blue. When the button is inactive, the chain acts as a normal hierarchical chain.

When you set up the hierarchical chain between objects, it is helpful to be able to see the links between objects. You can do this with the Link Display rollout at the bottom of the Display command panel (see Figure 17.8).

FIGURE 17.7
The Inverse Kinematics button turns MAX's interactive IK solver on and off.

The first option in this rollout, Display Links, draws a bone-like structure that represents the links for all selected objects. When the second option, Link Replaces Object, is enabled, the object is replaced by the link, which makes it easier to understand how IK works. In Figure 17.9, you can see the arm scene with both types of displays. When the links are visible, you can select either the link object or the object with which you want to work. When you transform one, the other is transformed also.

FIGURE 17.8
The Link Display rollout enables you to display the links between objects in a hierarchy.

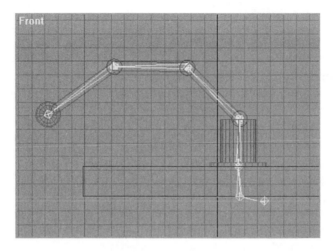

FIGURE 17.9   *A mechanical arm, showing the links between objects in a hierarchy.*

To adjust the IK parameters for an object, you first select the object and then click the IK button on the Hierarchy command panel. The resulting IK panel is shown in Figure 17.10.

The five rollouts—Inverse Kinematics, Object Parameters, Auto Termination, Sliding Joints, and Rotational Joints—are described next, with their options.

The Inverse Kinematics rollout enables you to solve the motion for an IK chain attached to a *follow object* (another object in the scene that has been animated). When you bind a portion of a kinematic chain to an object, that object becomes a follow object for the kinematic chain. Whenever an object in the kinematic chain is attached to a follow object, the motion of the follow object is translated into the kinematic chain. Solving the kinematic chain finds all of the joint position and rotation keys necessary to make the animation occur correctly. The Inverse Kinematics rollout provides the following options:

- **Apply IK.** Solves the kinematic chain for follow objects.
- **Apply Only to Keys.** Calculates the IK solution only at the frames where keyframes exist for the follow objects.
- **Update Viewports.** Updates viewports as the IK solution is solved.
- **Clear Keys.** Removes all keys from the kinematic chain prior to calculating the IK solution.
- **Start, End.** Defines the range of time for which the solution is created.

tip

You can use dummy objects in your hierarchical chain to define joints or points of rotation. Dummy objects, found on the Create command panel under Helpers, do not render, but add another link to the chain when necessary.

In the Object Parameters rollout, you can define the objects in the chain and their precedence, bindings, and order. This rollout offers the following options:

- **Terminator.** Defines the end of the IK chain by selecting one or more objects. After you have selected an object as a terminator, objects above the terminator in the chain are not affected when objects are moved beneath it.

- **Bind Position.** Binds the position of the selected object to the position of the follow object. Turning on the R button next to Bind Position maintains the selected object's position relative to the follow object. Turning it off moves the object to the follow object's position.

- **Bind Orientation.** Binds the orientation of the selected object to the orientation of the follow object. Turning on the R button next to Bind Orientation maintains the selected object's orientation relative to the follow object. Turning off the R button rotates the object to match the follow object's orientation.

- **Bind to Follow Object.** Binds the selected object to a follow object. Then, when you animate the follow object and click Apply IK, the IK chain is animated. Any object can be used as a follow object, but dummy objects generally are used because they do not render.

- **Precedence.** Sets the priority of the object in the kinematic chain. Precedence defines an object's importance in the solution to the IK chain. The higher the Precedence value, the more important the object.

Figure 17.10

The IK rollouts, where you can specify the parametrs to use for Inverse Kinematics.

- **Child-Parent.** Sets the priority for the entire chain as child and then parent. When Child-Parent is selected, all child objects have a higher precedence than their parents.

- **Parent-Child.** Sets the precedence for the entire chain as parent and then child. When Parent-Child is selected, all parent objects have a higher precedence than their children.

- **Copy, Paste.** Performs a copy and paste of rotating and sliding joint parameters between objects.
- **Mirror Paste.** Used when pasting constraints to mirror the constraint values.

In the Auto Termination rollout, you can specify whether to have interactive IK automatically terminated and, if so, how far up the chain you want the terminator.

The Sliding Joints rollout enables you to set the restrictions for sliding joints and to define how those joints act when IK is enabled. A sliding joint can move in any defined axis. If rotating joints are enabled, the joint can rotate as well as slide. By default, sliding joints are disabled and rotating joints are enabled. The Sliding Joints rollout offers the following options:

- **Active.** Defines whether the selected object can slide in the selected axis. The axis is defined by the parent coordinate system for the object.
- **Limited.** Restricts the motion of the sliding joint.
- **Ease.** Enables the joint to resist movement as it nears the limits of its motion.
- **From, To.** Enables you to define the upper and lower limit of motion for the object in the selected axis.
- **Spring Back (checkbox).** When Spring Back is turned on, the spring force pulling the object back to the rest position gets stronger as the object moves farther from its rest position.
- **Spring Back (field).** Sets the rest position for the joint.
- **Spring Tension.** Sets the strength of the "spring."
- **Damping.** Diminishes the strength of the motion of the object, making it more resistant to IK forces. Values range from 0 to 1 (with 1 the highest damping force). You dampen the motion of an object to simulate real-world situations, such as inertia.

The Rotational Joints rollout enables you to set the restrictions for rotating joints and to define how those joints act when IK is enabled. The options on this menu are the same as those on the Sliding Joints menu, except that the To and From fields are measured as angles. Rotational joints are similar to your knee, elbow, and shoulder joints.

The following exercise shows you how to use IK to animate the arm scene in this chapter.

Using IK to Animate a Scene

1. Load the file **MF17-01a.MAX** that you created earlier in this chapter. (If you did not complete the earlier exercise, load the file provided on the accompanying CD.)

2. Select one of the middle arm segments and rotate it quickly to see how it affects the rest of the object. As you can see, objects above and to the left of the selected arm also rotate. (This is forward kinematics.)

3. Choose Undo.

4. Select the entire mechanical arm except the ground object and click the Hierarchy command panel tab. Choose Child-Parent to set the joint precedence in this order.

5. From the Main Toolbar, set the reference coordinate system to Parent.

6. Select the first circular joint on the left and move up the rollouts until you can see all of the rotational joint parameters. Deactivate the X and Z axes and turn on Limited for the Y axis. Set the From value to 110 and the To value to –10. (If you use the spinners, you can see the joint move interactively, making it easier to define the limits.) Turn on Spring Back and set the Spring Back value to 74.

7. Select the next circular joint to the right. Deactivate the X and Z axes and turn on Limited for the Y axis. Set the From value to 75, the To value to –60, and the Spring Back value to 30. Turn on Spring Back.

8. Select the next circular joint to the right. Deactivate the X and Z axes and turn on Limited for the Y axis. Set the From value to –54, the To value to 0, and the Spring Back value to _45. Turn on Spring Back.

9. Select the large cylinder beneath the last circular joint. Deactivate the X and Y axes.

10. Select the base the arm sits on (object Box01). Deactivate rotation in all axes. Expand the Sliding Joint rollout, activate the sliding joint in the X axis, and turn on Limited, Ease, and Spring Back. Set From to –110, To to 110, and Damping to 0.5.

11. For each of the remaining objects in the scene, turn off all rotating and sliding joints.

12. Choose Select and Move, and move the ball on the end of the arm. Notice that only the ball moves (because it is a child object with IK turned off). Choose Undo.

13. Turn on IK. Move the ball at the end of the arm again. Because IK is on, all the other arm segments now move correctly (as they would in real life). For correct animation, combine forward and inverse kinematic techniques.

    The file as it should appear at this point is on the accompanying CD as **MF17-01b.MAX**; you can check your work against it, if you want.

    To animate the arm, simply turn on the Animate button and begin setting position keys. The rest of the arm should now react appropriately and position itself correctly. Always create the animation by adjusting the position of the last object in the chain.

    Another way to animate a kinematic chain, shown in the next set of steps, is to use a follow object.

Using the Follow Object to Animate a Scene

1. Click the Create command panel tab and choose the Helpers button.

2. In the Front viewport, create a dummy to the left of and slightly below the sphere.

3. Set the animation slider to frame 100 and turn on Animate.

4. Move the dummy object vertically 170 units and turn off Animate.

5. Select the ball on the end of the mechanical arm. Click the Hierarchy command panel tab and choose Bind to Follow Object, Bind.

6. Click the ball, drag over to the dummy object, and let go when you see the cursor change. The Bind Position option is selected automatically. Click the R button next to Bind Position to make the bind relative.

7. Choose Apply IK.

Now, having created the animation and position keys for all objects in the IK chain, you can create a camera and a light and render the animation.

As seen in the previous example, using character animation is typically easier with inverse kinematics than with forward kinematics. If you use forward kinematics, you must work your way up the hierarchy, placing or rotating each individual object. As you work out toward the children, you might discover that a previous object wasn't positioned properly, requiring you to start over from that object. If you use inverse kinematics, you can simply place the child or follow objects, and the parents are automatically placed in the proper position.

Using the Bones System

In the previous sections, hierarchical chains were defined by creating a series of objects and then using Select and Link to link the objects together. An alternative method for creating a hierarchical chain is to use the MAX Bones system. In a Bones system, no actual geometry is created: The hierarchical links themselves are displayed in the viewports. You can link other objects to the hierarchical links, after which any animation of the Bones system is reflected in the linked objects.

MAX Release 3 provides an IK system controller. In a system controller, a slave controller is applied to each object in the system, and a master controller is used to control the slave controllers. As a result, the interactions between multiple objects are handled by the master controller. This is exactly what is needed for IK, and the IK system controller is now the default controller for creating Bones systems.

When you use the IK system controller, the IK solution happens in real time and there is no need to use Apply IK to follow another object. To animate a Bones system by using the new IK system controller, you animate the position of special end effectors. An end effector is similar to a follow object, but it is created as part of the Bones system. When you create a Bones system, an end effector can be created automatically at the end of each kinematic chain. You can also create and animate end effectors at any level in the kinematic chain. Sliding and rotational joint restrictions are applied to individual portions of the kinematic chain, as described earlier. When you use the IK system controller, icons represent joint axes and any limits you have set. This direct feedback of the limit positions makes the limits easier to set.

Bones systems are created by selecting the Create command panel tab, clicking Systems, and then clicking the Bones button. The Bone Parameters rollout is displayed in Figure 17.11. The IK Controller area contains the following options for using the new IK system controller to create a Bones system.

- If Assign To Children is turned on, the IK controller is used while creating bones; if it is turned off, PRS (Position, Rotation, and Scale) controllers are assigned to each bone.

- If Assign To Root is turned on, the IK controller is assigned to the root (top bone in the chain); if it is turned off, a PRS controller is assigned to the root. In character animation, you will often want a PRS controller assigned to the root (allowing you to move the torso of the character) and the IK controller assigned to the rest of the character for animating the hand and foot positions.

- If Create End Effector is turned on, an end effector is created automatically at the end of each kinematic chain (the feet and hands, for example).

In the Auto Boning area, you can create a Bones system based on an existing hierarchical chain. For example, if you have a jointed character mesh already linked together (in which each body part is a separate object), you click Pick Root and then click the torso of your character. MAX subsequently builds a Bones system with the same structure as your linked model. If the Auto Link option is turned on, MAX relinks the body parts to the appropriate bone after creating the Bones system. If Copy Joint Parameters is turned on, all joint parameters are copied from your model to the appropriate bone. If Match Alignment is on, the local axis of the bones is the same as for the matching body part.

FIGURE 17.11
The Bone Parameters rollout, where you can create Bones systems.

Using the IK System Controller

1. Load the file **MF17-01b.MAX** from the accompanying CD.

2. Click the Create command panel tab, click Systems, and then click the Bones button.

3. Click Pick Root, and then click the large base on which the arm sits (object Box02). A Bones system is created to match the object hierarchy, as shown in Figure 17.12. Right-click in the viewport to turn off Bones creation.

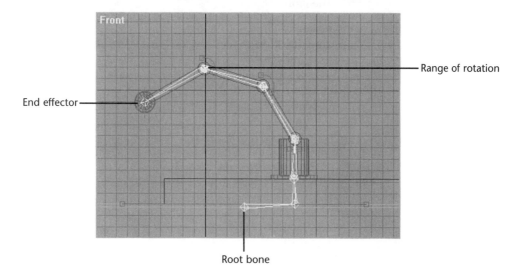

FIGURE 17.12   *The Bones structure created for a mechanical arm, using Auto Boning.*

4. If the Inverse Kinematics button in the toolbar is activated, turn it off so you can move or rotate the bones.

5. Because Create End Effector was on, an end effector was created at the end of the kinematic chain: the sphere (the end effector is shown as a blue + over the sphere). Advance to frame 100 and turn on Animate. Choose Select and Move. In the Front viewport, move the end effector up about 140 units. As the end effector is moved, the IK solution for the hierarchy is solved in real time.

6. Play back the animation. Note that the end effector and the sphere move in a straight line between the start and end positions.

7. In Figure 17.12, you might have noticed the orange arcs located near the circular joints. These arcs represent the range of rotation for the joint. Select the link from the first to the second circular joint (counting from the left), as shown in Figure 17.13.

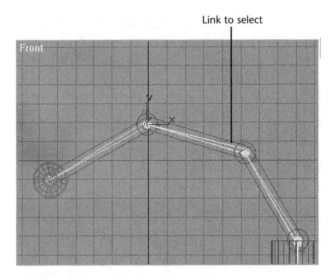

FIGURE 17.13 *The Bones link associated with the top rotational joint.*

8. Click the Hierarchy command panel tab and drag the panel up to display the Rotational Joints rollout. Because Copy Joint Parameters was turned on, the Y-axis rotational constraints were copied to the bone. Adjust the From and To values to see how the range limit display changes.

9. Select the root bone as shown in Figure 17.13 and move it. Note that the base of the arm moves, but the end effector at the arm does not.

10. Click the Motion command panel tab and select the end effector. The IK system controller parameters are displayed, as shown in Figure 17.14. In the IK Controller Parameters rollout, click Link in the End Effectors area and then click the root bone. Now select and move the root bone. The end-effector position remains constant relative to the root bone.

   This technique for linking end effectors to the root bone is useful for character animation, where the head and hand end effectors are linked to the root bone at the character's torso. When you move the root bone, the upper portion of the body moves, but the feet remain at their original location.

For more information on the IK system controller and its uses, refer to your MAX documentation and to New Riders' *Inside 3D Studio MAX 3.0, Volume III, Animation.*

Creating Skeletal Deformations

MAX 3 now has several built-in tools that enable you to perform skeletal deformations without the need of a third party plug in such as Physique or Bones Pro. Skeletal deformations are usually used on characters or objects that are a single mesh. You can animate the face by using the Morph controller, or you can set up the face to animate with a skeletal deformation tool.

MAX provides two main skeletal deformation tools: Skin and Flex. Both are implemented as object modifiers and are generally the last modifiers applied to an object. With Skin, you can use other objects in the scene to deform the mesh. Flex, on the other hand, is used to simulate soft body dynamics such as waving antennae on a bug. Skin and Flex may be used separately or together. The next section takes a closer look at them.

Using the Skin Modifier

The Skin modifier can be used on top of most types of geometry, including Mesh, Patch, and NURBS geometry. For the purposes of this book, Skin will only be used on a Mesh object, but consider the possibilities of using Skin with the Surface modifier.

Skin works by using other objects in the scene as "bones" to deform the mesh to which the modifier is applied. You can use just about any type of object, short of helper objects; for example, you can use primitives or splines to deform the mesh. When a bone is assigned to the mesh, it is automatically assigned a set of vertices within the Skin object. Then, when you move the bone, the vertices move as well.

FIGURE 17.14

The IK Controller Parameters rollout in the Motion command panel specifies the parameters for an IK system controller.

Skin provides a complete set of controls for modifying which vertices are applied to which bones through the use of *envelopes*. By adjusting the envelope around each bone, you can control how the bone is applied to the mesh. This enables you to create many different bones for different purposes. For example, think about how many bone objects you would want to create for a face.

Skin is available as an object space modifier. After it is applied to an object, you see the rollout shown in Figure 17.15.

The Skin Parameters rollout is divided into five parts. Each part is listed below and briefly described:

- **Add Bones.** Here, you can select objects in the scene to use as bone objects. You can also select objects to use as cross-sections (see MAX documentation for more on cross-sections). A list of selected bones appears in the list window. By selecting a bone, you can determine which envelope is available for editing when you're using Envelope sub-objects.

- **Envelope Properties.** This section is available only when the Envelope sub-object mode is active. You can adjust the envelope's size, falloff, and visibility, and whether it is an absolute or relative envelope. When absolute, all vertices inside the envelope are affected. When relative, vertices can have varying degrees of influence, much like a soft selection.

- **Weight Properties.** With these tools, you can "paint" weights onto the vertices to make them more or less influenced by the currently selected bone.

- **Filters.** Enables you to define what is shown in the viewports.

- **Advanced Parameters.** In this section, you can reset bones to their original state if you make mistakes when setting them up. You can do the same for vertices as well.

FIGURE 17.15

The Skin Parameters rollout, where you can define how bone objects are used to deform the object to which the Skin modifier is applied.

It's time to learn how to use the Skin modifier. The following exercise uses the Skin modifier on a head. (Later in this chapter, you will use the Morph controller to animate this same head. When you have finished that section, compare the technique to Skin. You will find both very useful.)

Using Skin to Deform a Head

1. Load the file **MF17-02.MAX** from the accompanying CD. Figure 17.16 shows you the scene at this point, which contains a mesh head and a spline.

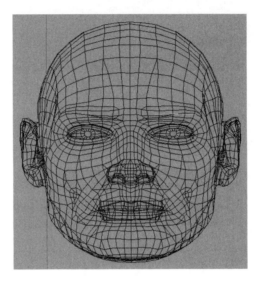

FIGURE 17.16   *A mesh-based head object with a spline. You will use Skin to deform the head with the spline.*

2. Select the Head object.

3. Go to the Modify command panel and click the More button. Select Skin from the list and choose OK.

4. In the Skin Parameters rollout, click Add Bone. A Select By Name dialog box appears. Select the Line01 object and choose Select.

   At this point, the spline deforms the mesh. To see this, select the spline, choose Move, and move the spline around in the viewport. As you do, watch the mesh deform. Choose Undo when you are finished. Now, adjust the spline's influence to better match its usage here. Reselect the Head object and return to the Modify command panel.

5. Enable Sub-Object mode in the Modify command panel. When you do, notice that a group of vertices in the head turn red and a cage appears around the spline, as shown in Figure 17.17.

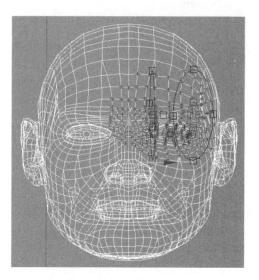

FIGURE 17.17   *The envelope that surrounds the spline.*

6. In the Envelope Properties section of the rollout, click the A button. It turns into an R and sets the envelope type to Relative. Now the vertices change colors, with red at the center and blue toward the edge. Red is more under the influence of the bone than blue.

7. Take a close look at the envelope itself and see the two sets of circles, representing an inner and an outer envelope. If you click one, it turns pink to indicate it has been selected. Select one of the outer circles.

8. In the Modify command panel, you will find a Radius spinner in the Envelope Properties section. Adjusting this spinner changes the size of the selected envelope circle. With the outer circle still selected, adjust the spinner to 0.134.

9. Select the Inner circle and adjust the spinner to 0.050.

10. Repeat steps 8 and 9 for the other side of the envelope. When you finish, the envelope should be centered around the eyebrow and just touching the upper lid of the eye, as shown in Figure 17.18.

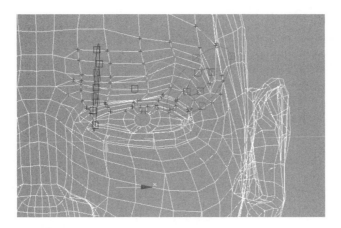

FIGURE 17.18   *The spline bone envelope after adjusting its influence on the mesh.*

11. Close the Sub-object mode.

12. Select the Spline shape in the scene. Activate Vertex sub-object mode. In the Front viewport, move the vertices of the spline to form the shape shown in Figure 17.19.

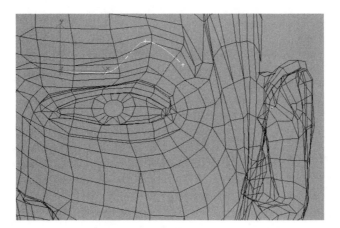

FIGURE 17.19   *The spline bone after adjusting its shape.*

13. Choose Zoom Extents and switch the Front viewport to a Shaded view. Notice that the left eye looks angry and the right eye is pleasant and happy.

14. Save the file as **MF17-02a.MAX**.

The previous exercise showed you a simple example of how to use skin and bones to affect a mesh. You might take this opportunity to apply more bones to the head mesh. Work on it until you feel you have generated enough controls to create any type of expression you like. By the time you finish, you will not only have learned how to use Skin, but you will have created a highly controllable facial animation, as well.

Using Flex

Flex is another skeletal deformation tool that is fun to use. Flex works with a selection of vertices. When these vertices are animated, Flex delays their motion slightly to give them a sense of weight and flexibility. Like Skin, Flex is implemented as an object space modifier and can be applied to just about any type of object. When you apply Flex, you get the rollout shown in Figure 17.20.

The Flex rollout is divided into four sections, which are listed below and briefly described:

- **Parameters.** The basic parameters for controlling the Flex effect. These define the flexibility of the selected vertices.

- **Paint Weights.** Enables you to paint weights onto the selected vertices to make them move more slowly or quickly.

- **Vertex Weights.** Enables you to assign and enable vertex weights.

- **Advanced.** Here, you can select space warps for use in conjunction with Flex. An example might be using the Wind space warp to make a tree blow in the wind.

Now see how to make use of Flex in a real-world situation. The following exercise shows you how to apply Flex to the head you worked on in the last exercise.

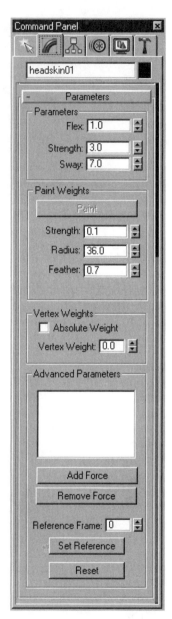

FIGURE 17.20
The Flex rollout, where you can define how the vertices will react when animated.

Using Flex on the Head

1. Load the file MF17-03.MAX from the accompanying CD. This is the same file you worked on in the last exercise, with one exception: The head has been animated to rotate left and right. Play back the animation to see the result.

2. Select the Head mesh and go to the Modify command panel.

3. Select Mesh Select. This enables you to pass a selection of sub-objects up the stack to the Flex modifier. In other words, this enables you to select the vertices you want to have affected by Flex.

4. Enable Vertex sub-object mode. In the Front viewport, select the vertices for the ears of the head, as shown in Figure 17.21.

FIGURE 17.21   *The head, with the vertices of the ears selected for use with Flex.*

5. In the Modify command panel, click the More button. Select Flex and choose OK from the list. This applies the Flex modifier to the selection, which is indicated by the * next to the Flex entry in the stack.

6. Set Flex to 1.5 and Sway to 20.

7. Play back the animation. As it plays back, watch the ears closely. You will see that they now act as if they are flexible and rubbery.

   As you can see from the previous exercise, Flex is very easy to use. When you combine it with Skin, you have the basic tools to create very realistic facial and body animations.

Using Space Warps

A *space warp* is a nonrenderable object that affects other objects as they move through the space influenced by the space warp. Space warps act as force field generators that can deform the mesh of other objects or apply force to objects and particles. For example, a space warp can pull or push particles as gravity does, or it can cause an object to explode. When you create a space warp, an icon for the warp appears in the scene. For an object to be affected by a space warp, you must bind the object to the warp by using the Bind to Space Warp tool in the Main Toolbar.

FIGURE 17.22
The Bind to Space Warp button to bind an object to a space warp.

To create a space warp, first choose the Space Warp button in the Create command panel and select the appropriate space warp category from the Category drop-down list. Then, select the space warp type to create and click in a viewport (or click-and-drag for some types).

To bind an object to a space warp, click Bind to Space Warp (see Figure 17.22), click the object you want to bind, drag the cursor to the space warp, and let go. Both objects are highlighted briefly to indicate the acceptance of the binding. Multiple objects can be bound to the same space warp, and multiple space warps can be applied to the same object. When you bind an object to a space warp, the binding is applied at the top of the object modifier stack (see Figure 17.23).

Space warps come in three categories: Geometric/Deformable, Particles & Dynamics, and Modifier-Based. Geometric/Deformable space warps deform the mesh of objects bound to them apply. Particle & Dynamics space warps forces to the individual particles in bound particle systems, and most can be used with Dynamics (described in the "Animating with Rigid-Body Dynamics" section later in this chapter) to apply forces such as gravity and wind to objects. Instead of deforming the mesh of the object, these forces are applied to the entire object. Finally, Modifier-Based space warps are similar to Geometric/Deformable space warps in that they deform the mesh of objects bound to them.

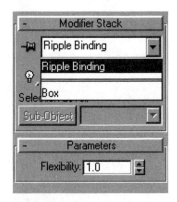

FIGURE 17.23
The Ripple binding in the modifier stack for an object bound to a Ripple space warp.

Geometric/Deformable and Modifier-Based Space Warps

Figure 17.24 shows the Object Type rollout for the Geometric/Deformable space warp. Figure 17.25 shows the Object Type rollout for the Modifier-Based space warp.

Except for the Bomb and Conform space warps, all Geometric/Deformable and Modifier-Based space warps duplicate object modifiers available in the Modify command panel. The parameters associated with these Geometric/Deformable and Modifier-Based space warps are the same as those for the corresponding modifiers and are described in Chapter 5, "Mesh Modeling Fundamentals."

For some of the Geometric/Deformable space warps (Ripple, Wave, and Conform), there is an additional area in the Parameters rollout called Display, which controls the detail or size of the Space Warp icon. The parameters in the Display area affect only the display and not the space warp's effect on objects.

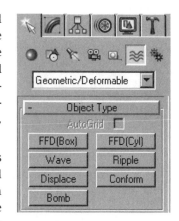

FIGURE 17.24
The types of Geometric/ Deformable space warps.

For the Modifier-Based space warps, there is an additional rollout called Gizmo Parameters (see Figure 17.26). When you apply the modifier on which these space warps are based, the Modifier gizmo is automatically sized to the bounding box of the object. Because Modifier-Based space warps are created independent of the objects, the size is set by the size of the space warp when it is created in the viewport. The Gizmo Parameters rollout provides spinners for adjusting the size of the space warp. The Gizmo Parameters rollout also includes a Decay spinner in the Deformation area. If you set the Decay spinner to 0, there is no decay and the space warp affects its bound objects regardless of their distance from the space warp. If you increase the decay, the effect on the bound objects falls off exponentially with distance.

As mentioned earlier, when you bind an object to a space warp, the binding is placed at the top of the modifier stack. For the Ripple and Wave space warps, a Flexibility parameter is associated with this binding, which acts as a multiplier of the space warp's effect on the object. Flexibility can be adjusted individually in each bound object's stack. Because this parameter belongs to each binding, it doesn't appear with the space warp parameters but is adjusted in the Modify command panel. To adjust flexibility, you select the object and then select the binding in the object's modifier stack (see Figure 17.27).

FIGURE 17.25
The types of Modifier-Based space warps.

In the following example, you create a space warp and bind it to an object.

Creating and Using a Ripple Space Warp

1. In the Top viewport, create a box that is approximately 100 units by 100 units by 1 unit tall. Set the Length and Width segments to 20.

2. Click the Space Warp button and choose Ripple.

3. In the Top viewport, create a Ripple space warp by clicking to the side of the box and dragging out until the ripple's Wave Length parameter is approximately 30. Release the mouse button and move the mouse up slightly to set Amplitude 1 and 2 to approximately 10.

4. Choose the Bind to Space Warp button and drag from the space warp to the box (or vice versa). Figure 17.28 shows the resulting object.

5. Animate the properties of the space warp over time. To accomplish this, turn on the Animate button and adjust any parameter in the Ripple area at any frame you want.

6. Select the box and click the Modify command panel tab. Adjust the Flexibility value up and down to see the effect of this parameter on the box. This parameter can also be animated.

7. Move the box around in the viewport. As the relationship between the box and the Space Warp icon changes, the effect on the box changes.

FIGURE 17.26
The Gizmo Parameters rollout for Modifier-Based space warps.

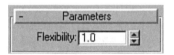

FIGURE 17.27
The Flexibility parameter in the Ripple and Wave space warp bindings.

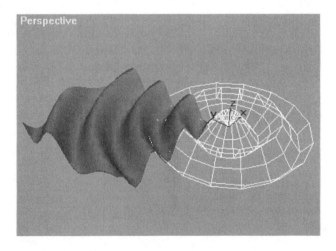

FIGURE 17.28 *The effect of a Ripple space warp on an object.*

For all Geometric/Deformable space warps, the geometry of the mesh is affected by the relative position of the space warp to the objects. This is also true for the Modifier-Based space warps and several of the Particle space warps. For the Bomb space warp, the space warp's position acts as the center point of an explosion.

Bomb

The Bomb space warp is the only Geometric/Deformable space warp not based on a modifier or compound object. Bomb is used to explode one or more objects into their constituent faces (fragments). To be effective, the objects need to have enough faces to show the explosion effect well. The Bomb Parameters rollout is shown in Figure 17.29.

To create a Bomb space warp, click anywhere in the scene. The location of the Bomb space warp is the location of the blast center (bound objects will be exploded away from or toward this point). Then, use the Select and Bind tool to bind objects to the Bomb space warp. Only objects bound to the Bomb space warp will be affected by it.

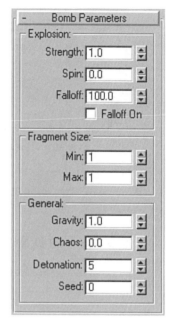

FIGURE 17.29
The Bomb Parameters rollout for Bomb space warps.

In the Bomb Parameters rollout are three areas: Explosion, Fragment Size, and General. In the Explosion area, the Strength parameter specifies how strong the explosion will be. This value can be positive, which pushes the fragments away from the Bomb, or negative, which pulls the fragments toward the Bomb. The Spin parameter specifies how fast the fragments rotate. If Falloff On is turned on, the Falloff parameter specifies the radius of the explosion force. Objects beyond this radius are broken into fragments but are not affected by the explosion force. They are, however, affected by the Gravity parameter. If Falloff On is turned off, all object fragments are affected by the explosion force.

In the Fragment Size area, the Min and Max parameters specify the limits on the number of object faces to be included in each fragment. Each fragment becomes an element of the original object. Smoothing is retained across the faces of a fragment but is not retained across fragments.

In the General area, the Gravity parameter specifies the force of gravity on the fragments. This force is always applied along the world Z axis and can be either positive or negative. All fragments, including those outside the Falloff radius, are equally affected by gravity.

The Chaos parameter adds random variation to the trajectory and spin of fragments after the explosion. The Detonation parameter specifies the time at which the bound objects are broken into fragments and specifies the explosion and gravity forces to be applied to the object fragments. The Seed parameter determines random number generators internal to Bomb, which select the faces and spin for each fragment. The Seed parameter is also used when applying chaos.

The following example shows how to use the Bomb space warp to cause an object to explode.

tip

Use Particle Array (PArray), the Particle Bomb (PBomb) space warp, and the Gravity space warp together to produce a very effective explosion effect. The fragments created by the PBomb space warp do not interact with the scene, so you cannot have them bounce off the ground or other objects. If you use the deflector space warps, the fragments created by using PArray can bounce and break up into smaller particles. In addition, PArray can give the fragments thickness, which Bomb cannot do.

Using the Bomb Space Warp

1. Load file **MF17-04.MAX** from the accompanying CD. The scene is based on the bowling alley you created in earlier chapters.

2. Advance to frame 0:0:21, just before the bowling ball hits the lead pin.

3. Create a Bomb space warp in the Top viewport, with the Bomb space-warp center next to the lead pin on the side where the bowling ball is located.

4. Using Bind to Space Warp, bind the lead pin to the Bomb space warp. As seen in the Left viewport, fragments of the pin are already being shot up and away from the pin's position.

5. With the Bomb space warp selected, go to the Modify command panel and set Detonation to 0:0:21.

6. Advance to frame 0:0:22 to see the first frame of the detonation. The pieces of the pin are moving much too fast. Decrease Strength to 0.2. To stop the fragments from flying so high, set Gravity to 4.0. To make the fragments larger, set Min to 5 and Max to 20. To give the fragments some spin, set Spin to 1. Finally, to add some extra randomness, set Chaos to 0.5.

7. Play back the animation in the Camera viewport.

   In this section, you have seen how to use the Geometric/Deformable space warps to deform the meshes of objects. In addition to the Geometric/Deformable space warps, several sets of space warps are designed for use with Particle Systems. Many of these space warps were covered in Chapter 9, "Working with Particle Systems."

Animating with Morphs

Morphing is the process of transforming one object into another over time. Many morphing effects were used in the movie *Terminator 2* to create the T-2000 Terminator made of liquid metal. In MAX, you can easily morph between multiple *morph targets*. The object being created by the morphing is called the *morph object*.

There are two restrictions on the morph targets: All morph targets must have the same number of vertices, and the order of the vertices must match. As the morph is generated, MAX simply moves the

vertices in the morph object to match the location of the same vertices in the morph targets. To illustrate the second restriction, if you have two face models with the same number of vertices but in a different order, a vertex on the nose of the first model might correspond to a vertex on the chin of the second model. Although MAX would enable you to morph between these morph targets, you would probably not be happy with the results. In practical application, one master object is created and copies of this object are made. The copies are then modified to form the morph targets without creating or deleting vertices, thus ensuring the same number and order of vertices.

With the original Cubic Morph controller, each key represents a single morph target, so at the frame associated with a particular key, the morph object always looks exactly like that single morph target. With the Barycentric Morph controller, each key represents a series of weights for all morph targets; therefore, one barycentric key represents a morph object that is a blending of all morph targets. The Barycentric Morph controller is a superset of the Cubic Morph controller and is the default morph controller. If you import scenes created in Release 1, they still use the Cubic Morph controller, but you can replace a Cubic Morph controller with a Barycentric Morph controller in Track View without a loss of data.

To create a morph, you first need to create each of the morph targets. Then, with one of the morph targets selected, you enter the Compound Objects object category in the Create command panel and click the Morph button. The Morph panel is shown in Figure 17.30. The object selected when you click Morph is set as the first morph target. To add an additional morph target, first select how the morph target is to be used (Reference, Copy, Instance, or Move). Then, click Pick Target to enter the pick mode and click each morph target. After selecting the morph targets, you can choose a morph target in the Morph Targets list and click Create Morph Key to create a key at the current frame. This key sets the influence of the selected morph target to 100% for the current frame.

In the Morph Target Name field, you can rename morph targets. You can delete a morph target by selecting the target in the Morph Targets list and clicking the Delete Morph Target key.

To adjust the influence of morph targets to other than 100%, you need to edit the morph keys in Track View. Figure 17.31 shows a Track View with a morph object. Figure 17.32 shows the Key Info dialog box for a Barycentric Morph controller key. The interpolation method for morph controller keys is a Tension/Continuity/Bias (TCB) controller. The top of the Key Info dialog box shows the parameters for the TCB interpolation parameters.

Below the TCB parameters is a list of morph targets, showing the percent influence each target has on the morph object. By selecting a target in this list, you can change its percent influence in the Percentage field. At the bottom of the dialog box is an option called Constrain to 100%. If this option is turned on as you adjust the influence percentage for one target, the influence percentage on the remaining targets changes to maintain a constant total influence percentage of 100%. It is recommended that you leave this option on because total influence percentages other than 100 can scale the morph object up or down.

In the following exercise, you use the Morph controller to perform facial animation of a character.

FIGURE 17.30
The Morph compound object command panel, where you create the morph object and select morph targets.

Creating a Morph Object

1. Load file **MF17-05.MAX** from the accompanying CD. This scene consists of five heads in various poses. A sixth head below the other five is a copy of the head farthest to the left.

2. Select the head at the bottom of the screen. In the Compound Objects object category in the Create command panel, click the Morph button.

3. Click Pick Target and then select the right-most four heads.

4. Open Track View and expand the hierarchy to the Morph controller.

5. Right-click the Morph controller key at frame 0.

6. Select one of the morph targets in the Key Info target list and change its percentage. Note that as you change the percentage, the morph object in the viewport updates to reflect the change.

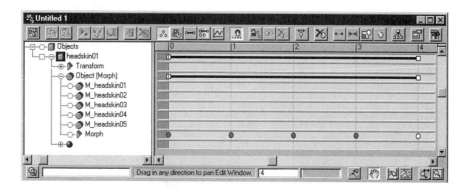

FIGURE 17.31   *The tracks for a Morph compound object in Track View.*

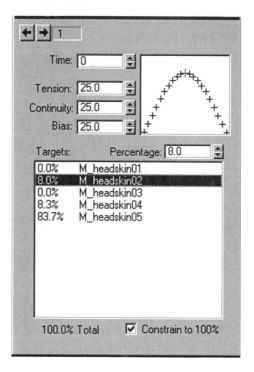

FIGURE 17.32   *The Track View Key Info dialog box for a Barycentric Morph controller key.*

In the previous exercise, you saw how to deform the face based on several different morph targets. To model a complete character, you will usually use the Physique portion of Character Studio or use Bones Pro to deform the character mesh based on the underlying skeleton. It is usually easier to use the Morph controller below Physique or Bones Pro to perform detailed facial animation of a character.

Animating with Rigid-Body Dynamics

The Dynamics utility is used to create animations that simulate real-world physics. Realistic object motion can be achieved, based on the object's physical properties and the forces acting on the object. The Dynamics utility shipped with MAX is a rigid-body dynamics package. In rigid-body dynamics, an object's positions and rotations are calculated based on the forces acting on the object, but no deformation of the object occurs.

To perform a dynamic simulation, you must specify the following information:

- The objects included in the simulation
- The properties of the objects
- The object collisions to look for
- The external forces generated by space warps acting on the objects
- Any initial motion of the objects

To create a dynamic simulation, click the Utilities command panel tab and choose Dynamics. The Dynamics utility rollouts are shown in Figure 17.33. To define a new simulation, choose New to initialize a new dynamic simulation. To specify a preexisting simulation, select the simulation name from the Simulation Name drop-down list.

Kinematic chains can be used in dynamic simulations; however, their use is beyond the scope of a Fundamentals book. For information on using kinematic chains in dynamic simulations, refer to your MAX documentation.

FIGURE 17.33
The Dynamics rollout, where you define the parameters for dynamic simulations.

Specifying Objects in a Dynamic Simulation

To specify the objects to include in the simulation, choose Edit Object List to display the Edit Object List dialog box shown in Figure 17.34. Only objects included in the simulation will be considered in the dynamics solution. This includes stationary objects with which other objects in the simulation can collide.

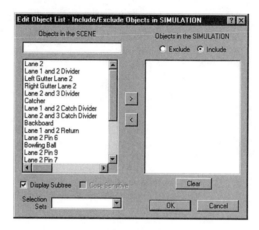

FIGURE 17.34   *The Edit Object List dialog box, where you define the objects to be included in the dynamic simulation.*

Specifying Dynamics Properties for Objects

To specify the properties for objects in the simulation, click Edit Object to display the Edit Object dialog box shown in Figure 17.35. To specify the object for which you are defining properties, use the Object drop-down list at the top-left corner of the dialog box. In the Misc Dynamic Controls area, you can turn on the Use Initial State option to take into account the motion and rotation of the object at the start time of the simulation. If the object is not moving, turn off this option. If you turn on This Object is Unyielding, the object is not assigned any motion or rotation in the simulation. You want to turn on this option for solid, fixed objects such as walls and floors. By using the Move Pivot to Centroid button, you can move the object's pivot point to the mass center of the object. The method by which the center of mass for the object is calculated is based on the Calculate Properties Using option.

tip

If you plan to animate the rotation of an object outside the dynamic simulation time period, you should use Move Pivot to Centroid before animating the rotation. An object rotates around its pivot point, so if you first animate the rotation and then change the location of the pivot point, the way the object rotates will change.

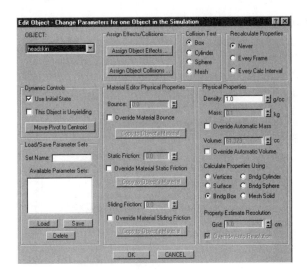

FIGURE 17.35   *The Edit Object dialog box, where you define the dynamics properties for the objects in a dynamic simulation.*

The distribution of an object's mass around its center of mass affects how the object rotates. The classic example is an ice skater: if the skater is rotating and pulls her arms in, she rotates faster than when she extends her arms. The distribution of an object's mass can be calculated several ways in MAX, using the Calculate Properties Using option in the Physical Properties area. For objects other than simple boxes, spheres, and cylinders, you can calculate the center of mass by using one of the bounding methods: Vertices, Surface, or Mesh Solid (listed in order of increasing accuracy).

You can move the object's pivot point to the center of mass, as described previously, and you can also automatically move it during simulation. How often the mass distribution is calculated during the simulation is specified in the Recalculate Properties area. Which option to use depends on whether the shape of the object is animated and, if so, how fast the shape is changing. If the shape of the object is not animated, choose the Never option. If the shape is changing slowly, choose the Every Frame option. If the shape is changing rapidly, choose Every Calc Interval.

In the Collision Test area, you specify the object boundaries used during collision detection. The choices are Box (the object's bounding box is used), Cylinder (the object's bounding cylinder is used), Sphere (the object's bounding sphere is used), and Mesh (the actual faces of the object are used). For the Cylinder method, the height axis of the cylinder is aligned with the object's local Z axis. The Mesh method is extremely calculation intensive and should be used only if the object's shape is complex or the results from other methods are inaccurate.

In the Physical Properties area, you specify the physical properties of an object. The Density parameter specifies the density of the object and is used to calculate the object's mass. The higher the mass of an object, the more resistant it is to changes in motion or rotation due to external forces (collisions and space warp forces). The Bounce parameter specifies how much an object will bounce after a collision. A ball made of lead, for example, would have a low Bounce value, and a rubber ball would have a high Bounce value. The Static Friction parameter specifies how hard it is to get a stationary object to move. The Sliding Friction parameter specifies how hard it is to keep a moving object in motion. To experience the difference between these two types of friction, press down on a table and push your hand along it. You need more force to start your hand moving than to keep it moving.

Typically, the Mass parameter is calculated based on the object's density and volume. You can override the automatic calculation of Mass and specify a value, if you desire. Similarly, the Volume of an object is typically calculated based on the Density value and the Calculate Properties Using selection.

You can specify the Bounce, Static Friction, and Sliding Friction values either in the Edit Object dialog box or in the object's material. It is usually easiest to use the values from the object's material if you have several identical objects with the same material (for example, pins in a bowling alley). For objects that are not the same, it is usually easiest to set the values in the Edit Object dialog box.

To set the property values in an object's material, open Material Editor and select the material. The bottom rollout for the Standard material type is the Dynamic Properties rollout shown in Figure 17.36. In this rollout, you can set the Bounce Coefficient, Static Friction, and Sliding Friction values, which will then be used for all objects that use the material. You can also set different property values for different object faces by using the Multi/Sub-object material type.

tip

If you need to use the Mesh method on an object for collision detection, consider placing an Optimize modifier on the object. You can usually use a fairly high Face Threshold value to reduce the number of faces significantly but retain the overall shape of the object. After solving the dynamic simulation, turn off or delete the Optimize modifier.

tip

If you calculate mass with Calculate Properties Using set to either Vertices or Surface, the internal volume of the object is not considered, resulting in a much lower calculated mass. You should not use the Vertices or Surface setting on objects for which collisions are being detected unless you override the automatic mass calculation. The motion resulting from a collision of two objects is dependent on the relative masses of the objects. If one object's mass is calculated by using Vertices or Surface and the other's by using a bounding object or Mesh Solid, the relative masses of the objects will be incorrect and will result in incorrect motion after the collision.

In the same way that the individual materials are applied to object faces based on their material ID, the dynamic properties are applied to the matching faces.

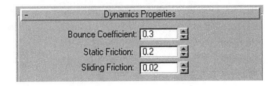

FIGURE 17.36   *The Material Editor Dynamics Properties rollout.*

Assigning Object Effects and Object Collisions

An *object effect* is a Particles & Dynamics space warp, such as Push or Gravity. You can assign effects to individual objects or to all objects, but not both. To assign effects to all objects, turn on Global Effect in the Effects area of the Dynamics rollout and click Assign Global Effects to display the Assign Global Effects dialog box shown in Figure 17.37. All space warps in the scene that can be used for dynamics are displayed in the list of Effects in the Scene. You can select effects for inclusion or exclusion of all objects in the scene, in the same manner that you selected objects in the Edit Object List dialog box.

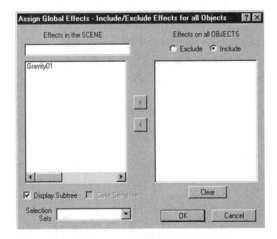

FIGURE 17.37   *The Assign Global Effects dialog box, where you define the space warp forces to be applied to all objects in the dynamic simulation.*

To assign effects on an object-by-object basis, turn on Effects by Object in the Effects area of the Dynamics rollout. In the Assign Effects/Collisions area of the Edit Object dialog box, click Assign Object Effects. This displays the Assign Object Effects dialog box, identical to the Assign Global Effects dialog box.

tip

If you have a lot of objects specified as Unyielding, assign collisions on an object-by-object basis. The dynamic simulation will be solved much faster.

An additional effect that applies to all objects in the simulation is Air Resistance Density. Air resistance pushes against object faces pointing in the direction of the object's motion, causing an object to slow down or flutter. The higher the Density value, the more drag is applied to the objects in the simulation.

Because collision detection is CPU intensive, you need to specify which object collisions to detect. Much as you assign effects to objects, you can globally specify a group of objects among which to detect collisions, or you can specify for each object certain objects with which to detect collisions, but not both.

Solving the Dynamic Simulation

After setting up the parameters necessary for the dynamic solution, actually solving the solution is easy: simply set the time range for the simulation and click the Solve button in the Dynamics rollout. The Dynamics utility calculates the motion of the objects at the first frame of the simulation and then steps through the time range, calculating the position and rotation of each object based on the object's previous motion, the forces applied by space warps, and the forces resulting from object collisions. Keys are generated for each object to store its position and rotation. Depending on the number of objects in the scene, the number of object collisions to detect, and the collision test methods, solving the dynamics solution can take anywhere from seconds to days.

If you are using collision detection in your simulation, you might find that objects are passing through one another. If this is the case, increase the Calc Intervals Per Frame, which specifies how many times per frame the object motions are solved. The higher this value is, the more accurate the simulation will be, but high values result in longer execution times. Finding the right number to use is a matter of experimentation; however, a value of two to four is usually a good starting point.

tip

If you know that a large number of objects aren't affected by the dynamics solution until near the end of the simulation time range, try to break the simulation into several parts. In each part, include only the objects for which you need to have the dynamics calculated.

In the following exercise, you use the Dynamics utility to model a ball rolling down a bowling alley and hitting the pins.

Creating a Dynamic Simulation

1. Load file **MF17-06.MAX** from the accompanying CD. This scene is a simple bowling alley with pins, lanes, and returns.

2. Create a Gravity space warp in the Top viewport.

3. Click the Utilities command panel tab and then click Dynamics.

4. Choose Simulation Name, New.

5. Click Edit Object List. In the Objects in Scene list, select Lane 2 and Bowling Ball and click the right arrow to include these two objects in the simulation. Click OK to close the dialog box.

6. Click Edit Object. In the Edit Object dialog box, choose Lane 2 from the Object drop-down list if it is not already the object shown. In Dynamic Controls, turn on This Object is Unyielding. Turn on Override Material Bounce and set Bounce to 0. Turn on the overrides for both friction parameters and set each friction value to 0.02. In the Load/Save Parameter Sets area, type Lane into the Set Name field, and then click Save.

7. Choose Bowling Ball from the Object drop-down list. Turn on Override Mat'l Bounce and set Bounce to 0. Turn on the overrides on both friction parameters and set each friction value to 0.02. Set Density to 8. In Collision Test, turn on Mesh. In Physical Properties, choose Calculate Properties Using, Bounding Sphere. Type Ball into the Set Name field and click Save.

8. In the Assign Effects/Collisions area, click Assign Object Collisions, select Lane 2, and click the right arrow. Click OK to close the dialog box. Click OK again to close the Edit Object dialog box.

9. In the Dynamics rollout, turn on Global Effects and click Assign Global Effects. Turn on Exclude and click OK to close the dialog box. If you turn on Exclude without adding any effects to exclude, all the effects in the scene are applied to the object.

10. Set Start Time to 1 and Air Resistance to 100. Turn on Update Display w/Solve and click Solve. This dynamics solution should take only 10 to 30 seconds. When the solution is complete, advance the frame until the bowling ball intersects the first pin (this should be frame 16).

11. Click New to create a new simulation. Click Edit Object List, turn on Exclude, and click OK.

12. Click Edit Object. In the Edit Object dialog box, choose Lane 2 from the Object drop-down list if it is not already the object shown. Click Lane in the Available Parameter Sets and then click Load.

13. In the Edit Object dialog box, choose Lane 1 and 2 Divider from the Object drop-down list. In Dynamic Controls, turn on This Object is Unyielding. Turn on Override Material Bounce and set Bounce to 0. In the Load/Save Parameter Sets area, type `Vertical Wall` into the Set Name field, and then click Save.

14. Select Left Gutter Lane 2 from the Object drop-down list. Select Lane in the Available Parameter Sets, and click Load. In the Collision Test area, turn on Mesh. Type `Gutter` into the Set Name field and then click Save.

15. Select Right Gutter Lane 2 from the Object drop-down list. Click Gutter in the Available Parameter Sets and then click Load.

16. Select Bowling Ball from the Object drop-down list. Click Ball in the Available Parameter Sets and then click Load. Click Assign Object Collisions, choose Exclude, and click OK to close the dialog box.

17. Select Lane 2 Pin 6 from the Object drop-down list. In Misc Dynamic Controls, turn off Use Initial State. In Collision Test, turn on Cylinder. In Physical Properties, set Density to 11.8 and set Calculate Properties Using to Mesh Solid. Under Property Estimation Resolution, leave Override Auto Resolution checked and set Grid to 1.0. Type `Pins` into the Set Name field and then click Save.

18. In the Assign Effects/Collisions area, click Assign Object Collisions, choose Exclude, and click OK to close the dialog box. Turn on Move Pivot to Centroid and select the next pin from the Object drop-down list. When you select the next pin, the object properties are calculated for the pin and the pin's pivot point is moved to the pin's center of mass. When the dialog box shows the new pin, click Pins in the Available Parameter Sets and then click Load.

19. Repeat step 18 for all the pins.

20. For each of the remaining objects in the simulation, load Vertical Wall to set the object parameters. These remaining objects are Lane 2 and 3 Divider, Catcher, Lane 1 and 2 Catch Divider, Lane 2 and 3 Catch Divider, Backboard, Lane 1 and 2 Return, Lane 2 and 3 Return, and Pit Wall. When you have set the parameters for these objects, click OK to close the Edit Object dialog box.

21. Open Material Editor and select the material applied to the pins. This material is Bowling Pin, shown in the sample slot as a white sphere with a red stripe. Open the Dynamics Properties rollout and set Bounce Coefficient to 0.3, Static Friction to 0.2, and Sliding Friction to 0.02. Close Material Editor.

22. In the Dynamics rollout, turn on Global Effects and click Assign Global Effects. Choose Exclude and click OK to close the dialog box.

23. Set Start Time to 15 (you want to start on the frame before the collision occurs) and set Calc Intervals Per Frame to 3. Set Air Resistance to 100. Turn on Update Display w/Solve and click Solve. Due to the large number of object collisions involved in the simulation, the dynamics solution should take two to three hours to solve. When the solution is complete, play back the animation in the Camera viewport.

24. Open Track View and expand the hierarchy tree to show the position track for Lane 2 Pin 0. Select the position key at frame 0 and right-click it. In the Key Info dialog box, click and hold on the Out tangent type button and select the Step tangent type from the flyout. Close the Key Info and Track View dialog boxes. Switching to the Step tangent mode eliminates the motion of the pin between the frame 0 and the first frame for which the second simulation was solved.

25. Save the file as **MF17-06B.MAX**.

The completed scene is included on the accompanying CD as file **MF17-06a.MAX**. If you run into problems, you can load this file and look at its settings.

As you can see in the preceding example, calculating the dynamics solution can take quite a long time if there are a lot of objects in the scene that can collide with one another. The key to working with dynamics is to experiment with the object parameters, using a subset of the objects in the simulation to determine which parameter values to use. When you are in the ballpark on these values, start adding new objects to the simulation and experimenting with their parameter values. Although it can take several hours or even a day to set up and solve the simulation, the alternative is to manually keyframe the animation, which can take several days and still not look totally realistic.

Conclusion

MAX provides many advanced tools to assist you in creating animations that would be difficult or impossible to achieve by simply keyframing individual objects over time. From this chapter you should have a basic understanding of the following tools and techniques:

- Creation and animation of object hierarchies
- Types of space warps and their effect on objects and particles
- Mesh deformation, using Morphing tools
- Mesh deformation, using Skin and Flex
- Setting up and solving dynamic simulations

Although it might take some time to become proficient with these tools, you should consider this an investment in becoming a professional animator. This chapter wraps up most of the animation topics covered in this book. Now, it's time to take a look at some special effects tools that are pretty cool, namely the Video Post and Render Effects, both of which are covered in the next chapter.

CHAPTER 18

Exploring Post Processing Techniques

Up to this point, you have seen many basic features of 3D Studio MAX, from modeling to rendering to animation. The last feature to take a look at is Video Post, which you use to apply special effects to various parts of a scene. A lens flare from a bright light is an example of a Video Post effect. This chapter focuses on how to make use of the Video Post features of 3D Studio MAX. In particular, this chapter focuses on the following:

- Post Processing
- What Is the Video Post?
- Working with Video Post
- Working with Image Filters
- Working with Compositors
- Working with Optical Effects
- Working with Render Effects

Post Processing

MAX 3 provides you with two methods for post processing images. *Post processing* is the capability to modify an image after the rendering process. Examples of post processing include lens flares, glows, highlights, blurs, and film grain. Such effects are handled after the rendering process because, for the most part, they are two-dimensional image-processing effects.

The two methods MAX provides for working with post processing are Video Post and Render Effects. Video Post has been around since MAX release 1 and Render Effects is new to MAX 3. A Video Post effect is applied after the MAX rendering engine has finished generating the image and has saved it to an image buffer. Render Effects, on the other hand, are tacked onto the end of the rendering process. Thus, Render Effects are slightly faster and have access to more scene information than Video Post routines.

Many of the Video Post routines have already been implemented as Render Effects, such as the Lens Effects package. Functionally, it is the same in both the Video Post and Render Effects, but the interfaces are completely different. Eventually, the Video Post will probably disappear from MAX and all Video Post filters will be ported to Render Effects.

At this point, you might be asking why this is important to a beginning animator. Well, the answer is simple. Many real world effects, such as depth blurring, can only be achieved as post process effects. Depth blurring is important for simulating real world camera lenses with low F-stop settings. Unless you want to purchase a high-end post-processing program such as Digital Fusion, Adobe AfterEffects, or Discreet's Effect, you will need to use one of MAX's built-in post-processing methods.

What Is the Video Post?

The Video Post (or VP) is a post-production special effects suite. Through VP, you can composite images or apply image filters through the use of a timeline and a Video Post queue, as shown in Figure 18.1.

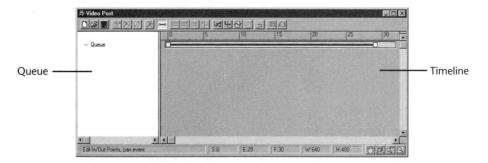

FIGURE 18.1   *The Video Post dialog box, showing an empty queue and timeline. By adding events to the queue, you can create special effects.*

Video Post is essentially a post-production routine. In other words, when MAX finishes rendering an image, it hands the image to Video Post, along with other pertinent data such as Z-Buffer data or Object Channel data. Video Post then processes the image by using a wide variety of filters or compositors. Using Video Post is similar to using filters in Photoshop to adjust an image. As a matter of fact, most Photoshop filters (if they are 32-bit filters) can be used inside of the Video Post as image filters.

Video Post filters can apply special effects—such as blurs, highlights, or glows—to specific parts of your scene. This is accomplished through some of the extra data that is passed to the Video Post from MAX. This data includes the Geometry Buffer and the Material Effects Channel. The geometry buffer (called G-Buffer) assigns an ID number to a specific object. Then, you can use this number to apply filters to that object. The Material Effects Channel works the same way, but at a material level instead of an object level. Figure 18.2 shows you an example of a scene without Video Post effects. Figure 18.3 shows the same scene after applying a few Video Post effects.

Figure 18.2   *A scene without any Video Post effects.*

Figure 18.3   *The same scene after applying a few Video Post effects. Notice how much different the scene looks with Video Post in use.*

As you can see from Figures 18.2 and 18.3, Video Post is a powerful image-processing program you can use to add that little extra bit of realism and flare to make your scene stand out from others.

When you use Video Post, all scenes are set up and rendered from Video Post instead of by using the Render Scene command. Because the same controls that are in Render Scene are within Video Post, this should not present any problems. If you do not render from Video Post, no Video Post effects will appear in the scene.

Working with Video Post

You access the Video Post module of 3D Studio MAX by selecting Render, Video Post to open the dialog box shown in Figure 18.1. This dialog box, which is the heart of the Video Post system, is divided into three sections: a toolbar, the VP Queue, and the VP Timeline.

The Video Post Queue

VP is based on a queue analogy in which you add events to the queue. These events are then processed in the order in which you entered them. You will almost always have at least three events in the queue when rendering in the Video Post. The first event is a scene event, which tells Video Post which view you want to render and with what parameters. Second, you will have at least one filter or compositing event that processes the image after rendering (often you will have more than one filter or compositor). The last event is always an output event so you can save the file in any format supported by MAX.

To add a Scene event to the Video Post, choose the Add Scene Event button on the VP toolbar. You are then prompted with the Add Scene Event dialog box, where you can select the view and set the Rendering Options, which are defined by the currently selected rendering engine. You can also set the length of time for the VP queue, if you wish. The length of time is given in frames in VP.

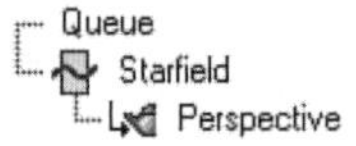

After you have added a Scene event to the VP queue, you add one or more filters or compositors. You can accomplish this in either of two ways. First, you can select the Scene event and add the filter directly on top of the event, which creates a hierarchy as shown in Figure 18.4. Second, you can add the filter event directly after the Scene event, Figure 18.5.

tip

Although you will often use Video Post at rendering time, you can substitute an input file event instead of the Scene event to process a series of still images that have already been created.

FIGURE 18.4
The Video Post queue with a hierarchical filter setup. Here, the filter is applied directly to the Scene event.

You must choose one method or the other, depending on the type of filter you use. The Starfield filter, for example, requires the first method, whereas all of the Lens Effects filters require the second.

A compositor is a filter that combines two images into a single image by compositing one image over the top of the other. To make use of a compositor filter, you must have at least two input events in the queue. Usually, these two events are a Scene event and an Image Input event. By selecting both queue events, you can apply the compositor filter.

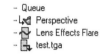

FIGURE 18.5

The Video Post queue with a linear filter setup. Here, the filter is applied in the order of the VP queue.

You apply filters and compositors by selecting the appropriate button on the VP toolbar. This brings up the Add Image Filter Event (or Add Image Layer Event) dialog box shown in Figure 18.6.

FIGURE 18.6   *The Add Image Filter Event dialog box, where you can select the filter and set up the parameters associated with that filter.*

Each filter you add to the VP queue can be given its own name. You can have multiple glow filters applied to your image, for example. Instead of seeing multiple Lens Effect Glow entries, you can rename them with more specific titles, such as Outdoor Light Glow or Car Headlight Flare.

There is a drop-down list where you can select the filter you want to apply. MAX ships with 13 filters from which you can choose. Many of the plug-ins for MAX are also Video Post filters and appear in this list when they're loaded. After you select a filter type, you can choose the Setup button to set up the parameters associated with the filter. Some filters have no parameters at all and others have several hundred.

Figure 18.7 shows you the setup parameters for the Lens Effects filter—one of the most complex filters available but easy to use. After you set up the parameters associated with the filter or compositor, choose OK to return to the Add Image Filter Event dialog box. Then, choose OK to return to Video Post.

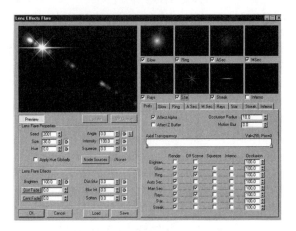

FIGURE 18.7   *The Lens Effects Flare setup dialog box. Notice how much control you have over the various features of the Lens Effects filter.*

The Video Post Timeline

After an event is added to the queue, this event has an associated timeline, which defines in time where this filter is active. When an event is unselected, the timeline is blue; when an event is selected, the timeline is red. Each timeline entry has a start point and an end point that you can adjust by simply clicking the start or end and dragging it along the timeline to adjust its position. If you need to adjust the timeline to a position that is not visible in the VP dialog box, you can use the View control buttons in the lower right of the dialog box to control the view. All of this should be familiar because the actual workings of VP are very similar to Track View.

After the input, filters, and output events are set in the VP queue, you can select the Execute Sequence button from the toolbar to render the queue. Figure 18.8 shows the dialog box that appears when you choose Execute Sequence. When the queue is selected, MAX processes the VP queue frame by frame, using the VP queue order that you defined.

VP queue sequences can be saved and loaded into other scenes at any time. The first three buttons on the VP toolbar can start new queues, load existing ones, or save them. Saved queues have a .vpx extension.

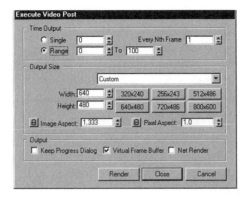

FIGURE 18.8   he Execute Video Post dialog box, where you can set the output size, range, and a few other parameters.

Working with Image Filters

An Image filter is a processing algorithm that modifies a 2D image in some way. Examples of Image filters are blur, contrast, fade, glows, highlights, and lens flares. Many of these effects can be applied in other packages, such as Photoshop, but applying them in VP is much easier.

Some Image filters can process an entire image, and others only process specific objects or work at specific depths in a scene. The Z Focus filter, for example, can blur objects behind other ones, making the image look as though it was filmed through a camera with a relatively low F-stop setting for a slower shutter speed.

The control of where Video Post filters work is handled through three different mechanisms in MAX: the Geometry Buffer (G-Buffer), the Material Effects Channel, and the Z-Buffer.

You control the G-Buffer ID of an object by selecting the object and accessing the Object Properties dialog box. Here, you will find a G-Buffer spinner that you can adjust to set a specific G-Buffer number for use in Video Post. You can then set a Video Post filter to work only with objects that have a particular G-Buffer number.

You set the Material Effects Channel number in the Material Editor by selecting the Material Effects button at the bottom of the preview window. These numbers work just like the G-Buffer but are limited to materials instead of objects. If you have an object with Multi/Sub-Object materials applied, you can set the filter to affect only one of those materials, if you want. Sometimes, the Material Effects Channel is referred to as the Material ID, which is different from the Multi/Sub-Object Material ID number. Material IDs in the Material Editor are limited to 16, thus limiting the number of VP effects you can use.

The last method of selecting objects for use in VP is the Z-Buffer, which is simply the distance that an object is from the camera. This information is automatically transferred to VP by MAX, so you do not have to do anything other than set the Z-Buffer settings in the Image filter, if it supports such an option.

The following exercise shows how to apply a Starfield background as a Video Post filter to the background of a nighttime scene of a water fountain. (The water has been removed from the scene for the sake of speed).

tip

Almost all Video Post filter parameters can be animated through Track View. To accomplish this, you need to open Track View and adjust the animation after you have added the Video Post filter to the VP queue.

Applying a Starfield Image Filter to a Scene

1. Load the file **MF18-01.MAX** from the accompanying CD (see Figure 18.9).

FIGURE 18.9   *The Water Fountain Scene before adding the Starfield background.*

2. Select Rendering, Video Post to access Video Post.

3. Choose Add Scene Event.

4. Select the Camera view as the view and choose OK. You might want to check the Render options. They are set for optimal image quality.

5. Choose OK to return to VP.

6. Select the Camera entry in the VP queue.

7. Choose Add Image Filter Event.

note

The files in this chapter take a substantial amount of time to render. To speed this up, you can turn off the raytraced materials in the Copper and Water materials and turn off shadows in the rendering options.

8. Choose Starfield from the drop-down list to select the Image filter you want to use.

9. Choose Setup. This displays the Starfield Setup dialog box.

10. Set the Dimmest Star setting to 40. Set the Count spinner to 20000 and Compositing to Background.

11. Choose OK to return to Add Image Filter Event. Then, choose OK again to return to VP.

12. Choose Execute Sequence.

13. Set the Time Output to Single and the size to 640×480. Make sure Virtual Frame Buffer is checked and choose Render. The image is rendered as shown in Figure 18.10. Compare it to the image in Figure 18.9.

note

The park benches and street lamps in the water fountain scene have been provided by Nsight Studios (www.nserve.com/nsight) from their Model collection.

FIGURE 18.10   *The Water Fountain scene after adding a Starfield background. Notice how the added context increases the scene's realism.*

As you can see from the last exercise, setting up a simple Video Post queue is not that difficult. Many filters in VP do not provide previews, however, so many times the only way to see the effect is to render the scene. (Most of the Lens Effects filters do provide their own previews.)

Filters are a powerful method of adding many optical effects to MAX scenes that you could not otherwise generate. Another option is to use Video Post to composite two or more image sources into a final image.

tip

If you have Photoshop or Premiere, you can use many of the 32-bit plug-ins from these programs as Image filters, providing you with an almost limitless number of choices and effects you can create.

Working with Compositors

Compositing filters are different from Image filters because they are used to combine two or more images into a single image. Usually, this is done by making use of the alpha channel of one or more of the images being composited.

The alpha channel is an extra eight bits of image data (making the image 32 bits) that represent 256 levels of transparency in an image. Images that have alpha channels are usually generated by a program such as MAX. This transparency data can be used to composite the image over the top of another. This type of compositing is useful any time you want to composite a rendering over a still image or series of still images and have the images blend together well.

You can accomplish a similar task by using the Environmental controls and applying a bitmap as the background. You will find, however, that VP Compositing filters are a little more accurate when it comes to transparent objects or small, thin objects that are difficult to composite.

The following exercise shows how to use VP to composite the fountain scene over a sunset. The fountain scene has been modified slightly to match the sunset image.

Compositing a Sunset into a Scene

1. Load the file **MF18-02.MAX** from the accompanying CD. This is the water fountain adjusted to match the sunset.
2. Choose Rendering, Video Post.
3. Select Add Image Input Event.
4. Choose Files and select the Sunset92.tga file from the CD.
5. Choose OK to return to the VP.
6. Choose Add Scene Event and add the Camera view to the queue.
7. Select both the Input and Camera events. (You can do this by holding down the Ctrl key and clicking each entry.)
8. Choose Add Image Layer Event.
9. Select Alpha Compositor and choose OK.
10. Choose Execute Sequence and render the first frame to 640×480. Figure 18.11 shows the resulting image.

tip

If you have Adobe Premiere 4.2 or later for Windows, you can use many of the Premiere transitions and filters inside of Video Post. VP provides you with much of the power of Premiere, without the need to actually use it. These transitions and filters provide you with many special effects.

Figure 18.11   *The Water Fountain scene composited against a sunset.*

Compositors are as easy to set up and use as Image filters. Just make sure, if you want to composite existing images over others, that they have alpha channels.

Working with Lens Effects (Video Post)

One of the features of MAX that gives Video Post so much power is the optical effects package that provides lens effects. If you're used to viewing the world through a camera lens, you have probably become used to seeing many effects that are only present when using a camera. A lens flare, for example, occurs when you have a bright light in front of the camera—the flare is simply a result of light bending off of the camera lens. In real life, without a camera lens, flares don't really exist, but we are so used to seeing them that many scenes don't look quite right without them.

Other optical effects, such as Z Focus, are necessary to make scenes look more realistic by blurring objects at various depths in the scene or focusing attention on a specific part of a scene. MAX 2 has four filters that handle four different optical effects: Lens Flares, Glows, Highlights, and Z Focus. The flare and glow modules are touched on here; you can explore the others on your own.

Lens Flares

A lens flare—an optical effect seen in many movies and commercials—occurs when a bright light source at any angle causes reflections in the camera lens. The result is a bright spot with smaller glowing spots crossing over the image. Most of the time, lens flares are seen when the sun or other bright source of light is in the image.

The MAX Lens Flare filter provides complete control over every part of a lens flare. As a matter of fact, the Lens Flare filter is composed of six different parts: Glow, Ring, Auto Secondaries, Manual Secondaries, Star Streak, and Inferno.

When you set up the Lens Flare, the first thing to do is select the Node source (the source of the lens flare). Generally, this is a light object but can be any object in MAX. The Node Source button spawns a Select By Name dialog box where you can select the source.

After you have selected the Node source, turn on the Preview and VP Queue buttons. A sample version of the scene in the VP queue is rendered and the flare is applied. Be careful; scenes that take a long time to render can take a few minutes to appear in the preview. When the preview is generated, you can use the Update button to update the preview. Most of the time, the preview updates automatically after you have changed a parameter.

To the right of the main preview window you will find the individual preview windows for each part of the lens flare. Each preview window has its own check box that enables or disables that particular preview. Then, all you have to do is set the various flare properties.

First, you should set the lens flare size, given as a percentage of the overall image size. Usually, a size of 20 or 30 is sufficient to generate a good lens flare. Other properties include the angle, hue, brightness, and squeeze. *Squeeze* produces anamorphic (gradual) squeezing when unusually large aspect ratios are used during rendering. A film resolution rendering, for example, usually has a 2.35 to 1 aspect ratio and the lens flare can be squeezed to match this.

After the general properties are set, you can use the Preferences tab in the lower-right corner of the dialog box to set whether or not each part of the lens flare is rendered. The Offscene column of check boxes determines whether portions of a lens flare appear when the source is off the screen or otherwise not visible (in real life, flare effects appear even when the source is not onscreen). Each option can also be squeezed according to the settings under Lens Flare Properties, and each part of a flare can have an Inferno or fractal noise effect applied. Last, you can set the occlusion for objects, to correctly hide the flare when the flare source goes behind an object in the scene.

tip

The Preview windows in the Lens Effects modules are excellent help, but they unfortunately render the entire scene to show the VP queue preview. This can be rather time-consuming. To help alleviate this problem, hide all objects in the scene except the objects to which you are going to apply the effect.

When the preferences are as you want them, you simply set each portion of the lens flare, such as the glow or star, as you see fit. Use the smaller preview windows to refine each part and the main preview window to see the result.

Glows

The Glows portion of the lens effects package is heavily used. Glow applies a radiance around any object according to its G-Buffer setting, Material ID, Color, Z-Buffer depth, Surface Normal angle, or other parameters. The glow routine is essentially the same as the glow portion of the lens flare but can be applied separately.

Glows can have Inferno effects applied, as well as occlusion. Also, as with the Lens Flare module, you can use the preview window to view the scene with the glows applied and before rendering.

The following exercise shows how to apply a few glows to the water fountain scene you worked on earlier. These glows are centered around the lights in the scene, which would normally have an aura around them at night.

Adding Glows to the Water Fountain

1. Load the file **MF18-03.MAX** from the accompanying CD.
2. Hide all of the objects in the scene, except for the lampposts, which are named Lightpost1 through Lightpost 8 and are treated as groups.
3. Open Video Post. You will see the Camera event with a Starfield applied. Deselect the Camera event, if it is selected.
4. Choose Add Image Filter event.
5. Select Lens Effects Glow and choose OK.
6. Double-click the Lens Effects Glow entry in the Queue and then choose Setup. (You must add the Glow event before entering setup to view the preview correctly.)
7. Turn on Preview and VP Queue. The preview takes a few seconds to appear.
8. Set the Source to Effects ID and the spinner to 2. You should see the Preview update almost immediately.
9. Go to the Preferences tab and set the Size spinner to 5. Figure 18.12 shows the resulting preview.
10. Choose OK to return to the Video Post queue.
11. Hide the lamppost objects and unhide the Tower Light01 object.
12. Unselect any entries in the queue and choose Add Image Filter event. Add another Glow, choose OK, and return to the setup.
13. Enable the Preview and VP Queue buttons.
14. Set the Object (G-Buffer) ID to 3.
15. Under the Preferences tab, set the size to 30. Figure 18.13 shows the preview at this point.

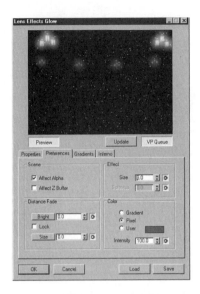

FIGURE 18.12   *The Glow preview after applying a glow to the lamppost lights. Notice how much more realistic the scene appears.*

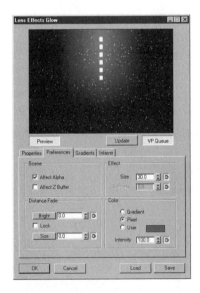

FIGURE 18.13   *The Glow module, with a preview showing the glow around the tower lights.*

16. Choose OK to return to the Video Post.

17. Unhide all objects and choose Execute Sequence to see the final results.

18. Save the file as **MF18-03b.MAX**.

As you can see from the previous exercise, using the Glow module is not difficult at all. After the G-Buffer or Material Effects Channel is set up, you can apply the glow and use the preview to see exactly what is going on as you make changes to the glow parameters.

Working with Render Effects

As mentioned at the beginning of this chapter, Render Effects are similar to Video Post filters, perform many of the same functions, and will eventually replace Video Post. On the other hand, applying a Render Effect is much easier than using Video Post. You access Render Effects by choosing Rendering, Effects from the pull-down menus. When you do, you see the dialog box shown in Figure 18.14.

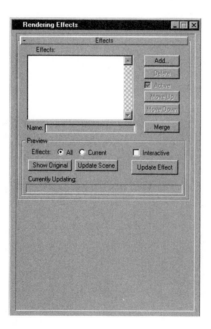

FIGURE 18.14   *The Rendering Effects dialog box, where you can set up and define the various effects you want to use on your scene.*

The first thing you might notice is that the Render Effects dialog box looks a lot like the Environment dialog box. They are also similar in function. You can add Render Effects to the Effects list and they are processed in the order in which they appear in the list. You can also set up the properties for each effect. When you select an effect from the list, its properties appear as rollouts at the bottom of the dialog box.

To illustrate how easy Render Effects are to use, you can redo the last exercise as a Render Effect instead of as a Video Post routine.

Using Render Effects to Add Glows to a Scene

1. Load the file **MF18-04.MAX** from the accompanying CD.

2. Choose Rendering, Effects from the pull-down menus.

3. Choose Add.

4. Select Lens Effects from the list of Effects and choose OK.

5. You receive two rollouts, a Lens Effects Parameters rollout and a Lens Effects Globals rollout. In the Parameters rollout, select Glow and press the right-arrow key. A glow is added to the scene and a new set of rollouts appears at the bottom of the panel.

6. In the Preview section of the Effects dialog box, turn on Interactive. The scene is rendered by the regular MAX rendering engine. When that is complete, scroll down to the Glow Element rollouts.

7. Click the Options tab. Click the Image check box and then set the Effects ID spinner to 2. Note: The scene might re-render at this point.

8. Go to the Parameters tab and set the Size spinner to 10 and the Intensity spinner to 20. Figure 18.15 shows the resulting preview.

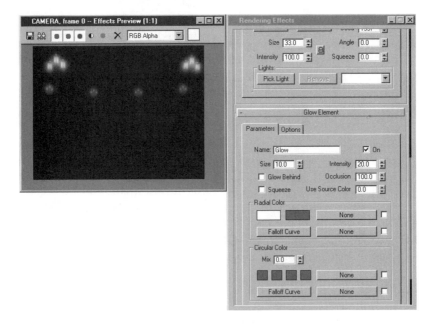

FIGURE 18.15   *The scene after applying a glow to the lamppost lights. Notice how much more realistic the scene appears.*

Unlike Video Post, in Render Effects you can now close the Effects dialog box and render the scene as normal, with the effect automatically added to the end of the rendering process. And in MAX 3, you no longer have to go through Video Post to render.

MAX 3 ships with seven different Render Effects, listed below and briefly described:

- **Lens Effects.** This is the Render Effects version of the Video Post Lens Effects. Unlike Video Post, where you have different filters for glows, highlights, and flares, they are all integrated here into one effect. You simply add the specific parts of the flare you need. (Glows and highlights are just parts of a flare, anyway.)

- **Blur.** This effect enables you to add blurring to individual objects or the entire scene.

- **Brightness and Contrast.** This commonly used effect enables you to add or remove brightness or contrast from your scene. Many scenes look better with a little more contrast.

- **Color Balance.** This effect enables you to change the colors in the entire image. This can be handy if you have a complex scene that needs a slight color adjustment. It's much easier than adjusting a lot of material and light settings.

- **Depth of Field.** This effect is used to simulate camera lens blurring for low F-stop settings. You've probably seen photographs where the subject matter is in focus and everything in the background isn't. Depth of Field provides this type of effect for you in MAX.

- **File Output.** Just like the File Output options in Video Post, you can save files out of Render Effects.

- **Film Grain.** This last effect enables you to add grain to your images to match film grain for backgrounds or to make the animation look as though it was shot on film instead of digitally recorded.

Each effect has its own set of parameters to set up and use correctly. Overall, however, Render Effects are much easier to use than Video Post, and a lot more powerful, thanks to being able to access more scene data than a Video Post filter.

Conclusion

Video Post is a special effects package that enables you to perform some basic nonlinear editing and image filtering, all of which is controllable. Render Effects is similar to Video Post, but applying a Render Effect is much easier than using Video Post.

This chapter focused on how to make use of both 3D Studio MAX Video Post and Render Effects. In particular, you learned about:

- Post process images
- Compositing two images
- Adding optical effects to a scene

Up to this point, you have seen many of the features and aspects of MAX 3, but there is one feature that you have been using off and on and probably didn't even know it. That feature is MAXScript, the scripting interface for MAX. It is highly integrated into MAX 3 (much more so than previous versions of MAX) and is the subject of the next and last chapter.

CHAPTER 19

A Brief Introduction to MAXScript

MAXScript is a complete programming language with which you can automate many aspects of MAX, including object creation and animation. MAXScript was designed specifically for MAX and provides access to the same internal functions in MAX used by plug-in developers.

This chapter provides you with a brief introduction into how to make use of MAXScripts and how to create them. Actual script writing is beyond the scope of this book, but this chapter does cover the following topics:

- What is MAXScript?
- Loading and Running Scripts
- The MAXScript Listener
- Using the MAXScript MacroRecorder

What is MAXScript?

MAXScript is an easy-to-use programming or scripting language for MAX. MAXScript has been a part of MAX since Release 2, but comes into its full glory with Release 3 of MAX. Many of the commands you find on the toolbars and the right-click menus of MAX are actually simple MAXScript commands.

With MAXScript, you can access nearly all the functions available in the user interface (UI), as well as some functions not available. You can create all the object types available in the Create command panel or you can create an editable mesh for defining the individual vertices and faces.

You can apply modifiers to objects, link objects into hierarchies, create and assign materials, apply or change controllers on objects, create animation keys, and create custom controllers. You can even use MAXScript to link MAX to external programs; for example, you can link to a spreadsheet and use its data to control an animation in MAX.

MAXScript accommodates MAX-specific syntax, including wild-character path names for selecting objects in the object hierarchy and context prefixes for setting the animation state, time, and reference coordinate system. MAXScript also provides tools with which you can perform sophisticated programming tasks. Vector and matrix algebra are built in, enabling straightforward calculation of values to be used in an animation. MAXScript's use of collection sets enables you to perform operations easily on large groups of objects in a single statement.

MAXScript even enables you to generate your own interfaces from command panel rollouts to floating dialog boxes and right-click menu access. With MAXScript, if you don't have a plug-in for a particular task, you can probably write a script to handle the task just as easily. A good example of this might be Render Effects. If you remember from Chapter 18, "Exploring Post Processing Techniques," a Render Effect is a post-rendering image process, and you can even write scripts to make your own Render Effects. First, take a look at how to load and run scripts.

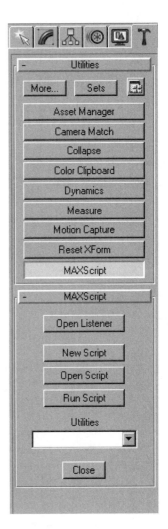

FIGURE 19.1

The MAXScript rollout in the Utility command panel. Here you can load, run, and even create your own scripts.

Loading and Running Scripts

MAXScript enables you to access scripts from a large number of places in MAX. The most common place is through the Utility command panel, where you will find a MAXScript button. When you click this button, the MAXScript rollout appears, as shown in Figure 19.1.

In the MAXScript rollout, you will find four buttons and a drop-down list:

- **Open Listener:** Opens the MAXScript Listener, where you can view and edit scripts. The Listener is covered later in this chapter.

- **New Script:** Launches a modified version of the Windows Notepad application, where you can create your own scripts. Notepad is used because scripts are just text files.

- **Open Script:** Enables you to open a script without running it. This is most commonly used to view or modify the contents of a script. (Scripts have .ms, .mse, or .mcr extensions and are generally saved in the Scripts directory under your MAX installation.)

- **Run Script:** Enables you to load and run a script. The drop-down list shows any scripts that are currently loaded and accessible in the Utility command panel. Not all scripts are launched from the command panel, so when you run a script, you might need to go to a different place in the UI to actually access it.

- **Pull-down menu:** In addition to the Utility command panel, MAXScript now has its own menu entry on the pull-down menus. Figure 19.2 shows you this menu.

FIGURE 19.2
The MAXScript pull-down menu, where you can access many of the commands found in the Utility command panel version of MAXScript.

Now that you have an idea of how to load and run a script, it's time to see how to actually do it. In the following exercise, you load and run a couple of the sample scripts that ship with MAX 3.

Loading and Running Scripts

1. In MAX, go to the Utility command panel and click the MAXScript button to access MAXScript.

2. Click the Run Script button. A File Open dialog box appears and places you in the Scripts directory.

3. Double-click Samples and choose the ObjectPaint.ms script. Choose OK to launch the script. You will now see the ObjectPaint entry in the MAXScript drop-down list.

4. Create a teapot in the scene and return to the Utility command panel.

5. Select ObjectPaint from the drop-down list. A new rollout appears at the bottom of the Utility command panel, as shown in Figure 19.3.

FIGURE 19.3
The ObjectPaint rollout, which was generated by the Object Paint script itself.

6. Select the teapot in the scene.

7. Click the Paint button.

8. Click and drag the mouse around in the scene. As you do, copies of the teapot are created. Essentially, you can now paint objects into the scene, if you like.

As you can see from the previous exercise, loading and running a script is not difficult. This script, which can be useful in certain circumstances, is not even a complicated script. The actual script is shown here:

```
utility ObjectPaint "ObjectPaint"
(
    spinner spn_spacing "Spacing:" range:[0, 99999, 20] align:#center
    checkbutton btn_paint "Paint" width:116

    tool ObjectPaint prompt:"Paint using selected object as brush"
    (
        local lastObject

        on mousePoint clickno do
        (
            if selection[1] != undefined and clickno == 1 then
            (
                lastObject = copy selection[Random 1
➥selection.count] pos:worldPoint — Added Frank D
            )
            else
            (
                btn_paint.state = off
                #stop
            )
        )

        on mouseMove clickno do
        (
            lastObject = copy selection[Random 1 selection.count]
➥pos:worldPoint — Added Frank D

            if clickno == 2 then
            (
                local vec = worldPoint - lastObject.pos
                local distSquared = vec.x*vec.x + vec.y*vec.y +
➥vec.z*vec.z
                if distSquared >
➥(spn_spacing.value*spn_spacing.value) then
                (
                    vec = Normalize vec
                    lastObject = reference $ pos:(vec *
➥spn_spacing.value + lastObject.pos)
                )
            )
        )
```

```
        on mouseAbort clickno do
            btn_paint.state = off
    )

    on btn_paint changed state do
        if state == on then StartTool ObjectPaint
        else StopTool ObjectPaint
)
```

These 30 lines of scripting can save you a lot of time modeling. Imagine using this tool to create a flowerbed in your scene.

ObjectPaint is a good example of a utility-based script. This means it is accessed through the Utility command panel. Now, take a look at some scripts that are not accessed in the Utility command panel. The following exercise shows you how to access a batch-rendering script that enables you to render multiple MAX files.

Running a BatchRender Script

1. In MAX, click the Rendering tab of the shelf. This tab is chosen for this exercise because it has room for additional buttons and the batch renderer goes well on this toolbar.

2. Right-click the toolbar and choose Customize. This launches the Customize User Interface dialog box shown in Figure 19.4.

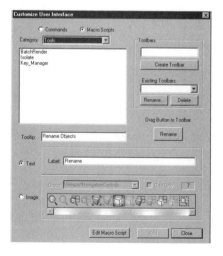

FIGURE 19.4   *The Customize User Interface dialog box, where you can add commands and customize toolbars.*

3. At the top of this dialog box, you will find radio buttons for Commands and MacroScripts. Select MacroScripts if it is not already selected.

4. Click the Category drop-down list and select Tools.

5. In the list window, you will see several scripts appear. Select BatchRender; notice that the sample button on the middle-right of the dialog box now says BatchRender.

6. Click and drag this button and drop it onto the Render toolbar, where it appears as a button labeled BatchRender.

7. Close the Customize User Interface dialog box.

8. Click the BatchRender button to launch the command. When you do, you get the floating dialog box shown in Figure 19.5.

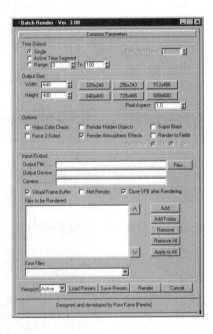

FIGURE 19.5   *The BatchRender dialog box, where you can set up multiple MAX files to render in succession.*

As you can see from the dialog box shown in Figure 19.5, you can add multiple MAX files to be rendered successively. You can even set some of the rendering options. Other rendering options need to be set in the individual MAX files before you set them up to render with BatchRender.

BatchRender represents a different kind of script than ObjectPaint. BatchRender is a MacroScript—a script that can be applied to a toolbar and launched with a single click. If you desire, regular scripts can easily be converted to MacroScripts.

Some scripts are not so straightforward to find. The following exercise shows you a script that appears as a Render Effect.

Running a Render Effect Script

1. In the MAXScript pull-down menu, select Run Script. (You can also do this from the Utility command panel, if you like.)
2. In the File dialog box, go to the Samples directory. Select FrameNumber.ms and choose Open.
3. When the script is loaded, go to the Utility command panel and look at the drop-down list. Notice that FrameNumber does not appear.
4. Choose Rendering, Effects from the pull-down menus.
5. Choose Add. At the bottom of the list of Rendering Effects, you will find a Frame Number Stamp entry. Select this and choose OK. When you do, the Frame Number rollout appears at the bottom of the dialog box, as shown in Figure 19.6.
6. Click the Update Effect button and you will be able to see the Frame Number Stamp effect in action.

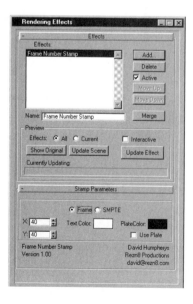

FIGURE 19.6   *The Frame Number Stamp dialog box, where you can set up the rendering effect script.*

By now, you have a good sense of how to run many of the scripts that ship with MAX. As you might realize, you probably need to know a little about a script before you run it, so you know where it will appear in the MAX interface. MAX has several other scripts that are worth looking at. Here's a quick overview of the scripts and where to find them:

- **Modifier Presets.** Found in the Customize User Interface dialog box under Preset Systems. Enables you to save the modifier settings for a modifier applied to the currently selected object. Then, you can apply these settings as a preset to other objects.

- **Light Lister.** Found on the Lights and Cameras tab of the Main Toolbar. This script enables you to edit multiple lights simultaneously.

- **Isolate.** Found in the Customize User Interface dialog box under the Tools section. This script enables you to isolate the currently selected object from the rest of the scene so you can work on it (you can hide the other objects in the scene and zoom in on the selected one). When you exit the isolation, the other objects in the scene are restored, as well as the viewports.

- **Key Manager.** Found in the Customize Toolbars dialog box under the Tools section. This script provides you with a nice way to edit the In and Out points of multiple keys.

- **Object Rename.** Found in the Samples directory. This script enables you to rename multiple objects at the same time.

There are many other examples of scripts used in MAX 3, from the right-click menu to other buttons on the toolbars. In addition, many MAX users around the world write their own scripts and make them available on the Internet, giving you access to many scripts that may be useful to you. Check out the Discreet webboard to find some of these (`http://support.ktx.com`).

Now that you have seen how scripts work, take a look at how to create one by exploring the MAXScript Listener.

The MaxScript Listener

The Listener is an interactive window for working with scripts. You can access it by choosing MAXScript, MAXScript Listener from the pull-down menus or by pressing the F11 key. When you do, you see the dialog box shown in Figure 19.7.

The MAXScript Listener is divided into two sections. The upper part is the MAXScript MacroRecorder. When it's enabled, you will see all the commands you can execute in MAX recorded there. Later in this chapter, you will see how to use this feature to quickly make a MacroScript.

FIGURE 19.7   *The MAXScript Listener, where you can work with and create scripts.*

The lower part of the Listener is an interactive MAXScript Interpreter. What this means is that you can type a MAXScript command into this window and immediately see the result. As a test, type **2+2** into this window and press Return. A **4** should appear below the equation, showing you the result.

A more complicated example might be to type **Sphere radius:15**. When you type this command and press Enter, a sphere is created with a radius of 15 units at 0,0,0 in the scene. All other aspects of the sphere are generated, based on the current defaults for a sphere. The Interpreter indicates this by displaying the sphere name and its location, as shown in Figure 19.8.

```
Welcome to MAXScript.

2+2
4
Sphere radius:15
$Sphere:Sphere03 @ [0.000000,0.000000,0.000000]
```

FIGURE 19.8   *The MAXScript Interpreter, showing the results of creating a simple sphere with a radius of 15.*

Thus, the Interpreter can be used to test MAXScript commands and algorithms that you invent, before you insert them into a script. As mentioned earlier, actually writing a script is beyond the scope of this manual, but using the MacroRecorder is not, and it is the easiest way to create a script.

Using the MAXScript MacroRecorder

When you open the MAXScript Listener, the MAXScript MacroRecorder is turned off by default, cutting down on the overhead of tracking every command you do. However, the MacroRecorder is also easily enabled. When the Listener is open, simply click the MacroRecorder drop-down menu and choose Enable. The drop-down menu is shown in Figure 19.9.

The MacroRecorder drop-down menu also enables you to define exactly how commands are recorded. The options in this menu are listed here by section and are briefly described:

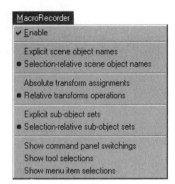

- **Object Naming.** You can select either scene-explicit or scene-relative object naming. With scene-explicit naming, the commands are recorded with the exact name you gave the object when you created it. Thus, these types of recorded scripts will work only on similarly named objects. Scene-relative scripts, on the other hand, use naming schemes that are not explicit and can be used on other objects. Scene-relative is the default.

- **Transform assignments.** Much like names, transforms can be interpreted as absolute or relative. In absolute transform recording, the X, Y, and Z coordinates are recorded. With relative, it's the change in the X, Y, and Z coordinates that is recorded. Relative is the default.

- **Sub-Object selection sets.** As with object naming, you can have explicit or scene-relative sub-object sets. Works the same as object naming.

- **Show.** You can use the last three entries in the MacroRecorder menu to enable the recording of options such as command panel switching, tool selections, and menu accesses by showing these in the MacroRecorder.

Now, see how to make use of the MacroRecorder to record a sequence of steps when applying a couple of modifiers to a teapot.

Creating a MacroScript

1. Start a new scene in MAX and choose MAXScript, MAXScript Listener from the pull-down menus.

2. In the Listener, click the MacroRecorder and choose Enable.

3. Create a teapot with a radius of roughly 20 units.

4. Go to the Modify command panel and apply a Taper modifier. Set the taper amount to –0.60.

5. Apply a Bend modifier and set the bend amount to –45 degrees.

6. If you have been watching the Recorder section, you will have seen all these commands being recorded as you selected them. Now, you will take the commands and create them as a button on the Render toolbar.

7. Click the Rendering tab of the shelf. Rendering is used only because it has room for more buttons. You can delete this button after the exercise, if you like.

8. In the Recorder section of the Listener, highlight everything below the teapot command, as shown in Figure 19.10.

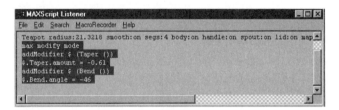

FIGURE 19.10   *The correctly highlighted sections of the Recorder in the Listener.*

9. Click the selected text and drag-and-drop it on the Interpreter window. Then, reselect the text and drag-and-drop it on the Rendering toolbar. A new button appears on the toolbar.

10. Create a new teapot in the scene. With the teapot still selected, click the button you just created. Notice that the teapot immediately has the selected modifiers applied to it.

As you can see from the previous example, creating a MacroScript is not particularly difficult when you use the MacroRecorder. After you have played with MAX for a while, you will find yourself doing the same things over and over again. When this happens, create a MacroScript instead — you will save yourself an enormous amount of time.

If you add a MacroScript to the toolbar as shown in the previous exercise, it can be edited just like any other command. You can change the button appearance, change the flyout name, or edit the script for further changes.

Scripting is a powerful, yet complex addition to MAX. Creating scripts with the MacroRecorder simplifies this process, but if you want to learn more about how to write scripts, consult the MAX documentation or attend a training session on MAXScript.

Conclusion

This chapter introduced you to the basics behind scripting in MAX. Specifically, it taught you the following:

- Running scripts
- Recording commands
- Adding scripts to toolbars

Unfortunately, we have come to the end of the journey for the Fundamentals of MAX 3. By this point, you should be familiar with the MAX interface and how to use MAX. Remember, if you are just starting out in your journey with MAX, there's much more to learn. Have patience, and above all, enjoy and explore the software—it's very powerful and a lot of fun. Enjoy!

Glossary

Many of the terms in MAX might be unfamiliar to you. The following is a list of the terms used most frequently, with their definitions.

3D Acceleration Video hardware enhancements that dramatically speed up the display of 3D scenes. MAX 3 supports cards that support OpenGL 1.1, Heidi, or Direct3D (Under 95 or NT 5.0).

3D Digitizer A mechanical arm with sensors that determines the physical position of a key point on an object and creates a 3D version based on that data.

3D Object Library Stock 3D objects in a variety of formats and resolutions, as an alternative to modeling.

3D Paint Software Software program or plug-in that enables you to paint texture maps or materials directly onto the surface of an object.

Align A command that brings object surfaces flush with each other or centers multiple objects along one or more axes.

Alpha Channel An optional layer of image data that provides an extra eight bits of information about transparency. The alpha channel is used as a mask for compositing one image over another.

Ambient Color The hue an object reflects if it isn't directly illuminated by a light source. Ambient color is intended to be representative of the color of the light reflecting off the objects in a scene, but only radiosity can truly accomplish this.

Ambient Light In theory, the cumulative effect of all the light bouncing off of all the objects in an area. Generally set as a global value that illuminates all objects in the scene equally.

Angle of Incidence The angle at which a light ray strikes a surface and is reflected into the viewer's eyes.

Animated Texture A video or animation file used instead of still images as a texture map, causing the texture on an object to change over time when the scene is rendered.

Animation In 3D graphics, the modification of any kind of object, light, material, or camera by moving or changing it over time. The creation of action or movement with inanimate objects.

Animation Controller Any of a number of different methods for creating or modifying animation keyframes or object behavior. Controllers include TCB, Bézier, audio, noise, and expression.

Anisotropic Refers to a shading model in which the specular highlight can be noncircular. This type of shading is commonly seen in metals or highly curved objects.

Antialiasing   A method of softening the rough edges of an image by adding or modifying pixels near the stair-stepping points. These create a blend between the object and background colors.

Anti-aliasing Filter   One of a set of routines you can select to define how the image is antialiased during render time. Different filters have different effects on the rendering. MAX ships with a predefined set, but you will also be able to purchase filters in the future.

Array   A matrix or pattern of objects extrapolated from a single object or group of objects. Usually found as radial or linear arrays, but can also be three-dimensional.

Aspect Ratio   The relationship between width and height of an image, expressed as a decimal ratio. Aspect ratio is calculated by dividing the width by height; for example, an image 4" by 3" would have an aspect ratio of 1.3333.

Atmospheric Effects   Camera- or light-dependent effects such as fog or volume lights that are added to a scene.

Attach   A command with which you can join separate elements into one object.

Attenuation   The decay of light over distance from the original light source, used to simulate light over long distances.

Axis   An imaginary line in 3D space that defines a direction. The standard axes used in 3D programs are X, Y, and Z.

Backface Cull   The removal of faces from the backside of an object in a viewport. Culling results in more realistic, less confusing views of scenes.

Bank   The rotation (or roll) an object or camera might perform when it moves through a curve in a path. This simulates the results of centrifugal force on a real-world object as it executes a turn.

Bend   A modifier that deforms an object by applying torsion around the selected axis.

Bevel   A flat transitional plane located between two other planes, usually set at an angle that is half the difference between the two.

Bézier Spline   A type of spline on which the control points always exist on the resulting curve. Extending from the control points are tangent points that allow the curve to be modified without moving the control points.

Bias   In a TCB animation controller, the bias adjusts the location of maximum extreme point (or peak) of the motion path or control curve in relation to the keyframe.

Bind Vertex   In editable spline, a command used to attach a vertex to the midpoint of a spline segment. When the spline segment moves, so does the bound vertex.

Bitmap   An image encoded as a series of dots or pixels. TIF, Targa, JPEG, and GIF are examples of bitmap file formats.

Blinn   A shading method that provides smoothing and specular highlights that are not quite as bright as Phong highlights. Named after its inventor, Jim Blinn.

Bluescreen   A blue background that serves as a stage for actors. The blue can be removed after filming and replaced with a different background. Costumes and props shot on a bluescreen stage cannot contain blue or purple pigments because the compositing process would cause any blue or purple elements to become transparent. An alternative is a greenscreen, which allows blue and purple objects but no green ones.

Bones Deformation   A technique of animating an object (usually a character) by defining and animating an internal skeleton that automatically deforms the surrounding mesh. Character Studio and Bones Pro are two plug-ins that perform this function.

Boolean Operation   A set of commands that adds or joins one object to another or subtracts an object from another, commonly used to reshape objects or "drill holes" in them.

Bounding Box   A stand-in in the shape of a box that has the same overall dimensions as the object. Bounding boxes replace mesh-intensive objects during movement or other translations so that the system won't be bogged down by redrawing a large amount of mesh.

Box Coordinates   A type of mapping coordinate system well suited to rectangular objects. Applies the image coordinates from six different directions, one for each surface on the object.

Bump Map   A grayscale image that varies the apparent surface roughness of an object by manipulating the normals.

Camera   In 3D graphics, an object that is used to simulate viewing a scene as a real-world camera would. In general, these objects have controls similar to cameras, such as field of vision (FOV) and lens length.

Camera Target   The point in 3D space at which a camera is looking, indicated by a small box attached to the camera object.

Center Point   The geometric center of an object, the center of the coordinate system, or the center of a selection set.

Chain   A series of linked objects using the hierarchical parent-child relationship but extending it by additional generations to grandchild, great-grandchild, and so forth.

Chamfer   See Bevel.

Channel   An individual attribute of a material that can accept images or be set to affect the appearance of the object to which the channel is applied. Typical channels include Diffuse, Bump, Opacity, Shininess, and Self-Illumination.

Character Animation   The process of imbuing objects not only with movement but with personality. Virtually any object can take on personality if character animation techniques are applied to it.

Child   An object linked to another that is closer to the beginning of the hierarchical tree (see also Parent).

Chroma   The color of an object determined by the frequency of the light emitted from or reflected by the object.

Chroma Key   A process that electronically removes a solid color (usually blue or green) and allows it to be replaced with another image. Often used to composite virtual characters into virtual environments. In some cases, a video "super black" signal is used instead of a visible color.

Clipping Plane   Also known as the viewing plane. A user-definable cut-off point that makes everything on the camera's side of it invisible during rendering.

Clone   A method of copying an object in MAX. Objects can be cloned as copies, instances, or references.

Closed Shape   A shape that has an inside and an outside, separated from each other by an edge.

CMYK (Cyan Magenta Yellow blacK) The colors of ink in the four-color printing process that are applied as tiny dot patterns to form full-color images.

Codec (Compressor Decompressor) Any one of a number of methods for compressing video and playing it back. Digital video file formats such as AVI and QuickTime are designed to accept plug-in compression technologies in the form of codecs.

Color   The hue of an object, determined by the frequency of the light emitted by the object. In computer graphics, color is determined by the combination of Hue, Saturation, and Value in the HSV color model or Red, Green, and Blue color levels in the RGB color model.

Color Depth   The amount of data used to display a single pixel in an image, expressed in bits. For example, an 8-bit image contains 256 colors or levels of gray.

Color Temperature   A value, in degrees Kelvin, that is used to differentiate between near-white and spectrums of light.

COM/DCOM   A set of interface controls that enable developers to write their own Network rendering programs. Available only to developers through the MAX SDK.

Compositing   The process of combining elements into a single scene. This might refer to combining still photos or bluescreen video with computer graphics backgrounds, or to any process in which separate images are combined.

Compositor   A Video Post filter used to perform compositing within MAX. Compositors require two input events in the Video Post queue to function correctly.

Compression Rate   The speed at which digital video data is encoded for playback, defined in kilobytes per second (KB/s). For the movies to play back properly, the target system must be capable of pulling the movie data off of the storage medium and displaying it at that speed.

Constraint   A restriction placed on the movement of an object in inverse kinematics to force the object to behave like a physical joint.

Continuity   In a TCB controller, continuity adjusts how tangential the path is to the control point. In filmmaking, it is the process of maintaining a smooth flow of consistency in props, costumes, action, and direction from shot to shot in a scene.

Control Vertices (CVs)   Control points that exert a magnet-like influence on the flexible surface of a patch, NURBS spline, or NURBS surface, stretching and tugging it in one direction or another.

Coordinate System   Two or three sets of numbers that use a grid-based system to identify a given point in space.

Crossing   A method of selecting objects with a region, circle, or polygon. All objects within or touching the region are selected.

Cylindrical Coordinates   A mapping coordinate system that wraps an image around one of an object's axes until it meets itself, like the label on a soup can.

Decal   An image that can be scaled and moved around on an object independent of any other texture mapping.

Default Lighting   The startup lighting in MAX, which enables you to begin rendering without having to define a light source. The default lighting in MAX is two omni lights.

Deform Fit   A type of deform modifier for a loft object that enables you to define the shape of an object by using an X-axis outline, a Y-axis outline, and one or more cross sections.

Degradation   The reduction of geometry detail based on viewport playback speed. When the minimum playback speed is compromised, the shading level of the viewport is reduced to restore the speed.

Depth of Field   The portion of an image that is properly focused. In photography, depth of field is controlled by the aperture setting. In 3D graphics, depth of field is normally infinite, but can be controlled through the use of Video Post image filters.

Detach   An operation that disconnects an element of a larger object, separating it into two objects. The opposite of Attach.

Diffuse Color   The hue assigned to an object. This is the color that is reflected when the object is illuminated by a direct lighting source.

Diffuse Map   A mapping channel used to change the object's color from the color defined by the color settings—usually a pattern or image.

Digital Retouching   The process of using 2D paint programs to modify photographic stills or movies.

Digitizing   The process of transforming images, objects, or sounds into a digital form that the computer can manipulate.

Directional Light   Also called a distant light. A virtual illumination source for simulating far-away light sources, such as the sun. It projects light along one axis only and all of the light rays (and, hence, shadows) are parallel.

Displacement Map   Also known as a deformation map. A grayscale image applied to an object that actually distorts the mesh, deforming it according to the gray value. Often used to create terrain models.

Dithering   The process of reducing the number of colors in an image while trying to maintain the highest quality image. MAX commonly dithers 48-bit renderings down to 24-bit imagery.

Dolly   In filmmaking, a wheeled platform on which a camera is mounted; also, the process of moving the camera around on the floor during the shot. In 3D, it means a camera movement made toward or away from the subject.

Dongle   A hardware key, which is a physical device plugged into the parallel port of a computer.

Double-Sided Object   An object with normals on both sides of the object's faces, allowing it to be seen from any viewpoint, even inside.

DPI (Dots Per Inch)   Resolution expressed in the number of dots or pixels the medium can display in one inch. A common laser printer output resolution is 300 dpi.

Dummy Object   An object that does not render, so it can be used as an invisible component of a chain or as a reference point for establishing remote axes of rotation.

Dynamics   A system used to simulate real-world physics such as gravity, friction, and collisions in a computer animation. For example, a bowling ball striking bowling pins is a great dynamics simulation.

Ease From   A keyframe parameter that controls the acceleration of the object or event as it leaves the keyframe.

Ease To   A keyframe parameter that controls the acceleration of the object or event as it enters the keyframe.

Edge   The visible line between two vertices that form a face.

Emitter   A simple polygonal shape that acts as a point of origin for particles in a particle system.

Environment   The backgrounds or atmospheric effects that are present in a scene.

Exclude   A feature that enables listed objects to be unaffected by the selected light source.

Export   Saving a file in a cross-program or cross-platform format, such as DXF.

Extrude, Extrusion   The process of pushing a 2D shape into the third dimension by giving it a Z-axis depth.

Face   The area enclosed by the edges of a polygon, forming a three- or four-sided surface.

Face Extrusion   A process that takes a selected face (or faces) and extrudes it in toward or out from its current position.

Face Mapping   An image-mapping type that tries to conform the image to individual faces on an object.

Falloff   The portion or range of a light source that is at a reduced or 0 intensity setting. Also, a set of transparency options that set how much more or less transparent an object is at its edges.

Fetch   Retrieves scenes that have been saved with the Hold command.

FOV (Field of View)   The angle, in degrees, that encompasses everything that can be seen through a lens or virtual camera viewport.

Field Rendering   An output option that renders images in the same way a television displays them in two alternating passes, one with every odd scanline rendered and the other with every even line. Compare with Frame Rendering.

File Format   The manner in which data is organized in a computer file. Common image file formats include BMP, PICT, and TGA. Popular 3D file formats include 3DS, DXF, and OBJ.

Fillet   Also called a radius edge. An arcing transition between two planes or lines.

Film Grain   Grainy dots that appear on imagery shot on film. MAX provides a Render Effect that simulates these.

Filter   A Video Post routine that applies image-processing techniques to the final rendering.

First Vertex   In a shape, the vertex that is used for orientation during skinning operations. Usually the one that was created first, but it can be any vertex assigned as such.

Flat Shading   A display or rendering mode that shows off the surface and color of the objects in a faceted manner because the polygons aren't smoothed.

Focal Length   The distance in millimeters from the center of the lens to the image it forms of the subject (assumed to be an infinite distance in front of the lens). Short focal lengths result in wide-angle images, and long ones are used for telephoto shots.

Forward Kinematics   The default method of animating linked objects, in which the movement of the parent object affects all the offspring down the chain.

Frame   In filmmaking or animation, a single still image that is part of a sequence. Also, the visible portion of a scene when viewed through a camera or viewport.

Frame Rate   The speed at which film, video, or animated images are displayed, in frames per second (FPS).

Frame Rendering   The default output option that renders the entire image. Compare with Field Rendering.

Freeze   A command that leaves an object visible in a scene but prevents it from being selected or changed.

Function Curve   A graphical way of displaying object transformations or other animatable parameters.

G-Buffer   Also called a geometry channel. A number assigned to an object so it can be referred to or selected in Video Post filters.

Gamma   In a computer display, refers to the overall brightness of the screen. Also, a measure of brightness for all output technologies as a way of predicting their appearance when the image is viewed on a color display.

Geometry   General term for 3D objects.

Ghosting   A viewport display option that displays faint images of animated objects before and after the current frame, so you can see where the object came from and where it is going in the animation.

Gizmo   A helper object used to apply various modifier effects to an object. For example, a gizmo is used to determine the location, scale, and orientation of mapping coordinates.

Glow   A Video Post or Render Effect that creates a soft halo of light around selected objects or materials.

Grid   Cross-hatched lines visible in the viewport and used like graph paper for determining scale when creating objects.

Group   A command that enables you to select a related collection of objects and then temporarily combine them into a whole.

Helper   An object used in conjunction with other commands to create certain effects. A Dummy Object is an example of a Helper.

Hidden Line   A display or rendering mode that draws the edges of an object, as in a wireframe display, but only ones that would be visible if the object were opaque.

Hide   A command that makes an object invisible.

History   A record of all modifiers and settings applied to an object. Also known as the Stack.

Hold   Saves the scene to a temporary buffer. Commonly used when you are not sure if a particular operation will be successful. Scene can be retrieved with the Fetch command.

Hotspot   The portion or range of a light source that is at the full intensity setting.

HSV (Hue, Saturation, Value)   A color selection interface used in MAX that enables you to adjust the hue (chroma), saturation (intensity), and value (brightness) to select a color.

IGES   A common geometry file format for exchanging 3D geometry with other programs such as Maya or SolidWorks. MAX supports the importing of IGES files only.

Import   Loading a file saved in a cross-program or cross-platform format, such as DXF.

Include   A light source option that enables you to select a list of objects that the specified light will affect. All other objects in the scene are ignored (see Exclude).

Instance   A type of duplication of an object, light source, map, animation controller, or camera in which changes to one are adopted by all.

Intensity   A measure of the brightness of a light source.

Inverse Kinematics (IK)   Method of controlling linked objects by moving the far end of the hierarchical chain, which then causes the rest of the chain to conform.

Keyframe   A user-defined point where an animation event takes place. MAX then tweens the events from keyframe to keyframe.

Lathe   Process of spinning a 2D shape around an axis, extruding it in small steps as it is rotated.

Lens Flare   The pattern of bright circles and rays seen when you point a camera lens at the sun or other bright light source.

Link   A hierarchical connection between two objects.

Local Coordinates   Coordinate system that uses the object itself as the basis for the axes.

MacroScript   A script that can be added to a toolbar and executed with a single click. Can also be prepackaged scripts that are ready to run. Most scripts created with the MacroRecorder are MacroScripts.

MacroRecorder   A script recorder that, when enabled, records most of the commands you select. This enables you to record often-repeated sequences of commands and save them as scripts.

Map   A bitmapped image, either scanned or painted, that gives a material unique qualities not available by simply varying surface attributes. Can also refer to procedural maps.

Mapping   The process of developing material attributes and assigning them to an object.

Mapping Coordinates   A set of coordinates that specify the location, orientation, and scale of any texture applied to an object.

Mask   A black-and-white or grayscale element used to prevent certain areas of an image from being affected by a process.

Material   The encompassing term for all of the images and settings that can be assigned to an object's surface.

MAXScript   The built-in scripting system for MAX. Enables you to write routines that automate many tasks.

Mesh   Slang term for a 3D object or scene, called that because it resembles a wire mesh sculpture.

Mesh Optimization   The process of reducing the density of a mesh object by combining closely aligned faces.

Metal   A rendering mode that simulates the specular highlights and surface characteristics of polished metal surfaces.

Mirror   A Transform that reverses an object or copies a reversed version of it along a specified axis.

Modifier   A routine applied to an object to modify its appearance or properties.

Morph   Animated 2D or 3D technique that makes one image or form smoothly transform into another.

Motion Blur   The smearing of an image or object when the subject or camera is in motion.

Motion Path   A spline that represents the path of an object, used for reference when making adjustments to the animation.

Multilayer   A type of material that enables you to layer two different specular highlights onto the surface of an object.

Multiplier   A light source setting that increases the intensity of the light past the RGB setting limits.

Named Selection Set   A set of objects referred to by a single name so they can easily be selected in the future.

Network Rendering   The process of rendering individual frames of an animation on different machines across a network.

Noise   Random variations applied to materials, colors, or animation parameters to give a more natural look or motion.

Normal   Imaginary marker that protrudes from a polygon face and indicates which side of the polygon is visible and what direction it's facing.

NTSC   American video standard, which is 29.97 frames per second.

NURBS (Nonuniform Rational B-Splines)   A type of spline that has control points residing on or away from the resulting curve. Curves can be used to form surfaces, which are also controllable with control points.

NURMS (Nonuniform Rational Mesh Smoothing)   A type of smoothing in the MeshSmooth modifier that results in much more refining of objects.

Objects   Individual meshes in a scene that have a single name.

Opacity   The degree to which light rays cannot penetrate an object.

Opacity Map   A grayscale image loaded into a material's opacity channel, making the object's surface appear to vary from opaque to transparent.

Operand   An object or shape being used in a Boolean operation.

Origin Point   The center point of the cyberspace universe, where the central axes meet. Identified by the coordinates 0,0,0.

Output   The stage in 3D production when a file, photographic slide, section of video tape, or other medium is used to store the image or animation.

Overshoot   A technique that turns a spot-light into a point light, but with shadows cast only in the areas defined by the Hotspot and Falloff regions.

PAL   The European video standard.

Palette   The full set of colors used or available for use in an image. Usually refers to images with 256 or fewer colors.

Pan   A side-to-side rotation of a camera around its vertical axis.

Parametric Modeling   Modeling system in which objects retain their base geometry information and can be modified at almost any point by varying the parameters that define them.

Parent   In a chain of linked objects, the object that is closer to the base of the hierarchy than the other object attached to it (see Child).

Partial Lathe   A lathe operation in which the cross-sectional shape is not revolved a full 360 degrees.

Particle System   An animation system that enables you to generate and control the behavior of a vast number of tiny objects. Used to simulate natural effects such as water, fire, sparks, or bubbles.

Patch Modeler   A modeling system that uses a network of control points to define and modify the shape of the patch, which is usually a lattice of either splines or polygons.

Phong Shading   A shading method that retains the smoothness of Gouraud shading but adds specular highlights for more realism.

Pivot Point   User-defined rotational center of an object, often the point where the three local axes meet.

Pixel   PI(X)cture ELement. The smallest unit of graphics a video adapter generates, usually about the size of a pinpoint. Pixels can be nearly any color, depending on the capabilities of the adapter.

Planar Coordinates   A type of mapping coordinate system well-suited to flat objects. It applies a set of rectangular image coordinates from a single direction.

Plug-in   An add-on feature that works within MAX. Plug-ins are popular for adding new capabilities to products without generating a new version of the software.

Point   In 3D space, the smallest area that it is possible to "occupy" is called a point. Each point is defined by a unique set of three numbers, called coordinates (see also Coordinate System).

Polygon (poly)   A closed shape with three or more sides. Also refers to two faces with a shared side that are treated as a single face. Sometimes called a quadrilateral.

Polygonal Modeling   The basic type of 3D modeling, in which all objects are defined as groups of polygons.

Polyline   A line with more than one segment (at least three vertices).

Post-Production Effects   Also known as Video Post and Render Effects. In MAX, this refers to transitions, color manipulations, or special effects applied to frames of an animation after it has been rendered.

Preview   An output mode that creates a fast-rendering test animation, or a display mode that generates a simplified version of the scene in real time.

Primitive   Any of a number of basic 3D geometric forms, including cubes, spheres, cones, and cylinders.

Procedural Object   An object generated by a mathematical formula, such as a Procedural Texture.

Procedural Texture A mathematically defined texture that can be used to simulate wood, marble, and other materials but usually doesn't look as realistic as scanned textures.

Quad (Quadrilateral) A four-sided polygon commonly used in 3D programs.

Radiosity The property by which light reflecting off an object goes on to illuminate other objects as well. Also, a rendering method that takes into account the color and shape of all surfaces in the scene when calculating illumination level and produces images of a near photographic quality.

RAM Player A command that enables you to load a sequence of images into RAM and play them back in real time. This command is only limited by the amount of available RAM in your system.

Raytracing A rendering method in which the color and value of each pixel on the screen is calculated by casting an imaginary ray backward from the viewer's perspective into the model to determine what light and surface factors are influencing it. Raytracing is implemented as a material in MAX.

Reactor An animation controller that enables objects in the scene to respond to the actions of other objects in the scene.

Real Time The immediate processing of input data and graphics so that any changes result in near-instantaneous adjustments to the image.

Reference Similar to an instance, a duplicate of an object in which changes to the original affect all references, but changes to the references are independent.

Reference Coordinate System The coordinate system around which Transforms are performed, such as world, screen, or local coordinates. This is user-selectable.

Reflection Map An image or process used to create an environment for a reflective object in order to roughly simulate the effects of Raytracing on reflective objects.

Refraction The bending of light waves when they move through different types of materials.

Refraction Mapping A material option used as a means of simulating the effects of light refraction in programs that don't offer Raytracing.

Refresh Rate The number of times per second that the screen image is repainted on the monitor, measured in cycles per second or Hertz (HZ).

Rendering The process wherein the computer interprets all object and light data and creates a finished image from the viewport you have selected. The resulting image can be either a still or a frame in an animation sequence.

RGB (Red-Green-Blue) The three primary colors in the additive (direct light) color model. Computer monitors vary the brightness levels of red, green, and blue pixels to create the gamut of displayable colors.

Roll To rotate a camera around its viewing axis, making the scene appear to spin.

Rotate A Transform that spins an object around the selected axis.

Rotoscoping The process of adding film or video to animation, either as a finished element or for use as a reference for the animated characters.

Safe Frame   A defined area of a frame that will not appear cropped when viewed on a television screen. Appears as a box outline in the selected viewport.

Saturation   Also called intensity. The measure of how concentrated a color appears to be. A fully saturated red, for example, cannot be any more red than it is, whereas a red with a low saturation begins to turn gray.

Scale   A transformation that adjusts the size of an object. Also, the mathematical relationship between the size of a subject in reality and the size of its representation on paper.

Scanline Rendering   Typical rendering method used by MAX. Renders the image as a series of horizontal lines.

Schematic View   A dialog box that enables the display of a scene as a diagram, showing hierarchical relationships between objects, modifiers, space warps, materials, and more.

Scripting   The process of programming specific actions into the MAX system. Usually used when you need added functionality or find yourself repeating the same set of commands over and over.

See-Through   An object display mode by which objects in the viewports are displayed as a gray shade so you can see objects inside of them. Commonly used in conjunction with the Skin modifier when setting up bones for skeletal deformation.

Segment   A step or division in an object, similar to the way a building is divided into floors.

Self-Illumination   A material channel or control that adjusts the degree to which an object appears to be lit from within.

Self-Illumination Map   A grayscale image loaded into the material's self-illumination channel, creating the impression that some portions of the object are lit from within.

Shadow Map Size   A setting that adjusts the amount of memory the system can use to create a given shadow map. The larger the map, the more refined and detailed it will be.

Shadow Mapping   A method of creating shadows in a scanline renderer that works by creating a grayscale texture map based on the lighting and mesh in the scene and then applying it to the objects at render time.

Shape   A collection of one or more splines combined to form a single object.

Shelf   A toolbar holder at the top of the MAX interface that divides different toolbars into tabs. Toolbars can be added to or removed from the shelf with ease.

Shininess   The overall reflective nature of the object—in other words, its glossiness.

Shininess Map   A grayscale image loaded into the material's shininess channel that varies the reflectivity of the surface. Used to make portions of an object dull or shiny.

Skeletal Deformation   A process by which you use objects in the scene to deform other objects. Most commonly used with single mesh characters. Skin and Flex are modifiers you can use to accomplish this.

Skew   A transform that forces one side of an object in one direction along the selected axis and the other side in the opposite direction.

SMPTE (Society of Motion Picture and Television Engineers)   In video and 3D graphics, a time format consisting of minutes, seconds, and frames (57:31:12 would be 57 minutes, 31 seconds, and 12 frames).

Snap   A feature that causes the cursor to move quickly from one position to another according to user-defined grid spacing or in reaction to various portions of an object, such as vertices, edges, or center points.

Snapshot   Creates a copy of an object at a specific point in time or converts a procedural object to a mesh object.

Space Warp   A 3D effect that affects only objects bound to the warp and within the influence field of the warp. A bomb explosion is an example.

Specular Color   The hue of any highlights that appears on an object at Phong shading levels or higher. Specular color is also affected by the shininess setting, or mapping, and by the color of the lights.

Specular Highlight   The bright reflections of light on glossy objects in Phong shading levels or higher.

Specular Map   An image loaded into the specular channel that varies the color and intensity of the specular highlights of the surface. Useful for creating the effect of prismatic or metal flake surfaces.

Spherical Coordinates   A mapping coordinate system that wraps an image around an object in a cylindrical manner and then pinches the top and bottom closed to surround it.

Spline   A line—usually curved—that's defined by control points. Bézier, B-Spline, and NURBS are common types of splines.

Spotlight   A directional light source that radiates light from a single point out into a user-defined cone or pyramid.

Squash and Stretch   Modified scale operations that treat the object as though it has volume. Squashing an object makes it spread out around the edges, while stretching it makes the object get thin in the middle.

Stack   A live history of changes made to an object. You may, at any time, go back in the stack and make adjustments to any modifiers. This makes MAX a parametric modeling system.

Steps   The number of additional vertices generated between control points on a spline or between predefined vertices on a poly.

Storyboarding   The process of visualizing a film or animation by breaking it down into a sequence of sketches that illustrate the key movements in the scene.

Strauss   A shading level good for simulating metal materials.

Strokes   A method of accessing commands in MAX by using simple mouse movements while holding down the middle mouse button.

Sub-Objects   Small elements that combine to form a larger object. For example, vertices, faces, and edges are sub-objects of mesh geometry.

SuperSampling   An antialiasing method for materials that contain bitmaps. SuperSampling provides additional control over antialiasing by processing the surrounding pixels of the rendered image.

SuperSampling Filters   Like Anti-Aliasing, SuperSampling has filters you can select and use for different types of SuperSampling.

Surface Approximation   A method for approximating NURBS and Patch surfaces with triangles for rendering purposes. More accurate approximations result in better renderings, but with longer render times due to larger face counts.

Surface Attribute   A basic material setting—such as color, shininess, or opacity—that affects all parts of an object equally.

Tangent Point   Also called a weight. The portion of a spline control system that acts like a magnet to attract the spline in its direction.

Taper   A Transform that compresses or expands an object along the selected axis.

Target   A positioning aid that enables you to see where a camera or light is pointed from any viewport.

TCB Controller (Tension/Continuity/Bias controller) One of the most common methods of providing control over the keyframe control points.

Teeter   A type of loft deformation that enables the cross section to be rotated around the X or Y axes perpendicular to the path.

Tension   In a TCB Controller, the amount of curvature the keyframe allows in the path before and after the keyframe.

Tessellation   The process of increasing the number of faces in a selected area by subdividing existing faces.

Texture Map   A bitmapped image, either scanned or painted, that gives a material unique qualities not available by simply varying the surface attributes.

Tiling   The technique of repeating an image to cover a large area.

Timeline   A graph-like interface for viewing and manipulating animation events.

Toolbar   A floating or docked palette of commands shown either as buttons or text. In MAX 3, you can create your own toolbars or dock them on just about any part of the screen. Examples include the Shelf and Command Panel.

TrackBar   A small bar located below the Animation Time slider. It displays all animation keys for the selected object.

TrackView   A dialog box where you can edit animation keys in a variety of ways.

Trajectory   The motion path for an object that already has animation applied to it.

Transform   A general term for an operation that alters the position, size, or shape of an object. Typical transforms include Move, Scale, and Rotate.

Triangle   A three-sided polygon, the basic polygonal shape used in MAX.

Tweening   Process in which MAX takes control of how the object is transformed or blended between keyframes.

Twist   A Transform that wrings an object around the selected axis.

Unclamped Colors   Under certain circumstances, it is possible for the MAX rendering engine to generated unclamped colors, which are colors that are whiter than 255,255,255. These usually occur under bright highlights. Unclamped colors can be selected for use with Lens Effects and other effects.

UV or UVW Mapping   UV or UVW coordinates look similar to the XY image coordinate system, but they conform to the mesh, no matter how it bends or twists. UVW coordinates are used for mesh objects; shifting them allows very precise repositioning of maps on an object.

Value   The lightness or darkness of a color (tinting or shading).

Vertex, Vertices   A single point in space through which parts of an object pass.

Video Post (VP)   A post-production routine by which you can filter, combine, or composite various events, scenes, and images.

Video-Safe Colors   Colors that fit into the luminance and saturation limits for television broadcast. Colors outside this range blur and distort the video signal.

VP Event   A placeholder for scene views, input images, filters, compositors, or output operations in Video Post.

VP Queue   The order in which Video Post events are processed.

View Coordinates   A coordinate system that uses the viewport as the basis for the X, Y, and Z axes. The axes remain the same no matter how the viewer's perspective on the 3D scene changes.

Viewing Plane   A plane surrounding the viewpoint at a perpendicular angle. It is an imaginary flat panel that defines the limits of the field of view.

Viewpoint   A position in or around cyberspace that represents the viewer's current location.

Viewport   A window that looks into 3D space.

Virtual Memory   The use of hard-drive space as temporary storage when the computer system runs low on RAM.

Volumetric Light   A light source with an adjustable 3D volume that can simulate the behavior of natural light in an atmosphere.

VRML (Virtual Reality Modeling Language)   A Web browser technology that enables you to explore simple 3D environments online.

Weight   See Tangent Point or Control Vertices (CVs).

Weld   An operation that combines the overlapping vertices of shapes or objects.

Window   A method of selecting objects, similar to Crossing, but here, objects must reside completely within the bounding region to be selected.

Wireframe   A display or rendering mode that draws objects by using lines to represent the polygon edges, which makes the object resemble a sculpture made of wire mesh.

World Coordinate   The fundamental coordinate system of 3D space, which is unchanged by the user's viewpoint.

XRef   An external reference object or scene. When added to a scene, an XRef does not add to the file size and generally cannot be changed other than transformed. You can use predefined blocks as XRefs, which are updated when you change the block. Also good for workgroup editing of scenes.

X Axis   Typically the horizontal or width axis, running left and right.

XY Coordinates   The normal coordinate system for 2D images and shapes. The X axis runs horizontally and the Y axis runs vertically.

Y Axis   Usually the vertical or height axis, extending up and down.

Z Axis   The axis normally associated with depth, running forward and back.

Index

SYMBOLS

T

W